BEST BIRDWA
DORSET

by
Neil Gartshore

This book is dedicated to my wife, Yuki, and to the three
budding birdwatchers in the family: Shaun, Amy and Fiona.

Illustrations by John Davis

BUCKINGHAM PRESS LTD

in
association
with

SWAROVSKI
OPTIK

Published in 2011 by:
Buckingham Press Ltd, 55 Thorpe Park Road, Peterborough
Cambridgeshire PE3 6LJ, United Kingdom
Tel/fax: 01733 561 739
e-mail: buck.press@btinternet.com
www.buckinghampress.co.uk

© Buckingham Press Ltd 2011

ISBN 978-0-9569876-0-0
ISSN 0144-364 X

Editor: David Cromack
Design and maps: Hilary Cromack
Publisher: Hilary Cromack

About the author: Neil Gartshore
Neil Gartshore grew up in Leicestershire where an interest in birds began at an early age. He spent nearly 25 years working in the nature conservation field, including time on the Farne Islands and in South Africa/the Sub-Antarctic. From 1991 until 2006 he was based at the RSPB's Arne reserve in Dorset.

He now works as a freelance bird surveyor, birdwatching guide and buys/sells out of print natural history books under the name of Calluna Books (www.callunabooks.co.uk).

When he can, he still travels in search of birds – South Africa, Spain and Japan are amongst his favourite birdwatching destinations. He has been a past Dorset County Bird Recorder and is currently the Chairman of the Dorset Bird Club.

About the artist: John Davis
John is a long-established member of the Society of Wildlife Artists and has illustrated many books and journals, including work for *BBC Wildlife* and *British Wildlife* magazines and the RSPB. He also provided the cover image and many of the black-and-white illustrations for the Buckingham Press book *Best Birdwatching Sites: Sussex*.

Landscape through the seasons and its wild inhabitants have been a constant inspiration for John and works in watercolour, acrylic and oils on these themes appear in a new book from Langford Press entitled *Jewels Beyond The Plough*.

To contact John, e-mail him at: johndavis.wildlife@tiscali.co.uk or phone 01243 512 351.

Cover: Dartford Warbler and other iconic Dorset species near Corfe Castle, by John Davis

Buckingham Press Ltd is registered in England and Wales, no 0533739.
Registered office: 55 Thorpe Park Road, Peterborough PE3 6LJ.

Printed and bound in Great Britain by:
Information Press, Eynsham, Oxford, UK.

CONTENTS

Dorset is blessed with an abundance of heathland sites, making it a stronghold for Nightjars in the UK.

Featured sites in Dorset

CONTENTS

AROUND 18 million people visit Dorset each year to enjoy its scenic delights, such as beautiful Lulworth Cove or the natural arch of Durdle Door as well as a mild climate. The Jurassic Coast, a World Heritage Site, is another major attraction – it has yielded many important fossils and today attracts many amateur fossil hunters hoping to make their own discoveries.

The county can actually boast the highest proportion of conservation areas in England, so it is no surprise that it is a popular destination for walkers and birdwatchers and we hope that this book will encourage both visiting birders and local people to explore all that Dorset has to offer.

It's location on the south coast makes Dorset an ideal landing point for migrant birds and places such as Portland Bill and Christchurch Harbour have formidable reputations for turning up rare species. The Purbeck coast, which includes sites such as Durlston Country Park and Winspit, is another migration hotspot that is so much more accessible than Shetland or Scilly.

However, Dorset has so much more to offer birdwatchers, including an extensive network of lowland heaths which are sanctuaries for attractive species such as Nightjars, Dartford Warblers, Woodlarks and Hobbies. Weymouth can lay claim to being Britain's best birding town as it boasts two fabulous RSPB reserves at Radipole and Lodmoor.

In common with the rest of the *Best Birdwatching Sites* series, this guide, written by a knowledgeable author, explores many different habitats to ensure readers are able to enjoy the very best that Dorset can offer.

As a company which is dedicated to bringing genuine benefits to the birdwatching community, Swarovski Optik is delighted to support this latest addition to a celebrated series of Buckingham Press books.

Peter Antoniou

Country Manager UK and Eire,
Swarovski Optik UK

SWAROVSKI
OPTIK

IT WAS EARLY one November on The Fleet when Jol remarked ...... "The weather this past week has been brilliant. I've seen Red-breasted Goose, Hen Harrier, Merlin, Great Grey Shrike and Redpolls. Where else could you see these things?" ......where indeed.

We had just spent a while scanning through 2000 dark-bellied Brent Geese looking for a single Red-breasted Goose. Earlier the same week I had been watching Bitterns at Radipole Lake and Hatch Pond, as well as seven Slavonian Grebes, a few Black-necked Grebes and a Great Northern Diver in Studland Bay. On Portland, a Dusky Warbler and a Richard's Pipit had just turned up. We were in Dorset, a county that has so much to offer birdwatchers of all abilities.

I first really arrived in Dorset in March 1991 – prior to then my only experience of the county was a trip to Bournemouth as a child before my birdwatching days had begun (and when Bournemouth was actually part of Hampshire!) and a long weekend spent visiting a friend on Brownsea Island in July 1984.

Over the past two decades I have come to know most parts of Dorset very well – especially the sites that I have worked on, or have been associated with, during my employment with the RSPB or as a freelance bird surveyor. Even now, there are still a few areas of the county that still produce a few surprises.

My first attempt to draw up a list of sites to feature in the book came up with 110. The list was then rationalised by 'lumping' some of them together – for instance the individual sites on the Studland peninsula have been treated as sub-sites under a single Studland listing, the same is the case for Portland.

On the other hand there are a number of sites that lie close, or adjacent, to each other that I have chosen to keep as separate listings, for example Hartland Moor & Stoborough Heath NNR and Middlebere.

I have, by and large, chosen what I consider to be the 'best' sites that Dorset has to offer but I have also tried to represent the habitats that are found in the county and to include as many suitable sites as possible away from the coastal hotspots – many of these inland sites have a broader natural history interest than just birds. For some habitats, such as heathland, it has been prudent to choose a selection of sites rather than to list all of them – those chosen have tended to be the larger/better accessed sites or sites in an area where fewer are found or access is difficult.

This book is intended to draw the reader not only to the enjoyment of the birding hotspots but also to encourage wider birding in the quieter corners of the county that are under-watched. Though I asked many local birders for their opinion of which sites should be included in the book the final choice has been mine.

Enjoy your visit!

Neil Gartshore
Wareham, August 2011

ACKNOWLEDGEMENTS

A book such as this cannot be written from the knowledge of one person alone and during the course of its production I have been fortunate to have the help of many of Dorset's birdwatchers and conservationists who have checked, advised and suggested on various sections of the book. My thanks to all of them and apologies to anyone missing off the list!

Mark Andrews, Chris Avanti, Derek & Kay Ball, Dominic Couzens, Nick Hopper, Kevin Lane, Paul Levey, John Lockwood, Jol Mitchell, Shaun Robson, Steve Smith, Richard Taylor.

Steve Groves (Abbotsbury Swannery); Gary Powell (ARC); Terry Elborn, Nick Woods (Borough of Poole); Dorset Bird Club; Danny Alder, Julien Cooper, Steve Davies (Dorset County Council); Robert Brunt, Andy Fale, Nicola Hoar, Emily Newton, Chris Thain (Dorset Wildlife Trust); Pam Martin (East Dorset Countryside Management Service); Justin Rylands, Mark Warn (Forestry Commission); Angela Peters, Peter Samson, John Sibthorp, Phil Stuckey (National Trust); Ian Nichol, Linda Smith (Natural England); Nick Quintrell, Nick Tomlinson, Mike Trubridge (RSPB); Linda McMullen (Semcorp Bournemouth Water); Ivan Tinsley, Marilyn Smith (Wessex Water); Robin Walter (Woodland Trust).

Sophie Lake and Doug Whyte: for general proof-reading of the final drafts.

David and Hilary Cromack, of Buckingham Press: for the opportunity to write this book and for the help and advice (and patience!) along the way.

Finally, I would like to say a special thank you to my wife Yuki and children, Shaun, Amy and Fiona, for putting up with me being 'in the office' for long periods of time and for keeping me company on some of the site visits.

HAVE YOUR SAY

If you would like to get in touch with me with any suggestions for sites which you feel should be added to future editions, or would like to pass on additional information that would improve a visit to a site, or would like to point out any corrections, I can be contacted through the publishers:

Neil Gartshore, c/o Buckingham Press, 55 Thorpe Park Road, Peterborough, PE3 6LJ or email me at admin@buckinghampress.com

WATCHING BIRDS IN DORSET

MEASURING JUST OVER 1,000 square miles, the county of Dorset (population 700,000) nestles between its larger neighbours of Hampshire to the east and Devon to the west on England's south coast. Away from the conurbation of the Poole-Bournemouth-Christchurch area, the county is very rural in character with small towns and many 'chocolate-box' villages.

At its widest points, Dorset is 50 miles from east-west and 40 miles from north-south, and has a coastline (excluding Poole Harbour) of 88 miles. The county town of Dorchester or the Saxon town of Wareham are good areas to base yourself for a visit, as you will be within an hour's drive of any of the sites in this book.

Dorset has a charm of its own with a wide variety of habitats and landscapes that draw people from near and far in pursuit of natural history, geological, historical and rambling interests …… as well as for sea-side visits. In the height of the summer, when the bird interest may not be at its best, there are plentiful opportunities to catch up with an array of dragonflies, butterflies, reptiles and other species groups.

The fact that Dorset is a coastal county means there is an obvious bias towards the coast for the birding hot spots – Christchurch and Poole Harbours to the east and Weymouth, Portland and The Fleet to the west – but inland sites shouldn't be overlooked. Though the number of specific inland sites to visit is low, the county has a major network of public rights of way which you can explore for yourself.

VISITING DORSET – SOME PRACTICAL POINTS

DRIVING

Though there are many alternative methods of getting to Dorset, the car is likely to be the choice of most birders, with the obvious flexibility of being able to get to the birding sites easily.

Driving in the county is relatively trouble-free on a well-signposted network of roads. It is worth bearing in mind though that many of the roads in the urban areas, such as around Dorchester, Weymouth and Poole-Bournemouth-Christchurch conurbation, can be very busy. The rural roads are generally very good but take extra care when driving around the narrow country lanes.

During the summer, bank holidays and on nice weekends at any time of the year, roads can suffer extra congestion as holidaymakers and day trippers swell the number of vehicles on them. Whatever time of the year you plan to visit allow enough time to get to the sites safely.

As with anywhere else in the UK, Dorset has its share of speed cameras – both static and mobile units, the latter can turn up anywhere!

Parking is another issue for the motorist - a proportion of sites in this book have parking charges. These charges are generally higher during the summer than the winter but the time when the changeover occurs varies from site to site. It is advisable to bring plenty of change with you on a trip to Dorset but also bring membership cards, if you have them, for the National Trust and the RSPB (free parking at selected sites on proof of membership).

I would strongly recommend that when you use pay-and-display car parks (either at sites or in the towns) you always buy a ticket, as they are patrolled regularly and you will certainly get a parking fine if you haven't displayed one!

PUBLIC TRANSPORT AND DISABLED ACCESS

If you don't want to come to Dorset by car there other means of getting here. Rail links from London are excellent with the Waterloo to Weymouth line (South West Trains) calling at the main centres of Bournemouth, Poole, Wareham, Dorchester and Weymouth, with a local change to Christchurch.

A second rail link runs from Bristol to Weymouth (First Great Western Trains) and stops at Dorchester. Long distance coaches from London drop off mainly in Poole and Bournemouth.

It is possible to visit a good proportion of the sites in this book by public transport. Those which can be relatively easily reached from towns/villages with reasonable public transport links are flagged up under their listing.

By the nature of some of the sites, disabled access can be limited. Again, those which offer a degree of access are flagged up under their listing. Depending on the nature of your disability it may be advisable to contact individual sites (where possible) to discuss your requirements.

ACCOMMODATION, FOOD AND TOILETS

Staying in Dorset is not usually a problem but bear in mind that in some areas where accommodation is less plentiful, or at time when there is an influx of holidaymakers, choices may be more limited.

There are a range of accommodation types to suit all pockets – from upmarket hotels to small family-run guest houses and B&Bs, from caravan parks and campsites to youth hostels. Contacting one of the local Tourist Information Centres is a good starting point if you are looking for accommodation. At busy times of the year it may be advisable to book accommodation in advance – I once had to find three beds for contractors working in Wareham in late-July and could only find a bunk room in Swanage as all the B&Bs were full!

There is no shortage of eating places around Dorset and, if sites don't have any catering facilities themselves, you won't be too far from a pub, a café, a restaurant or a shop.

Some of the sites have their own toilet facilities, but many do not. There are a number of public toilets scattered around the county, mainly in the towns and, but may have restricted opening times.

THIS CHAPTER aims to give an overview of what birds will be around during each month of the year and where to go to see them. Seawatching is dealt with separately.

JANUARY

Most birders get out bright and early to start off their New Year bird list. On a good day during the winter it is possible to see more than 100 species in a day. Our local January bird race record clocked up 129 species in the county. My own record is 106 but I restricted myself to within the Purbeck boundary, travelling only 40 miles during the day, but still managed to miss a few embarrassing birds ......how do you not see Canada Geese in Dorset?

The coastal areas are going to provide the largest numbers of species, particularly the Poole Harbour areas of Arne, Middlebere, Studland, Holes Bay, Lytchett Bay and the north shore. Numbers of wildfowl and waders are at their winter peaks. Avocets, Dunlins and Black-tailed Godwits reach into the thousands, with Oystercatchers, Grey Plovers, Lapwings, Curlews and Redshanks into the hundreds. All of these are generally widespread around the harbour.

Smaller numbers of Ringed Plovers, Knot, Sanderlings, Purple Sandpipers, Bar-tailed Godwits and Turnstones tend to be more localised with the north shore being the best area for most of them. A few Common Sandpipers, Spotted Redshanks and Greenshanks overwinter – Holes Bay is the best area to find all three on the same day.

Common wildfowl are found in the same areas – Brent Geese, Shelduck, Wigeon, Teal, Pintails and Red-breasted Mergansers are the most obvious, with a smaller number of Goldeneyes. Scan across open water anywhere around the harbour for the possibility of Scaup, Eiders, Long-tailed Ducks, Common or Velvet Scoters, especially out in Brand's Bay (Studland) and in the stretch of water between Arne and Brownsea.

Try to get out on an RSPB Birdboat around Poole Harbour sometime during the winter to get a good perspective its size and birdlife. A number of these sailings land on Brownsea Island for a couple of hours where you can see the lagoon at its best.

Kingfishers, which move down from the rivers into the harbours during the winter, are regularly seen, as are Little Egrets and Grey Herons. Spoonbills are a speciality of Poole Harbour, numbers often reaching into double figures, but they are irregular elsewhere. Peregrines can be seen buzzing the ducks and waders, often carrying one off for supper. Look for Marsh Harriers quartering the reedbeds and marshes.

Christchurch Harbour has a similar variety of birds. Numbers tend to be much lower, but it is a smaller harbour and easily covered on a winter's day, whereas Poole Harbour needs two, or even three, days to cover all of the areas. The Fleet holds large numbers of wildfowl (and a few waders), particularly Mute Swan, Wigeon and Brent Geese (usually with pale-bellied or Black Brant individuals among the dark-bellied birds).

Dorset's coastal waters are good for wintering divers, grebes, sea duck and gulls (including Mediterranean). Check out Hengistbury Head, Studland Bay, Durlston Country Park, Weymouth Bay, Portland/Portland Harbour and West Bexington ......it is possible to find three species of divers and five species of grebes in a day at this time of year.

Red-breasted Mergansers are the most likely sea duck encountered, with good numbers in Portland Harbour and at Ferrybridge. Common Scoters can be seen in all months, especially off Portland and Hengistbury Head and look out for the occasional Eiders, Long-tailed Ducks and Velvet Scoters.

A few seabirds may linger or pass along the coast during the winter including Fulmars, Cormorants, Shag, Gannets, Razorbills, Guillemots, regular gull species and Kittiwakes.

The freshwater bodies including Crichel Lake, Little Sea (Studland), Lodmoor, Longham Lakes, Radipole Lake, Sutton Bingham Reservoir, Swineham Gravel Pits and The Fleet (away from Ferrybridge) are more likely to hold Mallards, Shovelers, Pochards and Tufted Ducks than the harbours and there is a chance of a Ruddy Duck, a Goosander or, during a cold snap, a Smew.

Go inland to the cress beds in the Frome and Piddle Valleys for Green Sandpipers, Grey Wagtails and possibly a Water Pipit. Occasionally winter swans and grey geese (usually White-fronts) can be found along the floodplain, especially at Holme Bridge.

Lodmoor, Radipole Lake and Hatch Pond are reliable wintering sites for Bitterns, often two or three birds on each site and there is a good chance of seeing Snipe and Water Rails out in the open. Cetti's Warblers should be found on all three sites, Bearded Tits on the first two.

The chalk downland and farmland areas away from the coast are worth a visit. The short daylight hours mean that it is often easier to see hunting Barn Owls, especially around the Martin Down-Cranborne area. Corn Buntings and finches flock together – Maiden Castle is one of the best areas to look for them, as well as for Golden Plovers, Lapwings and Buzzards.

The heathlands are quite bleak at this time of year, compared to the summer. Most of Dorset's Stonechats head south for the winter but a few stay. Almost invariably if you find a Stonechat on the heath there will be a Dartford Warbler with it – look for a Stonechat on the top of a bush and for a Dartford under it. Hen Harriers favour the heaths in the winter and Merlin is regular – one of the best sites for these two is Hartland Moor.

One heathland speciality is the Great Grey Shrike. Numbers vary from year to year but Morden Bog (Wareham Forest) is a regular site and, less so, are Arne and Hartland Moor. Some of the mixed heathland/conifer forests areas including Avon Heath, Moors Valley and Wareham Forest hold Crossbills, Siskins and Redpolls, and Ravens are regular.

There are the usual suspects of resident passerines about and it should be possible to find Woodcock (often flushed from the woodland/heathland fringes), wintering thrushes, Black Redstarts (including Portland, Durlston), Brambling (Badbury Rings) and a possible over wintering Firecrest (Arne, Durlston, Portland), Chiffchaff or Blackcap.

FEBRUARY

Dorset starts to come out of its winter slumber as the days begin to draw out – birds will be very much similar to the previous month. Wildfowl and waders numbers begin to fall and with some of the species the majority of birds may have by left the end of the month, leaving just a few stragglers into March.

There are a number of Grey Heron colonies around the county and most birds will be on eggs by the end of the month.

On sunny days towards the end of the month, and into March, Dartford Warblers begin to sing more and they are joined by Woodlarks returning to their breeding areas including Arne, Avon Heath Country Park, Cranborne Common and Grange Heath.

MARCH

This is a bit of an in-between month as many of the winter visitors finally depart and the first of the summer visitors and migrants start to come through. Wader numbers are still dropping but some of the wintering birds are replaced by others passing through. Apart from the few ducks that remain for the summer, most of the wintering birds have gone.

Numbers of wintering divers and grebes along the coast also drop but some of the remaining birds start changing into their summer finery, particularly the Black-necked Grebes in Studland Bay. At Durlston Country Park and Portland Bill, Guillemots and Razorbills are making more frequent visits onto their breeding ledges.

The first migrants are invariably Sandwich Terns, Sand Martins, Wheatears and Chiffchaffs and they are all seen by mid-month, quickly followed by the first Swallows, Blackcaps and Willow Warblers by the end of the month. Winter thrushes leave.

Many of the resident birds are starting to nest and it is not unusual to see the first Blackbirds and Robins fledged by the end of the month.

APRIL

Now migration starts in earnest and the coastal headlands of Portland, Durlston Country Park and Hengistbury Head come into their own, but passage migrants can turn up anywhere along the coast. Some of the species, such as Grasshopper Warblers and Pied Flycatchers, peak during this month but most will continue moving through into May. These will include Cuckoos, hirundines, Tree Pipits, Yellow Wagtails, Nightingales, Redstarts, Whinchats, Wheatears, Ring Ouzels and a variety of warblers.

Migrant waders may include species such as Stone Curlew, Little Ringed Plover, Little Stint, Curlew Sandpiper, Ruff, Whimbrel, Common and Wood Sandpipers – Brownsea Island, Ferrybridge, Lodmoor and Stanpit Marsh are some of the best sites to find most of these. Look for Garganey on Lodmoor, Radipole Lake or on Stanpit Marsh.

The breeding season for the local birds is well underway - birdsong is everywhere – in the woods, on the heaths and over the downs.

Overshoots from the continent are likely in April (and May) and have included Night Heron, Purple Heron, Red-footed Falcon, Whiskered Tern, White-winged Black Tern, Alpine Swift, Red-rumped Swallow, Hoopoe, Bee-eater, Subalpine Warbler, Woodchat Shrike, Golden Oriole and Serin.

MAY

The breeding season is now in full swing with many of the summer visitors on eggs but migration still continues – this is usually the best month for the migrant spring waders, while Swifts and Spotted Flycatchers are late arrivals.

The seabird colonies are a hive of activity – Guillemots are clinging on to the ledges and the few Puffins left in Dorset can be seen flying into the cliffs or on the water at Dancing Ledge or at Portland Bill – try to get out on a coastal boat trip from Swanage in late May/June to get a close look at them. Peregrine sightings are almost guaranteed on these trips.

Venture away from the coast to some of the excellent inland sites: try the Dorset Wildlife Trust sites at Brackett's Coppice, Fontmell Down, Kingcombe Meadows and Powerstock Common for a good selection of common woodland and scrub birds. Go looking for Redstarts at Lambert's Castle or for Corn Buntings at Maiden Castle ......and enjoy the stunning countryside.

JUNE

This is always my favourite month to look for Nightjars on the heaths. All of the heathland sites listed in this book have them – my particular favourite area is around Wareham Forest where I go for a pre-dusk walk to look for Hobbies and Dartford Warblers before the Nightjars start their distinctive 'churring'. One word of warning: if you are going out to look for Nightjars make sure you have a torch with you and that you know how to get back to the car in the dark!

This is also a good time to go in search of Nightingales – either on the coast at Ringstead Bay/ White Nothe or inland on Lydlynch and Deadmoor Commons. This beautiful songster is likely to be heard first but with patience they will be seen ......listen, look and wait!

The coastal areas are now fairly quiet though there will always be something about. Sandwich and Common Terns are nesting on Brownsea Island, Common Terns also nest at Lodmoor and Abbotsbury and there is a small colony of Little Terns on Chesil Beach (at Ferrybridge) - eggs are hatching and chicks are growing. Many of the breeding seabirds on the cliffs are nearly ready to fledge.

Fledglings of all kinds are everywhere, some birds are even starting to flock up, particularly Starlings. This is a good time to hear Quail in the farming belt and listen for the soft purring of Turtle Doves around Martin Down. Look for Dippers on the rivers at Maiden Newton or Lyme Regis.

This can be one of the quietest months for birdwatching as birds are getting on with their business but there are plenty of other winged distractions in the form of butterflies and dragonflies. These are excellent through the summer: many of the sites are as important for them as they are for birds.

JULY

Where did the summer go? Birds are starting their autumn movements already!

The increase in waders is noticeable, both species and numbers. Common and Green Sandpipers are arriving at Lodmoor and other coastal sites and some of those expected for the winter are starting to return – there may be an early Avocet or Grey Plover.

Terns are fledging, the youngsters following the adults are constantly begging for food. The sea cliffs are virtually deserted – a few Fulmars and Herring Gulls hang on. Some of the smaller birds go quiet as they begin their post-breeding moult and the heat of the day can make birdwatching hard going at times.

By the end of the month though, migrants are beginning to move back through the coastal headlands. Initially it is a trickle and through August it can become a flood. Though rarities turn up all through the year, the autumn is especially a good time. Early migrants include movements of Wheatears, Grasshopper, Sedge and Willow Warblers and Pied Flycatchers.

The first autumn sightings of Ospreys cause some excitement. Sightings are reported along the coast but it is Poole Harbour where most of the records come from. Birds will be in the harbour now into October, usually one or two birds at anyone time but co-ordinated counts have produced up to six birds. They can be seen anywhere in the harbour but Middlebere is a particularly good spot for them.

AUGUST

This is the peak month for many migrants – certainly for Willow Warblers (interestingly Chiffchaffs peak in September) and it is time to watch the coastal headlands. One or two Melodious Warblers often turn up, usually on Portland.

Elsewhere, wader numbers continue to build up around the coastal sites. Whimbrels and Spotted Redshanks start passing through and Little Stints and Curlew Sandpipers may be picked out among the Dunlins – Brownsea Island or Stanpit Marsh are the best spots to get your eye in for them, a telescope is essential.

Inlands sites are all generally very quiet now, but many are still good for butterflies.

SEPTEMBER

This is another good month to be on the coast looking for migrants, with a greater chance of picking up a rarity or two amongst them. This can be a good month for finding a Wryneck, Tawny Pipit, Icterine Warbler, Barred Warbler or Ortolan Bunting.

This is a good month for passage Greenshanks in Poole and Christchurch Harbours and look for Honey Buzzards at points along the coast, especially on Portland. There is also some passage of Merlins, Marsh and Hen Harriers, while Hobbies will be leaving.

Birds are flocking up now in the woodlands – a good time to check out the mixed flocks of birds as they move around. Keep an eye out for the elusive Lesser Spotted Woodpecker among them at Arne, Sherford Bridge (Wareham Forest), Powerstock Common and Thorncombe Wood.

Farmland birds are also flocking up – look for groups of Skylarks, finches and buntings feeding in the stubbles and field margins.

OCTOBER

The wintering wildfowl and wader numbers continue to build up on the coastal sites. Hen Harriers and Merlin return to the heaths and this is a good month for wintering Great

Grey Shrikes to turn up. Inland Golden Plover and Lapwing flocks return to the downs and farmland.

This is the best month for Yellow-browed and Pallas's Warblers to turn up (they can arrive anytime from late September). Both are more or less annual visitors along the coast, on Portland and at Durlston Country Park in particular.

This is probably the best month for the phenomenon of 'vis migging', watching the skies for birds flying over ......visible migration. This activity can take place at any time of the year (but September-November is the best period). The activity can also take place anywhere in the county where there is a possibility of birds moving through. The main sites watched in Dorset though are coastal include Christchurch Harbour, Durlston Country Park and West Bexington.

Some species – Wood Pigeons, Skylarks, Meadow Pipits, Chaffinches, Bramblings, Goldfinches, Siskins and Linnets – can pass in their hundreds, if not thousands. Interesting sightings may include Woodlarks, Tree Sparrows, Crossbills, Hawfinches, Lapland Buntings – you will definitely need to have your ears tuned in to pick up some of these.

NOVEMBER

We are now well into winter, with short days and mixed weather. This month is virtually a mirror image of January, with may be a lingering Yellow-browed or Pallas's Warbler adding some interest.

Winter thrushes begin arriving in earnest but unless there is really bad weather further north numbers are generally small.

DECEMBER

If the country is in the grip of a freeze at any time during the winter, it may be hard to get out, but there can be a massive influx of birds such as Skylarks, Fieldfares and Redwings. Duck numbers often increase during these events, or could just as easily disappear if the water bodies freeze up ......I have seen parts of Poole Harbour frozen!

This month is also virtually a mirror image of January and is the last chance to add those final birds to the year list ...... there could be a chance of a last minute Smew, a Goosander or maybe an influx of Waxwings to round off the year.

The annual Dorset list over many years has averaged around 270 species, so there is always going to be plenty to see. If you are visiting Dorset there is no best time of the year to come as each month is different and it will depend on what you want to see,

I am lucky to live here and so I don't have to plan visits around holidays and weekends but if I had to pick one time of the year to come birdwatching in Dorset I would definitely go for the winter ......or maybe the spring, ...or possibly the autumn, ...but then again the summer also has some great butterflies and dragonflies. Phew, I'm glad that I don't have to make the choice!

SEAWATCHING IN DORSET

SEAWATCHING is a bit like Marmite – you either love it or hate it. Seawatching can be an exhilarating experience or hours of quiet contemplation. Weather conditions play an important role in what may be seen and you have to be prepared for all weathers. Even if you are in the right spot and conditions are ideal birds still may not turn up.

Seawatching tends to be a communal activity, especially as the number of top seawatching sites and the timings when the conditions are right are limited. Be prepared to listen for directions from others and to shout out your own observations.

TOP SEAWATCHING TIPS

- A telescope is essential – birds can often be quite a way out.
- Get your eye in – look for any features on the sea, such as marker buoys or passing boats.
- Get your head around giving directions – most people use the clock system, 1 o'clock, 2 o'clock etc from a point of reference. It takes some getting used to but not impossible.
- Remember that birds can move fast and by the time you are looking in the right area it may have moved – try going beyond the direction they are heading in and work your way slowly backwards.
- Wrap yourself up well against the elements and try to keep your telescope as dry as possible ......a misty lens doesn't see much.
- Try to predict when birds might be moving – the time of year, the right winds.
- Early mornings are generally best with numbers of birds easing off through the day (but there are exceptions so don't discount seawatching if you can only arrive later in the day).
- Expect the unexpected but get used to identifying the common species such as Fulmars, Manx Shearwaters and Kittiwakes – sizes of birds can be confusing without anything to directly compare them with.
- Call out birds when you see them to get other people on to them – don't worry if you get the identification wrong, the more eyes the better.
- Keep you own notes of birds seen, weather conditions etc - over time you will learn the trade and you will get hooked!
- Other birds, such as wildfowl, divers, grebes and waders, fly by during seawatches and passerines may come in off or head out to sea. I have heard stories of people seeing Storm Petrels but suddenly realising that they have picked up a Nightjar over the sea!
- Don't forget to look out for cetaceans, seals, basking sharks and watch out for the flotsam and jetsam floating around on the water.

KEY SITES FOR SEAWATCHING

Despite the length of Dorset's coastline, good seawatching sites are very limited. It is always worth having a scan offshore whenever by the coast but especially if a good onshore wind is blowing. Seabird 'wrecks' can occur especially during autumn gales when birds are blown closer to shore.

Portland

The Bill is the top seawatching spot in the county. Birds regularly pass on their way through the Channel. In the spring, mid April to mid May is the best passage time when there is a SW-SE onshore wind (it doesn't have to be too strong). In the autumn, unsettled weather can be good for passing birds. When birds are moving, also check out Chesil Cove - this often a good site if a 'wreck' has occurred.

West Bexington

Moderate SE-SW winds in the spring and the autumn (which is generally better) may bring birds passing across Lyme Bay closer to the shore.

St Aldhelm's Head & Durlston Country Park

The cliffs at St Aldhelm's Head are very high which can make seawatching a little difficult, the vantage point at Durlston Country Park isn't so high. Generally these sites will get the same birds under the same conditions as Portland, but in smaller numbers.

Branksome Chine

This site is in tucked well in against the mainland and so seabird passage is not a regular event. With good S or SE winds though, birds may be pushed up into Poole Bay during the spring or autumn.

Hengistbury Head

Birds need to be pushed into the shore as this headland is well away from the usual passage route. Birds tend to go to the south of the Isle of Wight rather than through the Solent which separates the island from the mainland. The best conditions here are when the winds are from the SE in the spring or the SW in the autumn. Winter gales can be productive.

BIRD SPECIES THAT CAN BE EXPECTED

I have listed here the main seabirds that may be picked up during a seawatch. I have not included divers, grebes, ducks, geese, waders or coastal gulls so bear in mind that they could be seen during a seawatching session at the right time of year. The main time of year for sightings and the months when the peak numbers occur are in brackets.

Fulmar (all year) - Breeding, local birds move away to moult for a short time in late autumn/ early winter. Some passage movements are noted. Occasionally 'blue' phased birds are seen.

Sooty Shearwater (Aug-Nov, peak numbers Sept) - Scarce autumn migrant and rare winter visitor.

Manx Shearwater (Mar-Oct, peak numbers Apr/May) - Common spring and summer visitor, scarce in autumn and rare in winter.

Balearic Shearwater (May-Nov, peak numbers July-Sept) - Regular summer and autumn visitor, can be recorded during the winter.

Storm Petrel (May-Jul) - Regular summer visitor and scarce migrant offshore, occasional autumn records.

Leach's Petrel (Oct/Nov) - Usually associated with 'wrecks'.

Gannet (all year). - A regular passage of birds.

Cormorant (all year) - Breeding, non-breeding resident and migrant.

Shag (all year) - Breeding, non-breeding resident and migrant.

Pomarine Skua (Apr-Nov, peak numbers Apr/May, Oct/Nov) - Uncommon but a regular spring migrant, fewer in the autumn and occasional winter visitor.

Arctic Skua (Apr-Oct, peak numbers Apr/May, Aug-Oct) - Regular spring and autumn migrant, occasional in winter.

Long-tailed Skua - Rare spring/autumn migrant.

Great Skua (Apr-Oct, peak numbers Apr/May, Aug-Oct) - Regular spring and autumn migrant, occasional winter visitor.

Sabine's Gull - Rare offshore migrant, especially autumn - often storm driven.

Kittiwake (all year, peak numbers winter) - Breeding, common migrant and winter visitor.

Little Gull (all year, peak numbers Apr/May, Oct/Nov) - Uncommon passage migrant and winter visitor.

Little Tern (Apr-Aug, peak numbers Apr/May) - Breeding, scarce spring and autumn passage migrant.

Black Tern (May & Aug/Sept) - Scarce spring and autumn passage migrant.

Sandwich Tern (Mar-Oct, peak numbers Apr/May & Aug/Sept) - Breeding, passage migrant.

Common Tern (Apr-Oct, peak numbers Apr/May & Aug/Sept) - Breeding, passage migrant.

Roseate Tern - Scarce passage migrant, mainly in spring.

Arctic Tern (Apr/May & Aug-Oct) - Fairly common spring and autumn passage migrant.

Guillemot - Breeding, common winter visitor.

Razorbill - Breeding, common winter visitor.

Little Auk - Rare autumn and winter visitor.

Puffin (Apr-Jul) - Scarce breeding visitor, occasional winter visitor

Other seabirds on the Dorset bird list are Black-browed Albatross, Cory's Shearwater, Great Shearwater and Macronesian Shearwater – these would have been seen during seawatches but are very unlikely ......but you never know what may turn up! Rare gulls/terns and Black Guillemots, which are also on the bird list, are more likely to be found in harbours or on beaches rather than to be seen during a seawatch.

DURING the preparation of this book I visited many places, including some that didn't find their way onto the final list of sites. I found on many occasions that I was totally distracted by my surroundings – Dorset has some of the most stunning landscapes in the UK and it was easy to forget that I was writing a book about birdwatching and not a book about walking!

Dorset's landscapes have been shaped by man's use over thousands of years. There are many examples of early Iron Age settlements across the county with a number of hill forts dominating the countryside. Eggardon Hill, Pilsdon Pen and Woodbury Hill didn't make it onto the list but others did, including Maiden Castle, Hambeldon Hill and Badbury Rings.

Small towns and villages are scattered through the county. Many, including the Roman town of Durnovaria (Dorchester) and the Saxon walled town of Wareham, have a long history of settlement. Others are relatively new – Bournemouth grew out of what would have been heathland, becoming a recognised town in the 1870s.

Dorset is well known for its geological interest, especially along the Jurassic Coast, a World Heritage Site. The diversity of its underlying geology is one of the reasons why there is such a good variety of habitats through the county.

Coastal Harbours, Marshes, Headlands, Cliffs & Bays

The Dorset coastline is the county's most prized asset. Many of the sites along it take in sections of the 630 mile South West Coast Path that starts at the entrance to Poole Harbour and finishes at Minehead, in Somerset.

Close to the Hampshire border, the headland of Hengistbury Head shelters the waters of Christchurch Harbour and Stanpit Marsh. The area is of particular interest at migration times when anything can turn up and during winter there is always a good selection of wildfowl and waders to be seen.

Poole Harbour has many places of interest. The mudflats and saltmarshes hold an impressive number of wintering wildfowl and waders, including the second largest population of Avocets. Brownsea Island is the jewel in the crown – its lagoon is an important high water roost for wintering waders and during the summer Sandwich and Common Terns breed here.

The southern shore of the harbour is relatively undeveloped from Studland, through Rempstone Forest and around to Middlebere and the Arne peninsula. The northern shore in contrast is more developed but shouldn't be avoided with Lytchett Bay, Holes Bay and the urban stretch of the harbour from Poole Quay to Sandbanks still providing a good variety of birds.

To the south of the harbour the coastal waters of Studland Bay are excellent for wintering divers, grebes (especially Black-necked), sea duck and Mediterranean Gulls. Beyond, the Purbeck cliffs hold breeding seabirds, including Puffin at Dancing Ledge, and the coastal hills and valleys from Ballard Down, through Durlston Country Park and round to Kimmeridge turn up plenty of migrant land birds in spring and autumn.

Nightingales breed on the edge of Ringstead Bay while Weymouth Bay, Portland Harbour and the coastal waters around Portland are good for divers, grebes and sea duck. The limestone outcrop of Portland is one of the UK's top hotspots for migrants with all manner of common, scarce and rare birds passing through in spring and autumn. A few seabirds nest on the cliffs near The Bill which is consistently the best place to seawatch in the county.

Heading west from Portland to West Bay is Chesil Beach. The Fleet, sheltered behind its shingle, holds important numbers of wintering wildfowl. Waders are fewer in number than the other coastal sites but all the regular species turn up. Dorset's only breeding colony of Little Terns are found on the beach at Ferrybridge.

From West Bay, the cliffs rise above the shoreline all the way to Lyme Regis and the Devon border. Fulmars, Peregrines and Ravens are common along here. Lyme Bay, covering the area from Portland to Lyme Regis, is an important wintering area for Red-throated Divers and good for seabird passage at times, particularly off West Bexington.

Rivers Valleys, Water-meadows & Freshwater Bodies

Typical birds of the rivers include Mute Swans, Moorhens, Kingfishers and Grey Wagtails while the shorter, fast-flowing rivers of West Dorset still hold a few pairs of Dippers. A number of cress beds are sited by the clear waters of the chalk rivers in the Frome and Piddle Valleys. Green Sandpipers are virtually guaranteed in the autumn/winter and there is also a chance of Water Pipit.

Together with a number of smaller rivers, Dorset's three main rivers, the Avon, Frome and Piddle, create a number of floodplains. Changes in agricultural practices has seen a sharp decline in breeding numbers of Lapwing, Snipe and Redshank while Yellow Wagtails has disappeared altogether as a breeding bird.

Wintering Bewick's Swans and White-fronted Geese are less frequent on the floodplains now than they used to be and numbers of wintering ducks, Lapwings and Snipe have also fallen in many areas.

There are a few larger freshwater bodies scattered around the county including Crichel Lake, Longham Lakes, Sherborne Lake, Sutton Bingham Reservoir and Swineham Gravel Pits – all good for a selection of wintering wildfowl and for breeding Great Crested Grebes.

Woodland - Coniferous & Deciduous, Scrub & Common

Dorset has around 10% of its area under woodland. The largest areas of coniferous forest (just over 40% of Dorset's woodland) are generally found on the acidic 'heathland' soils and include Wareham, Rempstone, Hurn and Ringwood Forests. Pure stands of conifer have a limited value to birds: Crossbills and Siskins do well, but a greater number of species are found in areas of mixed or deciduous woodland.

Common woodland birds are found throughout this habitat including Wood Pigeon, Tawny Owl, Great Spotted Woodpecker, Wren, Robin, Dunnock, thrushes, warblers, tits, Goldcrest, Nuthatch, Treecreeper, Jays, and finches.

Among the more interesting species, Woodcocks like a mixture of forestry and damp woodland with Cranborne and Sopley Commons and Whitesheet Plantation the more reliable sites to find roding birds. Lesser Spotted Woodpecker, Wood Warbler and Redpoll are now very scarce breeding birds and Redstarts are limited to two main sites, Lambert's Castle and Morden Bog (Wareham Forest).

Lydlynch and Deadmoor Commons hold breeding Nightingales and Turtle Doves are still found in the scrub and woodlands of the chalk downland areas, including Martin Down.

Heathland

Dorset's internationally important heathlands are centred on the Poole Basin area and stretch eastwards into the New Forest. The mosaic of heather, acid grassland and woodland is reminiscent of Egdon Heath from the novels Thomas Hardy. Though the area of heathland has declined from around 40,000ha in the 1700s to around 6,000ha today, the county contains some of the largest tracts of this valuable habitat outside of the New Forest.

Much of what remains is fragmented but most areas are now protected with many owned and/or managed as nature reserves. The target birds here are Nightjars and Dartford Warblers, both widespread and generally found in good numbers, and the more localised Woodlark.

Other species found on the heaths in summer include Hobbies, Tree Pipits, Stonechats and Linnets, while Hen Harriers and the occasional Merlin or Great Grey Shrike turn up in the winter.

Chalk Downland

The main area of Dorset's 'chalklands' stretches from the north-east to the south-west through the centre of the county and along the Purbeck ridge. Many of the original areas of chalk downland thrived under the grazing regimes of the wool trade but as this trade began to die out many areas were converted to arable, improved grassland or, in later years, to forestry.

Areas that have escaped conversion tend to be where it was too steep to plough, such as Fontmell Down. Martin Down, on the Dorset border, remains one of the largest areas of chalk downland in the country. Grazing, to maintain a short sward, ensures that these areas are ideal for chalk grassland plants which provide food for many species of specialist butterflies. Scrub is usually found on the downs but needs to be managed so it doesn't take over.

Lapwing, Grey Partridges, Skylarks, Stonechats, Linnets, Yellowhammer and Corn Bunting are typical breeding birds of the open downs but many are in decline. Turtle Doves hang on but Stone Curlew no longer breeds in the county. This habitat has the best areas to look (or at least to listen) for Quail. In winter, large flocks of Golden Plovers and Lapwings wander around the downs and the surrounding farmland.

Reedbeds

There are many reedbeds scattered around the county, especially along the coast, but none are particularly large or of commercial value. They may be tidal (or brackish), like those around the harbours of Poole and Christchurch, or freshwater, along the rivers or around lakes and ponds, such as parts of the River Frome and Hatch Pond. The most accessible reedbeds to visit are the RSPB reserves at Lodmoor and Radipole Lake in Weymouth.

Water Rails, Reed and Sedge Warblers and Reed Buntings are common and widespread, Cetti's Warblers and Bearded Tits are more localised. A number of Bitterns now winter and are regularly seen at Hatch Pond, Lodmoor and Radipole Lake and Marsh Harriers have bred recently on the last two sites, after an absence of nearly 50 years as a breeding species in Dorset.

Farmland (improved grasslands/crops), Parks and Gardens

There are few specific areas of farmland where I can direct you to go looking for birds but this habitat shouldn't be overlooked. Many of Dorset's 3,000 miles of footpaths, bridleways and byways run through farmland and with the aid of an OS map it could be worthwhile doing a little exploring of your own.

A walk around it will usually produce a good mixture of common species including Whitethroat and Yellowhammer. Others, such as Corn Bunting, Grey Partridge and Quail are scarce and Tree Sparrow is now all but extinct but is occasionally reported from the north of the county.

Any of Dorset's parks and gardens will have a good selection of common birds to see – I have had over 60 species in or flying over my own garden in Wareham since 2008, including Spotted Flycatcher, Brambling and wintering Chiffchaff and Blackcap.

Even towns turn up interesting birds. When Waxwings reach Dorset they are usually found around the towns' parks and gardens and one of the most spectacular bird events I have ever seen in Dorset happened in Poole in early 2011 – tens of thousands of Starlings roosted close to the town centre.

BIRDS ASIDE, there are plenty of other reasons for the birdwatcher and the natural history enthusiast to come to Dorset. The county caters for a wide range of natural history interests with many local groups active in the area.

Invertebrates number into the thousands of species ......among them flies, sand wasps, grasshoppers and beetles. These include many rare species, such as the Purbeck mason wasp and heath tiger beetle, restricted in Dorset to its heathlands.

Nearly 50 resident species of butterflies have been recorded within the county, only Devon and Hampshire can match this number. Though many are widespread, others such as Lulworth and silver-spotted skippers, marsh fritillaries and wood white have a very restricted range. The chalk grasslands are of particular importance for this group. (www.dorsetbutterflies.com)

Amongst the moths, Dorset probably has the largest macro-moth tally anywhere in the UK at over 700 species, in addition to the 200 or so species of Pyralid. As with birds, some interesting migrants turn up from time to time, especially along the coast. (www.dorsetmothgroup.org.uk)

Dragonflies are another well represented group in the county with around 30 species recorded. The Dorset heathlands, particularly sites such as the Arne RSPB reserve, are among the best in the UK. (www.british-dragonflies.org.uk)

The heathlands are also the prime area for reptiles – with all six of the UK's native species, including smooth snake and sand lizard, found on them. Amphibians are also well represented including natterjack toad and great crested newt. (www.arc-trust.org)

Many mammals are widespread, such as badger, fox and roe deer. Others are more localised, such as sika deer in Purbeck and red squirrels on Brownsea Island. Bats are well represented with a number of rare species, including greater horseshoe and Bechstein's. Many of Dorset's rivers still hold populations of water voles and otters are making a comeback. Bats: (www.dorsetbatgroup.org.uk), otters: (www.littleowl.org.uk)

The richness of Dorset's natural history continues in the plant world. More than 2,000 species of vascular plants & ferns, more than 400 species of mosses & liverworts, 650 species of lichen and 1,500 species of fungi have been recorded. The 10km recording square around Wareham is the most botanically diverse in the county. (www.derc.org.uk/local/dfg.htm)

Looking beyond the land, Dorset has a bountiful marine flora & fauna. There are opportunities to see some of this underwater world by going out on a boat trip off the coast to look for seabirds and cetaceans or on a glass-bottomed boat on the lower reaches of The Fleet. The Purbeck Marine Wildlife reserve at Kimmeridge Bay is great place for rock pooling or if you like snorkelling, you can follow and an underwater nature trail. (www.marine-life.org.uk)

HOW TO USE THIS BOOK

HERE is a typical layout of the site guide pages. Once familiar with the layout, you will be able to extract the information you need quickly and painlessly.

Title of site. Sites are listed in alphabetical order and numbered.

Key points: Opening times, terrain, suitability for wheelchair users and other useful tips. ALWAYS check opening times with the site managers before you visit.

Target birds and the likelihood of seeing them: Lists the species for which the reserve is most noted. The percentage figure gives a rough idea – based on the author's experiences at the site – of how likely you are to see the target species, provided you visit the site at the correct time and stay for a reasonable amount of time. Where you see 'winter raptors (25%)' this means that you have a 25% chance of seeing each species of raptor at the site.

Other possible species: A guide to some of the commoner species you are likely to see, season-by-season, though space does not allow 100 per cent to be covered. Under the *Occasional birds* sub-heading you will find a list of rarer species which are not recorded enough to be included in the Target Birds section.

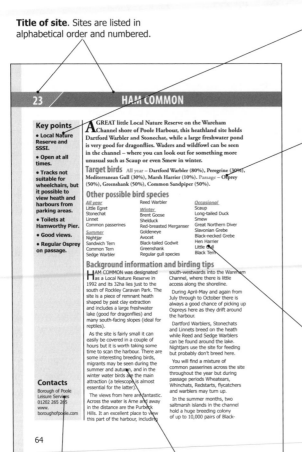

Useful contacts: Phone numbers to confirm access details etc.

Background information: Generally, this section will take you through the walk, with details of the birds that you might see and handy tips to help you see them. It might contain more information on points which have been briefly mentioned in previous sections, e.g. more extensive bird lists, more detailed information about terrain etc.

Best time of year to visit. There may be things to see at other times of year but this season is likely to produce the best results.

Relevant OS Landranger map number

Grid reference(s) of parking area(s) giving easiest access to site.

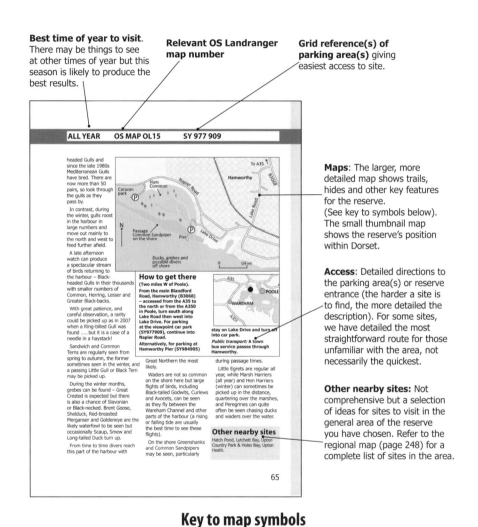

ALL YEAR   OS MAP OL15   SY 977 909

headed Gulls and since the late 1980s Mediterranean Gulls have bred. There are now more than 50 pairs, so look through the gulls as they pass by.

In contrast, during the winter, gulls roost in the harbour in large numbers and move out mainly to the north and west to feed further afield.

A late afternoon watch can produce a spectacular stream of birds returning to the harbour – Black-headed Gulls in their thousands with smaller numbers of Common, Herring, Lesser and Greater Black-backs.

With great patience, and careful observation, a rarity could be picked up as in 2007 when a Ring-billed Gull was found .....but it is a case of a needle in a haystack!

Sandwich and Common Terns are regularly seen from spring to autumn, the former sometimes seen in the winter, and a passing Little Gull or Black Tern may be picked up.

During the winter months, grebes can be found – Great Crested is expected but there is also a chance of Slavonian or Black-necked. Brent Goose, Shelduck, Red-breasted Merganser and Goldeneye are the likely waterfowl to be seen but occasionally Scaup, Smew and Long-tailed Duck turn up.

From time to time divers reach this part of the harbour with

Great Northern the most likely.

Waders are not so common on the shore here but large flights of birds, including Black-tailed Godwits, Curlews and Avocets, can be seen as they fly between the Wareham Channel and other parts of the harbour (a rising or falling tide are usually the best time to see these flights).

On the shore Greenshanks and Common Sandpipers may be seen, particularly

during passage times.

Little Egrets are regular all year, while Marsh Harriers (all year) and Hen Harriers (winter) can sometimes be picked up in the distance, quartering over the marshes, and Peregrines can quite often be seen chasing ducks and waders over the water.

How to get there
(Two miles W of Poole).
From the main Blandford Road, Hamworthy (B3068) – accessed from the A35 to the north or from the A350 in Poole, turn south along Lake Road then west into Lake Drive. For parking at the viewpoint car park (SY977909), continue into Napier Road. Alternatively, for parking at Hamworthy Pier (SY984905) stay on Lake Drive and turn off into car park.
Public transport: A town bus service passes through Hamworthy.

Other nearby sites
Hatch Pond, Lytchett Bay, Upton Country Park & Holes Bay, Upton Heath.

Maps: The larger, more detailed map shows trails, hides and other key features for the reserve. (See key to symbols below). The small thumbnail map shows the reserve's position within Dorset.

Access: Detailed directions to the parking area(s) or reserve entrance (the harder a site is to find, the more detailed the description). For some sites, we have detailed the most straightforward route for those unfamiliar with the area, not necessarily the quickest.

Other nearby sites: Not comprehensive but a selection of ideas for sites to visit in the general area of the reserve you have chosen. Refer to the regional map (page 248) for a complete list of sites in the area.

65

Key to map symbols

Road	Water	)(Bridge	𝖵 Reeds
Track	Trees	Lighthouse	Conifer forest
Footpath	Mud	Marsh	Broadleaf woodland

Viewpoint   (P) Parking

0 ½ Scale (miles)

● Train station

Key points

- Owned by the RSPB.
- Over 220 bird species recorded.
- Expect 40-60 species depending on time of year.
- Parking for 70 cars (please do not park on road verges).
- Access at all times but car park locked at dusk.
- Pay & display charge (RSPB members free).
- Allow two to three hours for the Shipstal trails.
- Allow an hour for the Coombe trail.
- Picnic area and toilets available.

Contacts

RSPB Arne office
01929 553 360
www.rspb.org.uk/
reserves

THIS TRADITIONAL stronghold for Dartford Warbler is one of the UK's top nature reserves, with a unique transition from the mudflats and saltmarsh of Poole Harbour to extensive areas of lowland heath. This most attractive site is definitely a place for the all-round naturalist, so a visit at any time of year will impress. The reserve gives excellent vantage points to view Poole Harbour's wintering wildfowl and waders.

Target birds

All year – Little Egret (90%), Dartford Warbler (90%), Raven (20%), Lesser Spotted Woodpecker (10%), Crossbill (10%). *Summer* – Nightjar (95% hear, 75% see), Hobby (30%), Woodlark (30%). *Winter* – Black-tailed Godwit (90%), Brent Goose (80%), Avocet (75%), Spoonbill (30%), Hen Harrier (25%).

Other possible bird species

All year	*Winter*	
Stock Dove	Woodcock	Whitethroat
Tawny Owl	Kingfisher	Spotted Flycatcher
Green Woodpecker	Rock Pipit	Pied Flycatcher
Meadow Pipit	Winter thrushes	*Occasional*
Stonechat	Brambling	Divers & rarer grebes
Marsh Tit	Siskin	Long-tailed Duck
Common woodland birds		Merlin
	Passage	Marsh Harrier
Summer	Osprey	Hoopoe
Sandwich Tern	Whimbrel	Wryneck
Common Tern	Yellow Wagtail	Black Redstart
Cuckoo	Wheatear	Firecrest
Reed Warbler	Whinchat	Great Grey Shrike
Summer warblers	Redstart	

Background information and birding tips

ARNE LIES in the south-west corner of Poole Harbour, and has been managed by the RSPB since 1965 when it held two pairs of Dartford Warbler (20% of the UK population!) Now it covers 535ha of lowland heath, acid grassland, woodland, saltmarsh, reedbed and farmland.

The habitats, and its location within Poole Harbour, ensures that Arne is a highly designated site by UK (SSSI), European (SPA, SAC) and International (Ramsar) legislation.

It is the RSPB's most visited reserve in the South West region, with more than 90,000 visits p.a., but even at the busy times of year I find that it is possible to walk around with a feeling of seclusion.

The wonderful views over Poole Harbour and Purbeck add to an exciting experience at any time of the year with the heathland specialities and the harbour's wintering wildfowl and waders two of the main birdwatching attractions.

A visit to Arne begins in the car park from where a number of well established trails are way-

How to get there

(Four miles E of Wareham).

From Wareham take the B3075 to Stoborough over the south bridge and causeway. Just past the petrol station (on your right) turn left down Nutcrack Lane and continue for about three miles until you reach the RSPB car park on the right.

Alternatively bypass Wareham on the A351 towards Swanage, turn left onto the B3075 into Stoborough, heading back towards Wareham. Take first right (New Road) towards Ridge and right again towards Arne and the RSPB car park.

No public transport available to site.

Low water feeding waders and wildfowl

Arne Bay

High water roost inc. Spoonbill

Sika deer on salt marsh

Scan for small grebes and unusual duck

Big Wood

View point

Arne | Arne Farm

Dartford Warbler

Winter finches

Shipstal Heath

Visitor Centre

Woodpeckers (inc possible Lesser Spotted)

To A351 (Wareham)

Osprey on dead trees (spring/autumn)

Coombe Heath

Dartford Warbler and Nightjar

Marsh (all year), Hen (winter) Harriers over marsh

Scan for harriers and Osprey

Middlebere Lake

Waders and wildfowl follow tide (inc. Avocet, Black-tailed Godwit)

marked. Spend a little time here to start picking up some of the woodland species – Nuthatches and Marsh Tits are regularly seen here, while Tawny Owls can sometimes be heard during the day.

On a cautionary note watch out for sika deer in the car park (and elsewhere) – give them a wide berth, as they can be aggressive.

The Shipstal area has four way-marked trails (pick up a map/follow the posts). My preference is to turn right just after leaving the car park. The path passes through a wooded strip between open farmland on one side and heathland/ harbour on the other before continuing through a piece of larger woodland to Shipstal.

This is a good spot in the spring for woodpeckers. You should find Great Spotted and Green but look/listen for Lesser Spotted (in the autumn/winter search among woodland bird parties for this elusive species).

Since the mid 1990s I have heard Woodlark regularly on this stretch from late March through to June – listen for them as you walk by the heath

and then search skywards.

At the end of this woodland, turn right to get your first close views of the harbour. The path follows the edge of the saltmarsh before giving the option of continuing on to the heath (and eventually to a viewpoint) or to turn off along

27

Key points

- **Small reception building/ information in car park.**

- **Trail leaflet available.**

- **Events organised (see RSPB website for details).**

- **Difficult to reach by public transport.**

- **Wheelchair access limited (contact RSPB).**

- **A wealth of other wildlife. Sika deer can be aggressive so do not approach.**

the beach. Take the heath option and you should find Dartford Warblers relatively easily – their scratchy song or harsh call notes are good clues, so keep your ears open as well as your eyes.

Over the years two or three pairs have usually nested in this area. There are a couple of loops over the heath to walk to give you a chance of finding them. At least one pair of Nightjars also breeds here.

The path following the cliff edge provides a good vantage point over the harbour (with better views than from the beach). A lot of the birds can be picked up with binoculars but a telescope would increase your tally.

The harbour is at its best in winter and this is one of my favourite spots to view it. A variety of duck species can be seen off the Point (and around the corner in Arne Bay), including good numbers of Pintail, Wigeon and Teal.

It is worth scanning the open water towards Brownsea Island for something a little more unusual, including smaller grebes, divers, Scaup, Long-tailed Duck and Eider (a telescope will definitely help as they can be distant).

Waders are well represented. Curlews, Oystercatchers and Redshanks are around all year. From September through to March, Avocets, Black-tailed Godwits (a few over-summer), Dunlins and Grey Plovers are common, with less regular sightings of Bar-tailed Godwits, Knot, Ringed Plovers and Turnstones.

Whimbrels, Spotted Redshanks and Greenshanks are regularly picked up on spring/autumn passage.

When the tide is out, birds feed on the exposed mud in Arne Bay, but fly out of the bay or move up on to the adjacent saltmarsh as the tide rises.

When the tide is low walk a little way out onto the mud from the beach by Shipstal Cottages to get a better view into the bay (but don't walk in front of the cottages as you will just disturb the birds).

Arne is one of the best sites in Dorset to see a Spoonbill. They are regular visitors, mainly in autumn/ winter (usually one or two, occasionally more) – in particular look out on the spit in Arne Bay or across the bay to Patchins Point.

All-year-round Little Egret sightings usually outnumber those of Grey Heron while, in summer, Common and Sandwich Terns regularly come by and, in winter, Kingfisher and Rock Pipit are around the saltmarsh and creeks.

From Shipstal Heath viewpoint, cross the main track and walk through Big Wood, stopping at the hide overlooking Arne Bay and the spit (albeit quite distant). The woodland will produce more common species.

The trails then heads back to the car park, with a choice of two routes, both of which pass through Arne Farm. In winter look out here for finch flocks in the planted strips within the deer fence and the hedgerows. There are usually good numbers of Chaffinches and Linnets but look among them for Bramblings and Reed Buntings.

The farm is also a good place for passing Yellow Wagtails (autumn), especially when there are cows in the fields.

Another trail from the car park heads out to Coombe Heath.

This shorter, circular route leads down to the northern side of Middlebere Lake (a channel of the harbour) and is probably the most scenic walk on the reserve. A hide provides shelter but I find viewing better from the paths.

Depending on the state of the tide, you'll find a similar selection of species to those found at Shipstal, together with a wintering flock of dark-bellied Brent Geese (always worth a scan through them for pale-bellied and Black Brant) – they are often in the fields on the Middlebere side (site 38).

In the early part of the winter (from late-September) this is a favoured area of some of the harbour's Avocets (and Black-tailed Godwits). The birds move around depending on the state of the tide and the weather conditions but they can often be seen flying into Middlebere on a falling tide or leaving on a rising tide.

The small spur just to the north of the hide is the best place to watch the spectacular sight of rows of Avocets flying in/out low across the water.

Ospreys are regular visitors to Poole Harbour and Middlebere is a particular favourite area – check the dead trees across the large reedbed to the south-west for a perching bird or two (the trees can also be seen from site 38). Water Rails are often heard, and sometimes seen, in the reeds on the edge of the channel and Reed Warblers sing from the reeds in the summer.

Over the years I have seen an increasing number of Yellow-legged Gulls in the channel, so check through the large gulls carefully. The heath holds Dartford Warblers (more pairs than Shipstal), while Stonechats and Nightjars also breed in reasonable numbers on this trail.

In general, look out for Hobbies (summer), Ravens (all year), Crossbills (all year although they have good and bad years) and, during the winter, Hen Harriers and Woodcocks (the latter are usually only seen when flushed).

You may also be lucky to see a Merlin, Short-eared Owl or a Great Grey Shrike, which are all species that turn up on occasions.

A good variety of common birds breed at Arne but non-breeding passage birds are relatively sparse. Annually these usually include small numbers of Whitethroats, Redstarts, Whinchats, Wheatears, Spotted and Pied Flycatchers, while Ring Ouzels (the autumn is generally better than the spring), Grasshopper Warblers and Wood Warblers are more irregular visitors.

Unusual species do turn up from time to time — I have seen Red Kite, Hoopoe, Wryneck, Black Redstart and Firecrest (almost annual) on more than one occasion.

The reserve's bird list stands at more than 220 species, so a visit at any time of the year should produce a good tally. However, Arne is as well known to the all-round naturalist as much as the birdwatcher.

The reserve is one of the best RSPB sites in the country for dragonflies and a good selection of common butterflies can be seen, with a healthy population of silver-studded blues on the heath. Though they are usually more difficult, but not impossible, to see, all six species of British reptile are found here.

Other nearby sites

Creech, Stoborough & Grange Heaths, Hartland Moor & Stoborough Heath NNR, Middlebere, Wareham Meadows & Swineham Point.

Key points

- SSSI owned by Dorset County Council.

- Pay and display car park.

- Car park gates locked overnight.

- Visitor centre and gift shop, toilets (disabled access) and café in North Park.

- Trails, some can be wet.

- North Park trails offer wheelchair access.

- Information leaflet available.

- Events programme (see website for details).

Contacts

Avon Heath Country Park
01425 478 082 (rangers);
01425 478 470 (visitor centre). www.dorsetforyou.com

A S A GOOD example of a heathland in a semi-urban setting, this site is next to the A31, one of the main routes into Dorset, and is worth a stop to stretch the legs and to take a break after a long drive. Within a short walking distance you could be watching your first heathland birds including Dartford Warbler and Woodlark.

Target birds *All year* – Dartford Warbler (80%), Woodlark (80%). *Summer* – Nightjar (90% hear, 75% see), Hobby (30%).

Other possible bird species

All year		
Sparrowhawk	Siskin	Tree Pipit
Buzzard	Crossbill	Chiffchaff
Tawny Owl	Common woodland birds	Willow Warbler
Green Woodpecker		Linnet
Meadow Pipit	*Summer*	*Winter*
Stonechat	Woodcock	Winter thrushes
	Cuckoo	Redpoll

Background information and birding tips

IN THE EARLY 1990s Avon Forest Country Park changed its name to Avon Heath Country Park to more accurately reflect the habitat and vision for the park. Avon Heath (230ha) is part of the network of Avon Valley heathlands which includes Sopley Common/ Ramsdown Plantation (site 52) and Town Common & St Catherine's Hill (site 59) to the south.

Owned by the County Council, this is Dorset's largest country park and consists of two main sections: North Park and South Park – separated by MoD land (private). Generally, South Park's landscape has more of an open feel about it than North Park.

Public car parking is now limited to the main car park in North Park, adjacent to the visitor centre, children's play area, café and toilets. The entrance gate opens at 8am and closes at 6.30pm or dusk (whichever is sooner) and the exit gate closes at 7.30pm.

If you turn up before the car park opens, or if you want to stay after it has closed, then there is a small lay-by just past the entrance that can be used. There are two smaller car parks – one on Birch Road (off the A31) and the other on Boundary Lane but parking in both is by annual permit only.

If you can, it is worth getting to the park as early as possible because it often gets very busy (especially North Park which is a popular place for dog walkers and families). The park rangers put on an excellent programme of events through the year, including many aimed at children.

The habitat across the park is predominantly heathland with areas of acid grassland and pine and birch woodland. There is a good network of paths and tracks including a number of marked trails of just under a mile to 2.5 miles if you want to follow a fixed route.

The North Park paths start from behind the visitor centre, while access to the north-west corner

How to get there

(Two miles SW of Ringwood).

The Park is signposted from the main road. From the A31 (from Ringwood or Poole directions) turn in to Brock's Pine Road at the St Leonards roundabout and continue into the car park (through the lorry park). From Bournemouth, head north on the A338 turning left on to the A31 and continue as above.

Public transport: **The Ferndown to Ringwood bus service (Wilts & Dorset) stops at St. Leonards – a walk of half a mile from the park.**

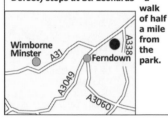

of South Park is a 600m walk from the car park through to Boundary Lane (take care when crossing the road here). There are some areas of private land within the park boundary – please do not enter them. You'll find the usual heathland specialities – Nightjars, Dartford Warblers and Woodlarks – across the site.

This is the best site in Dorset to see Woodlarks, which are found here in very good numbers. Areas of recently cleared woodland/scrub and the acid grassland are particularly good places to look for them.

More often than not, I usually pick them up by their song which carries across the heath – February and March are particularly good

months to hear them. Look out for them singing in flight, often quite high, or from the top of song perches. Tree Pipits, Stonechats and Linnets also breed here.

Woodcock probably breed in the area so listen out for them 'roding' at dusk while on your foray to find Nightjars – you should hear Tawny Owls at this time as well.

Crossbills can be seen at any time of year, and may breed from time to time, but their frequency depends on whether it is a 'good' Crossbill year or not.

Siskins are likely all year round but ever scarcer Redpolls are more likely in

winter when flocks of both species may be present. Buzzards are common, Sparrowhawks regular and, in the summer, Hobbies are seen from time to time.

If the visitor centre is open (11am-4pm) have a look at the displays and check out the 'indoor hide' which overlooks a small wildlife area with bird feeders – a good place to look for some of the park's common birds including Great Spotted Woodpecker and Nuthatch.

Apart from the birds, Avon Heath holds a good number of dragonflies and the six species of British reptile are present.

31

Key points

- Owned by the National Trust.
- Two car parks, free parking.
- No wheelchair access, but Rings can be viewed from NT car park.
- Dogs not permitted inside the Rings.
- Nearest toilets in Wimborne/ Blandford Forum.
- Good butterfly site.
- 11 species of orchid.

Contacts

The National Trust
01202 840 630
www.nationaltrust.
org.uk

Other nearby sites

River Allen - Crichel Lake, Holt Heath.

DOMINATED by the earthworks of an Iron Age hill fort, Badbury Rings is a great place to listen to the songs of Corn Bunting, Tree Pipit and warblers in springtime. However, in winter birders switch their attention to a magnificent two-mile avenue of beech trees to the south of this scenic site, because it has proved to be one of the county's best sites for large numbers of Brambling.

Target birds *All year* – Green Woodpecker (90%), Corn Bunting (50%). *Summer* – Tree Pipit (90%), Whitethroat (90%). *Winter* – Fieldfare (80%), Redwing (80%), Brambling (50%).

Other possible bird species

All year	Linnet	Winter thrushes
Buzzard	Yellowhammer	*Occasional/passage*
Kestrel	*Summer*	Barn Owl
Stock Dove	Cuckoo	Hobby
Skylark	Blackcap	Lesser Spotted
Nuthatch	Willow Warbler	Woodpecker
Common woodland	Chiffchaff	Wheatear
birds	*Winter*	Wood Warbler

Background information and birding tips

BADBURY RINGS is located mid-way between the towns of Blandford Forum and Wimborne, and has some commanding views over the surrounding countryside. The site forms part of the National Trust's Kingston Lacy Estate – the main house and gardens are close by on the same road.

The main attraction here is the chance of wintering Brambling. In good years I have seen flocks reaching 100+ birds, but some years they can be absent or may only be present in very low numbers.

The avenue of beech trees along the road is their favoured area, but as cars travel very fast here it is safer to stop in one of the car parks. Walk along the wide grass strips between the trees and the fields, or view part of the avenue from the fields below the Rings. Watch out for flocks of finches in

the trees or nearby on the ground.

At the same time of the year winter thrushes can be seen on the open grassland and in the hedgerows. Redwings and Fieldfares are plentiful, usually joined by good numbers of Mistle Thrushes, Song Thrushes and Blackbirds.

The main part of the site is an area of open (grazed) grassland dominated by the earthworks of the Iron Age hill fort that has even earlier settlement origins.

The top of the earthworks is covered with open woodland holding a number of common woodland species including Nuthatches and, in spring, Chiffchaffs and Willow Warblers. I usually find Tree Pipits here – look out for their song flight as they come into land on the trees on the edge of the woodland.

The spring is also the time to listen out for the jangling song of the Corn Bunting. This species has declined in the county, as elsewhere, in recent times but one or two pairs are still found in the area. For the best chance of finding them you will need to walk a circuit beyond the Rings to the edge of the farmland.

A full circuit will also take you past woodland and hedgerows as well as the open country thereby increasing your chances of a good species count.

Summer visitors are taking up territory from early April and the first Cuckoo is usually heard by mid-month. The woods hold Blackcap but also listen out for Wood Warbler which has occasionally been heard.

Common woodland birds should be plentiful – with luck there is a chance of Lesser Spotted Woodpecker – and along the hedgerows look out for Whitethroat and Yellowhammer.

I suggest taking the footpath from the main car park northwards across the downs and past the edge of The Oaks woodland. At the northern edge of the woodland turn south past King Down Farm and continue south to the minor car park before following the line of beech trees back to the main car park.

For a longer walk (four miles) turn left past King Down Farm along King Down Drove. Turn right (south) at the next track down to the road and turn right along the line of beech trees to the main car park. Whichever route you take, don't forget to spend some time among the Rings themselves.

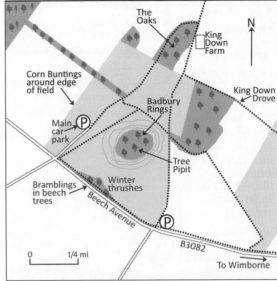

How to get there
(Four miles NW of Wimborne Minster).

Take the minor B3082 from either Wimborne Minster or Blandford Forum. Continue in either direction until you reach the car parks. There are two car parks - the main one is sign posted with a brown tourist sign from the road (opposite a turning to Shapwick), the other is

by the road at ST974021 (opposite a turning to Sturminster Marshall).

Wheatears are a regular passage birds from late-March/April (returning in the autumn) and there is the possibility of Whinchats during the same period or a passing Hobby (April to September).

Local Barn Owls are more often encountered during the shorter days (especially when you are driving along the roads).

Badbury Rings is also worth a visit for its butterfly interest, in particular from late-July to early September. Chalkhill blue, brown argus and dark-green fritillary are found on the open grassland which is also good for orchids – 11 species have been recorded here.

33

Key points

- National Trust ownership for most of area.

- Open access at all times.

- Allow two to three hours for circular walk.

- Can be muddy with some steep slopes, so not suitable for wheelchair users.

- Parking, toilets and refreshments in Swanage and Studland.

- Parking free for NT members in car park by Bankes Arms.

- Autumn visible migration can be spectacular.

BALLARD DOWN marks the eastern end of the Purbeck Hills which stop abruptly where vertical chalk cliffs fall into the sea by Old Harry Rocks, one of Dorset's most iconic landmarks. Throughout the year it is an interesting place for birding and walking and can be exceptionally good at spring and autumn passage times when, among the common migrants, there is always a chance of something more unusual turning up – recently this has included Stone Curlew, Wryneck and Hoopoe.

Target birds
All year – Peregrine (75%). *Autumn* – Ring Ouzel (20%), Grasshopper Warbler (10%), other species on visible migration. *Winter* – Great Northern Diver (50%), Red-throated Diver (25%),

Other possible bird species

All year	Whitethroat	Whinchat
Cormorant	Summer warblers	Wheatear
Shag	Linnet	Lesser Whitethroat
Kestrel	*Winter*	Firecrest
Red-legged Partridge	Divers	Spotted Flycatcher
Skylark	Grebes	Pied Flycatcher
Rock Pipit	Scoter species	Brambling
Yellowhammer	Mediterranean Gull	*Occasional*
Common passerines	Winter thrushes	Hoopoe
Summer	Chiffchaff	Wryneck
Fulmar	Firecrest	Tree Sparrow
Sandwich Tern	*Passage*	Hawfinch
Common Tern	Hirundines	Lapland Bunting
Stonechat	Redstart	

Background information and birding tips

LYING TO THE south of Purbeck's heathland are the Purbeck Hills, a chalk ridge stretching about 14 miles from Lulworth eastwards to Studland where it disappears into the sea before emerging again on the Isle of Wight (visible in the distance).

Though birds may be seen along the length of the ridge, the best area is found at its eastern end – Ballard Down. The birding, and the great views, can easily be combined with a visit to the adjacent Studland area.

Ballard Down is best approached from the village of Studland, but it can also be reached on foot from nearby Swanage. It is a pleasant walk at any time of the year but at its best for birds in the spring and autumn when birds are on the move.

I recommend combining birding with a circular walk from Studland to get the best out of the area but a shorter option is to retrace your steps after reaching Old Harry. The track can be muddy at times and the walk involves a number of fairly steep slopes in places. It can also be very busy with walkers.

Contacts

The National Trust
01929 450 123
www.nationaltrust.org.uk

The walk itself is straight-forward. From the National Trust's South Beach car park (by the Bankes Arms) walk the short distance down the road to the public toilets where the path out to Old Harry begins.

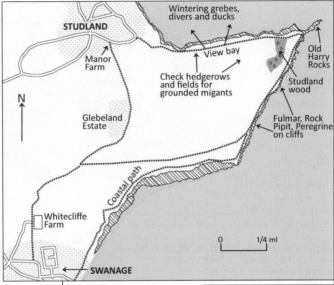

The first section of the walk, enclosed by trees and scrub, is a good starting point to search for common passerines and in late autumn/early winter look out especially for Firecrest or a lingering Chiffchaff.

In the spring, Blackcaps, Chiffchaffs and the occasional Willow Warbler fill the woodland areas with song, while Whitethroats are the commonest warbler in the scrub areas.

After 500 metres the path opens out with a hedge on the right and scrub above the cliffs on the left. Where there are breaks in the cliff-side scrub scan out into Studland Bay.

Though the birds are best seen from the Studland (site 53) it is possible to find birds on the water from here, particularly from late autumn and into the winter – Great Northern is the most likely diver species with the occasional Red-throated. Black-throated Divers are scarce.

Also look out for Black-necked and Great Crested Grebes, Brent Geese, Red-breasted Mergansers, Common Scoters and check out the gulls for Mediterranean Gull.

How to get there

(Immediately N of Swanage)

Head into Studland village on B3351 from Poole/ Bournemouth (via the Sandbanks ferry) or Corfe Castle (or by going north out of Swanage). Turn down the minor road by the shop/ Post Office until reaching the National Trust car park next to the Bankes Arms pub. There is very limited roadside parking along this road outside the main summer tourist season.

Public transport: **The Bournemouth-Sandbanks-Swanage bus service stops at Studland village (Wilts & Dorset).**

On foot (from Swanage):

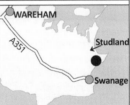

The South West Coast Path runs north from Swanage – from the seafront head north along Ulwell Road and Redcliffe Road, turning right into Ballard Way and on towards Ballard Down.

An alternative route is to take Whitecliff Road (off Ulwell Road), past Whitecliff Farm and continue northwards up onto the downs.

In the spring, just before the point, it is worth a detour through Studland Wood which is almost purely hazel.

Though you probably won't find too many birds in here, the ground is carpeted in wild garlic – the smell is out of this world, but only if you like garlic I suppose!

This stretch of the walk

Ballard Down has a good reputation for attacting vagrants – a Hoopoe was spotted recently.

turns up a variety of resting migrants in the bushes and on the open ground – look out for Wheatears, Whinchats, Grasshopper, Reed and Sedge Warblers, Ring Ouzels (especially in the autumn), Whitethroats, Lesser Whitethroats and winter thrushes.

I have seen Wryneck here and Stone Curlew has been seen in the adjacent fields. Hirundines overhead can pass in their hundreds and often in their thousands.

Mid-September through October is excellent for visible migration along this part of the Dorset coast and Ballard Down can be a good spot to watch this spectacle of the birds flying over. Pipits, wagtails, thrushes and finches can pass through in their hundreds while Wood Pigeon movements can be staggering.

Among the common species something a little more unusual is often picked up, including Woodlark, Brambling and Crossbill, while the calls of scarce Dorset birds such as Tree Sparrow, Hawfinch and Lapland Bunting give away their presence.

At the point, scan out to sea: Shags and Cormorants are usually seen and in the spring through to late summer local Fulmars can be seen floating by the cliffs.

Kestrels are often here – look out for them hovering on the updrafts at eye level. The locally breeding Peregrines regularly pass by (both here and elsewhere on the walk) and

Rock Pipits are found on the cliffs.

The walk continues southwards along the cliff top, in spring the air is full of Skylark song. Where the path splits go through the gate to take the path along the top of the ridge (the other path continues along the cliff edge and down into Swanage).

Check out the bushes on the ridge for Stonechat and Whitethroat (in the summer). After walking westwards along the top of the ridge for about a mile, a footpath turns to the north-east and heads down to the Glebeland Estate (while the tracks to the south go down into Swanage).

This can be a good spot to watch the visible migration as birds fly over the ridge. The path descends down the hill past Glebeland, eventually reaching the road by Manor Farm. On the way down check out the hedgerows and fields for birds, including Red-legged Partridges (scarce now) and Yellowhammers.

From the farm turn right and follow the road back to the car park. For an interesting detour take a look inside the Norman church and check out the trees in the churchyard for migrants – it's a good place for Pied and Spotted Flycatchers in the autumn.

Other nearby sites

Brownsea Island (via Sandbanks), Corfe Common, Dancing Ledge, Durlston Country Park, Studland.

SCATTERED around Dorset are a number of working cress beds that are attractive to Green Sandpipers from the autumn through to early spring. There is also an outside chance of a Water Pipit, while Grey Wagtail is virtually guaranteed at this cluster of sites, located between Wareham and Dorchester. All of the sites are private but can be viewed from public paths, roads or parking areas.

Target birds   *Autumn/winter* – Green Sandpiper (75%), Water Pipit (10%).

Other possible bird species

All year	Common finches	*Occasional*
Meadow Pipit	Yellowhammer	Little Egret
Grey Wagtail	*Autumn*	Snipe
Stonechat	Hirundines	Kingfisher

Background information and birding tips

UNDER NO circumstances should you enter any of the working areas where people and machinery will be operating out in the beds. Though this obviously causes disturbance, there are usually plenty of undisturbed areas still viewable where the birds can settle and be watched.

A visit to any of these sites will not produce many species (unless you spend a little time walking around the adjacent land), so it is unlikely that you will spend much time at them. However, it is worth calling in to at least one of them to look for their main target bird – Green Sandpiper.

Although this species is quite widespread around the county, the cress beds will give you the best chance of seeing one, and at reasonably close quarters. Each of the sites regularly has one or two birds.

The other bird of particular interest is Water Pipit. There have been a number of records from each of the sites over the years but they are by no means recorded

annually (though it is possible they could be overlooked). A telescope is useful here to scan the pipits to see if one can be picked out from the plentiful Meadow Pipits that are common around the beds.

Another bird of interest that you should see at any of the sites is Grey Wagtail and there is always a chance of Kingfisher passing through.

Snipe is another possibility, with an outside chance of Jack Snipe – so scan the beds carefully. During the autumn, hirundines hawk over the beds, often building up into quite large numbers.

Of the three sites, Bere Regis is the one you are most likely to pick up other birds in the immediate area. One viewing area into the cress beds is from the edge of farmland (after passing through Court Farm).

Here, a mixture of common finches, Stonechat and Yellowhammer can be found along with other common passerines. An over-wintering Blackcap or Chiffchaff may also be possible.

Key points

- Please do not enter any of the cress beds, view from the boundaries.

- Parking for Bere Regis/ Tincleton is on the nearby roads.

- Parking at Waddock Cross is by Wessex Trailers.

- There are no toilets in the immediate vicinity.

- Wheelchair access by the parking areas.

- Only Bere Regis can be reached by public transport.

Other nearby sites

Higher Hyde Heath, River Frome, Holme Bridge, Tadnoll & Winfrith Heath, Wareham Forest

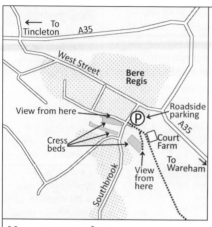

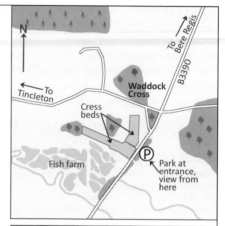

How to get there

Bere Regis SY 848 947

(6.5 miles NW of Wareham).

From Wareham take the road minor just north of the town, across Wareham Forest, to the A35 – turn left towards Bere Regis. Take the left turn at the roundabout, stay on this road as it veers to the left (Southbrook Road) then take the first right turn into Elder Road. You can park on the roadside here overlooking the eastern end of the cress beds. Walk back to the turning into Elder Road, cross over the road and follow the public footpath into Court Farm, and around to the right. Just past the large barn you can look back into the western side of the cress beds. This track can be very muddy.

Tincleton SY 767 918
(5.5 miles E of Dorchester).
From the north-eastern side of the Dorchester bypass (A35) take the minor road off the roundabout to Kingston Maurward College/ Stinsford, staying on it until reaching Tincleton. At Tincleton Cross turn right onto Watery Lane – the cress beds are just along this road. Park carefully by the roadside and scan from the road/gates.

Waddock Cross SY 797 908
(7.5 miles E of Dorchester).
Follow the same route from Dorchester. At Tincleton Cross continue straight on until the Waddock Cross crossroads. Turn right here on to the B3390 and almost immediately on the right pull off the main road into a parking area

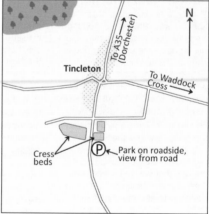

for the cress bed offices and Wessex Trailers. View from here.

Public transport:
A Poole-Dorchester bus service runs through Bere Regis. (Wilts & Dorset, operated by Damory Coaches).

No bus services to Tincleton/Waddock Cross.

THE SONG of the Nightingale has become less common in Dorset but the Vale is still the best bet to catch up with this delightful songster – there are still good numbers on both Lydlinch Common and Deadmoor Common. Nearby is Piddles Wood, a very good example of traditionally managed oak/hazel coppiced woodland, which holds a number of typical woodland birds. Each site is also worth a visit for their spring flora and to catch up with a number of uncommon butterflies.

Target birds   *Summer* – Nightingale (90% hear, 30% see).

Other possible bird species

All year	Willow Warbler	Spotted Flycatcher
Common woodland birds	*Occasional*	Willow Tit – now gone?
Summer	Hobby	*Winter*
Blackcap	Cuckoo	Woodcock
Garden Warbler	Lesser Whitethroat	Redwing
Chiffchaff	Whitethroat	Fieldfare

Background information and birding tips

THESE THREE sites within the Blackmoor Vale in the north of the county are relatively small but can be combined in a visit as they are located within easy reach of each other.

Though Nightingale is likely to be your target bird on a visit here (but not present in Piddles Wood), you will also pick up a good mixture of common woodland birds across the sites.

The pick of these are Marsh Tit, Nuthatch, Treecreeper and Bullfinch.

Garden Warbler, Blackcap, Willow Warbler and Chiffchaff are present in the summer. Willow Tits have been recorded in the past at Lydlinch and Deadmoor. Though probably no longer on either site there is always an outside chance they could still be present, but unrecorded.

① Lydlinch Common (ST 736 135)

LYDLINCH COMMON, a Site of Special Scientific Interest, has long been the best site in Dorset where Nightingale is virtually guaranteed. Though numbers fluctuate from year to year, it is worth making a spring visit to go to see/hear this attractive songster. They are likely to be heard first but with a little patience they can be seen – often giving great views.

The Common isn't very large (ca 30ha) and it is divided by roads

into three sections. The habitat consists of herb-rich grassland, fen meadow and scrub. A lack of management in recent years is now being addressed by contractors and volunteers from the local branch of Butterfly Conservation: scrub clearance and the introduction of grazing is pushing this SSSI back towards favourable condition.

There are no formal footpaths around the site, so feel free to wander around any promising

Key points

- Open access at all times.
- Deadmoor Common very wet underfoot.
- No wheelchair access to any site.
- Small sites – all easily visited in a day.
- Nature trail & leaflet at Piddles Wood.
- Good for Nightingale at Lydlinch and Deadmoor.
- Good selection of common birds.
- Good butterfly interest.
- Toilets available at Girdlers Coppice.

Contacts

Piddles Wood – Dorset Wildlife Trust
01305 264 620
www.dorsetwildlifetrust.org.uk/reserves

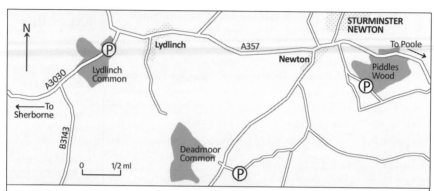

How to get there

Lydlinch Common (Ten miles NW of Blandford).

Deadmoor Common (Nine miles NW of Blandford).

Piddles Wood (Seven miles NW of Blandford).

For all sites: take A350 north from Blandford, turning left at the Durweston Bridge traffic lights on to A357 and head towards Sturminster Newton.

For Piddles Wood turn left into Common Lane (Broad Oak), just before the traffic lights at Sturminster Newton, take the next left hand fork (Copse Hill) and continue about a quarter of a mile to the car park (on the left).

For Deadmoor Common continue on A357 past the Sturminster Newton traffic lights and take the next left (Glue Hill) towards Woodrow. There is no parking at this site so, at Woodrow, turn left on to the minor road heading towards Fifehead Neville and park up carefully somewhere on this road.

Walk back to the junction and cross the road to the entrance track to the common.

For Lydlinch Common continue

on A357 towards the village of Lydlinch. Just past the village take A3030 towards King Stag and park up at the first small lay-by/gate on the left.

Public transport: None of the sites can be reached easily by bus.

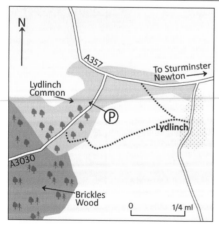

areas. Two species of butterflies in particular that will benefit from the clearance work are marsh fritillary and high brown fritillary, both important species listed under the SSSI citation.

2 Deadmoor Common (ST 757 110)

DEADMOOR COMMON (ca 40ha) is a typical example of damp, broad-leaved woodland in the Blackmoor Vale area – and damp is the right word to describe the site! On the occasions I've visited in the spring, wellingtons have been essential.

You will reach the south-east corner of the wood from Woodrow by taking the footpath from the road, past the cottages and across the field to a stile. From here the main

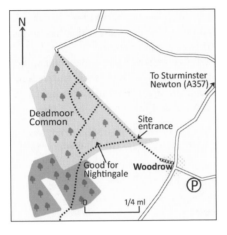

footpath runs north-westwards along the eastern boundary. As with Lydlinch Common, Nightingales are likely to be heard first, but for a good chance of seeing them, take time to look into the scrub by the open clearings as you walk along the main footpath.

An alternative footpath from the same stile is worth following as well – turn left on entering the wood and follow the southern boundary (the path leaves the wood after a short distance). In the past I have tended to find more Nightingales along this stretch than along the main footpath which is far more enclosed.

You can wander around the woodland but it can be tricky negotiating your way around if conditions are particularly wet as there are no marked trails to follow.

3 Piddles Wood (ST 792 128)

WOODLAND in this area named in the Domesday Book was probably Piddles Wood. Today it is classed as a semi-natural ancient woodland and is owned by the Hinton St. Mary Estate.

An area of 24ha of its total 62ha is leased to the Dorset Wildlife Trust in two sections: Piddles Wood south of the A357 and Girdlers Coppice north of the road adjacent to the River Stour.

From the small car park, a main track runs through the wood down to the A357. A circular way-marked trail leads off this main track to the right and takes you through the woodland types, including stands of hazel coppice, found in the area.

Look out for butterflies in the open areas including purple hairstreak, silver-washed fritillary and white admiral.

For access to Girdlers Coppice, turn off the A357 toward Fiddleford Mill where there is a car park. Just past the traffic lights, and the turning to Sturminster Newton, is a parking area overlooking the river where a Kingfisher is sometimes seen. There are toilets here.

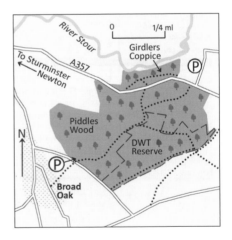

Other nearby sites

Duncliffe Wood, Fontmell Down, Hambledon Hill & Hod Hill, Sherborne Lake.

Key points

- Owned by Dorset Wildlife Trust.
- Designated SSSI.
- Ancient woodland (partial).
- Expect to see 20-25 species.
- Limited parking available.
- Access available at all times.
- Leaflet available.
- Information board.
- Paths are wet for most of year.
- Disabled access difficult.
- No public toilets nearby.

Contacts

Dorset Wildlife Trust
01305 264 620
www. dorsetwildlifetrust.org. uk/reserves

THIS SMALL Dorset Wildlife Trust reserve holds a nice mixture of typical woodland bird species, which has in the past included Wood Warbler. The woodland is dominated by oak high forest and has smaller areas of hay meadow and wood pasture, which provide habitat for some interesting butterflies. The stream running through the site usually turns up sightings of Kingfisher and Grey Wagtail and there is possibly a Dipper.

Target birds *All year* – Grey Wagtail (75%), Marsh Tit (75%), Kingfisher (50%), Dipper (<10%). *Summer* – Garden Warbler (50%), Wood Warbler (<10%).

Other possible bird species

All year	Common woodland	Redwing
Sparrowhawk	birds	Song Thrush
Buzzard		Mistle Thrush
Tawny Owl	*Summer*	Siskin
Great Spotted Woodpecker	Blackcap	
Nuthatch	Chiffchaff	*Occasional*
Treecreeper		Woodcock (winter)
	Winter	
	Fieldfare	

Background information and birding tips

DORSET Wildlife Trust has managed this 40ha site since the mid 1960s and bought it in 1985. Its habitat comprises of deciduous woodland, wood pasture, hay meadow and there is a small fast-flowing stream running through it.

There is limited parking and though access is open at all times a spring/summer visit is likely to provide the best birding.

The underlying clay bed means that the ground tends to remain wet underfoot most of the year and, together with the terrain, makes the site unsuitable if you have walking difficulties.

A series of footpaths and permissive paths offer a selection of routes across the site from the car park.

The deciduous woodland is the main habitat and walks will take you through a mixture of the dominant, unmanaged, high forest and areas of managed coppice (with standards).

Birds here are what would be expected: tits (including Marsh), Nuthatch, Treecreeper, Great Spotted Woodpecker and thrushes.

In summer, warblers are present with Blackcap and Chiffchaff the most common species, along with smaller numbers of Garden Warbler.

The site was traditionally known for Wood Warbler. There have been no recent records, though they may just be overlooked and could still be here in spring and summer.

The small stream running through the wood is fairly steep-sided and during heavy rain can become torrential.

Dipper is another species of the past with no recent records, and again they could simply be overlooked. Grey Wagtails and Kingfishers can still be seen along the course of the stream. Buzzard, Sparrowhawk and Tawny Owl are often seen or heard.

Outside of the breeding season the common resident birds will still be found and are joined by Siskins, most likely feeding on the alder in the wetter areas.

Winter thrushes moving around the area call in from time to time and there is a chance of flushing a Woodcock or two from the woodland floor.

Part of the woodland is considered to be of ancient origin, so though the bird interest is typical of this habitat, a visit in the spring will definitely be enhanced by the floral display.

In the summer butterflies become a big attraction and include silver-washed and marsh fritillaries. The open areas of hay meadow and wood pasture are particularly good for both of these groups. The autumn usually produces a good show of fungi.

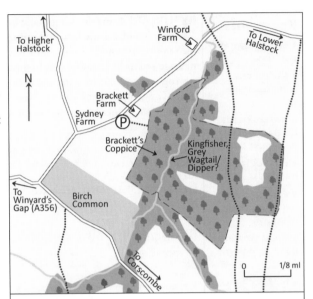

How to get there

(18 miles NW of Dorchester).

From Dorchester take the A37 then the A356 towards Maiden Newton. Continue on the A356 towards South Perrott (Somerset).

At Winyard's Gap, turn right on to the minor road heading towards Higher and Lower Halstock. Go just past the turn to Higher Halstock to where there is the entrance to a small car park (just before Brackett Farm). Walk down the track to the entrance of the reserve.

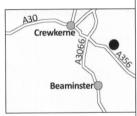

Other nearby sites

Cattistock Churchyard and Maiden Newton, Kingcombe Meadows, Powerstock Common, Sutton Bingham Reservoir.

43

Key points

- Pay & display parking.

- Restaurant/ café, open all year.

- Toilets (with disabled facility) in the car park.

- Bus route nearby.

- Easy access for wheelchair users.

- Good viewing point into Poole Bay.

- Better chance of birds on a S or S-E wind.

- Telescope essential.

THIS AREA, overlooking Poole Bay, is best known for its beach and seaside facilities but can be a good watchpoint for seabirds given the right conditions. It is possible to record passage seabirds, including shearwaters, petrels and skuas, during strong onshore winds as well as the regular terns and gulls. In winter, grebes, divers and ducks are possible offshore. Migrant passerines are sometimes found in the trees at the back of the car park.

Target birds *Spring/autumn passage* (if conditions right) –

Great Northern Diver (50% in spring), Red-throated Diver (40%), Arctic Skua (30%), Manx Shearwater (20%), Leach's/Storm Petrel (20%), Great Skua (20%), Arctic Tern (20%). *Winter* – Great Northern Diver (30%), Red-throated Diver (25%), Black-throated Diver (10%).

Other possible bird species

All year	Guillemot	Balearic Shearwater
Fulmar	Razorbill	Storm Petrel
Gannet	*Winter*	Leach's Petrel
Mediterranean Gull	Common Scoter	Grey Phalarope
Kittiwake	Great Crested Grebe	Pomarine Skua
Spring through autumn	Black-necked Grebe	Little Gull
Whimbrel	Auks	Little Tern
Sandwich Tern		Black Tern
Common Tern	*Occasional*	Little Auk
	Velvet Scoter	

Background information and birding tips

THIS PARTICULAR area of Poole Bay lies between the entrance of Poole Harbour and Hengistbury Head to the east.

Before reaching Hengistbury Head there are several places where you can stop along the seafront to view the bay but Branksome Chine, within the Borough of Poole, is the site most frequently watched by the local birders.

As with most seawatching sites the opportunity to see good birds relies on the right weather conditions. This site is tucked in against the mainland and with no obvious headland, passage seabirds are not a regular occurence.

With a good south or south-easterly onshore wind though, birds may be pushed up into the bay instead of passing further out to sea and a stop here can be worth the effort.

If you take shelter among the buildings to keep out of the worst of the weather, it is possible to seawatch in relative comfort.

As with all seawatches, you need to put in the time scanning out to sea and even if conditions are right you still may not see very much – sometimes it is just the luck of the draw!

It can be worth calling in at any time of the year but spring (April/

Other nearby sites

Brownsea Island (via Sandbanks), Poole Harbour – Poole Quay to Sandbanks, Studland.

May) and autumn (September/ November) passage times are more likely to turn up some good birds. At these times it is also worth having a look in the small piece of woodland on the northern edge of the car park for any passing migrants.

All four skuas have been recorded from here with Arctic Skua and Great Skua seen annually. Pomarine Skuas are seen less regularly, while Long-tailed Skua has been reported on a couple of occasions.

Spend time searching through the 'Commic' terns – though the majority of birds will be Common Terns, I have occasionally picked up Arctic Terns among them.

On a good day, Storm and Leach's Petrels may be pushed close inshore, with May/June and October/November usually the best months respectively.

Little Gulls and Whimbrels can pass through in good numbers, with October being the peak month for the former and April for the latter.

The summer months tend to be quiet but Common and Sandwich Terns that breed on nearby Brownsea Island may be foraging offshore and June/July can be the better months to see Manx Shearwaters here.

During the winter it is worth a visit to see if anything is lingering offshore. Great Crested Grebes are likely and perhaps the odd Great Northern Diver or two.

Sea-duck or auks may be in the vicinity, usually flying by. Any scoter you see is likely to be Common Scoters but check them carefully as Velvet Scoters are noted from time to time.

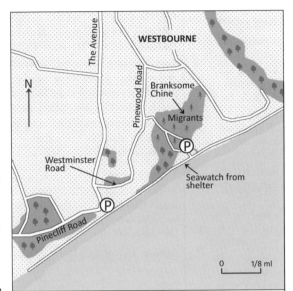

How to get there

(Between Poole and Bournemouth, to NE of Sandbanks).

From the Poole to Sandbanks harbour road (Shore Road/ Banks Road) take the B3065 (Haven Road) towards Westbourne.

On reaching a roundabout turn right (still Haven Road) and continue along for three-quarters of a mile to where the road descends, past a car park on the sea front, before rising again.

Just after this car park turn right into Westminster Road (which forks into Pinewood Road) and turn right again after about a third of a mile into the Branksome Chine beach pay and display car park.

Alternatively, leave the Wessex Way at the roundabout, where the

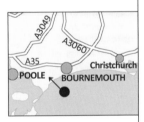

A35 and A338 meet at Westbourne, on the B3065 (The Avenue) to Sandbanks. At the end of The Avenue, just before the bottom of the hill, turn left into Westminster Road.

Public transport: The regular Swanage/Sandbanks-Bournemouth bus service passes close by. The Poole-Sandbanks bus service runs to Canford Cliffs, a mile from this site (Wilts & Dorset).

Key points

• **Owned by the National Trust.**

• **100ha leased by Dorset Wildlife Trust.**

• **Highly designated: SSSI, SPA, SAC, Ramsar.**

• **More than 250 bird species recorded.**

• **Reached by a boat from Poole or Sandbanks.**

• **Wheelchair users need to be able to walk a few steps to access boat boarding gates. Check with booking kiosk for other restrictions.**

Contacts

The National Trust
01202 707 744
(Brownsea Island) www.
nationaltrust.org.uk

Dorset Wildlife Trust
01305 264 620
www.dorsetwildlifetrust.
org.uk/reserves

Dorset Wildlife Trust
01202 709 445
(Brownsea Island)

THE LARGEST of five islands in Poole Harbour is the only one with public access and it holds many attractions for birdwatchers. The non-tidal brackish lagoon has Dorset's only breeding colony of Sandwich Terns, while in autumn and winter it holds a spectacular high-water roost of waders, including internationally important numbers of Avocets and Black-tailed Godwits. Many rarities have turned up, with White-rumped and Stilt Sandpipers being more recent visitors. Brownsea also has a population of Golden Pheasant and is renowned for its red squirrels.

Target birds

All year – Spoonbill (80% winter/ 20% summer). *Summer* – Sandwich Tern (100%), Common Tern (100%), Yellow-legged Gull (75%). *Winter* – Avocet (>95%), Black-tailed Godwit/ Icelandic race (>95%), Knot (75%), Spotted Redshank (75%), Greenshank (75%), Peregrine (50%), Firecrest (30%).

Other possible bird species

All year	(exc. Common)	Common Gull
Shelduck	Tawny Owl	Kingfisher
Gadwall	Green Woodpecker	Siskin
Tufted Duck	Raven	Redpoll
Golden Pheasant	Reed Bunting	*Passage*
Little Grebe	Common woodland birds	Little Stint
Cormorant		Curlew Sandpiper
Little Egret	*Summer*	Whimbrel
Grey Heron	Nightjar	Common Sandpiper
Sparrowhawk	Reed Warbler	
Buzzard	Chiffchaff	*Occasional*
Water Rail		Merlin
Moorhen	*Winter*	Ringed Plover
Coot	Brent Goose	Lapwing
Oystercatcher	Wigeon	Wood Sandpiper
Snipe	Teal	Little Tern
Curlew	Grey Plover	Roseate Tern
Redshank	Sanderling	Lesser Spotted
Mediterranean Gull	Dunlin	Woodpecker
Regular gull species	Woodcock	Crossbill
	Bar-tailed Godwit	
	Turnstone	

Background information and birding tips

THE NATIONAL TRUST, owners of this 1.5 mile by 0.75 mile island, leases 100ha to the Dorset Wildlife Trust (DWT) to manage as a nature reserve – this includes a 28ha brackish, non-tidal lagoon - the 'jewel' in Poole Harbour's crown. Brownsea is open to the public from April (or Easter if earlier) to October (10am-5pm) – check exact dates with the National Trust (NT).

A number of ferry companies are licensed to land on the island and

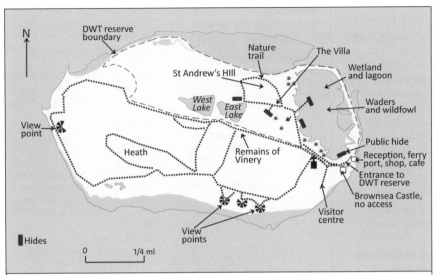

How to get there

(Located in Poole Harbour).

There are plenty of car parks signposted around Poole town centre and Poole Quay is a short walk down the High Street from bus and railway stations.

A number of ferry companies offer sailings to Brownsea – check the sailing details with the sales kiosks.

A shorter crossing operates from a kiosk on the Sandbanks side of the chain ferry. To reach Sandbanks from Poole town centre, take the A350 (Parkstone Road) to the main Civic Centre roundabout and follow the road signs to Sandbanks along the B3369 ¬ parking can be difficult in Sandbanks at busy times.

If approaching from Studland, park in the National Trust car park in Shell Bay and cross on the chain ferry as a foot passenger.

Public transport: Poole is easily accessible by rail and bus (sailings from Poole

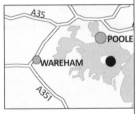

Quay). Alternatively, the Bournemouth-Sandbanks-Swanage and Poole-Sandbanks bus services stop by the Sandbanks kiosk (Wilts & Dorset).

boats leave from Poole Quay or Sandbanks. Not all the sailings land/pick up on the island, so check with the sales kiosk. There is a charge for the ferry.

Though closed in winter, when the bird numbers on the lagoon are at their best, there are some visiting options. Some of the RSPB Birdboat (site 41) sailings around the harbour land for a couple of hours and the DWT run a few sailings for members.

Recently there has been limited opening during some weekends but, again, details should be checked with the NT. Alternatively, why not offer your services on a DWT or NT work party to see the birds at close quarters?

Visitors must pay a landing fee on arrival on Brownsea (not payable by NT members or DWT members who are only visiting the DWT reserve).

Non-DWT members need to pay a separate entrance fee to visit the reserve at The Villa. Don't forget to take your membership cards or you will be charged!

Key points

- **Open Apr-Oct, limited access Nov-Mar.**

- **Charges apply (some free for NT/DWT members).**

- **Choice of walks.**

- **Visitor centre, shop, café & toilets.**

- **Leaflets & information boards.**

- **Guided walks and events.**

- **Reasonable disabled access across parts of the island.**

It is certainly worth exploring the whole island as it has an interesting history – including being the birthplace of the Scout and Guide movement. There are plenty of NT facilities (a visitor centre, shop, café, toilets and a public hide overlooking the south end of the lagoon) and there is reasonable disabled access.

The NT side of the island can get very busy but there are plenty of paths leading to quieter areas. Leaflets are available and walks, and other events, are run through the season.

The DWT reserve is quieter. The entrance is a short walk from the Quay, signposted along a boardwalk through an area of wet woodland. Once through the main gate the path leads up to The Villa, passing two hides on the way. The hides give a great view over the lagoon and many of the birds can be seen at very close quarters.

A telescope is useful though, especially to scan through the more distant waders during the autumn/winter. Waders are present all year round – no sooner does the spring finish than the autumn begins!

The best months on the lagoon are October through to February/March – I have regularly seen up to 15 species of wader on a single visit. Oystercatcher, Dunlin, Avocet and Black-tailed Godwit produce the highest numbers – the last two reaching peaks well in excess of 1,000 birds.

These are followed in number by Grey Plover, Bar-tailed Godwit, Curlew and Redshank (sometimes reaching three figures) and smaller numbers of Lapwing, Ringed Plover, Knot, Greenshank, Spotted Redshank and Turnstone. Check the edges of the reeds for Snipe.

Rare waders have turned up from time to time, but Whimbrels, Common Sandpipers, Little Stints and Curlew Sandpipers are regular passage visitors, mainly in the autumn.

Make sure you visit both hides, because some species favour the north end of the lagoon, others the south. If possible, time your arrival at the lagoon with a rising/high spring tide when birds are more likely to return from other parts of the harbour to roost/feed here.

Flocks of birds frequently take flight, swirling around the lagoon ......quite a sight. When this happens, scan around in case there is a bird of prey about – more often than not, a Peregrine. As the tide falls, many of the birds leave the lagoon to feed out in other parts the harbour.

Joining the waders will be a good selection of duck (Shelduck, Gadwall, Teal, Shoveler and Wigeon), a few Dark-bellied Brent Geese, gulls – including Mediterranean (particularly in early spring), Cormorant (have topped 600 birds), Grey Heron, Little Egret and Kingfisher (late summer onwards).

The lagoon is the top Dorset site for Spoonbill, with usually one or two birds on display, but in October 2006 12 turned up, only to be outdone a year later when there were 26! Numbers subsequently have dropped off but still peak into double figures.

The summer months are a lot quieter for numbers of species – there will still be a selection of waders about, albeit in small numbers. The main attraction on the lagoon at this time of the year is the tern colony. Dorset's only colony of Sandwich Tern breeds here (around 200-250 pairs) along with about 200 pairs of Common Tern – both can be seen at close quarters from the MacDonald hide.

Roseate Tern, an annual visitor, made a successful breeding attempt in 2009 and the lagoon has held Britain's only breeding pair of Yellow-legged Gull for many years.

The track from the entrance gate to The Villa (pay your entrance fee here if you are not a DWT member) is part of a nature trail that continues around the reserve. Turn right after leaving The Villa ......on your left is an area of permanently flooded woodland, with a boardwalk through it to a hide in a reedbed.

Water Rails, Reed Warblers and Reed Buntings breed in the reeds and Siskins and Redpolls feed on the alder seeds in the winter. A total of 23 species of dragonflies have been recorded on the reserve – this is a particularly good area for them and if you are lucky there is a chance of seeing water vole.

Return to the start of the boardwalk and turn left. The remainder of the trail follows a circular walk around the (mainly coniferous) woodland which includes areas of former rhododendron ......an invasive alien that has now been eradicated from the DWT reserve after decades of clearance work.

The first part of the woodland walk reaches a hide overlooking East Lake (freshwater) – Little Grebes breed and there may be a duck or two, usually Tufted Duck (breeds/winter) or Pochard (winter). The trail turns uphill away from the lake to an arboretum (planted in the 1800s), on to St. Andrew's Hill (where there are great views of the lagoon and beyond) and back down to The Villa.

There is no access beyond the trail to the west but listen in the spring for Grey Herons in the heronry – as the youngsters grow, the noise gets louder! Storms in the late 1980s destroyed many mature trees and as a consequence the size of the heronry has fallen from over 100 pairs to less than ten pairs

today. The UK's first Little Egrets bred here in 1996 and the colony steadily grew until 2005 when a pair of Ravens wiped out the colony by taking the young ......there has been no confirmed breeding since then.

The remainder of the island is managed by the NT. It is a less interesting from a bird perspective but still worth the time to walk around, especially to pick up a variety of the common birds which should include Jays, Nuthatches and Treecreepers.

There are a number of walks of varying lengths (mainly through woodland), access to the southern shore and a number of viewpoints with spectacular views across Poole Harbour to the Purbeck Hills.

The target bird for this area is Golden Pheasant. It is usually very secretive, more often heard than seen, so it is worth getting to the island as early as possible to check out the woodland paths before too many people arrive. The area around the remains of the Vinery is worth checking first before heading further west.

With the removal of so much cover on the island – the rhododendron will soon be eradicated from the NT side – it will be interesting to see how the pheasants will modify their behaviour.

Brownsea's star attraction is not a bird but the red squirrel – the island has a population of around 200. The area around the DWT Villa is one of the best places to look for them but they are spread around the island.

They are seen throughout the year but the autumn is a particularly good time to find them as the leaves fall from the trees and they are very active storing food for winter.

Other nearby sites

Poole Harbour – Poole Quay to Sandbanks, Studland, Upton Country Park & Holes Bay.

Key points

- A large area of heathland mainly owned by the Borough of Poole.
- Events programme – see Borough of Poole website.
- Wheelchair-friendly gates (RADAR keys needed). Contact Council for details.
- Nearest public toilets in Adastral Square, Canford Heath.
- Other heathland wildlife.

CANFORD HEATH is synonymous with heathland conservation in Dorset, as it is here that the tide of destruction caused by housing development was halted in the mid 1980s. Today it is one of the largest blocks of heathland in the county with Nightjars and Dartford Warblers in good numbers, regular Hobby sightings and a good selection of other interesting species (both avian and non-avian) that you would expect on this type of habitat.

Target birds
All year – Dartford Warbler (80%), Raven (50%). *Summer* – Nightjar (95% hear, 75% see), Hobby (75%).

Other possible bird species

All year	Siskin	Woodcock
Buzzard	*Summer*	Redpoll
Green Woodpecker	Cuckoo	*Occasional*
Meadow Pipit	Chiffchaff	Woodlark
Stonechat	Willow Wabler	Tree Pipit
Common woodland birds	*Winter*	
Jay	Snipe	

Background information and birding tips

DURING the mid 1980s conservationists won the battle to stop further housing development onto the heath. While there are still many pressures on the site due to the urban nature of its surroundings, don't let this put you off making a visit.

Canford Heath covers about 380ha and is the fourth largest block of heath in Dorset. The site has a number of landowners but the majority is owned and managed by the Borough of Poole. One unwelcome 'claim to fame' is that it has probably had more fires annually (more often suspected arson than not) than any other areas of heathland in the county.

A major fire in 2006 resulted in many properties being evacuated and nearly 200 firemen in attendance before it was brought under control. These fires can have a devastating effect, especially if they coincide with the breeding season as they often do. However, both Nightjar and Dartford Warbler numbers remain high and they are widespread across the heath. Woodlark is a casual visitor but Hobbies are regularly seen and usually breed on the heath or nearby.

The majority of the heath is dominated by calluna/bell heather and western gorse (dry heath) with smaller areas of wet heath and mire. As well as the heath there are areas of deciduous and coniferous woodland which will add variety to the birds seen.

There are plenty of paths across the site, many of them are signposted but I find the best way to enjoy a visit is to just go where the flow takes you. Despite the close proximity to its urban surroundings the site is large enough to give you a sense of the wilderness that heathlands provoke.

Contacts

Borough of Poole Leisure Services
01202 265 265
www.borough of poole.com

Initially from the lay-by, walk across to 'South Walk' (the main bridleway) which runs across the heath in an east-west direction along Lodge Hill. From this track you can explore the paths off to the north and south. The ground to the south drops away into the Canford Heath housing estate so the walks here are fairly short and will take you along the edge of the houses – highlighting how housing has encroached onto the heath. The paths to the north allow a variety of shorter or longer walks to be taken.

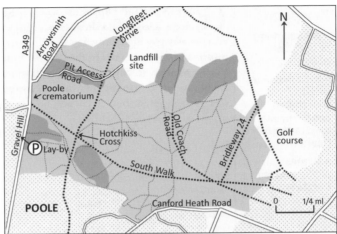

The wooded areas hold a good mixture of common woodland species, including Treecreeper, Nuthatch and Jay. Siskin (breeds) and Redpoll (scarce now) may be found, particularly in flocks during the winter. Small numbers of Crossbills can turn up through the year but they are erratic.

Other breeding birds include Green Woodpecker, Meadow Pipit, Stonechat, Willow Warbler and Linnet but Tree Pipit is very scarce. Cuckoos can be heard in spring and Wheatears pass through in spring and autumn.

Look out for Buzzards and the occasional Raven overhead. Woodcock and Snipe can be occasionally flushed from the tracks during the winter, usually from the woodland and heathland areas respectively.

An irregular visitor to Dorset

How to get there

(Three miles N of Poole).

Heading south on A31 from Ringwood head towards Wimborne. On reaching Wimborne stay on the A31 until the Merley roundabout. Turn left onto A349 towards Broadstone. Turn right at the next roundabout on to Oakley Hill – which runs into Gravel Hill. Continue on to, and over the Dunyeat's roundabout (past Poole Crematorium) and pull in to the lay-by on the left and access the heath from here.

From Poole (A35/A3049) take the A349 north from the Fleetsbridge roundabout towards Broadstone. Stay on the A349 and after passing

Poole Grammar School (on the right) look for the lay-by on the right hand side of the road.

Public transport: The Poole-Wimborne and Poole-Bournemouth bus services run along Gravel Hill. You can reach the south of the site from two Canford Heath bus services.

which can turn up in good numbers during 'bad' winters is the Waxwing. The ornamental shrubs of the streets and gardens around the Canford Heath housing estate are as good a place as any to look for them. They can stay in an area for

a while, at least until they have exhausted the supply of berries, before they move on.

As well the bird interest there is a good suite of other heathland species here, including reptiles and dragonflies.

51

Key points

- Easy parking at both sites.

- Wheelchair access possible through churchyard and along main road in Maiden Newton.

- Nearest public toilets in Dorchester.

HAWFINCH and Dipper are scarce species in Dorset, so if you are keen to add them to your list a visit to these two villages may pay dividends. However, be warned, a sighting is by no means guaranteed. In the past the Cattistock churchyard has been a regular wintering site for Hawfinches while Dippers are often seen on the river at Maiden Newton.

Target birds *All year* – Dipper (50%). *Winter* – Hawfinch (<10%).

Other possible bird species

All year		
Buzzard	Common corvids	Siskin
Sparrowhawk	Bullfinch	Redpoll
Great Spotted	*Summer*	*Occasional*
Woodpecker	Blackcap	Little Egret
Grey Wagtail	Chiffchaff	Kingfisher
Goldcrest	Spotted Flycatcher	Raven
Marsh Tit	*Winter*	Brambling
Nuthatch	Fieldfare	Yellowhammer
	Redwing	

Background information and birding tips

CATTISTOCK CHURCHYARD

NOWADAYS your best chance of a Hawfinch sighting in Dorset is during the autumn at a coastal site as birds move through on migration.

This wasn't the case when I had my first experience of the bird in the county in the early 1990s – then the place to go to find this elusive species was the churchyard in the west Dorset village of Cattistock.

For most of the 1990s birds turned up regularly during the winter. November through to January were the favoured months, with occasional sightings in February and early March.

Since 2000 sightings have become more erratic but birds are still reported from time to time, so if you are in the area during the winter it may be worth calling in.

While you wander around the churchyard you should find a few common passerines, with the possibility of a good flock of Siskins in the alders by the southern gate, and Bramblings have been seen here on rare occasions.

As an alternative to Cattistock a trip over the Hampshire border into the New Forest is likely to prove more productive for Hawfinch at this time of the year.

The Blackwater Arboretum (on the Rhinefield Ornamental Drive – car park at SU267046) is an excellent site where the Hawfinches usually gather an hour or so before dusk, giving good views before going off to roost.

There are also other birds here including Siskins and Redpolls and, occasionally, Crossbills and Bramblings.

MAIDEN NEWTON

DIPPERS can be found at a number of sites in the west of the county but sightings at some of the traditional ones are now few and far between, so it is worth checking out Maiden Newton, where the River Hooke joins the River Frome.

Scan the river both north and south of the bridge on the main road (near the shops).

It is possible to follow the river for a short distance in both directions. To the south, a footpath leaves the main road a little further along from the bridge (away from the main shops). Scan the river where you can – after a few hundred yards a road bridge over the river takes you back to the main road.

To access the north side of the river take the Cattistock road and walk past the church. At the end of the church wall there is a gate with a footpath to Chilfrome – this path follows the river north for about half a mile before it veers away.

Young Dippers have been seen at this site, so a spring trip may be more productive. The river may be in flood during the winter. Little Egrets and Kingfishers are sometimes seen on the river and Grey Wagtails breed here.

Marsh Tits, Goldcrests and Bullfinches are among the common passerines in the area, while Buzzards and Sparrowhawks can pass overhead.

Other nearby sites

Brackett's Coppice, Kingcombe Meadows, Powerstock Common, Sutton Bingham Reservoir.

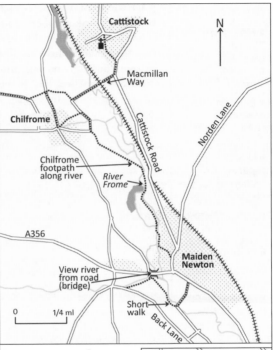

How to get there

(Maiden Newton 8.5 miles, Cattistock 10 miles NW of Dorchester).

Maiden Newton lies on A356 between Dorchester and Crewkerne. Take A37 Yeovil road from Dorchester, turning left on to A356 just past Grimstone.

Alternatively, from Crewkerne pick up A356 to South Perrott and stay on this road to Maiden Newton. Park by the shops on the main road, in a small car park signposted opposite the shops or on roadside around the corner (signposted to the station).

For Cattistock take the road signposted to the railway station and follow the road signs north to the village.

Once in Cattistock park on the road by the children's playground and walk the short distance down the lane to the churchyard.

Public transport: A Dorchester -Yeovil bus service stops at both villages, (South West Coaches). The daily Weymouth to Bristol train service stops at Maiden Newton – from Dorchester use the Dorchester West station (First Great Western Trains).

Key points

- More than 320 species recorded, with over 200 seen annually.

- Parking at Stanpit Marsh (free).

- Parking at Hengistbury Head & Mudeford (pay & display).

- Some Stanpit Marsh paths can be inundated at high tide.

- Good tarmac road for wheelchairs on Hengistbury.

Contacts

Bournemouth Borough Council 01202 420 909 www.bournemouth.gov.uk

Christchurch Countryside Service 01425 272 479 www.dorsetforyou.com

Christchurch Harbour Ornithological Group www.chog.org.uk

THIS HARBOUR is compact and is easily covered in a day. Though peak numbers of birds don't match those of Poole Harbour, most of the waders and wildfowl are common to both. The variety of habitat, plus the coastal headland, ensures that common migrants pass through annually. Sub-rarities and rarities regularly turn up – in recent years these have included Cattle Egret, Glossy Ibis, Black Kite, Corncrake, Kentish Plover, Wilson's Phalarope, Sabine's Gull, Barred Warbler, Ortolan Bunting .....the list could go on!

Target birds
Autumn – Visible migration. *Winter* – Wildfowl and waders. *Passage* – Seabirds, rarities and sub-rarities.

Other possible bird species

All year	*Winter*	Great Skua
Mute Swan	Brent Goose	Little Gull
Shelduck	Wigeon	Little Tern
Common Scoter	Gadwall	Sandwich Tern
Gannet	Teal	Common Tern
Cormorant	Pintail	Turtle Dove
Little Egret	Shoveler	Short-eared Owl
Grey Heron	Goldeneye	Hirundines
Sparrowhawk	Goosander	Water Pipit
Kestrel	Red-throated Diver	Yellow Wagtail
Water Rail	Great Northern Diver	Black Redstart
Oystercatcher	Avocet	Redstart
Ringed Plover	Grey Plover	Whinchat
Black-tailed Godwit	Lapwing	Wheatear
Bar-tailed Godwit	Purple Sandpiper	Ring Ouzel
Curlew	Dunlin	Firecrest
Redshank	Jack Snipe	Spotted Flycatcher
Mediterranean Gull	Snipe	Pied Flycatcher
Auks	Turnstone	Brambling
Green Woodpecker	Regular gull species	Siskin
Skylark	Kingfisher	Redpoll
Meadow Pipit	Winter thrushes	
Rock Pipit		*Occasional*
Stonechat	*Passage*	Eider
Cetti's Warbler	Garganey	Long-tailed Duck
Dartford Warbler	Manx Shearwater	Red-necked Grebe
Corvids	Spoonbill	Sooty Shearwater
Linnet	Osprey	Balearic Shearwater
Reed Bunting	Hobby	Bittern
	Knot	Spotted Redshank
Summer	Sanderling	Pomarine Skua
Fulmar	Little Stint	Black Tern
Cuckoo	Curlew Sandpiper	Arctic Tern
Nightjar	Ruff	Wryneck
Sand Martin	Whimbrel	Nightingale
Summer warblers	Greenshank	Yellow-browed Warbler
	Arctic Skua	Bearded Tit

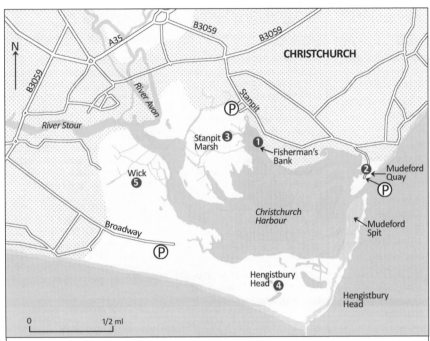

How to get there

(S outskirts of Christchurch).

The A35 runs to the north of Christchurch

North side: Leave A35 at the large Purewell roundabout onto B3059 towards Mudeford. Cross over the next roundabout into Stanpit and look for the car park (right hand side of road) for Stanpit Marsh. Fisherman's Bank can be accessed a little further along this road and is viewed from the footpath that runs along this section of foreshore – it is best approached on foot from Stanpit Marsh car park.

For Mudeford Quay continue along Stanpit into Mudeford, then turn right into Chichester Way, following the road into the car park.

South side: Leave A35 off Barrack Road, turning onto B3059 into Stour Road (heading towards Southbourne). Cross straight over the next two roundabouts (and the river bridge in between them) before turning left into Broadway (signposted Hengistbury Head). Follow this road to the end and into the Hengistbury Head car park.

If visiting both northern and southern parts I would recommend sticking to the A35 to pick up the turn-offs mentioned, rather than to trying to drive around smaller roads through the town.

Public transport: The Poole-Bournemouth-Christchurch-Somerford bus service (Yellow Buses) runs by Broadway (with a walk of just over a mile to the Hengistbury Head car park). The Yellow Buses

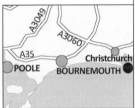

service linking Hurn and St Catherine's Hill runs through Christchurch and Stanpit/Mudeford.

Nearest railway station is Christchurch (two miles from Stanpit and Hengistbury).

Other nearby sites
Coward's Marsh, Sopley Common, Ramsdown Plantation & Avon Causeway, Town Common & St Catherine's Hill.

Key points

- **Refreshments and toilets at Mudeford Quay & Hengistbury.**
- **Visitor centre at Stanpit Marsh.**
- **Leaflets and events information from visitor centre.**
- **Can be reached by public transport.**
- **A wealth of other wildlife.**
- **Geological and archaeological interest.**

Background information and birding tips

BEFORE the boundary changes in 1974, Christchurch Harbour was part of Hampshire but now the whole area lies within Dorset. It is an extremely well watched site that has its own dedicated birders who run an excellent up-to-date website and produce a comprehensive annual bird report.

Christchurch Harbour lies between the conurbations of Bournemouth and Christchurch, so to reach areas within the site can take a little effort but it is certainly worth it.

The harbour can be conveniently divided into north and south sections, mostly covered by the 350ha SSSI designation.

The natural harbour is fed by the Rivers Stour and Avon running into its western end and the sea through the narrow entrance to the harbour between Mudeford Quay on the north shore and Mudeford Spit on the south. Christchurch has a double high tide system (with a slight drop in the tide between the two highs).

The habitats here include a good mixture of saltmarsh and mudflat, reedbed, freshwater marsh, drier grassland, heathland and woodland. The harbour's bird list stands at just over 320 species, with more than 200 species recorded annually. The site offers a good selection of waders – a rising tide is the best time to see them as they are pushed closer to the shore – and seawatching can be good in the right conditions.

The headland of Hengistbury Head is an important migration route. As well as grounded birds, it is a good viewpoint for watching birds flying through (Vis Mig). Most of the common migrants can be expected, and there are always a scattering of sub-rarities and rarities annually, though most will only make a brief stop before moving on. An early morning visit is usually the most productive, especially after a 'fall' when birds have been grounded by poor weather.

All of the areas around the harbour can get very busy with people, so birds are prone to disturbance at any time of the day. Generally an early morning start will be quieter on the people front (and usually better for birds anyway). Recent new bylaws now make it compulsory for dogs to be kept on a lead over most of the area, so at least some of the disturbance has been reduced.

North Side: ❶ Fisherman's Bank (SZ 174 920)
❷ Mudeford Quay (SZ 183 917)

FISHERMAN'S BANK gives a good view over the northern part of the harbour and across to the east bank of Stanpit Marsh.

Waders are the main interest here but numbers tend to be quite low and are likely to be better from Stanpit Marsh. It is still worth calling in, especially during the spring and autumn – Dorset's first Marsh Sandpiper was seen from here in the spring of 2000. Black Redstarts sometimes winter.

Mudeford Quay looks over the

north-east corner of the harbour and should also be scanned for waders. A few birds may be picked up on the beach outside of the harbour or offshore. Look out for Common Scoters and check out any gulls for Mediterranean. The scrub around the car park area is worth checking for migrants.

3 Stanpit Marsh (SZ 171 924)

THIS 65ha SITE, owned and managed by Christchurch Borough Council, was designated as a Local Nature Reserve in 1964 and a SSSI in 1986. Generally the site is flat and reasonably easy to walk around but it is liable to flooding at high water. Some of the gravel paths, especially where inundated by the tide, are a little rough. A telescope is useful for scanning over the marshes and into the harbour beyond.

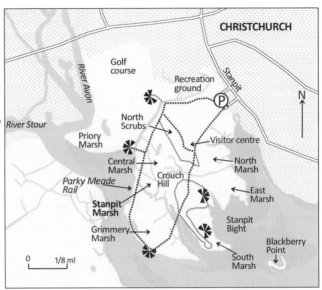

From the free car park, walk along the footpath to the south side of the recreation ground. Almost immediately you will be looking over reedbeds and the marsh. After 350m, the path reaches a purpose-built visitor centre (opened in 2008) which provides information about the site.

Running north-west from the centre is the main area of scrub on the marsh (North Scrubs) which is worth exploring, especially when migrants are about.

The main route follows a loop around the marshes. The ground initially rises a little across Crouch Hill. This sandy 'hill' is dotted with patches of gorse and is a good area for Linnets and passing Wheatears.

The fenced-off area on the hill is part of a successful breeding programme for the rare natterjack toad.

This is a good spot to scan over East Marsh, South Marsh and out into the harbour (towards Stanpit Bight and beyond to Blackberry Point sand spit).

In the winter, check the marshes for roosting waders and wildfowl, including Black-tailed Godwits and dark-bellied Brent Geese. Take time to scan across the Bight for birds feeding on the mud – two or three hours before high tide is the best time to watch.

A drier strip of land runs out from Crouch Hill along the west side of South Marsh allowing the best views – but be careful not to disturb any roosting birds by trying to get too close and do not go out any further than the last bushes.

Search through the waders carefully throughout the year, but especially in the autumn, for Little Stints, Curlew Sandpipers, Ruff and other less common passage birds.

The path continues down to the main channel before turning northwards along Parky Meade Rail, a reed-fringed bay. This is a good area for Water Rail in the autumn. Just north of here, to the left of the main track, is Priory Marsh.

It is no longer practical to follow the old path across the marsh, so the best option is to scan from, or just beyond, the gate (taking care not to disturb any birds on the pools).

Alternatively view the area from the edge of the golf course (continue on the main track through into the Recreation Ground, carrying on until you can cross over the creek on the left to reach the edge golf course).

Turn left along the fence, following it to beyond the clump of trees – scan the pools where possible through the scrub. Garganey, in spring and autumn, and some of the waders can favour this area.

You can return to the car park across the Recreation Ground but a better option is to walk through the North Scrubs back to the Visitor centre, looking for more small birds on the way, and leave by the way you came in.

South Side: ④ Hengistbury Head & ⑤ Wick (SZ 162 911)

BOURNEMOUTH Borough Council manage this 162ha site, which was declared a Local Nature Reserve in 1990. Aside from its natural history interest (birds, flora and invertebrates, especially beetles), the area is internationally important because of its coastal geology and its Stone Age and Iron Age archaeology.

The main car park is at the end of Broadway where there is a café (Hiker Café, open daily, 01202 428 552) and toilet block. A tarmac road (private) continues, beyond the turning circle, all the way down to Mudeford Spit (just over a mile) and is suitable for wheelchairs.

A 'land train' makes daily journeys to the Spit where there is another café (Beach Café – opening varies through the year, 01202 423 474) and toilets.

From the car park, walk east along the tarmac road. Scan across Wick Hams and the harbour to the north of the road and across Barn Field and Long Field to the south. Stonechats breed on the fields and if there are migrants about it is worth checking the scrub for them. Continuing along the tarmac, you enter the wooded area, first passing a private nursery/bird sanctuary.

The sheltered woodland can hold a good variety of birds at migration time, especially warblers and flycatchers, and is the place to pick up rarities and sub-rarities, including regular Yellow-browed Warblers. The woodland ends north of the tarmac, opening onto Holloway's Dock – a tidal lagoon linked by a channel to the harbour that is good for waders (I have regularly had good views of Avocets and Greenshanks here) and Little Egrets.

After the lagoon, the beach huts on Mudeford Spit loom ahead. The spit is actually outside the SSSI ......and is very busy, especially in the summer. I usually walk along to the end along the harbour shore and return along the seawards side – looking, in winter, for Purple Sandpiper on the groynes.

This is the best place for seawatching on Hengistbury, as you can use the shelter of the huts against the worst of the elements. The best conditions are when the winds are from the SE in spring and SW in the autumn and winter gales can be productive.

The summer is the best time for Gannets, Manx Shearwaters and Fulmars (the most likely seabirds to be seen). From the spring to autumn, Arctic and Great Skuas come through annually in small numbers and Pomarine Skua has become more regular recently. Winter grebes are fairly scarce but there is a good chance of seeing divers. Red-throateds are the most likely to be seen, but small numbers of Black-throateds and Great Northerns turn up as well.

Plenty of interesting seabird species have been seen on seawatches, Sooty and Balearic Shearwaters, Leach's Petrel, Sabine's Gull and Long-tailed Skua among them.

From the base of the spit, take the steps up the slope, to Warren Hill and the heathland. The main track runs to the west across the heath, eventually joining a tarmac track which runs around Barn Field and back to the car park. A few pairs of Stonechats and one or two pairs of Dartford Warblers breed on the heath and there are usually Nightjars around

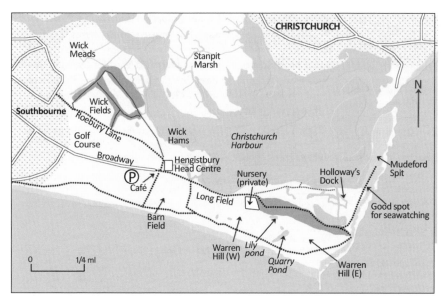

(possibly breeding). An alternative route back, especially if migrants are about, is a path through the top of the woodland.

Turn right at the top of the steps and follow the line of trees to a fork in the path to take you down to the Quarry Pond. Walk past the pond (on your left) and take the left fork followed by the right fork – past the Lily Pond.

After about 300m the path comes out of the woodland into the open and gives views down into the nursery/bird sanctuary area. There is a small heronry in here, containing a handful of Grey Herons (hanging on) and Little Egrets (increasing). After another 400m the path joins up with the main path.

There is an option of returning from the Spit to the car park by walking back along the beach but this won't be very productive for birdwatching.

Wick, which lies to the north of the car park, is a large area of meadows, some wet (in the northern part), with scrub and planted hedgerows and trees. From the car park head north from the turning circle towards the Hengistbury Head Centre.

At the entrance to the centre go through the gate by the signs and out into the fields, or alternatively turn left along Roebury Lane between the fields and the golf course, and turn to the right into fields at the end of the lane.

Along with a selection of common passerines, a good number of warblers breed on Wick – Cetti's, Reed, Sedge, Blackcap, Lesser Whitethroat, Whitethroat (the most numerous) and Chiffchaff. The area is good for migrants in the spring and autumn, so be sure to spend time walking around, checking the open ground, scrub and other suitable cover.

There are great 360-degree views from the top of the Head, which makes it a great spot for watching visible migration (Vis Mig - see the Trektellen website www.vismig.org).

Autumn movements of some species can be very high, especially in October, including Wood Pigeons, Skylarks and finches. Look out for something more unusual: Woodlarks (100+ counted on one day!), Tree Sparrows, Twite, Hawfinches, Lapland Buntings and Snow Buntings are all good Dorset records.

Key points

- SSSI managed by Dorset Wildlife Trust.
- Parking space is limited.
- Allow about two hours and expect 25-30 species in spring.
- Tracks can become very muddy and rough when wet.
- Site unsuitable for wheelchairs.
- Information board by main entrance to Coombe Heath.
- The walk around Lulworth Lake (Lulworth Estate) is permitted access only, not a right of way.
- If the ranges are firing it can be a little noisy!
- Nearest toilets in Wool or Wareham.

Contacts

Dorset Wildlife Trust
01305 264 620
(www.
dorsetwildlifetrust.
org.uk/reserves)

COOMBE HEATH is an important remnant of Purbeck heathland and is one of the more remote examples of the habitat in Dorset. Take a circular walk around the heath and you'll be almost certain to see Dartford Warbler at any time of year, while Woodlarks have bred and summering Hobbies are regularly seen. A walk around Lulworth Lake will produce a different range of species.

Target birds
All year – Dartford Warbler (80%), Yellowhammer (75%), Crossbill (25%). *Summer* – Nightjar (50%), Tree Pipit (50%), Hobby (25%), Woodlark (20%).

Other possible bird species

All year	*Summer*	Teal
Canada Goose	Cuckoo	Pochard
Mallard	Reed Warbler	Tufted Duck
Coot	Blackcap	
Meadow Pipit	Chiffchaff	*Occasional*
Stonechat	Willow Warbler	Greylag Goose
Common woodland		Hen Harrier
birds	*Winter*	Merlin
Linnet	Wigeon	Crossbill
Reed Bunting	Gadwall	

Background information and birding tips

FIRST OF ALL don't confuse this Coombe Heath, managed by the Dorset Wildlife Trust, with the part of the RSPB's Arne reserve also known as Coombe Heath!

This particular site is surrounded by forestry plantation and agricultural land in an area dominated by the MoD's Lulworth Ranges where there is little public access. Once you have navigated your way along the back roads you'll arrive at a dead end.

Leave your car at the end of the tarred road, just inside the woodland, taking care not to block the access, and walk to the entrance to the heath itself along the woodland edge.

You should find a good selection of common birds in this strip of woodland including summer warblers (possibly including Garden Warbler), Marsh Tits, Nuthatches,

and Great Spotted Woodpeckers – all species that are also widespread in the scrubby/wooded areas around the edge of the heath and the lake.

The entrance onto the heath by the main sign is uneven and can be very muddy but once through the first bank of gorse the heath opens out and walking is a little easier (but it can still be very wet). To your left, the heath stretches across to forestry blocks where red flags are usually flying. This MoD land is part of a firing range and when the guns are operating a walk can be very noisy.

Target birds are the heathland specialities. Nightjar, Dartford Warbler and Tree Pipit breed and could be anywhere on the 41ha site while Woodlark is in the immediate area and has bred.

A late-winter/early spring visit

should give an indication if they are around as this is a good time to listen out for them.

Meadow Pipits, Stonechats, Linnets and Yellowhammers are common and Hobby is usually in the area, especially if breeding nearby.

Walk south along the footpath to the south-east corner of the heath and leave by this gate onto a permitted path that runs off to the right. This will take you along the southern edge of the heath through to the south-west corner of the site where you can continue your walk across the heath back towards the main entrance gate.

I like to take a detour to nearby Lulworth Lake, just south of the heath among the farmland. This can be reached by staying on the public footpath after leaving the heath. Continue walking up the lane towards Home Farm and just before the farm, turn right along a permitted path that drops down to the lake.

A shorter alternative is to take the permitted path immediately after leaving the heath by the south-east gate and make a circuit from this path around the lake. Whichever route is taken, rejoin the permitted path along the southern edge of the heath and continue your walk back across the heath.

Lulworth Lake may produce a few water birds, including Tufted Ducks, Pochards, Mallards, Little Grebes and Coot, and is best for these during the winter months. Greylag and Canada Geese drop in from time to time.

The lake's main claim to fame was the regular appearance of a Ferruginous Duck that stayed

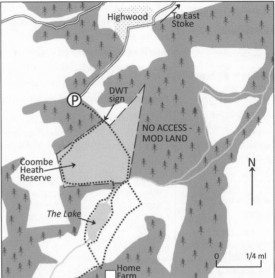

How to get there

(Three miles SE of Wool).

From Wareham take A352 towards Wool. At Holmebridge turn left on to B3070. Turn right at the crossroads at West Holme on to 'Holme Lane, leading to Bindon Lane' and signposted to East Stoke.

At the next crossroads turn left, signposted to Highwood. Continue on this narrow road to end of the tarmac. Park just inside the woodland and take the footpath signposted to Shaggs. After a few hundred yards you will be

at the entrance to Coombe Heath.

Alternatively, from Wool, turn off A352 by the railway crossing, passing the railway station and take the next left on to Bindon Lane. Continue on to the Highwood crossroads.

in Purbeck over a number of winters a few years ago. In the summer Reed Warblers and Reed Buntings nest in the marshy fringes.

If you take a winter visit across the heath to the lake, keep a look out for a passing Hen Harrier or Merlin and check any Snipe that you flush

for a possible Jack Snipe. Crossbills could be in the area at any time, especially in good Crossbill years.

Other nearby sites

Creech, Stoborough & Grange Heaths, River Frome, Tadnoll & Winfrith Heath.

Key points

- **Access available at all times.**

- **Allow at least one hour and expect 20-30 bird species.**

- **Leaflet available in NT shop and Castle View visitor centre.**

- **No wheelchair access.**

- **Limited roadside parking on B3069 (park with care).**

- **Pay and display car parks in West Street and at Castle View visitor centre (NT members free).**

- **Close to a bus route.**

- **Toilets in West Street car park.**

- **National Trust shop & tea room in the village.**

Contacts

The National Trust
01929 477 322
(www.nationaltrust.
org.uk)

THE ROMANTIC ruins of Corfe Castle attract thousands of tourists each year, and it is certainly worth exploring the castle and village before walking out onto the common where you'll enter a world of tranquil natural beauty. The common, the largest of its kind in Dorset, has been designated an SSSI because of its flora, but it also attracts a nice variety of common birds with a chance of something a little more unusual.

Target birds *All year* – Buzzard (90%), Stonechat (90%), Kestrel
(80%), Raven (75%), Yellowhammer (75%). *Summer* – Whitethroat (75%). *Passage* –Wheatear (50%), Whinchat (20%). *Winter* – Black Redstart (10%).

Other possible bird species

All year	*Summer*	Fieldfare
Skylark	Blackcap	Redwing
Meadow Pipit	Chiffchaff	
Stonechat	Willow Warbler	*Occasional*
Linnet		Barn Owl
Bullfinch	*Winter*	Redstart
	Snipe	Dartford Warbler
	Woodcock	

Background information and birding tips

THE HISTORIC village of Corfe Castle is dominated by a castle which has stood for more than a thousand years. The oldest surviving structure originates from the 11th Century, but there is evidence of some form of a stronghold pre-dating the Norman Conquest.

It remained a royal fortress until the 16th Century when it was sold by Elizabeth I. During the English civil war the Royalist Bankes family came under siege in the castle and after two attempts the castle fell in 1646. So it couldn't be used as a Royalist stronghold again it was 'slighted' (destroyed) by explosives.

If visiting the castle, be sure to take your binoculars with you: Raven has recently started to breed on the ruins and Black Redstart has been recorded – mainly in the autumn/winter.

The Common lies to the south of the village. It covers 140ha, and is divided into three blocks (West, Brickyard and East Commons), Its boundaries haven't changed for nearly 250 years and the site is well served by a series of footpaths, though you will get the best out of your visit by picking out your own route.

While walking around, look out for the Bronze Age burial mounds along the ridge on West and Brickyard Commons and enjoy the views of the castle.

The Common came under the ownership of the National Trust in 1982 and is managed by a combination of traditional grazing, using ponies and cattle, and scrub management.

While the scrub removal has been a contentious issue in the past, it is necessary to maintain the open aspect of the Common, which is a designated SSSI, of particular

How to get there

(Four miles SE of Wareham).

Corfe Castle lies on the A351 Wareham-to-Swanage road and can also be approached from Studland via the chain ferry across from Sandbanks.

There is limited roadside parking in the village but the main car park (pay and display) is located in West Street. There is more pay and display parking (free to NT members) at the Castle View visitor centre (SY 960 825) on the left as you approach the village from Wareham.

A number of entrances to the common can be accessed from the village.

Alternatively there is limited roadside parking on the B3069 Kingston road immediately south of the village (SY 962 807).

Public transport: The regular Poole-Wareham-Swanage bus service passes through Corfe Castle (Wilts & Dorset).

For a piece of nostalgia,

The Swanage Railway runs steam train services between Swanage and Norden, and stops at Corfe Castle. There is a park-and-ride facility at Norden for the railway.

Days/times of services vary depending on the time of year.

Phone 01929 425 800 or check the website at: www.swanagerailway.co.uk for further details.

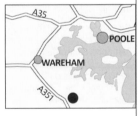

---

importance for its floristic interest.

The easiest options to get on to the Common are from the village at the end of West Street or off the Kingston road. If you have limited time you should concentrate

your visit on West Common, where from the entrance points the combination of open grassland, scrub and wet flushes can easily be seen.

In the spring Skylarks and Meadow Pipits will be in full aerial song but continue to

look skyward for Buzzards, Kestrels and Ravens, the latter more often than not picked up by their distinctive deep call.

The gorse scrub scattered around the Common holds Stonechats, Linnets, Yellowhammers and, usually,

63

Whitethroats, while Blackcaps, Chiffchaffs, Willow Warblers and Bullfinches are more often found around the boundary hedgerows. The common thrushes, tits and finches will make up the numbers on a visit.

During passage times Wheatears are regular visitors, with Whinchats and Redstarts less so, and more interesting sightings recently have included Red-backed Shrike and Short-eared Owl.

The wet flushes on the site are worth a look, particularly the areas to the south and west where the common is flanked by a branch of the Corfe River. Lapwing has bred here in the past and in winter Snipe may be flushed from these areas (I have had Jack Snipe on one occasion).

Winter is also a good time for a chance of Woodcock but, as with Snipe, they are more likely to be flushed.

Small flocks of wintering Redwings and Fieldfares will be more easily seen. Other casual sightings have included Dartford Warbler and Barn Owl.

If you have time, extend your visit to the other areas of the Common. The habitats in these areas are similar to those on West Common and you'll find a selection of the birds already mentioned.

Cross over the B3069 Kingston road to get to Brickyard Common. There is a good sized pond alongside the A351 to check for dragonflies. Unfortunately the pond has been colonised by two very invasive alien plants – New Zealand pygmyweed (Australian stonecrop) and parrot's-feather – despite efforts to remove them, they both remain.

The third part of the site, East Common, is best approached from the A351 to the south of the village. Follow the footpath in from the road - after about 200m check out the wet flush on the right. This is another good area for dragonflies, including southern damselfly and there is a possibility of Snipe in here in the winter.

The path continues over a railway bridge and into the main part of East Common (not part of the SSSI). This area was ploughed up as part of the war effort in the 1940s and 'improved' for agricultural use. These improvements continued until the early 1980s when the Trust instigated a natural reversion to its former state, including filling in drainage ditches to allow the wet habitats to return.

This is a good area to watch the steam trains passing by but be careful if you stand on the bridge when the engine goes underneath ......it can get a bit smoky!

Walk out across the Common, again checking out the scrub and wet flushes for birds. To leave, either retrace your steps over the bridge back to the main road or make your way to the north end where a path runs under the railway line and back to the main road through the village.

The Common is good for a number of butterflies including marbled white, small copper and large skipper.

Ravens can be seen at many Dorset coastal locations and have now started to nest on Corfe Castle.

COLD WEATHER or flooding have a tendency to concentrate wildfowl and waders along the Avon Valley at Coward's Marsh. Bewick's and Whooper Swans and Smew are scarce in the valley area but this site is a reliable place to see Goosander, a regular winter visitor. A spring/autumn visit will often turn up good birds, especially when it is wet, and may include Garganey, Water Pipit and a variety of waders.

Target birds *Spring* – Garganey (25%), Little Ringed Plover (25%). *Winter* – Goosander (50%), Green Sandpiper (50%).

Other possible bird species

All year	Hirundines	*Occasional*
Mute Swan	Whimbrel	Egyptian Goose
Greylag Goose	Common Sandpiper	Smew
Canada Goose	Yellow Wagtail	Spoonbill
Shelduck	Wheatear	Marsh Harrier
Mallard		Hen Harrier
Grey Heron	*Winter*	Peregrine
Little Egret	Gadwall	Merlin
Buzzard	Teal	Hobby
Lapwing	Pintail	Mediterranean Gull
Redshank	Tufted Duck	Little Gull
	Snipe	Sandwich Tern
Spring/autumn	Regular gulls species	Water Pipit
Ruff		
Greenshank		

Background information and birding tips

COWARD'S MARSH is an area of well-grazed common land on the Dorset side of the River Avon, which runs from Ringwood down to Christchurch and can easily be combined with a visit to nearby Town & Common/St Catherine's Hill (site 59).

Covering just 28ha, it is a small site but it does turn up some interesting birds. It has a mixture of lowland acid grassland with some birch woodland and heathland on its western edge.

The site should only be viewed from the gate at the entrance to the marsh (a telescope is useful) – don't try to walk out on to the marsh as you will only disturb the birds. With careful scanning over the area, most birds will be visible from the gate.

There are a number of ditches and low-lying areas, so the site is liable to flooding – conditions which usually provide the best chance of seeing interesting birds.

The main bird interest here is during the spring and autumn, especially if there are still plenty of wet splashes over the marsh. In the spring, Garganeys and Little Ringed Plovers are fairly regular visitors – usually in late March, early April.

Historically, Lapwings, Redshanks and Snipe have bred (now only the first two breed sporadically) but

Key points
• A small site, designated as SSSI.

• Scan for birds from the gate only.

• Habitat best when wet.

• Wheelchair access on tracks is possible, but pot-holes are often full of water.

• Less mobile birders can be taken by car along Marsh Lane and dropped by the gate.

all can still be seen at this site, particularly later in the autumn/winter.

Other waders might include Ruff, Greenshank, Whimbrel and, more regularly, Green Sandpiper and there is always a chance something more unusual – which has included Pectoral Sandpiper in the past.

In the winter there are usually a few duck about such as Mallard, Gadwall, Teal and Tufted Duck, but the main attraction for most birders will be Goosanders which can usually be seen on the river or sitting out on the river bank.

The occasional Smew may also turn up. Canada and Greylag Geese visit regularly and there may be an Egyptian Goose from time to time.

Among the more interesting small birds, Yellow Wagtails are more frequent in the autumn (no longer a breeding bird here, or in Dorset for that matter).

Any pipits you spot are worth scanning for Water Pipit especially in the late winter/early spring and Wheatears come through in both passage periods.

A number of species have, and do, turn up infrequently – these include Spoonbill, Hen and Marsh Harrier, Merlin, Hobby and Little Gull while Peregrine is a little more regular.

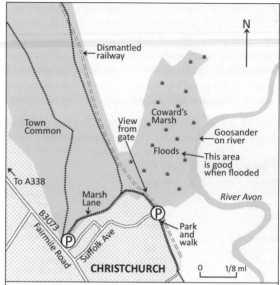

How to get there

(1.5 miles NW of Christchurch).

From A35 in Christchurch take B3073, off the Fountain Roundabout (heading towards Hurn) into Bargates Road which runs into Fairmile Road. After just over a mile, turn right into Suffolk Avenue and continue along to Marsh Lane. Park here and walk north along the track (also Marsh Lane) until reaching Marsh Cottage – this is the entrance to Coward's Marsh.

Please view from here so you don't disturb birds on the marsh.

Public transport: **The**

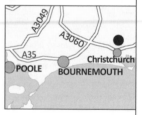

Bournemouth-Christchurch bus service runs through Fairmile, with a stop 150 metres from Marsh Lane and a further 650m walk to the viewing point (Yellow Buses).

Nearest railway station is at Christchurch, just under a mile from Suffolk Avenue, along Fairmile Road.

Other nearby sites

Christchurch Harbour, Sopley Common, Ramsdown Plantation & Avon Causeway, Town Common & St Catherine's Hill.

DORSET'S MOST NORTHERLY heathland is dominated by wet heath which can make access difficult in places, but it holds all the usual specialities of the habitat, including Nightjar, Woodlark and Dartford Warbler. Hobbies and Woodcock are occasionally seen, while in winter, Hen Harriers, Merlins and Great Grey Shrikes turn up from time to time. Crossbills, Siskins and Redpolls use the surrounding Ringwood Forest woodland areas.

Target birds *All year* – **Dartford Warbler (80%).** *Summer* – **Nightjar (90% hear, 75% see), Woodlark (75%), Tree Pipit (75%), Woodcock (50%).**

Other possible bird species

All year	Redpoll	*Occasional*
Buzzard	Yellowhammer	Hen Harrier
Kestrel	Common woodland birds	Peregrine
Tawny Owl	*Summer*	Merlin
Green Woodpecker	Cuckoo	Hobby
Meadow Pipit	Chiffchaff	Turtle Dove
Raven	Willow Warbler	Great Grey Shrike
Siskin		

Background information and birding tips

FROM THE parking area in Blackwater Grove, Alderholt, take the bridleway down the lane from the end of the houses, looking out for common woodland birds along the way.

Once out into the open, and after passing under the power lines, follow the track around to the left and keep going until you reach the gate onto the Common.

The bridleway continues south-westwards over the Common and out into the forestry on the other side. Half-way along the bridleway, a footpath crosses from north to south it but it is difficult to find.

Both the bridleway and the footpath are part of a wider network of routes in the area.

The heathland (43ha) consists predominantly of humid/wet heath, with purple moor grass (*molinia*) dominating the vegetation. The bridleway is frequently wet and muddy, though a stone track has been laid part of the way into the heath from the gate at the Alderholt end.

The site has open access but in reality walking is hard in many places because of the *molinia* tussocks.

The best option is to follow the bridleway to the far end, turning off to the right where the vegetation is shorter and where the ground rises into a drier area. Follow what looks like a mown track until you reach the forest fence on the northern boundary – listen for Woodlarks singing over this drier area.

Follow the fence a short way to the public footpath markers and you can then pick your way back over the heath to the bridleway.

Key points

- **Designated SSSI.**
- **Allow up to two hours for a birding visit.**
- **Paths can be very wet.**
- **Wheelchair access not possible.**
- **Roding Woodcock possible.**
- **Nearest public toilets in Fordingbridge (2.5 miles away).**

Other nearby sites

Holt Heath, Martin Down, Moors Valley Country Park, River Allen - Crichel Lake.

Allow about 90 minutes to walk this loop to/from the car, or to extend your walk venture out into the forest beyond the Common.

Dartford Warblers breed here – there is plenty of gorse scattered around so check it for them as well as for Stonechats and Linnets.

Nightjars breed here and in the adjacent forest, so if you are out at dusk looking for them keep your eyes (and ears) open for Woodcock 'roding' over the area and for calling Tawny Owls. Other summer visitors include Cuckoos, Tree Pipits and Willow Warblers.

Yellowhammer is a bird that I have seen decline around the Purbeck heaths over the years but it still appears to be here in good numbers.

Crossbills, Siskins and Redpolls can be found in the surrounding forest and over-flying the Common. Buzzards, Kestrels and Ravens are also regular overhead and a Peregrine is always possible.

Turtle Dove has been recorded from general vicinity in the past.

A visit in the winter can be fruitful with the possibility of Hen Harrier, Merlin and Woodcock, while Great Grey Shrike has been recorded.

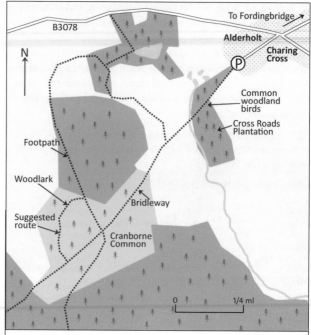

How to get there

(4.5 miles NW of Ringwood).

From Bournemouth head north on the A338 to the A31 Ashley Heath roundabout and turn right towards Ringwood. Keep in the left hand lane for the B3081 turn-off towards Verwood.

If approaching on A31 from the Wimborne/Poole direction, take the slip road up to the Ashley Heath roundabout and go straight over, keeping in the left hand lane for the B3081.

If approaching from Ringwood, keep in the left hand lane of the A31 and take the A3081 to Verwood (which passes back under the A31).

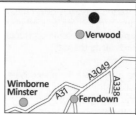

After three quarters of a mile along the B3081, take the right fork towards Alderholt. On approaching Alderholt, turn left into Ringwood Road then left again on to the B3078. Almost immediately, turn left into Blackwater Grove and drive to the end and park up on the road. Walk from here.

THESE THREE SITES form a continuous link of heathland that holds good numbers of Dartford Warblers and Nightjars. Grange Heath, though quite small, is one of my favourite heathland sites. Positive management work in the 1990s has turned it from a fledgling pine forest into a maturing open heathland that is now a great site for Woodlarks and worth a late summer visit to see the scarce marsh gentian in flower. Southern damselfly is a speciality at Creech Heath.

Target birds
All year – Dartford Warbler (90%). *Summer* – Nightjar (90% hear, 75% see), Woodlark (G: 75%), Tree Pipit (G: 75%). *G = Grange*

Other possible bird species

All year	*Summer*	
Buzzard	Cuckoo	Woodcock
Tawny Owl	Stonechat (uncommon	*Occasional*
Green Woodpecker	in winter)	Hen Harrier (G)
Meadow Pipit	Willow Warbler	Merlin (G)
Siskin	Linnet	Hobby
Crossbill		Jack Snipe
Common passerines	*Winter*	Great Grey Shrike (G)
	Snipe	

Background information and birding tips

DORSET HAS some of the largest tracts of heathland outside the New Forest. These three sites, sitting between the Arne-Hartland Moor/Stoborough Heath National Nature Reserve to the east and the MoD ranges to the west, are part of a continuous piece of heathland stretching just over 14 miles.

Though separated by minor roads and a railway line, the three sites can easily be combined and are treated here as a single unit.

Most of the land was owned by the English China Clay company which extracted ball clay from the heathlands here, and in the surrounding area, for decades.

The ball clay name is believed to derive from the time when the clay was mined by hand. Though cut into 15 to 17-kilogramme cubes,

the corners became rounded off in transit, leaving 'balls'.

In 1991, Stoborough Heath was purchased by the RSPB, while Grange Heath was leased by them in the early 1990s and purchased in 2005.

Creech Heath remains with the clay company (now Imery's) but has been leased to Amphibian and Reptile Conservation Trust (ARC) since the 1990s. Both organisations are actively managing the sites with a programme of scrub removal, bracken control, the introduction of stock grazing and heather/gorse management.

The typical heathland species are found here in summer – Nightjars and Dartford Warblers are widespread across the area, while Woodlarks are more localised, mainly on Grange Heath.

Key points
- RSPB own Grange & Stoborough Heaths.
- Creech managed by ARC.
- Open access at all times.
- Options of a short or long visit.
- Good selection of heathland species.
- Many access points.
- Paths can be very wet. Wheelchair access not possible.
- Within easy reach of Wareham.
- Good botanical and dragonfly interest.
- Tearooms and museum at Blue Pool.

Contacts
RSPB Arne office
01929 553 360
www.rspb.org.uk/reserves

ARC Office
01202 391 319
www.arc-trust.org

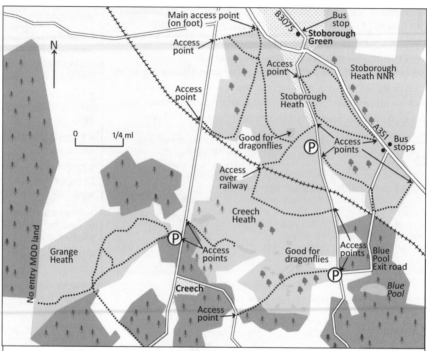

How to get there

(1.5 to two miles S of Wareham).

The sites have multiple entrances, but these directions will take you a suitable entrance point to each of the heaths.

For Stoborough Heath (SY 939 846), take B3075 south from Wareham through Stoborough to the roundabout and cross over into Furzebrook Road. Part of the site is immediately on the left but continue down this road until the houses on the right hand side finish. Park in the lay-by just beyond the last house and walk back to the entrance gate.

For Creech Heath (SY 931 835) continue along the road beyond the lay-by, over the railway line, past Furzebrook House, and pull in on the right hand side of the road just opposite the entrance to The Blue Pool (an old claypit that now offers walks, tearooms and museum). There is no actual parking space here so park with care.

For Grange Heath (SY 917 837) turn right at the roundabout on to the Wareham bypass, then take the next left turn into Grange Road. Half a mile after passing under the railway bridge the road dips. At the bottom pull off the road on the right hand side and park up carefully so as not to block the track. Walk down this track for about 300m to the heath.

Public transport: The nearest railway station is at Wareham where a bus can be caught to

Stoborough (Wilts & Dorset). Get off at Stoborough Green and walk through the small estate to the Wareham bypass – cross the road carefully (fast traffic) and enter the gate on to the site.

Alternatively, walk south for just over a mile from Wareham town centre, across the causeway to Stoborough/ Stoborough Green.

Meadow Pipits, Stonechats and Linnets should easily be found anywhere, while Tree Pipits and Yellowhammers (a bird that has disappeared from many heaths in the area) are more likely to be found on Grange Heath. Hobbies are often in the area in summer and Buzzards are common all year round.

There is no formal access or facilities on the sites (apart from a few information boards at key access points) but the area is criss-crossed by a network of paths.

Parking is very limited to a number of roadside locations and there are many gated access points dotted around. Due to past workings of the clay industry and the nature of the ground, the footpaths can be very wet, especially in winter.

From the Stoborough Heath parking entrance walk straight into the heath and stop at the large clay pit. This is good for dragonflies and there is usually a pair of Dartford Warblers about here – then, explore the many paths as the fancy takes you.

At 65ha, Grange Heath is the smallest of the sites and it is quieter (well away from the main Wareham-Swanage road which makes the eastern block of Stoborough Heath very noisy). From the parking area, once through to the heath, the main track runs the whole length of the site.

The track eventually stops at a fence onto MoD land – under no circumstances should you enter this area! From February, Woodlarks should be singing, with two or three pairs usually here. I often hear my first Cuckoo of the year here in early April and Crossbills are regular.

If you plan to visit the area in the summer you will be able to combine birding with watching dragonflies. The ponds dotted around the sites hold a wide selection of dragonflies and damselflies, including the scarce southern damselfly which breeds in the runnels by the main lily pond on Creech Heath. This can be found just along the track from the parking spot.

J.D.

Grange Heath is an excellent site if you want to see Tree Pipits.

A visit to the area in the winter shouldn't be overlooked. Though the sites have a bleakness to them (which in itself can be attractive), there is always a chance of picking up a few good birds.

Hen Harriers often pass through and I have seen Merlin a few times and also an occasional Great Grey Shrike. Snipe are regularly seen on the heath, I once flushed up 130 birds in a small area, and they are worth checking out for Jack Snipe.

There is also a good botanical interest here as well. The site is dominated by humid and wet heath/mire systems which are far more interesting than the dry heath found on the higher ground. Scarce plants include Dorset heath and marsh gentian.

Other nearby sites

Hartland Moor & Stoborough NNR, River Frome - Holme Bridge, Coombe Heath & Lulworth Lake, Wareham Meadows & Swineham Point.

Key points

- National Trust owned SSSI.
- Part of Dorset Heritage Coast.
- Part of South West Coast Path.
- Access available at all times
- Allow up to two hours and expect 25-30 bird species.
- Information boards at Spyway Farm.
- Steep slope to negotiate – no wheelchair access.

D ANCING LEDGE, one of the Purbeck coastal sites that can be visited in its own right or as part of a longer walk, is one of the few places in southern England where it is still possible to see Puffins in spring and summer. The birds are tucked away on the lower cliff ledges but can be seen as they fly into the cliffs or at rest on the water. Visit early in the season to see a good selection of newly-arrived migrants.

Target birds *All year* – Shag (90%), Yellowhammer (80%), Raven (75%). *Summer* – Peregrine (75%), Puffin (75%), Whitethroat (75%), Little Owl (10%).

Other possible bird species

All year	Skylark	Whinchat
Kestrel	Meadow Pipit	Wheatear
Regular gull species	Stonechat	Ring Ouzel
Rock Pipit	Blackcap	Brambling (autumn)
Linnet	Chiffchaff	Common finches
	Willow Warbler	
Summer		*Occasional*
Fulmar	*Passage*	Offshore seabirds
Guillemot	Fulmar	Migrant land birds
Razorbill (uncommon	Kittiwake	(rarities/sub-rarities)
here)	Hirundines	

Background information and birding tips

D ANCING LEDGE is one of two sites in Dorset where breeding Puffins are found, the other being on Portland (site 43), but be aware that their numbers barely reach double figures. They can be seen from early April (through to the end of June).

The site lies between Durlston Country Park (site 20) and the Worth Matravers coastal walks (site 65) and can be visited as an extension to either by continuing along the coastal paths from their respective ends.

The area can get very busy both on land and sea and I find that an early morning or late evening visit is often more successful because there is likely to be more bird and less human activity.

Don't be put off though if you can't make these times as the walk is worthwhile at any time of day and you will still have a good chance of seeing the target bird species.

The return trip to the ledge takes about 90 minutes (allowing some time to look for the birds) but, more often than not, I combine a visit here with the Seacombe Bottom section of the Worth Matravers coastal walks.

This makes a nice circular walk of about three hours and, by doing this in the spring, there is a better chance of finding some newly-arrived migrants.

The cliffs are about a mile from the nearest car park in Langton Matravers, with the last quarter mile being a steep descent to the ledge – remember, if you go down

Contacts

The National Trust
01929 450 123
www.nationaltrust.
org.uk

How to get there

(2.5 miles SW of Swanage)

Just as you leave Corfe Castle on A351, heading towards Swanage, turn right on B3069 towards Kingston/Langton Matravers. Once in Langton Matravers drive slowly looking (on right) for Durnford Drove and a signpost to Langton House.

Turn in here and follow the road to the track's end where there is a small car park (SY 998 783). Use the gate at the end of the car park taking the track south that eventually leads to the cliffs (via a small information shelter at Spyway Barn).

Public transport: **The Poole-Wareham-Swanage bus service runs through Langton Matravers on B3069 and a**

To Wareham • B3069 • N • Acton • Eastington Farm • To Worth Matravers • Seacombe Bottom • To Worth Matravers coastal walks • Migrants in valley • Priest's Way • Langton Matravers • Turn off here • Dunnford Drove • Langton House • P Park here • Spyway Barn • Watch for Puffins flying into the cliffs or sitting on the water • Peregrine • Dancing Ledge • Puffins breed on ledges under cliffs • Durlston Country Park • To Swanage • 0 1/4 ml • Studland • Swanage • A351

limited service runs from Swanage to Worth Matravers (Wilts & Dorset).

you need to get back up again! The walk from the car park crosses Spyway Farm, which was purchased in the 1990s by the National Trust, prior to which it was managed without the use of chemicals, a practice that the Trust is continuing.

With a mosaic of dry-stone walls, open fields and scrub, Whitethroats, Stonechats, Linnets and Yellowhammers should be found quite easily.

However, Little Owl sightings will need a little more work. Spend a little time looking for the owls around the farm buildings and scan carefully along the stone walls.

Once across the fields and through the last gate you will be looking at the sea and the steep slope, with the obvious path, down to Dancing Ledge. On the descent scan the

patches of scrub for birds (I have seen Little Owl on the open ground among this scrub in the past).

Skylarks will be in full song above the slopes in the spring and Kestrels regularly hunt over the area. In April/May, and later in September/October, the area attracts migrants – Wheatear in particular, but any common migrants are possible, with possibly something more unusual such as a Red-backed Shrike or a Ring Ouzel.

Unless you are going specifically to look for the Puffins, I would recommend Durlston Country Park or the Worth Matravers coastal walks in preference to Dancing Ledge as they are more likely to produce a greater number of migrant sightings.

Dancing Ledge's steep cliffs are fenced off and you should not climb over them to get better views of the Puffins – in fact, it is virtually impossible to see them on the cliffs as they are tucked away under overhangs.

I find the best viewing area is down on the ledge itself – sit off to the right hand side and look for auks flying to and from the cliffs as well as scanning the sea for birds floating on the water.

Guillemots breed here and are the auk species most frequently seen but with a little patience Puffin and possibly Razorbill (scarce on this section of cliffs) may be picked out.

Close inshore Shags and Herring Gulls are common, and Peregrines and Ravens often fly over the area. A spring (and autumn) seawatch may produce Kittiwakes and Fulmars (a few pairs breed along this stretch of coast), Gannets and possibly skuas, terns and shearwaters.

Seabird movements may be better with a stiff onshore wind, whereas the Puffins are more likely to be found and better viewed on a reasonably calm day.

As with migrants, there are more productive sites for seawatching locally but it is certainly worth a scan out to sea while you are here looking for the Puffins.

As an alternative way of viewing the Puffins at Dancing Ledge you could take one of the birdwatching cruises out of Poole or Swanage (see site 41) and improve your chances of seeing them closer to 90%. Sailings are, however, subject to the weather and sea conditions and there have been occasions when the sailings have either been cancelled or the boat has had to turn back.

All being well though, the boats can get reasonably close into the cliffs. Look for the Puffins tucked into a ledge or standing out on a rocky outcrop. Birds can also be seen flying into or away from the cliffs or might even be picked up sitting on the water.

The RSPB Birdboats have been running two coastal trips in late May/June for a number of years now. They depart from Poole Quay and so have to travel for quite a distance to get to the ledges. The return journey can take up to four hours but there is an opportunity to look over the lagoon at Brownsea Island (site 9) and to do some birdwatching along the way.

The Durlston Country Park staff act as guides on a number of boat trips out of Swanage (approx. mid-May to early July). The journey is much shorter (around two and a half hours).

Apart from the Puffins, other breeding seabirds such as Guillemots, Razorbills, Shags, Cormorants and Fulmars will be seen will be seen on the way from Durlston to Dancing Ledge. However, Kittiwakes are now restricted to nesting in Blacker's Hole (mid-way between the two).

Two or three pairs Peregrines breed along this stretch of coast and I haven't failed to see at least one bird on the trips that I've done in the past.

Remember to wrap up well if going out on a boat trip – it can get quite cold on the water. The boats have toilets and usually have a selection of refreshments available.

Other nearby sites

Corfe Common, Durlston Country Park, Worth Matravers coastal walks.

WITH A SPLASH of floral colour and birdsong filling the air, a spring visit to Duncliffe Wood is well worth considering. This ancient habitat contains the expected array of common woodland birds, including Marsh Tit and Bullfinch, while Buzzard and Raven are frequently seen soaring overhead. As the summer progresses and the birds quieten, the butterflies take over as the wood's main interest.

Target birds *All year* – Buzzard (90%), Marsh Tit (90%), Raven (75%), Bullfinch (75%), Little Owl (10%).

Other possible bird species

All year	Treecreeper	*Winter*
Kestrel	Common woodland	Fieldfare
Stock Dove	birds	Redwing
Tawny Owl		
Great Spotted	*Summer*	
Woodpecker	Blackcap	
Nuthatch	Chiffchaff	
	Willow Warbler	

Background information and birding tips

DUNCLIFFE WOOD, one of the largest woods in North Dorset, is in an area with few accessible birding sites. It sits on the double summits of Duncliffe Hill, dominating the landscape to the west of the town of Shaftesbury.

The site is known as a PAWS (Plantation on Ancient Woodland Site), extending to 92ha and has been a Woodland Trust reserve since 1984.

During the 1950s and '60s the wood was largely felled and replanted with a mixture of trees including native (oak), non-site native (beech) and non-native (Norway spruce and larch).

The Trust has worked towards removing many of these trees to restore Duncliffe to a semi-natural woodland and to conserve its Ancient Woodland key features.

A spring visit is likely to be the most productive for birding, while the summer is good for butterflies.

You will approach the wood from the parking area along an open track bounded by hedgerows with boundary oaks and fields. Little Owl is sometimes recorded from this area so check the oaks as you walk by. Kestrels may also be hunting over the fields.

Once inside the wood you have a choice to make as the site is criss-crossed by a series of paths and tracks, including two marked routes.

The route to the north of the main bridleway (the 'strenuous route') involves a little more climbing than the southern track (the 'medium route'). I tend to favour a longer circuit that covers both routes but missing out the main bridleway.

Allow three hours if you want to walk the full circuit, or allow about two hours for the 'strenuous' route, or 90 minutes for the 'medium route'.

Key points

- Access available at all times.

- Limited roadside parking (park with care).

- Expect 25-30 species in a two to three hour visit.

- Nearest toilets in Shaftesbury.

- Leaflet available at entrance to wood.

- Two routes marked out.

- Paths can be wet/slippery.

- Limited wheelchair access (slope involved).

Contacts

Woodland Trust
01476 581 111.www.
woodlandtrust.org.uk

How to get there

(Four miles W of Shaftesbury)

From Shaftesbury take A30 Sherborne road and head towards East Stour. A mile before you reach East Stour, turn left on to the unclassified road towards Stour Row.

Continue for half a mile until you reach a right hand junction (by New Gate Farm).

About 60 yards past this turning, there is a pull-in on the left where you can park. A footpath sign directs you to the wood from here (there is also a leaflet dispenser for the wood at this point).

Good views

Good views

Good bluebell area

Main bridleway

Dunchliffe Wood

Good views

N

To A30 Shaftesbury

P

0   1/8 ml

Alternatively, from Sherborne take A30 towards Shaftesbury. Once past East Stour take the unclassified road on the right signposted to Stour Row (as above).

A303

A350

Gillingham

Shaftesbury

A30

By mid-April the air is full of birdsong with the summering warblers (Willow Warbler, Chiffchaff and Blackcap) joining the resident thrushes, tits, Nuthatches and Great Spotted Woodpeckers. The birds are scattered throughout the woodland, so just keep your eyes and ears open for them as you walk around.

Marsh Tits are present in good numbers, while Jays and Bullfinches add a splash of avian colour to the bluebells, primroses and other ground flora.

Walking around you will notice a number of bird and bat boxes including Tawny Owl boxes – it's worth looking at the latter carefully in case an owlet is looking out.

From the main gate into the wood, walk up the main bridleway for about 150 metres and take the path on the left for the 'strenuous route'. Half way along this section there is a seat in the middle of a large bluebell area with a Tawny Owl box in the trees opposite (also look at the bat boxes – Treecreepers

sometimes nest in them).

At the end of this path turn right and climb up the steep hill (careful here as the ground can be very slippery when wet) until a gate takes you out of the wood (by a trig point).

Take in the wonderful views across the surrounding countryside before following the fence line to the second gate (go past the first gate) before re-entering the wood. In any of the open areas

When scanning the glorious countryside on the edge of the wood, you can expect to see Buzzards riding the thermals.

look skywards for Buzzards and Ravens circling overhead.

Back in the wood, continue down the hill to the bottom of this section, turn right and continue on until you reach the main bridleway. From here you have the option of returning to the main entrance along the bridleway or taking the next fork off to the left and to follow the 'medium route' around the southern edge of the wood.

If you select this 'medium route' turn left again at the next T-junction. At the southern boundary of the wood turn sharply right and stay on this path until you rejoin the main bridleway. Turn left on to the bridleway and return to the main gate.

Alternatively if you have less time, or want a less strenuous walk, just follow the 'medium route'. Take the main bridleway across to the far side and turn right just before the bridleway leaves the wood and follow the paths mentioned above.

There are a number of other tracks crossing the site that you may want to wander at your leisure instead of following either of these recommended routes.

The surface on the main bridleway should be passable for wheelchairs but bear in mind that there is a fairly steep slope to negotiate.

If you visit at dusk in June-July, look out for glow-worms along the main bridleway. Butterflies of particular interest include ringlet, silver-washed fritillary, white admiral and purple hairstreak.

There are also some 'notable' Dorset plants on the site that you might like to look out for, including moschatel, yellow archangel, wood speedwell and early purple orchid.

Other nearby sites

Blackmore Vale, Fontmell Down, Hambledon Hill & Hod Hill.

Key points

- National Nature Reserve owned by Dorset County Council.
- Allow half a day to cover the site.
- Leaflets available at visitor centre.
- Various trails – some wheelchair access but many slopes, so assistance may be required.
- Events programme (see website for details).
- Visitor Centre (toilets and refreshments).
- Pay & display parking.
- Guillemot webcam.
- Visible migration watch point.

SITTING JUST ABOVE the town of Swanage, Durlston Country Park forms part of the stunning Purbeck coastline and is one of Dorset's top migration hotspots. As well as being a great place to watch visible migration in action, its sea cliffs are one of the few sites in the county where its possible to see breeding seabirds. Its importance as a site for nature conservation was further recognised in 2008 when it became a National Nature Reserve.

Target birds

All year – Shag (100%), Peregrine (70%), Raven (70%). *Summer* – Guillemot (100%), Razorbill (100%). *Autumn* – Visible migration species. *Winter* – Black Redstart (75%), Merlin (30%), Firecrest (20%). *Passage* – Rarities & sub-rarities.

Other possible bird species

All year	Blackcap	Willow Warbler
Common Scoter	Garden Warbler	Spotted Flycatcher
Fulmar (exc. Aug-Oct)	Lesser Whitethroat	Pied Flycatcher
Gannet	Whitethroat	Manx Shearwater
Cormorant	Chiffchaff	Balearic Shearwater
Sparrowhawk		Arctic Skua
Buzzard	*Winter*	Great Skua
Kestrel	Red-throated Diver	
Herring Gull	Great Northern Diver	*Occasional*
Kittiwake	Regular gull species	Sooty Shearwater
Tawny Owl	Winter thrushes	Storm Petrel
Green Woodpecker	Firecrest	Pomarine Skua
Skylark	Brambling	Little Gull
Meadow Pipit		Mediterranean Gull
Rock Pipit	*Passage*	Arctic Tern
Stonechat	Whimbrel	Puffin
Linnet	Cuckoo	Wryneck
Bullfinch	Tree Pipit	Woodlark
Yellowhammer	Yellow Wagtail	Dartford Warbler
Common scrub birds	Redstart	Golden Oriole
	Whinchat	Tree Sparrow
Summer	Wheatear	Serin
Guillemot	Ring Ouzel	Hawfinch
Razorbill	Grasshopper Warbler	Lapland Bunting
	Wood Warbler	

Background information and birding tips

THE COUNTRY PARK, originally established by Dorset County Council in the 1970s, covers 113ha of sea-cliffs, chalk grassland, hay meadows, hedgerows and woodland.

As well as a bird list of more than 270 species, the park has recorded nearly 600 species of wild flowers and is one of the top ten sites in the UK for butterflies. A total of 34 species includes Adonis and chalkhill blues and the nationally rare Lulworth skipper (check out the excellent wildlife pages on the Durlston website).

Contacts

Durlston Country Park
01929 424 443
www.durlston.co.uk

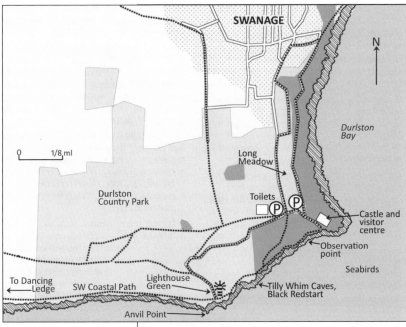

A major project to restore and refurbish Durlston Castle was completed in 2011 and it now provides an improved range of visitor facilities. The visitor centre is open all year round and the rangers organise a wide range of activities and events.

There are four way-marked trails in the park, which all start from the car parks. Leaflets which show the routes are available from the visitor centre.

As an alternative to driving, consider walking from Swanage town centre along The Victorian Trail (1.75 miles – route indicated by Queen Victoria markers). The trail starts at the Tourist

How to get there

(S of Swanage).

Drive from Swanage town centre, following the brown tourist signs to the country park.

By foot: **It is close enough to walk from the town centre ......up hill most of the way! Either walk up along the road or follow the coastal footpath (part of the South West**

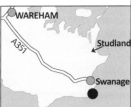

Coastal Path, overlooking Durlston Bay).

Information Centre on the seafront and follows the South West Coast Path, via Peveril Point, to Durlston, but be aware it is uphill most of the way.

Getting around the park is straightforward with a good network of paths (some surfaced), gates and stiles.

However, be aware there are some steep slopes to negotiate and the paths across fields can get muddy when wet. There are a number of paths suitable for disabled users, including a tarred road (quite steep) down to the Anvil Point lighthouse. A Tramper mobility vehicle is available for hire from the visitor centre).

The breeding seabirds, seen from the Cliff Top Trail (0.75 mile/Cormorant markers), are one of the obvious attractions of Durlston. Late March through to the end of June is the best time for them.

Guillemots are the most numerous, nesting on the lower ledges of the cliffs. Most can't be seen from the cliff top but you will see plenty of them as they fly to and from the ledges or loaf around on the water – check through them for Razorbill.

On very rare occasions I have seen a Puffin among them - likely to be a straggler from Dancing Ledge (site 18), 1.5 miles to the west. There is a webcam set up on the Guillemots in the visitor centre so that visitors can observe adults and chicks on their narrow cliff ledges.

Fulmars, Shags and Herring Gulls also breed, but Kittiwakes have long gone. A small colony of these dainty gulls hangs on in Blackers Hole, between the park and Dancing Ledge, so birds may be seen offshore.

Other birds to look for on the cliffs include Rock Pipits, Jackdaws and Feral Pigeons – the latter often attracting the attention of a Peregrine. Though Peregrines haven't bred in the park recently, there are usually two or three pairs along the Purbeck coast, so they are still regularly seen. In the winter, check

out the Tilly Whim cave area for a Black Redstart and look in the blocked-off entrance for adders in the spring.

The Cliff Top Trail provides a good vantage point for seawatching - use the Dolphin Watch hut if you need to shelter from the weather (the spring is the best time to look for dolphins passing through). Numbers of birds don't match up to those passing Portland but most species can be seen.

All three divers are recorded annually, with Red-throated the most numerous during the winter – I have seen 'flocks' pass by on occasions. Sightings of grebes on the other hand are very rare. Common Scoter is the most likely duck to be seen (in all months) – all other ducks are scarce.

Gannets are a common sight all year round, as are the local gulls, Shags and Cormorants. Manx Shearwaters are fairly common from spring to autumn, with larger numbers in April/May. Both Balearic and Sooty Shearwaters are scarce and are usually seen later in the summer/autumn when there is also a chance of Storm Petrels.

Skuas are more likely in the spring with Arctic the most regular, followed by Great and Pomarine.

Terns are around from mid-March and into the autumn – Sandwich is obvious but close 'Commic' Terns should be checked (likely to be Common but a few Arctics are picked up each year). There is always the chance of

Durlston is one of the few Dorset locations suitable for seawatching – Gannets are just one of the many species that may pass by.

something more unusual – maybe a Little Gull or even a Sabine's Gull.

Waders at Durlston are generally scarce and tend to be picked up flying along the coast during a seawatch, or passing over.

The main area of woodland habitat is just to the south of the car park/castle and along the eastern side of the park overlooking Durlston Bay. The Woodland Trail (0.75 mile/ tree markers) follows a route northwards along the wildflower-filled Long Meadow, returning through woodland where openings provide views out into the bay. These woodlands can be a good spot for wintering Firecrests, while the resident Tawny Owls are usually heard after dark.

The Wildlife Trail (one mile/butterfly markers) covers the downs (mainly in the south) but only a small part of the meadows (mainly in the north – it is worth extending your walk to cover the meadows more thoroughly). These grassland areas are excellent for butterflies and they hold an interesting flora, including nine species of orchid (early spider and bee among them).

The routes around the grasslands pass areas of scrub, hedgerows and many of the park's dry stone walls – all attractive to breeding birds and migrants. As well as the common scrub birds, there are also breeding species such as Green Woodpecker, Skylark, Meadow Pipit, Stonechat, Blackcap, Whitethroat, Lesser Whitethroat, Chiffchaff, Linnet, Bullfinch, Yellowhammer and, occasionally, Garden Warbler. Overhead, look out for Sparrowhawks, Buzzards, Kestrels and Ravens.

Spring passage starts in mid-March when the first Chiffchaffs and Wheatears appear – most of the common migrants are recorded annually.

Apart from those that stay to breed, hirundines come through in their hundreds while numbers of Cuckoo, Tree Pipit, Yellow Wagtail, Ring Ouzel, Redstart, Whinchat, Willow Warbler and Spotted Flycatcher vary from year to year depending on the weather conditions when the birds are moving.

Less common species, such as Turtle Dove, Grasshopper Warbler, Wood Warbler and Pied Flycatcher also turn up in small numbers.

The same species may return in autumn – August and September are the best times but individual birds may stay for longer periods of time than they do in the spring. An early morning visit can often be the most productive, especially after a 'fall' when birds have been grounded by poor weather.

In the spring and autumn there is always a chance of a local rarity or two – Honey Buzzard, Hoopoe, Wryneck amongst them – while Yellow-browed Warblers can turn up in the autumn. In 2011 Durlston recorded Dorset's second Red-flanked Bluetail and has the only UK record to date of Brown Thrasher, way back in the 1960s.

Migrants tend to be more numerous in the autumn than the spring when birds start to appear from the end of July (usually Swifts).

By October visible migration (Vis Mig) can be spectacular here (see the Trektellen website www.vismig.org). The numbers of birds, and species, involved can be staggering at times, with birds constantly flying overhead. Long Meadow, by the car park, can be a good spot to stand to watch for them and an early start is recommended, although movements can be picked up all around the park.

In October 2005 there was a staggering passage of Wood Pigeons along the Dorset Coast – a peak count of 73,000 was recorded in one day at Durlston.

Finches are one of the more obvious groups to come through, with many species reaching into the hundreds if not thousands. These include Bramblings, Siskins and Redpolls and on one day in October 2010 9,600 Linnets were counted.

In general, choose a day with light-ish winds (with some N or W in it) and good visibility – numbers will depend on time in the field as well. There is always a chance of something more unusual passing over – sightings have included Hawfinch, Tree Sparrow, Lapland Bunting and, in 2008 an Olive-backed Pipit ...... having a good ear is a help though!

Other nearby sites

Ballard Down, Corfe Common, Dancing Ledge, Studland, Worth Matravers coastal walks.

Key points

- Owned by National Trust & Dorset Wildlife Trust.
- Important chalk grassland SSSI.
- Car parking free of charge.
- Choice of walks.
- Some steep slopes – site not suitable for wheelchair users.
- Refreshments and toilet facilities at the Compton Abbas airfield.
- Leaflet and information boards in car park.
- Fantastic site for chalk grassland flowers and butterflies.
- Great scenery.
- Archaeological features.

Contacts

Dorset Wildlife Trust
01305 264 620
www.dorsetwildlifetrust.org.uk/reserves

National Trust 01672 539 167. www.nationaltrust.org.uk

FONTMELL and Melbury Downs are located on the steep slopes of the North Dorset Downs between Shaftesbury and Blandford and have spectacular views over the Blackmoor Vale. Its mosaic of chalk grassland, scrub and woodland will provide a few bird sightings but it is best known for its stunning display of flora and butterflies.

Target birds   *All year* – Raven (75%), Yellowhammer (75%).

Other possible bird species

All year	Bullfinch	Wheatear (passage)
Sparrowhawk	Common scrub birds	Blackcap
Buzzard	*Summer*	Garden Warbler
Kestrel	Tree Pipit	Chiffchaff
Green Woodpecker	Meadow Pipit	Willow Warbler
Skylark	Redstart (passage)	
Linnet	Stonechat	

Background information and birding tips

WALKERS and general nature lovers will really appreciate this Site of Special Scientific Interest (which is made up of 23 units) covering just over 260ha of land spread over this part of the North Dorset Downs. The area is largely under National Trust and Dorset Wildlife Trust ownership and management.

The selection of birds you see are likely to take a back seat to the flowers and butterflies along a number of walks across this important chalk grassland habitat.

The grassland survives on the steep slopes where it was impossible to plough for agricultural use.

The three main routes are all accessible from the main Spread Eagle Hill car park, and provide a good sample of the flora, butterflies and typical birds of the area. I tend to follow one of these routes and only make detours if anything catches my eye.

The first route (2.5 to 3.5 miles) covers most of the Dorset Wildlife Trust land and part of the National Trust's. From the car park, head south for 200m across the first field to reach the edge of a steep-sided natural amphitheatre with scrub in the bottom. Stay on the top of the eastern side of the slope, continue through the wooded area, and into open country at the southern end.

Head north along the western side which runs alongside a finger of farmland – there is less scrub/woodland here – to the bottom of the amphitheatre and spend a little time checking the scrub at the bottom of this valley.

By now you should have come across a number of common scrub birds including Willow Warblers, Linnets, Yellowhammers, and possibly Tree Pipits.

Continue to the small clump of woodland (start of the National Trust land), and then go back to the car park by either turning left and walking clockwise around the downs or by turning right, taking a shorter route.

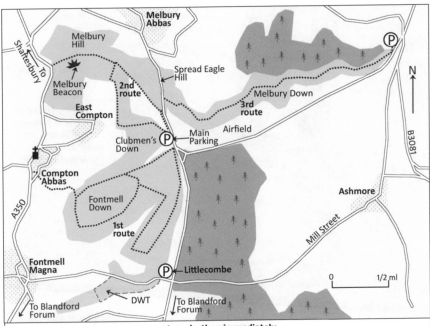

How to get there

(7.5 miles N of Blandford).

From the A350 Blandford Forum bypass take B3081 north, past the Sunrise Business Park, towards Melbury Abbas. After about seven miles there is a right hand turn to Compton Abbas airfield – just after this turning (on the left) is a small car park on Spread Eagle Hill with information boards and views looking down to the valley.

From Shaftesbury take A30 eastwards, then immediately turn right on to B3081 to Melbury Abbas and continue on through the village (20mph speed limit here and steep hills).

The car park is on the right hand side of the road after about two-thirds of a mile from the village (there is a small pull-in just before the car park – drive past this to the main parking area

Public transport: It is possible to take the Wimborne-Blandford-Shaftesbury bus

service to Compton Abbas where there is a public footpath out to the western side of the site (NORCAT).

The second route runs to the north of the car park, aiming towards Melbury Beacon – one of the beacons set up in 1588 to warn of the Spanish Armada. From the north-west corner of the car park take the track for about 350m, passing a small quarry on the way, and walk through a gap in the bushes onto the grassland.

Continue around the edge of the grassland/field, pick up the track at the northern corner of the field and head north-west to the beacon. Keep a look out for Stonechats that favours the area around the beacon. To return, go back to the corner of the field and follow the edge of the field back to the

83

When walking the open grassland areas, there's a good chance you'll see or hear Green Woodpeckers.

road and then the fence line to the car park (2.5 miles).

The third route lies to the east of the main road and takes the form of a linear walk of just over 2.5 miles (each way, five miles in total). Head north from the car park by walking adjacent to the road for about 600m. Cross the road carefully (vehicles travel fast along here) and walk eastwards along the base of the sheltered valley of Melbury Down.

The open grassland can be good for Wheatears in the spring and autumn and look among the scrub in the autumn for Redstarts. Note: There is a car park at the eastern end of this walk as an alternative to crossing the road.

Skylarks are seen and heard throughout the area and a Green Woodpecker should easily be found. Keep an eye out overhead for Buzzards, Kestrels, Sparrowhawks and Ravens.

There is a small additional area belonging to the Wildlife Trust just to the south of the site that is worth calling into. Garden Warblers and Blackcaps can be found in the woodland and scrub here. This can be reached by taking a detour from the southern end of the first route – continue heading south to the Fontmell Magna road and cross the road to the small car park (Littlecombe). Alternatively, the car park can be reached by turning off the B3081 onto this road.

The mixture of open chalk grassland, woodland and scrub will offer a good variety of butterflies. Around 35 species have been recorded here including Adonis and chalkhill blues, grizzled and dingy skippers, silver-washed, marsh and dark green fritillaries and Duke of Burgundy – but don't forget to check their flight periods before a visit.

Other nearby sites
Blackmoor Vale, Duncliffe Wood, Hambledon Hill & Hod Hill.

Key points

- **Designated SSSI owned by RSPB.**
- **Expect 20-25 bird species in spring.**
- **Open access at all times.**
- **Small car park (if parking on the road, do so with care).**
- **Allow up to two hours for the full trail.**
- **A series of short or long walks lead off from car park.**
- **Leaflet available.**
- **Events organised.**
- **No local public toilets.**
- **Wheelchair access limited (contact RSPB for more information).**

Contacts

RSPB Arne office
01929 553 360
www.rspb.org.uk/
reserves

GARSTON WOOD has a reasonable selection of common woodland birds but one of the main attractions is its spring floral spectacle dominated by bluebells, wood anemones and the pungent aroma of wild garlic. Since the late 1990s the woodland's ongoing management has improved the quality of the coppice and is worth a visit in the winter to see this work in action.

Target birds *All year* – **Marsh Tit (90%), Yellowhammer (50%).** *Summer* – **Garden Warbler (75%).**

Other possible bird species

All year	Common woodland	*Winter*
Red-legged Partridge	birds	Woodcock
Grey Partridge	Bullfinch	Winter thrushes
Sparrowhawk		
Buzzard	*Summer*	*Occasional*
Tawny Owl	Blackcap	Sparrowhawk
Great Spotted	Chiffchaff	Goshawk
Woodpecker	Willow Warbler	Turtle Dove (scarce now)
Nuthatch	Spotted Flycatcher	
Treecreeper	(scarce now)	

Background information and birding tips

GARSTON WOOD is part of the wider Cranborne Chase SSSI/AONB designated area and lies to the east of the main woodlands within the Chase, linked by a narrow corridor. Its 34ha consists predominantly of hazel coppice with oak, ash and field maple standards and smaller areas of high forest, glades and rides.

Since its purchase in 1986, the RSPB has restored much of the hazel into a coppicing cycle of 10 to 15 years and I was lucky enough to be involved with the site for a number of years during its re-instatement.

A number of rides criss-cross the wood, giving the options of short, medium or long walks. Garston Wood has been a working woodland from well before the early 1600s so its ancient woodland ground flora is some of the best in the county – to see this at its finest try to visit in late-March to early May (though the flowers do seem to 'go over' earlier each year!)

As you approach from the main Blandford Forum-Salisbury road into Sixpenny Handley, and onto the wood, look out for partridge in the fields – where it's safe to do so pull in and scan around. Both Red-legged and (less commonly) Grey may be seen. If you are really lucky, you may even hear Quail.

From the wood's car park it is worth heading north through the small gate in the corner into an area of scrub that was clear-felled and planted with pine and beech in the late 1970s. This is where Nightingales were mainly found (they have not been recorded since the mid 1990s – the last one I heard was in 1996 – but they are not too far away so keep your ears open).

As this planted area matured the Nightingales disappeared but Turtle Doves moved in (unfortunately these seem to have disappeared now). Bullfinch is often found in the car park area.

Alternatively, leave the car park by the main gate by the notice board and walk west along the main public footpath. Near the western end of the path (before the reserve boundary gate), head south along the ride to the first ride on the left (short route), second ride on the left (medium route) or continue to the southern gate before heading back north for the long route.

The main area of high forest in the centre of the wood is where Great Spotted Woodpeckers and Nuthatches are likely to be found.

The remainder of the wood is divided up into coupes (small blocks) that are coppiced on a cycle of between 10 to 15 years. As a result of this there will be a movement of birds through the woodland as the hazel matures.

This is a good site to get to grips with spring bird song – Blackcaps and Garden Warblers can be compared. Willow Warblers and Chiffchaffs are found in good numbers, but Spotted Flycatchers have become a little more irregular in recent years.

Tawny Owls breed and occasionally youngsters may be located. Look for Buzzards and Sparrowhawks overhead, I have seen Goshawk in the past. Willow Tits have not been recorded for many years.

Dormice are present in the wood and sometimes evidence, such as gnawed hazel nuts, can be found.

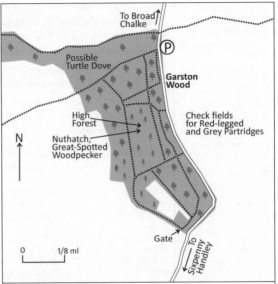

How to get there

(13 miles NE of Blandford Forum).

Garston Wood lies N of Sixpenny Handley along the Broad Chalke road. Leave A354 Salisbury-to-Blandford Forum road on B3031 into Sixpenny Handley.

Take the first right (Dean Lane) towards Broad Chalke and continue on this road for 1.75 miles until you come to the reserve's small car park (located in the NE end of the wood).

Public transport: The Blandford Forum-Salisbury bus service runs through Sixpenny Handley (Wilts & Dorset). It is a mile walk from there to the wood's southern gate.

Bats are well represented (check for events to see these special animals). The local fallow deer population use the wood – hence the internal fencing to protect freshly cut coppices. Later in summer, butterflies become the main interest, including both silver-washed fritillary and white admiral.

The winter months are less productive for birds but Woodcock, winter thrushes and the common resident woodland birds may be seen. This is also the time of year to see the reserve's woodland management activities in action.

Key points

- **Local Nature Reserve and SSSI.**
- **Open at all times.**
- **Tracks not suitable for wheelchairs, but it is possible to view heath and harbours from parking areas.**
- **Toilets at Hamworthy Pier.**
- **Good views.**
- **Regular Osprey on passage.**

A GREAT little Local Nature Reserve on the Wareham Channel shore of Poole Harbour, this heathland site holds Dartford Warbler and Stonechat, while a large freshwater pond is very good for dragonflies. Waders and wildfowl can be seen in the channel – where you can look out for something more unusual such as Scaup or even Smew in winter.

Target birds All year – Dartford Warbler (80%), Peregrine (30%), Mediterranean Gull (30%), Marsh Harrier (10%). Passage – Osprey (50%), Greenshank (50%), Common Sandpiper (50%).

Other possible bird species

All year	Reed Warbler	*Occasional*
Little Egret		Scaup
Stonechat	*Winter*	Long-tailed Duck
Linnet	Brent Goose	Smew
Common passerines	Shelduck	Great Northern Diver
	Red-breasted Merganser	Slavonian Grebe
Summer	Goldeneye	Black-necked Grebe
Nightjar	Avocet	Hen Harrier
Sandwich Tern	Black-tailed Godwit	Little Gull
Common Tern	Greenshank	Black Tern
Sedge Warbler	Regular gull species	

Background information and birding tips

HAM COMMON was designated as a Local Nature Reserve in 1992 and its 32ha lies just to the south of Rockley Caravan Park. The site is a piece of remnant heath shaped by past clay extraction and includes a large freshwater lake (good for dragonflies) and many south-facing slopes (ideal for reptiles).

As the site is fairly small it can easily be covered in a couple of hours but it is worth taking some time to scan the harbour. There are some interesting breeding birds, migrants may be seen during the summer and autumn, and in the winter water birds are the main attraction (a telescope is almost essential for the latter).

The views from here are fantastic. Across the water is Arne and away in the distance are the Purbeck Hills. It an excellent place to view this part of the harbour, including south-westwards into the Wareham Channel, where there is little access along the shoreline.

During April-May and again from July through to October there is always a good chance of picking up Ospreys here as they drift around the harbour.

Dartford Warblers, Stonechats and Linnets breed on the heath while Reed and Sedge Warblers can be found around the lake. Nightjars use the site for feeding but probably don't breed here.

You will find a mixture of common passerines across the site throughout the year but during passage periods Wheatears, Whinchats, Redstarts, flycatchers and warblers may turn up.

In the summer months, two saltmarsh islands in the channel hold a huge breeding colony of up to 10,000 pairs of Black-

Contacts

Borough of Poole
Leisure Services
01202 265 265
www.
boroughofpoole.com

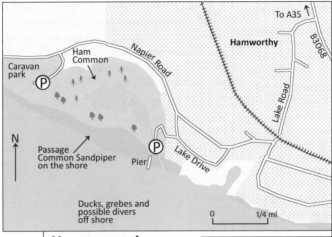

Passage Common Sandpiper on the shore

Ducks, grebes and possible divers off shore

0   1/4 ml

headed Gulls and since the late 1980s Mediterranean Gulls have bred. There are now more than 50 pairs, so look through the gulls as they pass by.

In contrast, during the winter, gulls roost in the harbour in large numbers and move out mainly to the north and west to feed further afield.

A late afternoon watch can produce a spectacular stream of birds returning to the harbour – Black-headed Gulls in their thousands with smaller numbers of Common, Herring, Lesser and Greater Black-backs.

With great patience, and careful observation, a rarity could be picked up as in 2007 when a Ring-billed Gull was found ......but it is a case of a needle in a haystack!

Sandwich and Common Terns are regularly seen from spring to autumn, the former sometimes seen in the winter, and a passing Little Gull or Black Tern may be picked up.

During the winter months, grebes can be found – Great Crested is expected but there is also a chance of Slavonian or Black-necked. Brent Goose, Shelduck, Red-breasted Merganser and Goldeneye are the likely waterfowl to be seen but occasionally Scaup, Smew and Long-tailed Duck turn up.

From time to time divers reach this part of the harbour with

How to get there

(Two miles W of Poole).

From the main Blandford Road, Hamworthy (B3068) – accessed from the A35 to the north or from the A350 in Poole, turn south along Lake Road then west into Lake Drive. For parking at the viewpoint car park (SY977909), continue into Napier Road.

Alternatively, for parking at Hamworthy Pier (SY984905)

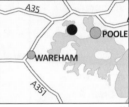

stay on Lake Drive and turn off into car park.

Public transport: **A town bus service passes through Hamworthy.**

Great Northern the most likely.

Waders are not so common on the shore here but large flights of birds, including Black-tailed Godwits, Curlews and Avocets, can be seen as they fly between the Wareham Channel and other parts of the harbour (a rising or falling tide are usually the best time to see these flights).

On the shore Greenshanks and Common Sandpipers may be seen, particularly

during passage times.

Little Egrets are regular all year, while Marsh Harriers (all year) and Hen Harriers (winter) can sometimes be picked up in the distance, quartering over the marshes, and Peregrines can quite often be seen chasing ducks and waders over the water.

Other nearby sites

Hatch Pond, Lytchett Bay, Upton Country Park & Holes Bay, Upton Heath.

Key points

- A National Nature Reserve (Hambledon) with leaflet box.

- Information boards at both sites.

- Steep hills to negotiate. No access for wheelchair users.

- Important Iron Age hill forts.

- Stunning scenery.

- Local pubs/ shops and nearest toilets in Blandford or Shaftesbury.

- Good for chalk grassland plants and butterflies.

Contacts

Natural England (Hambledon) 0300 060 6000 (ask for the reserve number). www.naturalengland. org.uk

National Trust (Hod) 01672 539 167. www.nationaltrust. org.uk

WITH SUPERB VIEWS over the surrounding countryside, the landscape here is dominated by two fine examples of Iron Age hill forts. Chalk grassland plants and butterflies provide the main wildlife interest at both sites, but birdwatchers can enjoy seeing a number of common species, plus Buzzards and Ravens flying overhead.

Target birds

All year – Raven (80%), Yellowhammer (80%), Stonechat (50%), Corn Bunting (20%). *Summer* – Tree Pipit (80%), Cuckoo (50%).

Other possible bird species

All year	Common passerines	*Passage*
Buzzard		Hirundines
Skylark	*Summer*	Redstart
Meadow Pipit	Chiffchaff	Wheatear
Stonechat	Willow Warbler	Spotted Flycatcher
Nuthatch	Blackcap	
Common corvids		*Occasional*
Linnet	*Winter*	Quail
	Redw ing	Corn Bunting
	Fieldfare	

Background information and birding tips

WHILE THE National Trust's Hod Hill is, at 22ha, Dorset's largest hill fort, it is the smaller of these two sites.

The main track from the car park runs along the eastern edge of the woodland, through a gate and out on to the hill fort, important in historical terms because it was re-used by the Romans.

This historic place is well worth exploring – I usually choose to walk around the ramparts for a good view over the surrounding countryside.

Woodland runs along the western edge of the hill and the path through it is an alternative route to the hill fort – follow the track south along the valley bottom (by the River Stour where it can be very muddy at times) to the end of the woodland.

Then turn left up to the south-west corner of the hill. Whichever route you take, there is a steep climb to get to the top of the hill!

Hambledon Hill, a National Nature Reserve, lies to the north-west of Hod Hill. It is possible to walk between the two along public footpaths (but allow a good three to four hours to complete the circuit).

One interesting feature you pass, if you take this walk, is a small yew woodland growing on the steep hillside. If you don't fancy a long walk, there are three main paths up onto the hill from along the roadside – the path to the north is the shortest route.

The chalk grassland, sitting between the Stour and Iwerne valleys, rises steeply but once at the top you won't be disappointed.

The NNR covers 73ha and is managed by Natural England. The hill top is encircled by an Iron Age earthwork and, as with Hod Hill, it is worth just exploring the ramparts yourself. Though the open grassland has the main wildlife interest, there are also areas of scrub where you'll pick up more birds.

On both sites, the south and west-facing slopes are particularly good for plants and butterflies, including chalkhill, small and Adonis blues.

A spring and summer visit will produce a good selection of birds and there is always a chance of something a little more unusual: Quail have been heard in the past and Corn Bunting is in the general area.

Early spring will find Skylarks in full song and the local Buzzards soaring above the hills. Chiffchaffs are the first of the migrants to arrive followed by Blackcaps, Willow Warblers, Tree Pipits and Cuckoos.

Hirundines can fly through in large numbers and Wheatears may stop off on the hillsides. You can bump up the numbers of species on a visit with a selection of common woodland and scrub birds.

In the autumn more migrants may pass through with a better chance of picking up a Redstart or a Spotted Flycatcher at this time of the year.

The winter months are rather bleaker on the hills but Redwings and Fieldfares will join the resident birds in the area.

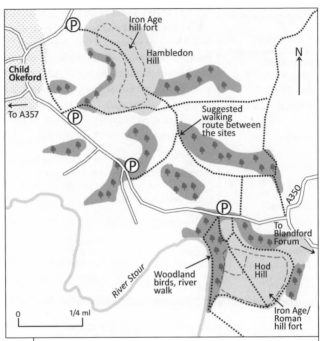

How to get there

(3.5 miles NW of Blandford).

From Blandford Forum take A350 towards Shaftesbury. Just beyond Stourpaine turn left to Child Okeford. The Hod Hill car park is about a mile down this road on the left. Continuing on, and before reaching Child Okeford, there are two lay-by parking areas on the right hand side of the road with footpaths up to Hambleton Hill.

For a third parking area (roadside), and the closest to the fort, drive through the village and take a right turn just after the Baker's Arms

pub, continuing on to the end of the houses on the right – another footpath leads up from here.

Public transport: The Blandford Forum-Sturminster Newton-Gillingham-Shaftesbury bus service runs through Child Okeford (Damory).

Other nearby sites

Badbury Rings, Blackmoor Vale, Duncliffe Wood, Fontmell Down

25 HARTLAND MOOR & STOBOROUGH HEATH NNR

Key points

- **National Nature Reserves with SSSI, SPA, SAC designations.**
- **Open access.**
- **Expect 30-40 species.**
- **Multiple free parking areas (Sunnyside Farm car park locked at dusk).**
- **Two good circular trails – allow two hours for each. Part of the tramway trails suitable for wheelchairs.**
- **Leaflet & information boards.**
- **Easy access from Wareham on foot/bus.**
- **Good for a variety of non-avian species.**

Contacts

Natural England 0300 060 6000 (ask for the reserve number)

THESE National Nature Reserves were on part of my route to work for five years and almost daily I would see something of interest. I frequently saw Dartford Warblers by the road and flushed a Hoopoe on a couple of occasions. It's a reliable site for summering Hobby, with Hen Harrier, Merlin, Woodcock and Great Grey Shrike possible in the winter. I've also seen a Montagu's Harrier and Lesser Grey Shrike in the area. This is one of only a handful of Dorset sites where the rare Purbeck mason wasp can be found.

Target birds
All year – Dartford Warbler (90%), Raven (50%), Peregrine (30%). *Summer* – Nightjar (95% hear, 75% see), Hobby (75%). *Winter* – Hen Harrier (75%), Merlin (25%), Woodcock (25%), Green Sandpiper (25%).

Other possible bird species

All year	Blackcap	Wheatear
Buzzard	Chiffchaff	Grasshopper Warbler
Kestrel	Willow Warbler	Garden Warbler
Lapwing	*Winter*	Lesser Whitethroat
Green Woodpecker	Snipe	Spotted Flycatcher
Skylark	Winter thrushes	*Occasional*
Meadow Pipit	Great Grey Shrike	Black-tailed Godwit
Stonechat	*Passage*	Wood Sandpiper
Linnet	Yellow Wagtail	Jack Snipe
Reed Bunting	Redstart	Woodlark
Summer	Whinchat	Pied Flycatcher
Cuckoo		

Background information and birding tips

WITH A COMBINED size of 350ha, the National Nature Reserves of Hartland Moor and the adjacent Stoborough Heath fit neatly between Arne (site 1), Creech, Stoborough & Grange Heaths (site 17) and Middlebere (site 38).

The landscape is dominated by open heathland and acid grassland – Soldier's Road, which divides the two NNRs, is a good place to get an overview of the sites.

There are a number of parking options, including a car park at Sunnyside Farm, but if you don't have transport the site can easily be reached from Wareham on foot (one mile) or by bus.

A large proportion of Stoborough Heath NNR consists of acid grassland but was heathland until the 1950s when it was 'improved' for agriculture. Since the site was designated as a NNR in 1985, re-instating the heathland has been the priority and the site is a good example of how this valuable habitat can be restored over time.

Hartland Moor NNR, on the other hand, is an amazing example of a heathland bog system and covers an entire drainage basin. It is unique in having a Y-shaped bog

92

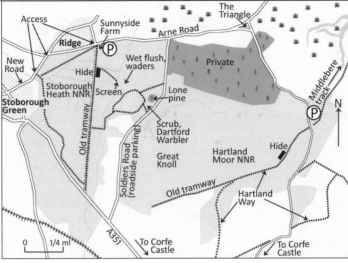

How to get there

(Two miles SE of Wareham).

From Wareham take B3075 to Stoborough over South Bridge and causeway. Just past the petrol station (on your right), turn left down Nutcrack Lane and continue through Ridge (towards Arne).

Alternatively bypass Wareham on A351 towards Swanage, turn left onto B3075 into Stoborough, heading back towards Wareham. Take first right (New Road) towards Ridge and right again through Ridge.]

There are three main parking areas off the Arne Road. For Sunnyside Farm (SY 927 863) turn right into the car park just after the junction into Sunnyside Road. For Soldier's Road (SY 925 856) take the next right turn after Sunnyside and park up along this road.

For Middlebere Track (SY 964 854) turn right at 'the triangle', signposted to Corfe Castle (there is an RSPB sign just beyond this turn). Follow

this road, over a cattle grid then, as the road starts to rise, pull in by the entrance track to Middlebere Farm (also the parking area for Site 38).

Public transport: The nearest railway station is at Wareham where you can catch a bus to Stoborough (Wilts & Dorset). Get off at Stoborough Green and walk back a few metres into New Road. Follow this road (caution: there is no footpath), just beyond the turn into Tucker's Mill Close, to the signed entrance gate at the western end of the site.

On foot: walk south from Wareham town centre, across the causeway to Stoborough and Stoborough Green (just

over a mile). Alternatively, follow the river from the south side of South Bridge to Redcliffe/Ridge. Walk up the tarred road past the farm to the junction and turn right. Walk along the road to the crossroads (there is a rookery on the corner) and access the site here (a mile).

which includes both acid and alkaline drainage systems. The forest on the higher ground immediately to the north of Hartland is under private ownership (with no access), but a large part of

the forest is being removed to restore it to heathland, as it was before the trees were planted in the 1960s.

An old tramway runs from Sunnyside Farm southwards across Stoborough Heath

and forms part of a circular walk (2.5 miles) through the heath and acid grassland (the first part is suitable for wheelchairs).

The scrub along the tramway, and around the field

93

boundaries, is good for migrants in the spring and autumn, particularly for warblers. Scan the field to the east for Yellow Wagtails in the autumn.

After 250m take the steps down into the field (there is also a hide just beyond here) and follow the boundary on your left to a small viewing screen. An old ditch has been blocked up here and it is now a large wet area which has produced some good birds. Lapwings and Redshanks have bred and it is a good spot for Green Sandpipers in the autumn and winter. Wood Sandpiper, Ruff, Black-tailed Godwit and Jack Snipe have also been seen here.

The tramway can also be joined from the west side of Soldier's Road. This area is very popular with dog walkers but sometimes Woodlarks can be found feeding on the ground, particularly in the winter.

I have always found the roadside gorse is very good for Dartford Warblers – even in years when numbers have been hit by cold winters there are usually birds here.

Just up the slope, on the edge of the grassland, is the 'Lone Pine' hill, which is a good place to sit in winter to watch for Hen Harriers (and Merlins). Look to the north for a Marsh Harrier over the Wareham Channel and Swineham; long distance views of Osprey are also possible in spring and autumn.

There are panoramic views from here, so always keep looking skywards. Peregrines and Ravens often drift over and Red Kites sometimes pass through in spring. One lucky local observer was watching a 'Buzzard' being mobbed by 'crows' until he realised that the latter were Buzzards and the former was an eagle, probably a White-tailed Eagle!

At dusk in winter look and listen for Woodcock and Snipe as they leave the forest/heath on their way to feed in the surrounding area.

On the eastern side of Hartland (opposite the parking by the Middlebere Farm entrance track) is the start of another dismantled tramway. The Hartland Way trail (3.5 miles) begins here – the first section is suitable for wheelchairs as far as a hide overlooking the heath.

This stretch is particularly good for Dartford

Warblers and Stonechats and the scrub along the tramway often funnels migrants through.

The trail leaves Hartland and heads south into National Trust land before circling round back on to Hartland, returning to the start of the trail. Most of the Trust land is 'improved' grassland and is under heathland restoration management.

As an alternative to following the trail, I tend to continue along the tramway which peters out but runs into more grassland and scrubby boundaries. This is another area which is often excellent for migrants, particularly in the autumn: likely species are Yellow Wagtail, Wheatear, Whinchat, Redstart, warblers (including Grasshopper) – but they are just as likely to be seen elsewhere across the site.

Other birds that should be found in the area include breeding Nightjars (in very good numbers), Hobbies (especially feeding over the mires) and Cuckoos in the summer and resident Green Woodpeckers, Skylarks, Meadow Pipits and Linnets.

Buzzards, Kestrels and Ravens are frequently seen overhead while Peregrines are regularly seen. Great Grey Shrikes don't turn up every year but I have seen them on Hartland many times over the years, especially around The Great Knoll area.

This is a great area to look for non-avian species, particularly heathland plants, reptiles, dragonflies and other invertebrates. One particular speciality is the rare Purbeck mason wasp found on the Hartland tramway. They feed on the larvae of a heathland moth and nest in burrows. In May to July, look for holes in the ground with a granulated (not fine) 'spoil heap'.

Other nearby sites

Arne, Creech, Stoborough & Grange Heaths, Middlebere, Wareham Meadows & Swineham Point.

DESPITE BEING tucked away in an industrial area of Poole, this little gem of a Local Nature Reserve is certainly worth a look, especially in the winter. There is usually a good selection of ducks and a mixture of gulls on the water but Bittern is the speciality of the site, regularly offering stunning views. In addition, Great Crested Grebes, Water Rails, Snipe and Cetti's Warblers are frequently seen or heard.

Target birds *All year* - Great Crested Grebe, (90%), Cetti's Warbler (90%) Reed Bunting (90%). *Winter* - Snipe (90%), Magpie (large evening roost 90%), Bittern (75%), Water Rail (75%).

Other possible bird species

All year
Mute Swan
Mallard
Gadwall
Little Grebe
Coot
Moorhen

Kingfisher
Summer
Reed Warbler
Winter
Wigeon
Teal
Shoveler

Pochard
Tufted Duck
Regular gull species
Occasional
Mandarin
Ruddy Duck
Jack Snipe

Background information and birding tips

THOUGH I have seen a Bittern within Poole Harbour a sighting there is a rare occurrence but nearby Hatch Pond is rated as one of the best sites in the county for seeing this wintering species, the others being Lodmoor (site 31) and Radipole Lake (site 47) in Weymouth.

This Local Nature Reserve site is managed by the Borough of Poole Leisure Services and is located between housing estates, commercial units and close to a busy road. At first glance you may not be inspired to stop, but do give it a chance.

Apart from the open water there are reed fringes along the western edge, opening out into a larger reedbed in the north of the site. Scrub around the edges with larger trees on parts of the boundary give the site a good mixture of

habitat. Though there are no visitor facilities, wheelchair access is possible along the tarmac path on the southern boundary.

It is best to visit Hatch Pond in winter as that is when Bittern can be seen: in recent years they have been annual visitors....with up to four birds! They are often viewed as it is getting dark – I usually arrive there at least half an hour before dusk and wait.

Stand in the small clump of pine trees on the eastern boundary and look across (and down) to the main reedbed where a small channel, known locally as 'Elborn's Cut', is kept open. As the evening draws in the birds usually appear in the open channel, either by emerging from the surrounding reeds or by flying in.

Sometimes they disappear quickly into the reeds while on other

Key points
● A Local Nature Reserve.
● Access available at all times.
● Wheelchair access along southern footpath.
● Nearest public toilets at Upton Country Park or Poole town centre.
● A key site for Bittern.
● Large Magpie roost.

Contacts
Borough of Poole Leisure Services
01202 265 265
www. boroughofpoole.com

95

occasions they put on a show for a good few minutes. If you can't arrange to be here at this time of day, a visit at any other time may still produce sightings – scan the edges of the reeds and watch out for a bird in flight.

While waiting for the Bittern there will be plenty other birds to keep you occupied. The site is excellent for Snipe, which can be seen/heard flying into or out of the pond.

You may see them on the ground by the edge of the reedbeds and, especially, in the reed channel cut for the Bittern, which is also a good spot to see a Water Rail.

You may also be treated to a burst of song from a Cetti's Warbler or two, Reed Buntings are regular, while a variety of common passerines are often heard/seen moving around the area.

One sight I always find quite amazing at Hatch Pond is the build-up of Magpie numbers as the evening draws in. It is here that I've seen the largest concentration of birds anywhere in the county - their numbers regularly reach into three figures.

Out on the open water you should find a selection of duck including good numbers of Gadwall and smaller numbers of Teal, Wigeon (occasional), Shoveler, Pochard and Tufted Duck.

Great Crested Grebes (they also breed here) and Little Grebes can also be found, together with Coots, Moorhens, Mute Swans, Grey Herons and Cormorants, and occasionally Little Egrets.

Look among the gulls that often

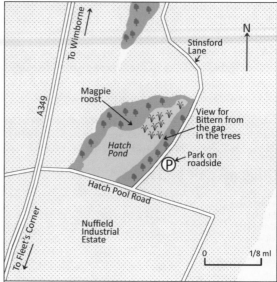

How to get there

(1.75 miles N of Poole).

Hatch Pond is located close to the Nuffield Industrial Estate just north of Fleet's Corner roundabout on the main A35. From the roundabout take A349 duel carriageway towards Wimborne (immediately passing a large Tesco store on the left and a set of traffic lights). Staying in the right hand lane, carry on to the next main traffic lights and turn right here – this is Hatch Pond Road. Hatch Pond is

on the left – continue to the next traffic lights and turn left in to Stinsford Lane and park up on the right hand side.

Public transport: Poole town bus services.

gather in a pre-roost flock – occasionally there will be a Mediterranean Gull lurking with the common species and in the past Iceland Gull has been recorded here.

Lesser Scaup (Nov-Dec), Purple Heron (Aug-Sept) and Black-throated Diver (Jan)

have been unlikely visitors to the site in the past and recently otter was recorded.

Other nearby sites

Canford Heath, Poole Harbour – Poole Quay to Sandbanks, Upton Country Park & Holes Bay, Upton Heath.

THIS DORSET Wildlife Trust's reserve west of Wareham is rich in wildlife, including specialist heathland birds, and is an interesting example of how past industrial workings can revert back to nature. It is the most undisturbed area along a four mile stretch of the Puddletown road, where sand extraction has changed the nature of the heathland landscape dramatically since the 1920s. A Night Heron here in 2006 was totally unexpected!

Target birds
All year – Stonechat (90%), Grey Wagtail (80%), Dartford Warbler (75%), Yellowhammer (50%). *Summer* – Nightjar (75% hear, 50% see), Tree Pipit (75%), Woodlark (50%), Hobby (25%). *Passage* – Wheatear (50%), Whinchat (25%).

Other possible bird species

All year	Summer	Winter
Little Grebe	Siskin	Snipe
Mallard	*Summer*	*Occasional*
Tufted Duck	Cuckoo	Water Rail
Moorhen	Reed Warbler	Jack Snipe
Coot	Blackcap	Woodcock
Pied Wagtail	Chiffchaff	Kingfisher
Common woodland birds	Willow Warbler	Redpoll
	Spotted Flycatcher	

Background information and birding tips

CLOSE TO THE parking area you'll see a hide overlooking one of the ponds created by past industrial workings and this is a good place to start your visit. The hide, and a small viewing area further along the track, is accessible to wheelchairs. The pond can be very good.

Grey and Pied Wagtails are usually about and various ducks come and go with Mallard and Tufted Duck often staying to breed, along with Little Grebe, Coot and Moorhen. Water Rail is seen, but more often heard. From time to time, and if lucky, you may pick up a flash of blue from a Kingfisher.

In the spring I always find that it is worth spending a little time in the hide watching the surrounding trees and bushes for small birds – a good mixture of common passerines can be expected but you never know what may turn up. A totally unexpected bird in the shape of a Night Heron put in an appearance in 2006.

From the parking area take the trail through an area of wet sallow woodland and out on to the edge of the heath. The sallow provide a nice mixture of common woodland birds, including Green and Great Spotted Woodpeckers and Spotted Flycatcher, and is an area where Siskin can be regularly found.

If you follow the marked trail you will eventually return to the main path next to the parking area hide.

The 54ha site has open access so you can explore at will. The central

Key points
• Access available at all times.

• Designated SSSI.

• Expect to see 20-30 bird species in a one hour visit.

• Leaflet available.

• Information board in parking area.

• Marked nature trail.

• Bird hide overlooking a pond.

• Paths are wet for most of year.

• Wheelchair access to first pool and bird hide.

Contacts
Dorset Wildlife Trust 01305 264 620 (www.dorsetwildlifetrust.org.uk/reserves)

area consists of humid and wet heath and so can be very wet underfoot and difficult to walk over.

This type of heath is far richer botanically than the dry heath – look out for the tiny sundews in the bare areas among the heather and for the more prominent yellow spikes of the bog asphodel. There is also a healthy silver-studded blue butterfly population here.

The main bird interest is on the dry heath towards the north end of the reserve. The drier slopes are dominated by the 'dry' heathers (bell and ling) mixed with stands of gorse and a few pine and birch and this is where you are likely to find breeding Woodlarks, Tree Pipits, Dartford Warblers and Stonechats.

You can reach this area by crossing the humid/wet heath from the trail. Alternatively, if you take the track beyond the hide and continue past the viewing area, you can pick your way over the rough ground to the edge of the dry heath. Crossbills are often seen, but more often than not you will hear them first as they fly over.

May, once the birds are holding territory, is a particularly good time to visit. A late evening visit is a good time to look for a Hobby feeding over the heath (they often breed in the area).

As daylight fades Nightjars become active – though they are usually heard rather than seen, you can sometimes pick up birds flying around before the light finally goes.

As with all Nightjar sites, if you do go out late in the evening

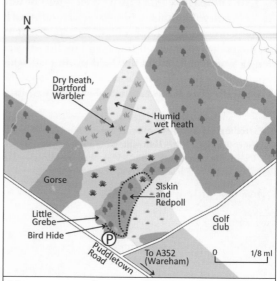

How to get there

(Five miles NW of Wareham).
Take A352 from Wareham towards Wool. Just after the Worgret Manor Hotel turn right along Puddletown Road.

After 3.5 miles there is a turn on the right to the Dorset Golf and Country Club. Immediately past this turn is a Hanson's facility – turn in here.

Set back in the entrance is a small DWT parking area – open the gate and park just inside.

remember to take a torch and work out your route back to the parking area before it is fully dark.

The site is at its best in the spring/summer but can be worth a visit in the winter. There is always a chance of

flushing Woodcock in the woodland and a Siskin flock, possibly with a few Redpolls, often feeds in the alders.

Out on the heath Snipe are regularly flushed – but look at them carefully as occasionally Jack Snipe are present.

Other nearby sites
Bere Regis, Tincleton & Waddock Cross Cress Beds, Tadnoll & Winfrith Heath, Wareham Forest, Wareham Meadows & Swineham Point.

HOLT HEATH & FOREST NNR, is one of the finest examples of heathland and bog habitat in eastern Dorset and the usual heathland suspects of Nightjar, Dartford Warbler, and occasionally Woodlark, are found here. More interestingly, Curlew breeds in the mires. The 72ha of ancient woodland within the National Nature Reserve is quite a rare habitat in Dorset – Holt Forest was mentioned in the Domesday Book.

Target birds
All year – Nightjar (95% hear, 75% see), Woodcock (75% roding), Dartford Warbler (75%). *Summer* – Hobby (50%), Curlew (50%). *Winter* – Hen Harrier (25%), Merlin (10%).

Other possible bird species

All year
Sparrowhawk
Buzzard
Tawny Owl
Green Woodpecker
Meadow Pipit
Stonechat
Marsh Tit
Siskin

Linnet
Yellowhammer
Reed Bunting
Common woodland species

Summer
Cuckoo
Skylark
Tree Pipit
Blackcap

Chiffchaff
Willow Warbler

Winter
Snipe
Redpoll

Occasional
Woodlark
Crossbill

Background information and birding tips

LOCATED to the north of Wimborne, the 500ha of Holt Heath and Forest NNR incorporates one of the more sizable blocks of heathland remaining in Dorset (411ha) and is one of my favourite sites.

It is part of the National Trust's Kingston Lacy Estate and has more of a New Forest 'feel' about it than a Dorset one.

As well as the general landscape, this is in part due to the large grazing unit. Cattle grids over the roads allow a much bigger area to be grazed and stock (cattle and ponies) have free range over the area – so drive with care!

The best access point onto the heath is via the White Sheet Hill car park in the south-western corner, which also allows easy access to the Forestry Commission's White Sheet Plantation. There are a few roadside parking places along Holt Road between Higher Row and Lower Mannington.

Parking at the western end of this road is useful to cover the heath to the north side of the road or to walk through to Holt Forest, while the eastern end provides closer access to Summerlug Hill.

A good circular route is mapped out from the car park – it consists of two loops giving the option of doing a six mile walk or a shorter three mile walk.

The full route covers the whole width of the heath, south of Holt Road, and takes in all of the heathland community types that are found on the site – dry heath, dominated by calluna, wet heath and the very important mires.

Key points
- National Trust (part of the Kingston Lacy Estate) and Forestry Commission ownerships.
- A National Nature Reserve and SSSI.
- Access at all times.
- Allow a minimum of two hours.
- A circular route is laid out around the heath, but is not accessible for wheelchairs.
- Nearest toilets in West Moors or Wimborne.
- Free car parking at White Sheet Hill.
- Can be busy with dog walkers.
- Information boards.
- A reliable site for roding Woodcock.

Contacts
The National Trust 01202 840 630. www.nationaltrust.org.uk

99

How to get there

(3.5 miles NE of Wimborne).

From Wimborne town centre take B3078 northwards towards Cranborne. Turn right just before leaving town (Burt's Lane) towards Colehill. Continue to the T-junction, turn right into Smugggler's Lane then left into Colehill Lane and follow this road to Broom Hill.

At Broom Hill, go straight over the crossroads (towards White Moor). Turn right where the road reaches the top of the hill and bends to the left (just after the fishing lakes), down a gravel track to the White Sheet Hill car park.

Alternatively, from A31 from Ringwood or A338 from Bournemouth take the Ashley Heath roundabout heading towards Ashley Heath and Three Legged Cross. Stay on this road and turn left after Three Legged Cross to Lower Mannington. This road crosses the heath (Holt Road) – at the crossroad turn left to Higher Row/Broom Hill. Just after crossing a cattle grid turn left into the White Sheet Hill car park.

Map labels: Holt Forest · Mannington · To Verwood · Lower Mannington · Lower Row · Holt Heath · Summerlug Hill · Higher Row · Main walk route · Woodcock · Access from West Moors · Main parking · Curlew · Broom Hill · White Sheet Plantation · To Wimborne Minster · Ferndown Forest · N · 0 — 1/2ml

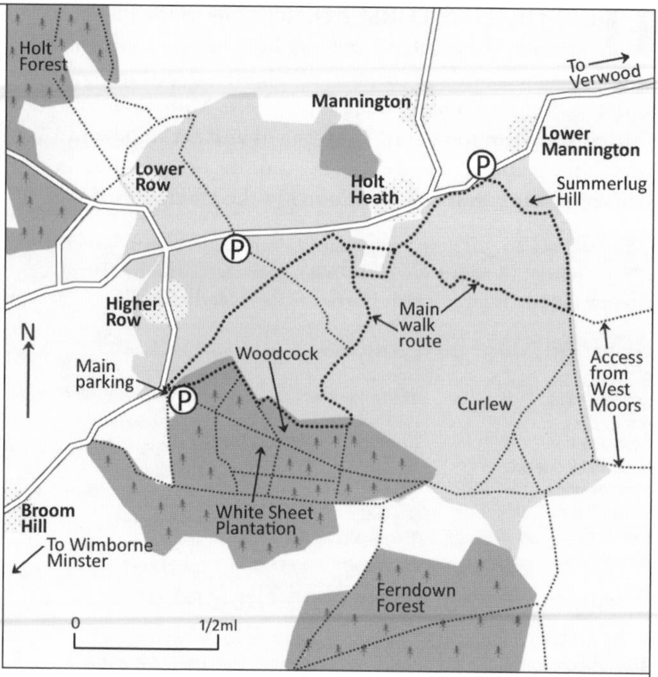

There are also alternative pull-in parking spaces along the road between Higher Row and Lower Mannington.

Public transport: The Bournemouth-Verwood and Poole-Verwood bus services stop at West Moors. A footpath from the Memorial Hall (Station Road) takes you to the SE corner of the heath (third of a mile). Alternatively, just over half a mile north of the hall, turn left into Newman's

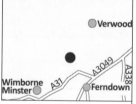

Map labels: Verwood · A3049 · A338 · Wimborne Minster · A31 · Ferndown

Lane – this path brings you out to the heath just south of Summerlug Hill (half a mile). (Wilts & Dorset).

It is in these mires where the Curlew breeds – usually one, but occasionally two pairs. It is virtually impossible to walk through the mires and it shouldn't be attempted – there are plenty of vantage points to look across this wet area. The birds are usually on territory from February and may be seen displaying over the mire, their bubbling call carrying across the heath.

The main area where they are found is in the south-east quarter – Summerlug Hill gives a good perspective over the area and it is possible to walk around the edge of the mire along footpaths and bridleways. Out on the open heath, you should find a good selection of breeding species: Skylark, Tree Pipit, Stonechat,

Dartford Warbler, Linnet, Yellowhammer and, at dusk, Nightjar.

Woodlark doesn't occur here regularly but is possible, especially in early spring in areas that have been burnt or cleared.

Later in the summer look out for a Hobby hawking over the mires, and for other summer visitors such as Cuckoos and Willow Warblers.

It is worth making a visit here during the winter. Dartford Warblers will still be about but there is also a reasonable chance of picking up a Hen Harrier or Merlin.

Snipe are more common at this time of year but usually are only seen when flushed off the heath – they may breed in the mires but are scarce in the summer.

Spring and autumn passage migrants are usually limited to a few Redstarts, Whinchats, Wheatears and hirundines but there is always an outside chance of something a little more unusual coming through.

White Sheet Plantation is an interesting area. Much of it burnt down in 1979 and its recovery, other fires and active management since then have created an interesting mosaic of habitats, including areas that are being restored to heathland.

The plantation is crossed by a series of rides and paths – just pick your own way round them. The wooded areas hold Siskins, Marsh Tits and other common woodland species and Crossbills may be seen from time to time.

This is probably the best site, or at least the most reliable, in the county to find a roding Woodcock. May and June, at dusk, is a good time to look for them as they display over the woodland rides and heath. Nightjars will also be found in good numbers and listen out for Tawny Owls.

Other groups of interest in the general area include all six species of the UK's reptiles, a range of heathland plants including marsh gentian, and a variety of butterflies and dragonflies.

Holt Forest was formally grazed wood pasture but grazing has ceased. The woodland is dominated by oak, with some areas of beech, and an understory of holly - many of the oaks trees are very old specimens with a history of pollarding. Take the bridleway from Lower Row (north-west corner of the heath) and continue into the forest.

There will be a nice selection of common woodland birds to add to the birds seen on the heath but nothing unexpected.

The ground flora here is poor because of the acidic soils, shade and past grazing practices but you may pick up some interesting butterflies – purple hairstreak and white admiral are recorded here.

Other nearby sites
Badbury Rings, Cranborne Common, Longham Lakes, Moors Valley Country Park, River Allen - Crichel Lake.

Dartford Warbler is one of the key species that visitors come to see on the open heath areas at this site.

Key points

- Designated SSSI owned/leased by Dorset Wildlife Trust.

- Expect 25-30 species in the summer.

- Way-marked trails and public rights of way.

- 'Tramper'route for mobility vehicles, but use with caution.

- Leaflet & information boards at Kingcombe Centre and DWT West Dorset Interpretive Centre.

- Events, walks and courses.

- Café selling local produce.

Contacts

Dorset Wildlife Trust
01305 264 620.
www.dorsetwildlifetrust.
org.uk/reserves

The Kingcombe Centre
01300 320 684.
www.kingcombecentre.
org

A S ONE OF Dorset Wildlife Trust's larger reserves, Kingcombe Meadows has a superb mixture of unimproved grassland, ancient hedgerows and a patchwork of small fields lying across the valley of the River Hooke. It is managed as a working farm but without the use of pesticides or artificial fertilisers, so is a fantastic example of what Dorset's rural past must have looked like. There area has a good mixture of birds, butterflies and flowers, with Dipper a possibility on the river.

Target birds *All year* – **Kingfisher (5%), Dipper (5%).**

Other possible bird species

All year	Bullfinch	Woodcock
Buzzard	Yellowhammer	Fieldfare
Kestrel	Common woodland birds	Redwing
Tawny Owl	*Summer*	Siskin
Green Woodpecker	Cuckoo	Redpoll
Great Spotted	Blackcap	*Occasional*
Woodpecker	Chiffchaff	Hobby
Grey Wagtail	Willow Warbler	Jack Snipe
Marsh Tit	*Winter*	Garden Warbler
Raven	Snipe	
Common corvids		

Background information and birding tips

V ISITING THE Dorset Wildlife Trust's 185ha reserve at Kingcombe Meadows is like taking a step back in time. An 1844 tithe map shows that many of the field systems have changed little and a lot of the old field names have been retained.

Two long distance paths, The Jubilee Trail and Wessex Ridgeway, run through the site and are incorporated into two way-marked routes. These follow a one-way system with arrowed marker posts pointing you in the right direction.

The circular route is the longer at 2.5 miles but there is the option of splitting this into two shorter circuits. The Tramper route is designed for mobility vehicle use and is about a mile long, but it should be used with caution.

Both walks start from Pound Cottage car park (where you can walk through to the Kingcombe Centre). Turn left out of the car park and walk 100m along the road (be watchful of passing cars). The route leaves the road on the bend and continues around the meadows. The flowers are allowed to set seed before cutting and provide a food source for butterflies. You can walk over the fields to look at them but take care when haymaking is underway or if they are being grazed.

The hedgerows, old boundary trees and scrubby areas hold a good selection of common birds. An early morning 'dawn chorus' visit is a good time to pick up what is around. Check the scrub for species such as Blackcap, Chiffchaff and Willow Warbler, while Whitethroat, Yellowhammer and Bullfinch are more likely to be found along the hedgerows.

Cuckoos, Green Woodpeckers and Marsh Tits are some of the more interesting species and there are occasional sightings of Hobbies and Garden Warblers.

The circular route crosses the River Hooke – it isn't very wide and is only visible for a length of about 100m.

The chalk rivers of West Dorset hold a few Dippers, Kingfishers and Grey Wagtails, all of which can be seen on this stretch of water, though a sighting is by no means guaranteed.

In the summer look out for the beautiful demoiselle damselflies as you wait for birds to appear. At the river the choice is to return to the car park or to continue on the second part of the circular route on the north side of the valley.

From the autumn, winter thrushes are in the meadows, while Siskins and Redpolls forage in the trees along the river. The resident woodland species should be located more easily as the trees are bare of leaves.

By the winter, Snipe can be seen (usually flushed) in the wetter areas of the meadows – watch out for Jack Snipe which has been recorded here. Another species likely to be flushed is Woodcock – particularly in the wet wooded areas. Tawny Owls can be very vocal during the short winter days.

The Kingcombe Centre is now part of DWT. In summer look out for Swallows, Swifts and House Sparrows nesting in the buildings.

As well as the facilities for day visitors passing through – toilets,

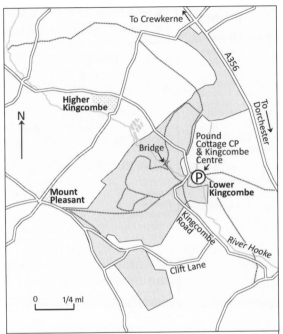

How to get there

(10 miles NW of Dorchester).
From Dorchester take the A37 Yeovil road and turn left onto A356 just past Grimstone. About a mile after leaving Maiden Newton turn left (Toller Lane) to Toller Porcorum.

In the village turn right and follow this road to the hamlet of Lower Kingcombe. Pound Cottage Information Centre and parking is the

first building on the right hand side of the road and just beyond is the Kingcombe Centre.

information centre and the Conservatory Café (I would recommend sampling some of the local produce) – the Centre runs a wide range of day and residential courses throughout the year and there are opportunities to

join guided walks out on the reserve.

If you are thinking of staying in West Dorset, the Centre can also offer B&B with/without meals. Contact them for further information.

103

Key points
- Free National Trust car park.
- Access available at all times.
- Occasional events (see website for details).
- No wheelchair access but the hill top area is relatively flat.

THIS PROMINENT hill fort, which lies close to the Devon border, has stunning views over the surrounding countryside. The site includes woodland, with some magnificent beech trees, which holds Redstarts and Wood Warblers in spring and summer, as well as open grassland and a small area of heathland, which has attracted breeding Nightjar.

Target birds
All year – Yellowhammer (90%), Raven (50%). Summer – Tree Pipit (90%), Redstart (90%), Nightjar (75% chance of hearing), Wood Warbler (10%).

Other possible bird species

All year		
Buzzard	Nuthatch	Chiffchaff
Meadow Pipit	Treecreeper	Willow Warbler
Great Spotted	Linnet	Spotted Flycatcher
Woodpecker	_Summer_	
Marsh Tit	Stonechat	
	Blackcap	

Background information and birding tips

OWNED by the National Trust, Lambert's Castle is designated a Site of Special Scientific Interest for the flora of its acidic grassland and heathland. The site itself is quite small and easily covered in a couple of hours. I find that it is worth zigzagging around to cover each habitat to pick up a decent tally of bird species.

The hill fort at the site's centre is marked out by an earth bank, and is dominated by open grassland and scrub. The western slopes are covered in mixed woodland while the eastern slopes feature a mixture of birch woodland and scrub. An area of heathland lies to the west of the car park.

Your main target species here are Redstart and Wood Warbler. There are usually two or three pairs of breeding Redstarts, and I've always seen them whenever I've gone looking for them. You should hear/see them within a few minutes' walk from the car park. I

find a pair often nests just inside the woodland.

Walk a few yards through the gate into the grassland and look at the tops of the trees on the edge of the wood, particularly those with dead branches (favourite song perches).

Records of the Wood Warbler have been more erratic in recent years. In some years breeding has been noted, in other years birds have been heard singing briefly in May, but quite often there have been no reports of birds at all.

From the car park, take a walk first through the western woodland following the contour path at the top of the slope, past the magnificent old beech trees, to the northern end of the site.

There is another chance of seeing Redstarts along this path and, if Wood Warblers are around, this is where they could be found.

You'll find a good variety of

Contacts
The National Trust
01297 489 481
www.nationaltrust.org.uk

common woodland birds here as well, including Nuthatches, Treecreepers, Marsh Tits and Great Spotted Woodpeckers. Spotted Flycatchers are still be found in this part of the woodland in reasonable numbers.

The Marshwood road runs along the bottom of the slope, so there can be quite a lot of background noise as cars pass by.

You may have to be patient for a quiet spell to listen to the bird song – if they are there, it's highly likely that you will pick up a Wood Warbler first by its song and then will have to track it down for a visual sighting.

At the end of the woodland path you come out into the open area of the hill fort. Head back towards the car park but walk along the eastern slope through the open birch woodland and scrub.

This is a good area for Tree Pipits – watch out for their aerial display, as well as for Whitethroats, Willow Warblers, Linnets and Yellowhammers.

Once you reach the gate to the car park, head back over the open grassland, following the edge of the western woodland to the northern end of the hill fort.

Here look out/listen for the Redstart again, keeping your eyes peeled for a male sitting on a favourite song perch. This part of the walk will give you a chance to see the man-made features of the hill fort itself.

Nightjars are known to have bred in recent years on the heathland – known as Lambert's Common – and are normally heard annually.

Obviously they are likely to be

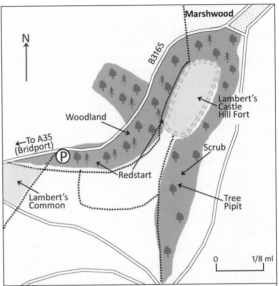

How to get there

(Seven miles NE of Lyme Regis).

From Bridport take A35 towards Honiton/Axminster, then turn off on B3165 towards Marshwood (there are two parts of the B3165 either side of the Dorset-Devon border near Raymond's Hill that join into a single road).

About a mile before Marshwood, look out for a track on the right (at SY 364 999) that leads to the car park.

There is a small National Trust sign by the road but it can be easy to miss – if you do, turn around in Marshwood and retrace your route for a mile – but watch carefully as the sign is obscured from this direction.

heard or seen at dusk, while Stonechats on the heath will be about during the day.

When you are in the open at any time, keep an eye skywards for a passing Buzzard or Raven and, in the spring, for early hirundines coming through.

Other nearby sites

Lyme Regis, West Bexington.

105

Key points

- An RSPB reserve and a designated SSSI.

- Allow two hours to complete the two-mile circular route.

- Over 260 species recorded here and Radipole Lake.

- Expect 40-60 species depending on time of year.

- Pay-and-display car parks either end of Lodmoor, off the main road (W&PBC).

- Access available at all times.

- Easy to reach by public transport.

- Wheelchair access.

- Trail leaflet available.

- Events organised.

Contacts

RSPB Weymouth Visitor Centre 01305 778 313
www.rspb.org.uk/reserves

A S THE 'WILDER' of the two Weymouth reserves managed by the RSPB, Lodmoor has developed into an excellent site for breeding ducks and holds a small colony of Common Terns on purpose-built islands that can be viewed from close quarters. Waders are better here than Radipole and I saw my first Dorset Aquatic Warbler in 1992 – birds may still come through occasionally, so keep your eyes open in the autumn. This is a good site for wintering Bitterns, while Marsh Harriers have started breeding.

Target birds *All year* – Cetti's Warbler (95% hear, 75% see), Little Egret (50%), Bearded Tit (25%), Peregrine (25%). *Summer* – Common Tern (95%), Reed Warbler (95% hear, 75% see), Sedge Warbler (95% hear, 75% see), Marsh Harrier (80%), Hobby (30%). *Winter* – Waders & wildfowl, Bittern (80%), *Spring/autumn passage* - Unusual waders and possible rarities.

Other possible bird species

All year	Cuckoo	Whimbrel
Mute Swan	Hirundines	Common Sandpiper
Shelduck	Blackcap	Green Sandpiper
Gadwall	Lesser Whitethroat	Greenshank
Shoveler	Whitethroat	Wood Sandpiper
Pochard	Chiffchaff (poss. winter)	Redshank
Tufted Duck	Willow Warbler	Yellow Wagtail
Little Grebe		Redstart
Great Crested Grebe	*Winter*	Whinchat
Sparrowhawk	Spoonbill	Wheatear
Buzzard	Merlin	Grasshopper Warbler
Kestrel	Regular gull species	(spring)
Water Rail	Kingfisher	
Mediterranean Gull	Water Pipit	*Occasional*
Stonechat	Winter thrushes	Scaup
Reed Bunting	Firecrest	Smew
Common passerines		Roseate Tern
	Passage	Arctic Tern
Summer	Garganey	Black Tern
Sandwich Tern	Little Ringed Plover	Short-eared Owl
Common Tern	Little Stint	
	Curlew Sandpiper	

Background information and birding tips

H ISTORICALLY, Lodmoor was open to tidal inundation but it is now enclosed behind a sea wall. However, there is still a brackish influence on the water, mainly in the southern part of the site.

Since 1983, Lodmoor has been managed by the RSPB and holds

a mosaic of wetland habitats – a large reedbed, open water, wet grassland, saltmarsh and areas of scrub dotted around the edges.

A visit here can easily be combined with Radipole Lake (site 47) and there is a seafront walk between the two along Weymouth

106

Bay (site 57). Lodmoor has good hardcore paths and the circular walk of just over 1.5 miles is easily negotiated. The main parking area to use is 'Lodmoor', signposted just off the A353, by the south-west corner of the site.

Alternatively, parking is available at Overcombe. Both car parks are council-owned and charges apply.

The entrance path is opposite the main car park and after a few metres there is the option of turning left or to carry straight on.

My own choice of direction usually depends on whether there is anything specific around – if there isn't, I tend to walk around clockwise. The 'tern islands' are the first feature of note and can be easily seen from the path by the entrance or from the viewing shelter a little further along.

The islands hold a growing number of nesting Common Terns, the numbers now becoming limited by the available space, and a pair or two of Oystercatchers usually find a spot to nest.

It is always worth checking out the terns for other species – Sandwich, in particular, but also Arctic and Roseate, which are seen from time to time. Whiskered and White-winged

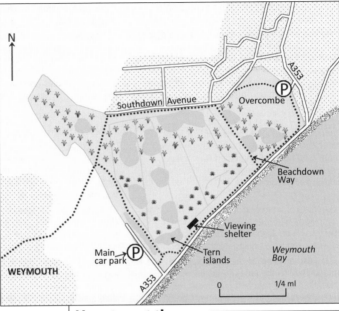

How to get there

(1.5 miles NE of Weymouth)

From Weymouth town centre drive 1.5 along the A353 towards Wareham.

Public transport: There is a frequent local bus service to Overcombe Corner and Lodmoor Country Park from the Weymouth seafront (by the King's statue).

Nearest railway station is

Weymouth, a mile from the reserve.

Black Terns have been seen in the spring, and Black Terns in spring and autumn.

An area of the remnant saltmarsh, with wet grassland beyond it, runs adjacent to the main road. Both of these habitats are crossed by a series of ditches and there are pockets of deeper open water among them (there is

another area of wet grassland by the Overcombe corner).

These areas are liable to flooding in the winter, and gradually dry out as the summer progresses. At all times of the year, but particularly during the spring/ autumn migration periods, they are well worth scanning. A telescope is very useful as

107

birds can disappear into the contours of the marshes.

Waders are very well represented at Lodmoor and it is the most productive site in the Weymouth area for this group of birds. Little Ringed Plover is one of the first summer migrants to arrive but something a little more unusual will turn up on passage, particularly in the autumn.

These may include Little Stint, Curlew Sandpiper and Wood Sandpiper, but scan carefully for any rarities that may be among them – recently a Long-billed Dowitcher (which actually stayed for a long time) and a Semipalmated Sandpiper (which stayed only briefly) were found.

Numbers of wintering waders are not particularly high but most of the common species will be seen during this period, Lapwing and Snipe being particularly obvious.

The northern part of the moor, and the area immediately to the east of Beachdown Way, is dominated by reedbed and pools. Reed and Sedge Warblers and Reed Buntings breed in good numbers and there are a few pairs of Bearded Tit but sightings of these can fluctuate – early autumn is a good time to look for them as they move around.

Duck breed in the reeds around the pools but their success is only apparent when ducklings are seen on open water – Pochard, Tufted Duck, Gadwall and Shoveler may be among them. Little and Great Crested Grebes and Water Rail also breed.

The birds to watch for in winter are Bitterns – look out for them flying and scan for them feeding along the edges of the pools/reedbeds. Looking down from vantage points along Southdown Avenue is a good practice, especially for birds in flight.

Marsh Harrier last bred in Dorset (in Poole Harbour) in 1962 but in 2009 a pair nested at Radipole Lake. In 2010 they nested at Lodmoor and in 2011 a male mated with two females – one here and the other at Radipole. Hobbies in the summer, Peregrines all year, and Merlins and Short-eared Owls in the winter may join the local Buzzards, Sparrowhawks and Kestrels over the moor.

The areas of scrub are worth checking, particularly along Beachdown Way. I virtually never fail to get Cetti's Warbler here all year round. Although they are usually heard, good views are always possible. They are joined in the summer by Whitethroats, Willow Warblers, Blackcaps and Chiffchaffs (the latter regularly over-winter and should be checked out in case there is a 'Siberian' about).

Hirundines pass through in large numbers and local birds regularly feed over the moor ...... worth checking out for a Red-rumped Swallow or an Alpine Swift in the spring! In the winter you may strike lucky and sight a Firecrest.

The bird list for Lodmoor (and Radipole Lake) stands at more than 260 species and, as this site is well watched, not much escapes the attentions of the local birders.

Other species of interest you should look for include Garganey on the pools in the spring/autumn, as well as Scaup and Smew in the winter, which is when a Spoonbill sighting is most likely.

Kingfishers appear from late summer through the winter, and occasional Water Pipits may arrive at anytime during the winter and into the spring.

Migrants turn up during both periods of passage (usually in larger numbers in the autumn), and include species such as Yellow Wagtail, Redstart, Wheatear and Whinchat. Spring is the better time to pick up Grasshopper Warbler though, as they 'reel' and in 2011 a Savi's Warbler stayed for a while. Keep an open mind when it comes to rarities as Lodmoor gets its fair share!

Other nearby sites

Lorton Meadows & Two-mile Copse, Portland Harbour & Ferrybridge, Radipole Lake, Ringstead Bay, The Nothe & Weymouth Bay.

A S BIRDS colonise new sites they create excitement for local birders and watchers at Longham Lakes' two reservoirs have already recorded 150 species. As well as a great selection of typical species associated with open freshwater, an ever-increasing number of more interesting birds are being recorded – including Bewick's Swan, Garganey, Smew, Goosander, Slavonian Grebe and Black Tern.

Target birds
All year – Grey Wagtail (75%), Mediterranean Gull (50%), Peregrine (25%). *Summer* – Hobby (50%), Little Ringed Plover (30%). *Winter/passage* – Green Sandpiper (50%), Kingfisher (50%).

Other possible bird species

All year
Mute Swan
Gadwall
Tufted Duck
Little Grebe
Great Crested Grebe
Cormorant
Little Egret
Grey Heron
Sparrowhawk
Buzzard
Lapwing
Regular gull species (exc Common)
Common passerines
Reed Bunting

Summer
Hirundines
Whitethroat
Reed Warbler
Sedge Warbler

Winter
Wigeon
Teal
Shoveler
Pochard
Common Gull
Kingfisher
Stonechat
Winter thrushes

Passage
Whimbrel

Common Sandpiper
Greenshank
Common Tern
Yellow Wagtail
Whinchat
Wheatear

Occasional
Black-necked Grebe
Slavonian Grebe
Smew
Goosander
Ruddy Duck
Osprey
Little Gull
Black Tern

Key points

• A new, maturing site, with more than 150 species recorded.

• Expect 30 to 50 species in a 90-minute visit.

• Parking just off site.

• Easy walking around the site.

• Unisex toilet outside study centre open to visitors.

Background information and birding tips

PERMISSION for gravel extraction and the construction of reservoirs at this site was given in 1994, with the north reservoir being completed in 2002, and the southern one in 2009.

Much of the bird recording on the site since 2002, especially in the early days, has been down to local author Dominic Couzens and it is worth checking out Dominic's website at www.birdwords.co.uk (follow the link to Longham Lakes for a fuller appreciation of what the site can offer.

Due to current planning restrictions there are no parking facilities on the site – the fisherman's car park and lakeside study centre is private and should not be entered. There is a single unisex toilet outside the study centre which may be used.

I recommend parking in the lay-by next to the Citylodge Hotel. First take a walk from the hotel to the bridge over the River Stour for a brief look.

Over the years, as I have driven over the bridge, I've seen Grey Wagtail and Little Egret many times and have occasionally picked up a

Contacts

Recreational Services Manager, Sembcorp Bournemouth Water Ltd 01202 444 646

flash of blue as a Kingfisher has whizzed through.

The public footpath (leading to Hampreston Church), which takes you to the lakes, starts opposite the hotel. Despite the site name, the lakes are actually reservoirs and are named Longham Reservoir North and Longham Reservoir South.

The path brings you to the eastern bank of the larger LR South. There are good hard paths around both of the reservoirs but because they follow the shore, and there is very little cover, birds are prone to some disturbance.

In addition, the smaller LR North is stocked for fishing, and open all year, so again birds can be disturbed. In reality though, the birds just tend to move to a quieter part of the reservoirs if the disturbance activity gets too close.

On arriving, it is worth scanning the water with a telescope for ducks and to check out the gulls for Mediterranean Gull (usually heard first).

Once you see what birds are out there, and how many people are around, you can decide which way to go. The path runs around the perimeter of both reservoirs with another path between them so you have plenty of flexibility when it comes to charting a good route.

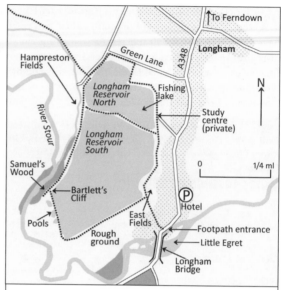

How to get there

(Five miles NW of Poole).

The site lies E of Longham village on A348 Ringwood Road, between Ferndown and Bear Wood. Park by the Citylodge Hotel on the Ferndown side of the Longham Bridge.

From the hotel, cross the road (with care as it can be very busy) and take the footpath signposted to Hampreston Church. Follow the footpath to the path that circles both lakes – return the way you came in.

Public transport: The Poole-Verwood bus service passes through Longham (Wilts & Dorset).

The southern end of LR South has, apart from an area of newly-planted trees, some rough grassland and small spillage pools which may attract Snipe and Green Sandpiper but look from a distance and approach quietly.

Beyond the pools there are glimpses of the River Stour and a small area of mature oak and beech woodland (Samuel's Wood) – look out here for woodpeckers and other woodland species.

Waders, which were attracted when the quarry workings were flooded, are now generally scarce. Little Ringed Plovers and Lapwings actually bred when the quarrying operations better suited their breeding requirements. There is now a large island on the northern part of LR South but it remains to be seen if it will be attractive to breeding (and passing/wintering) waders.

The scrub and fields around

Hobbies provide some of the most exciting birdwatching moments when they aerobatically pursue dragonflies on summer evenings.

the site (particularly East Fields, Hampreston Fields and the bushes along Green Lane) should provide a decent list of common passerines. In the summer Whitethroats are common but look out for Lesser Whitethroats as well.

Regular migrants in spring/autumn include Yellow Wagtails, Wheatears and Whinchats with the possibility of maybe a Ring Ouzel or Redstart.

The Hampreston Fields in particular can be very good for passage migrants and you should definitely find Stonechats if you look in this area in the winter.

The reservoirs can be good all year round for a selection of water birds, albeit in small numbers. Joining the resident Coots, Moorhens, Mallards, Little and Great Crested Grebes, both Tufted Ducks and Gadwall are seen in most months while Teal, Wigeon and Pochards are

regular in the winter.

Other interesting duck have included Garganey (passage) and Smew/Goosander (winter). In the summer, Reed Warblers breed in the reed fringes, Cuckoos may be seen/heard and hirundines often gather to feed.

More unusual birds that have been recorded include Great White Egret, Grey Phalarope, Hoopoe and Hawfinch. Maybe you can add to this promising site's tally on your next visit.

Other nearby sites

Canford Heath, Holt Heath, Sopley Common, Ramsdown Plantation and Avon Causeway, Town Common & St Catherine's Hill.

Key points

- Part of Lorton Meadows has SSSI designation.

- Visitor centre (open April-October) has toilets and disabled facilities.

- Leaflet available.

- See website for events programme.

- Limited wheelchair access.

- Two Mile Copse owned by the Woodland Trust.

Contacts

Dorset Wildlife Trust
01305 264 620
www.
dorsetwildlifetrust.
org.uk/reserves

Lorton Meadows
Visitor Centre
01305 816 546

Woodland Trust
01476 581 111
www.woodlandtrust.
org.uk

O N A VISIT to Weymouth don't overlook these two small reserves. They hold a nice mixture of woodland, unimproved grassland and scrub that offers different bird species to those you'll see at the town's more famous reserves – Radipole and Lodmoor. Expect a variety of common woodland/scrub birds all year round and in the summer Lesser Whitethroat breed at Lorton Meadows.

Target birds
All year – Green Woodpecker (80%), Yellowhammer (50%), Barn Owl (20%), Cetti's Warbler (20%). *Summer* – Lesser Whitethroat (90%).

Other possible bird species

All year	*Summer*	*Occasional*
Buzzard	Blackcap	Garden Warbler
Kestrel	Whitethroat	Firecrest
Tawny Owl	Chiffchaff	Raven
Nuthatch	Willow Warbler	
Common woodland birds		
	Winter	
	Winter thrushes	

Background information and birding tips

WHILE A VISIT to Weymouth usually involves the coastal sites, it is worth calling in to these two reserves for a different variety of birds.

Though you are most likely to see a mixture of common woodland and scrub birds, you never know what may turn up – a Pallas's Warbler appeared and stayed for a week in March 2008.

The Dorset Wildlife Trust's Lorton Meadows reserve consists of 34ha of unimproved grassland and scrub and has a Wildlife Centre (open April to October), where you can watch CCTV images of breeding birds (Barn and Tawny Owl in 2011).

The centre has facilities suitable for the disabled visitors, including parking, toilets, a picnic area, wildlife displays and a small shop.

A network of paths cross the reserve, including two way-marked trails from the Centre. The Green

Hill Trail takes about 30 minutes over fairly flat ground while the Ewe Leaze Trail (up to 1.5 hours) covers most of the reserve. The terrain is more uneven but this route gives good views over the surrounding area.

Barn Owls are among the resident birds here, so a late evening walk may produce a sighting. Kestrels breed on the reserve. I always find the site good for Whitethroats and there are usually a least a couple of Lesser Whitethroat territories as well.

Cetti's Warbler can sometimes be found on the south-east boundary where the reserve borders the northern end of the wider Lodmoor area.

Green Woodpeckers can be seen anywhere across the reserve and Greater Spotted Woodpeckers often nest in Coffin Plantation. Keep your eyes skyward for Buzzards and Sparrowhawks as well as Ravens that often pass over the valley.

The grassland is a good area for butterflies with a decent species list including marbled white, small and large skippers. More than 25 species have been recorded on the reserve.

The adjacent Two-mile Copse is owned by the Woodland Trust and consists of 6ha of ancient woodland. The wood can be entered through access points from Lorton Meadows, and inside you can follow a circular footpath around the wood.

All year round there is a good mixture of woodland birds, being joined in the summer by Blackcaps, Chiffchaffs and Willow Warblers. Outside the breeding season it is worth keeping a lookout for a Firecrest.

In 2009 work started on the Weymouth relief road after many years of objections and inquiries. Both sites have lost some land, which was compulsorily purchased, though some land in mitigation was added to Lorton Meadows.

From the summer of 2010, 30ha was leased to DWT, doubling the size of the reserve and linking it to the RSPB reserve at Lodmoor. Time will tell if this road will affect the wildlife interest of the sites though early indicatons are that the soundproof fences along the road are doing a good job and noise from the road is minimal.

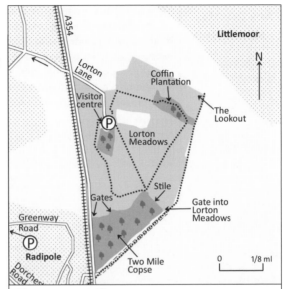

How to get there

Take A354 from Weymouth town centre towards Dorchester. Immediately after the roundabout by Morrison's supermarket turn right onto Greenway Road and park on the road.

Follow the bridleway, under railway and road bridges, for half a mile until reaching a gate taking you into Lorton Meadows.

Alternatively, continue along the Dorchester road towards Upwey and take a right turn into Lorton Lane. Follow the road/then the track for half a mile until you reach the DWT visitor centre car park. The two reserves lie adjacent to each other.

Note: when the relief road

is completed it will bypass the sites so you will need to travel on the old road (as directed above) to be able to get to them.

Public transport: The regular Weymouth-Dorchester bus service passes Lorton Lane (First Hants & Dorset). The site is close to Upwey station (South West Trains). The walk to the reserve entrance is 1.25 miles.

Other nearby sites

Lodmoor, Maiden Castle, Radipole Lake, Thorncombe Woods.

Key points

- Some National Trust land.

- Stunning scenery.

- Good walks – some steep slopes, so not suitable for wheelchairs.

- Wheelchair access OK at sityes in the town.

- All facilities in Lyme Regis.

- Parking at Charmouth & Seatown.

- Reasonable public transport access.

Contacts

National Trust 01297 489 481
www.nationaltrust.org.uk

Other nearby sites

Kingcombe Meadows, Lambert's Castle, Powerstock Common, West Bexington.

THE TOWN is a popular resort for people wanting to enjoy the Jurassic Coast World Heritage Site shoreline which is famed for its geology and fossils...... and there are a few interesting species to keep birdwatchers happy, too. Dipper is one of the speciality birds found on the River Lim, while Purple Sandpiper is a regular winter visitor to The Cobb. The area around Golden Cap is good for Peregrine and Raven.

Target birds *All year* – Dipper (75%), Peregrine (75%), Raven (75%). *Winter* – Purple Sandpiper (75%), Black Redstart (30%).

Other possible bird species

All year	Reed Bunting	Turnstone
Cormorant	Yellowhammer	Regular gull species
Shag	Common passerines	
Fulmar		*Occasional*
Buzzard	*Summer/passage*	Grey Phalarope
Kestrel	Hirundines	Great Skua
Rock Pipit	Wheatear	Little Gull
Kingfisher	Reed Warbler	Firecrest
Grey Wagtail		
Stonechat	*Winter*	
	Ringed Plover	

Background information and birding tips

LYME REGIS is an attractive coastal town and if you want to base yourself in the west of the county this is a good area to consider.

The town itself has two main birding attractions. The Cobb (harbour) is one of the regular wintering spots for Purple Sandpipers – check out the rocks around the harbour walls and on the beach. You should also see Turnstones, while Rock Pipits are present all year with an occasional Black Redstart in the winter/spring.

The sea front looks out into Lyme Bay but the occasional Shag or Cormorant and a few gulls are probably the best birds you will see. Stormy autumn weather with onshore winds may push something close to shore – Grey Phalarope has been seen fairly regularly over the years, along with the occasional Great Skua or Storm Petrel. It is worth checking the gulls during these conditions as Sabine's and Little Gulls have been recorded in the past.

The second attraction here is the River Lim that flows through the town and is home to breeding Dippers. The two areas that I normally check are the lower reach, just up from the sea front (and shops) and the stretch of river that flows into the town from the north.

From the sea front, walk to the eastern end of Broad Street, turn left into Coombe Street, left again into Mill Street and walk through to the river. Follow the river for as far you can go. Dipper is possible here but Grey Wagtail is almost certain.

The more reliable area for Dipper is approached from the north. Coming off the A35, and

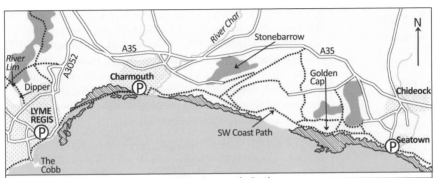

How to get there

(22 miles W of Dorchester).

There are three main access points to the area. In the west, for Lyme Regis, turn off A35 onto A3052 and drive into the town where there are a number of sign-posted car parks. In the centre, Charmouth can be reached from the A35 with turn-offs in either direction. Once in the village, turn down into Lower Sea Lane and follow the road to the beach car park. On the eastern side of the village the narrow Stonebarrow Lane will take you to a National Trust car park.

In the east, for Seatown, turn off A35 at Chideock (into Duck Street), bear right and then left into Sea Hill Lane and follow the road to the beach car park.

Public transport: The Poole-Exeter Coastlink bus service runs along the A35 (and to

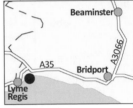

Lyme Regis) as does the Weymouth-Bridport-Axminster service (First: Hampshire & Dorset).

approaching the town on the A3052, turn right into Colway Lane, which crosses over the river. Park on the roadside and walk to the bridge. There is the option of walking along the river to the north (Ridgeway Trail) or southwards along the road. Again look out for Grey Wagtails here and there is a chance of Kingfisher.

It is worth checking out the stretch of coast to the east. If you are feeling energetic, you can walk the South West Coast Path from the town to Charmouth (two miles) and Seatown (5.5 miles) or, alternatively, you can drive around to these villages.

This stretch has some of the most stunning coastal scenery in Dorset, certainly on a par with the Purbeck coast. Large areas of land between Charmouth and Seatown, including Stonebarrow Hill and Golden Cap, are owned by the National Trust.

There are a number of footpaths to follow around the area and it is possible to walk along the pebble beaches, though these usually just hold the occasional Ringed Plover or Oystercatcher.

I like to park at Charmouth Beach and follow the coast path above the cliffs to Seatown, returning by an inland route (passing some of the wooded areas along the way). Where the River Char flows into Lyme Bay there is a small reedbed which holds Reed Warblers (summer) and Reed Buntings.

There is a good selection of birds in the area and they include Buzzard, Kestrel, Stonechat, Linnet, Yellowhammer and other common scrub and woodland species. Peregrines breed in the Golden Cap area and Ravens are regularly seen.

In spring and autumn a few migrants pass through – hirundines overhead, Wheatears on the ground and from time to time something more unusual, such as Red-backed Shrike or Firecrest, will turn up.

115

Key points

- More than 210 bird species recorded.

- Plenty of parking nearby.

- Disabled birders can view the 'pools' from the roadside.

- Information boards.

- Close to public transport.

- View on a rising tide/ telescope useful.

LYTCHETT BAY is an important inlet on the northern shore of Poole Harbour which holds a good variety of wintering waders and wildfowl and regularly turns up a few goodies, which included my first UK Purple Heron in the early 1990s. The 'Pools' attract some of the harbour's more unusual waders, such as Spotted Redshank and Green Sandpiper, and the fields here may turn up grey geese or winter swans. Marsh Harriers and Ospreys are annual visitors.

Target birds
All year – Peregrine (25%), Marsh Harrier (10%). *Autumn* – Osprey (25%). *Winter* – Black-tailed Godwit (90%), Avocet (80%), Kingfisher (50%). *Passage* – Whimbrel (80%).

Other possible bird species

All year	*Summer*	Regular gull species
Mute Swan	Sandwich Tern	
Canada Goose	Common Tern	*Occasional*
Shelduck	Reed Warbler	Whooper Swan
Mallard		Bewick's Swan
Cormorant	*Winter*	Great Crested Grebe
Little Egret	Wigeon	Hen Harrier
Grey Heron	Gadwall	Merlin
Buzzard	Teal	Hobby
Water Rail	Goldeneye (now rare)	Knot
Oystercatcher	Red-breasted Merganser	Ruff
Redshank	Little Grebe	Jack Snipe
Black-headed Gull	Grey Plover	Woodcock
Cetti's Warbler	Lapwing	Bearded Tit
Reed Bunting	Dunlin	
	Greenshank	

Background information and birding tips

THE BIRD LIST for Lytchett Bay, and the surrounding area, now stands at over 210 species – an amazing total considering the size of the site.

This high number is undoubtedly down to the fact that ringing has taken place in the bay for many years, sometimes picking up birds that may otherwise not have been recorded, and the dedication of Shaun Robson who has meticulously watched the site, and produced an excellent annual report, since 1992.

The bay lies to the north of the main body of Poole Harbour and to the west of Holes Bay (site 60). Access is limited in places, particularly along the north-west/ western shore, but it can be viewed from a number of places from the north-east corner and by walking along the eastern shore.

Use the Sports and Recreation Ground Car Park near Turlin Moor and take the track leading from the northern end of the car park through the white barrier and continue until the bay comes in to view (walking around the edge of the sports fields).

Contacts

ARC 01202 391 319
www.arc-trust.org

Follow the obvious path along the shore – stop frequently and scan out into the bay (early morning is best as the sun is behind you and a telescope is useful).

The NE corner of the bay can be viewed from three points. Just after the white barrier take the path to the right and follow it through to Border Drive (about 200m).

On the right of the path is an area of open scrub – good for picking up a selection of common passerines, while on the left there is a piece of boggy woodland – listen here for the explosive sounds of Cetti's Warbler. Once through to the road continue walking through an area of grass and bushes to the shore and scan over the bay.

Moving further west, walk along the road (keeping the bay on your left) to the road junction, turn left into Shore Lane and continue on to the next corner and to footpath No.12. Parking is available here at the junction of Lytchett Way and Shore Lane.

After a few metres the footpath splits – keep to the left and you'll reach the shore after 250m or continue through the gate on the right for about 350m (turning left at the end of the woodland).

It is worth going to the end of both paths to scan over the bay – particularly in the afternoon when the light is a little better. There is an evening roost of Linnets and Pied Wagtails in the vicinity of this spot in autumn and winter.

The bay is used by most of the species of waders and wildfowl found around Poole Harbour. Shelduck, Teal, Wigeon,

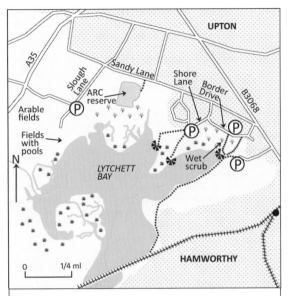

How to get there
(2.5 miles W of Poole).

From the A35 take B3068 into Upton, cross over the small double roundabout and head towards Hamworthy on Blandford Road.

For the eastern shore turn right into the Sports and Recreation Ground car park (opposite the garage and just before the traffic light turn into Turlin Moor). Park here and walk through to the eastern shore. You can also easily reach the NE shore from here.

For alternative parking, turn right off B3068 into Sandy Lane, take a left into Shore Lane – park up at the end of this road and follow the footpath (no.12) to the bay. Alternatively, turn left into Border Drive, parking near the information sign and walk to the bay.

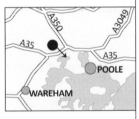

Half a mile from the Shore Lane turn is the entrance to the small ARC reserve (off Sandy Lane) and just beyond a left turn into Slough Lane (drive to the end and park up to view the pools).

Public transport: The Poole-Creekmoor-Upton and the Poole-Hamworthy-Turlin Moor bus services cover this area (Wilts & Dorset).

The nearest railway station is at Hamworthy.

117

Oystercatcher, Avocet, Black-tailed Godwit, Redshank and Curlew, can reach good numbers while others, such as Brent Goose, Pintail and Grey Plover – common enough in Poole Harbour – are scarce visitors here.

One benefit of having a well-watched site is that patterns emerge and whereas birds like the Avocet have been increasing in the bay, others such as Goldeneye, Red-breasted Merganser, Lapwing and Dunlin, have all shown declines over the years.

The winter months (November-February) are the best time for birdwatchers to visit as this is when birds reach their peak numbers. A few waders hang on into May and start returning from mid/late-July. A visit is best on a low or rising tide when the mud is exposed and birds are encouraged closer to the shore.

The bay can't be viewed from the western shore as the land here is private and should not be entered. However, there are two areas worth looking at. There is a small nature reserve managed by the Amphibian & Reptile Conservation Trust (ARC) off Sandy Lane – park in the small lay-by next to the entrance.

This small area of heathland has been completely overgrown but recent clearance work has begun to open it up again. There are a number of tracks that will take you around the heath, so you can look out for a few scrub birds including Linnets. By the shore listen out for Reed Warblers in the reeds. Dartford Warbler is recorded here and Nightjar occurs occasionally.

A little further along Sandy Lane, take a left turn into Slough Lane. The fields at the end of the lane are worth a look. They are private but can be viewed from the road where there is limited roadside parking.

The ' Pools' at the back of the field, to the left of the road leading up to the waterworks, often attract some interesting waders at high tide, including Greenshank, Spotted Redshank and occasionally Ruff. The fields can also turn up geese and swans, including Whooper (2010), and Little Egrets are regular. There is no access to the fields beyond the waterworks but scan from the gate.

It is worth having a walk along the lane (signed 'unsuitable for vehicles') checking out the arable field and hedgerows as you go for small birds, including mixed finch flocks and Reed Buntings. I saw my first UK Purple Heron from this road, in the field to the west of the arable field, in 1992.

In the spring and autumn small numbers of migrants pass through the bay area, so watch out for a mixture of hirundines overhead and Wheatears, Whinchats, Redstarts and a variety of warblers around the fields and hedgerows. Ospreys (especially in the autumn) and Whimbrels are regular visitors.

In winter, Jack Snipe and Woodcock are likely to be under-recorded as they are best seen when flushed but Rock Pipit is common on the saltmarsh and a Marsh Harrier sighting is more likely than Hen Harrier. Kingfishers may be seen in the bay from the autumn through to late winter and Chiffchaffs and Blackcaps sometimes overwinter in the hedgerows and scrub.

The gulls are worth scanning through. As well as the common species, Mediterranean and Yellow-legged are regular visitors, while Little, Ring-billed and Iceland have been picked up on more than one occasion.

Water Rails do well in the reedbeds - they are present all year and breed in good numbers, but as they like to keep under cover they are more likely to be heard than seen. There is also a chance of sighting a Bearded Tit, a sporadic breeder, at any time of the year.

Other nearby sites

Ham Common, Hatch Pond, Upton Country Park & Holes Bay, Upton Heath.

MAIDEN CASTLE is among the largest and most complex of Iron Age hill forts in the whole of Europe, holding commanding views over the surrounding countryside. This makes it well worth a visit for the place itself, but the birds are not bad either – it is a regular site for Corn Bunting, Golden Plover (winter) and there still a chance of finding Grey Partridge here.

Target birds *All year* – **Corn Bunting (80%), Yellowhammer (75%), Raven (50%), Red-legged Partridge (40%), Grey Partridge (20%).** *Winter* – **Buzzard (95%), Golden Plover (80%).** *Passage* – **Wheatear (80%), Redstart (20%), Whinchat (20%).**

Other possible bird species

All year	*Summer*	*Occasional*
Pheasant	Cuckoo	Quail
Buzzard	Whitethroat	Merlin
Stock Dove	Chiffchaff	Hobby
Skylark	Hirundines	Peregrine
Meadow Pipit		Mediterranean Gull
Stonechat	*Winter*	Barn Owl
Common corvids	Lapwing	
Linnet	Regular gull species	
Common finches	Fieldfare	
	Redwing	

Background information and birding tips

THE AREA to the south-west of Dorchester is dominated by Maiden Castle and I would recommend a visit to see this fabulous historical site for its own sake – the birds are almost a bonus.

The hill fort itself covers about 20ha but is surrounded on all sides by farmland and provides a great vantage point for scanning the area.

The word 'Mai Dun' (Maiden) is believed to come from the Celtic for 'Big Hill'– and that is what it is! Early human occupation dates back over 6,000 years but the castle was first laid out around 600BC over the remains of a Neolithic settlement.

In AD43 it was taken by the Roman army and its inhabitants (the local Durotiges tribe) moved to the new town of Durnovaria (now Dorchester).

Ever since I have known the site it has been the most reliable place in Dorset to find Golden Plovers. The numbers at Maiden Castle fluctuate but they usually reach the low hundreds and I have seen up to a thousand plus.

Their winter feeding areas can be spread widely around parts of inland Dorset that are relatively under-watched, so it is hard to work out how many birds actually winter in the county.

Numbers of Lapwings also reach into the hundreds and these two species provide a spectacular sight when up in the air and calling. The

Key points

- Owned by English Heritage.
- Expect to see 20 to 30 bird species in a two-hour visit.
- Free car park available.
- Access at all times.
- Information boards (at hill fort).
- Steep banks & ditches (around hill fort).
- No access for wheelchairs, but area can be viewed from car park.
- Monkey's Jump path can be very muddy when wet.
- Can be busy. Early morning visit recommended.
- Nearest toilets in Dorchester.

Contacts

English Heritage (SW Regional office) 0117 975 0700 (www.english–heritage.org.uk)

birds can move around the immediate area, so a little patience may be required to find them – scan all of the fields and watch out for birds on the move.

There are two options to access the site – either park in the main car park or go to the pull-in just past the Monkey's Jump roundabout. Whichever you choose it is worth walking along the footpath to/from from the Monkey's Jump end as this is where you have the best chance of being rewarded with a partridge or two.

Both Grey and Red-legged Partridges are found here but they can be elusive and mobile. Winter or early spring is a good time to look over the farmland before the crops/grass grow too high, making visibility more difficult.

There are still reasonable numbers of Corn Buntings in Dorset, especially spread through the north-east to south-west chalk belt, but at Maiden Castle they are almost guaranteed all year round.

The walk between Monkey's Jump and the hill fort is the best area to look for them. In the spring, they will be heard singing in the hedgerows or from the fences.

In the winter, check for Corn Buntings in the hedgerows or feeding in the fields either side of the footpath, where flocks often reach up to 50 birds, occasionally more.

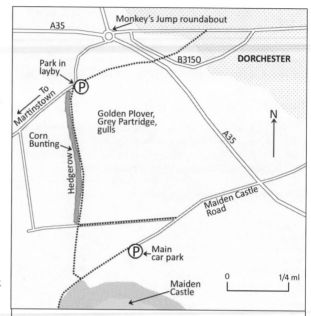

How to get there
(On the SW outskirts of Dorchester).

To reach the main car park from the A35(T), south of Dorchester, follow the brown tourist signs to 'Maiden Castle'. Take B3147 towards the town centre (passing Dorchester Town Football Club and Tesco). After about half a mile, turn left on to Maiden Castle Road and follow this road for 1.25 miles to the car park.

Alternatively, leave A35(T) by the Monkey's Jump roundabout (next to MacDonalds) and head towards Martinstown.

The road bends to the left then

the right where you need to park off the road (after 400 metres) at the small pull-in (SY 665 900). From the gate, take the footpath to the hill-fort.

Public transport: A town bus service runs to Castle Park (Coach House Travel).

You should also pick birds up when you make a circuit of the hill fort, particularly on the wire fences.

There are a good selection of common passerines here at any time of the year – finches, common corvids and scrub birds all year, summer visitors (including Cuckoos,

Whitethroats and passing hirundines) and winter visitors such as Fieldfares and Redwings.

During passage in the spring and autumn good numbers of Wheatears often move through, with smaller numbers of other migrants such as Whinchats and Redstarts.

The site attracts Buzzards all through the year but the winter is especially good. It is not unusual to regularly see up to 20 birds, or even more, in the area, either sitting in the fields, on the fence posts or circling overhead.

I always find the variations in colour quite interesting here with individuals ranging from very pale to very dark. Stand on the top of the hill fort and scan the area to the north (towards Dorchester) for them.

Less regular species turn up each year and may include Quail, especially in a good 'Quail year', but they are more likely to be heard rather than seen. As far as raptors are concerned there always a chance of seeing a Hobby in the summer, Merlin in the winter and Peregrine at any time of the year.

Barn Owls are also in the area and there is a chance of a hunting bird, probably more so during the shorter winter days. Good numbers of regular gull species use the farmland outside of

the breeding season and it is worth scanning among them for a Mediterranean Gull or two.

A circular walk around the hill fort from Monkey's Jump is about three miles but a mile less from the main car park. The hilly nature of the site means that there is no wheelchair access possible from the main car park.

Other nearby sites

Lorton Meadows & Two-mile Copse, Cattistock Churchyard & Maiden Newton, Thorncombe Woods, The Fleet.

Grey Partridge is a species in rapid decline in many parts of southern England, but Maiden Castle still provides a good opportunity to see this attactive game bird.

Key points

- **A National Nature Reserve – important for chalk grassland birds, butterflies and plants.**
- **Good for half a day or a full day visit.**
- **Good selection of scrub and downland birds.**
- **Information boards & leaflet available.**
- **Good network of footpaths and tracks.**
- **Some disabled access possible, especially on main tracks from car park.**
- **Two car parks.**
- **Main bus route passes entrance.**

Contacts

Natural England 0300 060 6000 (ask for the reserve). www.naturalengland.org.uk

www.hants.gov.uk

LOCATED on the border where Hampshire, Wiltshire and Dorset meet, Martin Down was the place Dorset birders went for their annual Stone Curlew tick. Sadly they haven't bred here for a number of years, but there is always the chance of spotting a bird on passage. The site is a fine example of chalk grassland with areas of scrub and woodland so there are plenty of other reasons to visit – Nightingales, Turtle Doves, Garden Warblers and Lesser Whitethroats will be in the scrub and woodland areas, and the site is excellent for butterflies and orchids.

Target birds *All year* – Yellowhammer (75%), Raven (50%), Corn Bunting (50%), Barn Owl (30%). *Summer* – Garden Warbler (95%), Lesser Whitethroat (95%), Turtle Dove (75%), Grey Partridge (25%), Nightingale (<10%).

Other possible bird species

All year	Common woodland	*Passage*
Buzzard	birds	Whinchat
Kestrel		Wheatear
Red-legged Partridge	*Summer*	
Green Woodpecker	Lapwing	*Occasional*
Skylark	Cuckoo	Montagu's Harrier
Stonechat	Blackcap	Stone-curlew
Linnet	Whitethroat	Hobby
Bullfinch	Chiffchaff	Quail
Common scrub birds	Willow Warbler	Little Owl

Background information and birding tips

THIS National Nature Reserve, jointly owned/managed by Natural England and Hampshire County Council, covers an area of 340ha. Its main habitat, chalk grassland, would have been far more extensive in the area historically but even so this site still remains one of the largest in the country.

As well as grassland, a mixture of woodland and scrub adds to the diversity of habitat, attracting a range of birds, plants and invertebrates.

The main car park off the A354, where there are maps and leaflets, is a good starting point and is a regular spot for Lesser Whitethroats in spring and summer, while Stonechats, Whitethroats, Linnets, Bullfinches and Yellowhammers will be close by.

A short walk beyond the car park will take you to the old rifle range, part of a more recent history. Carefully climb up on to the top of the butt and look out to the east over the site.

Annually one or two plots of ground are prepared for Stone Curlews and though they no longer breed here, the plots are worth checking out – I once saw three Dotterel here one spring. You might be lucky with a passing bird in late March/early April or at least you should find breeding Lapwings through the spring.

To the right of the rifle range is Bokerley Dyke, a linear earthworks running along the southern boundary – a defensive ditch and embankment thought to have originated in the Bronze Age or early Iron Age.

One of the main footpaths runs along the dyke and is a good option of a route to take if you want to cover the whole site in one go.

The reserve can be conveniently split into two. Grassland on the northern section was ploughed in the 1940s-1950s but the southern section has remained unploughed for centuries, and as a result is the more interesting part for flora and insects.

The grasslands as a whole have plenty of Skylarks and the air is full of their song in the spring. Both Red-legged and, if you are lucky, Grey Partridges may be seen. Sometimes Quail are heard – but will be very difficult to see. If visiting in late summer look for passing Wheatears and Whinchats.

Apart from around the car park, the northern area of grassland is largely free of scrub and has a number of footpaths and tracks running through it.

The scrub/hedgerow along the northern boundary, next to the adjacent farmland, held Nightingales in the past. This species has now become a very

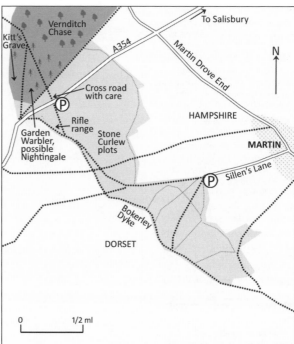

How to get there

(Nine miles SW of Salisbury).

From Blandford Forum take A354 towards Salisbury. The main car park is signposted (brown tourist sign) about three-quarters of a mile after the village of Woodyates, just past the Woodyates lay-by. Traffic moves quickly on this road, so be careful not to overshoot.

For alternative parking continue on A354 for another mile to a section of dual carriageway. At Martin Drove End turn right to the village of Martin. In the village take another right along Sillens

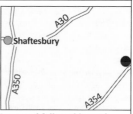

Lane and follow this road three-quarters of a mile to the car park.

Public transport: The Blandford Forum-Salisbury bus service runs along the A354 - a bus stop/gate on to the reserve is located near to the main car park (Wilts & Dorset).

scarce bird, and will take some finding – if it is present at all – so all areas of scrub

are worth checking.

You can reach the southern area of grassland from the

main car park or alternatively drive around to the village of Martin's Sillens Lane car park. Here again you'll find a series of footpaths that will allow you to walk circular routes. With more scrub and some woodland, this area usually proves more interesting for birds and is where I have seen (and heard) Turtle Doves more frequently.

Other species groups shouldn't be overlooked. Look for hares in the open areas. Butterflies are well represented (36 species regularly recorded!), including Adonis blue, silver-spotted skipper and dark-green fritillary.

Among the chalk-loving plants, 12 species of orchid have been found here. There are a few small areas where acid soils, created by underlying conditions, allow heath and chalk plants to grow side by side ......quite an unusual sight!

Another interesting area to visit lies to the north of the A354. Cross the road by the entrance to the car park ......take care crossing as vehicles are generally travelling fast ...... and take the track into Vernditch Chase on the other side.

The majority of the site is Forestry Commission land (some restrictions when felling) but the best area for birds (and butterflies) is the western section (referred to as Kitt's Grave), still part of the NNR.

You can walk a circular route around the Chase along footpaths and forest rides. The mixture of scrub and woodland clearings is good for Garden Warbler and a selection of common woodland birds will be found. Nightingales are probably more likely here than on the main part of the site – listen out for their song as they will be quite difficult to see.

Other nearby sites

Cranborne Common, Garston Wood, River Allen - Crichel Lake.

This part is good for butterflies including silver-washed fritillary and (now more rarely) Duke of Burgundy.

FURTHER AFIELD

The general area to the south of Martin Down has other good resident birds to offer, including Barn Owl (breeding), Little Owl and Corn Bunting. An alternative place to drop in on for a chance of some of these is the minor road to Monkton Up Wimborne. Head back toward Blandford Forum, cross straight over the Handley roundabout and take the next left, passing a pumping station – there is a car park about half a mile along the road.

Montagu's Harrier used to breed in this general area up until the early 2000s and I've heard more Quail here than anywhere else in the county. Fewer birds are found in the area during the winter but a Great Grey Shrike wintered near the pumping station in 2010/11.

MIDDLEBERE is one of the best, and most attractive, corners of Poole Harbour and offers a varied walk taking in heathland, hedgerows, farmland and reedbed before reaching the mudflats and saltmarsh of the harbour. All year round it is an excellent spot for waders, including significant numbers of Avocets and Black-tailed Godwits in the winter. The site has a great bird of prey pedigree – eight or nine species are recorded here annually and there is always a chance of two or three other species passing through.

Target birds
All year – Dartford Warbler (75%), Peregrine (50%), Barn Owl (20%), Marsh Harrier (10%). *Summer* – Hobby (30%). *Winter* – Avocet (80%), Black-tailed Godwit (80%), Yellow-legged Gull (75%), Pintail (50%), Grey Plover (50%), Hen Harrier (30%), Spoonbill (20%). *Passage* – Osprey (50%), Yellow Wagtail (50%).

Other possible bird species

All year	*Summer*	Winter thrushes
Little Egret	Hirundines	
Canada Goose	Reed Warbler	*Occasional*
Shelduck	Summer warblers	Merlin
Buzzard		Curlew Sandpiper
Sparrowhawk	*Winter*	Spotted Redshank
Kestrel	Brent Goose	Greenshank
Water Rail	Wigeon	Water Pipit
Stonechat	Teal	Black Redstart
Corvids	Green Sandpiper	Brambling
Bullfinch	Regular gull species	Crossbill
	Rock Pipit	

Background information and birding tips

MIDDLEBERE LAKE (a channel rather than a lake!) is one of the most important areas of Poole Harbour and a place where you can get close views of the waders and wildfowl that use it.

The channel is a lot quieter between mid-March and mid-July when most of the waders and wildfowl have left Dorset, but it is worth a visit at any time of the year.

The 'Avocet' hide is approached along a private track from Hartland Moor – park on the roadside (by the Middlebere Farm sign) and

walk – please do not drive down. At the end of the track, just before the National Trust holiday cottages, please take the path leading off to the right – this will allow you to get around the buildings without disturbing the guests.

Access to the hide, and its use, is permitted by the National Trust and is not a right of way. The track is a little rough but is not too bad for wheelchairs (three-quarters of a mile to the hide). Alternatively contact the Trust for permission to drive down to the cottages.

All year round, the walk to the

Key points
- **Open access at all times.**
- **Roadside parking.**
- **Do not drive down the track (disabled drivers should seek National Trust permission).**
- **Three hides.**
- **Wheelchair access to 'Avocet' hide.**
- **Important area of Poole Harbour.**
- **Good for birds of prey.**

Contacts
The National Trust
01929 450 123
(www.nationaltrust.org.uk)

125

hide always provides a good mixture of common passerines, including Bullfinches, using the hedgerows and scrub that runs the length of the track.

In the spring, look for newly arrived migrants including Redstarts, Whitethroats and other warblers, while in the winter, groups of winter thrushes feed on the berries, Bramblings turn up from time to time, and Chiffchaffs often stay.

The start of the track takes you by a section of heathland where you may see a Dartford Warbler or a Stonechat (if you don't, take a short walk on the Hartland Moor side of the road for them).

Once through the heathland, the track passes open grassland (a good area for wagtails, thrushes and corvids) before reaching a group of farm buildings.

Halfway down the track, before you reach the farm buildings, a small gate (on the right) leads up to the 'Harrier' hide, overlooking another part of the harbour (Wych). Though views are distant here, you certainly get a different perspective of the area.

The channel below the hide, depending on the time of year, may hold Lapwings, an occasional Greenshank, Common Sandpiper, Little Grebe or a Kingfisher, while in November 2000 a Long-billed Dowitcher was found.

The little copse of pine on the hill by the hide often has a few small birds in it, including Siskins, and, on occasions, Crossbills.

Once at the farm buildings, look out over the area of reed and grazing marsh to the left for Little Egret and harriers.

Marsh Harrier sightings are

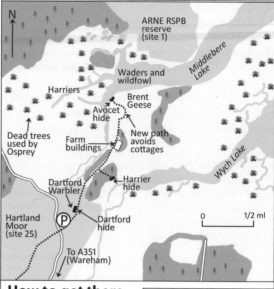

How to get there

(Four miles SE of Wareham).

From Wareham take B3075 to Stoborough over the south bridge and causeway. Just past the petrol station (on your right) turn left down Nutcrack Lane and continue for about two miles to 'the triangle' (there is an RSPB sign just past the turning) and fork to the right for Middlebere.

Follow this road, over a cattle grid then, as the road starts to rise, pull in by the entrance track to Middlebere Farm.

Alternatively bypass Wareham on the A351 towards Swanage, turn left onto the B3075 into Stoborough, heading back

towards Wareham. Take first right (New Road) towards Ridge and right again to 'the triangle'.

From Corfe Castle take A351, heading towards Wareham. At the roundabout turn right (to the Swanage Railway 'Park and Ride' facility at Norden) then immediately left on to the minor road that crosses Hartland Moor. After 1.75 miles you will reach the Middlebere track entrance.

possible all year, Hen Harriers are regular in the winter and I have also seen Montagu's here in the spring.

In the summer listen out for Reed Warbler, and through the year for squealing Water Rail.

Green Sandpipers use this area from the autumn through the winter and though occasionally seen on the ground they are more likely to be picked up in flight. I have also seen Black Redstart around the buildings.

Osprey is a regular sight around the harbour at the right time and Middlebere is a particularly favoured spot. They pass through in the spring but are more frequent in the autumn (from late-July to October – I've seen one as late as November 4).

Look left from the 'Avocet' hide (across to the Arne side) to a row of dead oak trees in the distance – this is where the Ospreys tend to perch, often eating fish. A pole has been erected (on the Arne side) in front of the hide which, if used, will bring the birds much closer.

Birds of prey can be outstanding at Middlebere. Apart from the harriers already mentioned, Kestrels, Peregrines, Sparrowhawks and Buzzards are regular at any time of the year, with a good chance of a Hobby in spring, summer and early autumn and a chance of a Merlin in the winter. I have also had a fly-over Honey Buzzard and Red Kite.

Barn Owls are around all year, breeding nearby, and can sometimes be seen hunting over the saltmarsh. Pipits in front of the hide during the winter months are worth scanning – most will be Meadow Pipits but Rock Pipits move into the harbour at this time and a Water Pipit could be among them.

If the tide is too high, you'll see a lot of water, no mud and few birds, while at low tide the mud will be exposed, but it is likely that the birds will be very distant or even absent from the channel. Try to time your visit mid-way between high and low water, preferably when the tide is rising so that the birds are brought closer as the mud is covered.

The lower section of the channel – towards the main part of the harbour – is best watched from the Arne side (site 1), while Middlebere is better for the upper section.

After watching the channel for 15 years from the Arne side, I 'found' the Middlebere side in 2006 and now, out of preference, will go to this side to view the channel – you can get closer to the birds (viewing from a hide) and the light is better as the sun is behind you (though viewing from Arne gives a wider perspective of the area).

In winter Teal are the most numerous duck here, with up to 300 birds not uncommon, while there are smaller numbers of Wigeon, Pintail, Mallard, and the occasional Gadwall. Shelduck are present all year round (including a few breeding pairs) but the winter has their largest numbers.

Canada Geese often visit the area, especially on the fields to the right of the hide. Over the years I've seen a number of feral geese species among them, including Barnacle, White-fronted and Bar-headed. The same fields are used by Brent Geese, usually later in the winter – check among the dark-bellied birds for pale-bellied or Black Brant races.

Among the waders, Avocet and Black-tailed Godwit provide the largest numbers (they can be into the high hundreds). Smaller numbers of Lapwings, Curlews, Oystercatchers, Grey Plovers, Dunlin and Redshanks (a few pairs of the latter also breed on the saltmarsh) are regular visitors.

From time to time something a little more unusual, such as Knot, Greenshank, Spotted Redshank or Curlew Sandpiper, may pitch up. Look out for Yellow-legged Gull among the regular gull species.

Look out for sika deer in the fields on the way down to the hide, as well as over the saltmarsh.

The beginning of the Middlebere track is one of the starting points for Hartland Moor & Stoborough Heath NNR (site 25), with which it can easily be combined.

Other nearby sites

Arne, Creech, Stoborough & Grange Heaths, Hartland Moor & Stoborough Heath NNR, Studland.

Key points

- **Access available at all times/car park locked at dusk.**

- **100+ species recorded.**

- **Expect 40 – 50 species (early spring) in a two hour walk.**

- **Ample parking (fees charged).**

- **Toilets, café & activities.**

- **Leaflets & information boards.**

- **Variety of way-marked trails.**

- **Ranger service.**

- **Events organised.**

- **Excellent disabled access.**

Contacts

Moors Valley Country Park 01425 470 721 www.moors-valley. co.uk

A BUSY Country Park, offering golf, fishing, children's play areas and aerial walkways among its activities, may not be an obvious birding location but along Moors Valley's forest trails you will find plenty of common species, including Siskin and possibly Crossbill. The two freshwater lakes offer breeding Great Crested Grebes and wintering Goosanders, so the park is definitely worth a visit, especially if you have children in tow.

Target birds
All year – Dartford Warbler (75%), Redpoll (50%), Crossbill (20%). *Summer* – Tree Pipit (75%). *Winter* – Kingfisher (50%), Goosander (<10%).

Other possible bird species

All year	Siskin	Tufted Duck
Mute Swan	Linnet	Moorhen
Canada Goose	Bullfinch	Coot
Mallard	Reed Bunting	Regular gull species
Great Crested Grebe		
Cormorant	*Summer*	*Occasional*
Sparrowhawk	Cuckoo	Merlin
Buzzard	Nightjar	Water Rail
Kestrel	Summer warblers	Woodcock
Green Woodpecker		Mediterranean Gull
Stonechat	*Winter*	Grey Wagtail
Common woodland birds	Gadwall	Raven
	Teal	Firecrest
	Pochard	

Background information and birding tips

MOORS VALLEY is a joint venture between East Dorset District Council and The Forestry Commission. There are no admission charges but parking charges apply, and vary, throughout the year. Take a ticket at the entrance barrier and pay at the machine by the centre before leaving.

Facilities include information centre, toilets, restaurant, snacks and a shop, while there are activities for all the family: children's playground, aerial walkways, fishing (Moor Lake only), golf, cycling (and bike hire) and a good programme of events.

The park is located at the southern end of Ringwood Forest but you can enter the forest itself from roadside parking points along the B3081 and Horton Road. Using one of these entrances will allow access into the area before the car park opens (at 8am) and before it gets busy (though they are popular with early morning dog walkers).

A late evening visit may also be quieter but remember that the car park closes at dusk. There are plenty of paths to follow throughout the forest, including a number of way-marked trails.

Despite how busy the place gets, it is still possible to see a decent selection of birds – in early spring you should expect 40 or 50 species in a couple of hours. More than 100 species have been recorded in the park, with more unusual birds turning up on occasions – these have included Merlin, Firecrest and Hoopoe.

For birdwatching, the park is really divided into two – the lakes/nature trail and the forest itself. The lakes in winter hold a few common duck including Gadwall, Teal and Pochard, while Goosanders are annual visitors. Check out the gulls for Mediterranean Gull.

Kingfishers tends to be winter visitors here but Great Crested Grebes are breeding residents and can be seen at fairly close quarters. Resident Reed Buntings are joined by Reed and Sedge Warblers in the summer.

A two-mile-long way-marked nature trail, which is suitable for wheelchairs, starts just north of Moor Lake and takes in Crane Lake and part of Potterne Woods......but watch out for golf balls as the trail cuts through the golf course!

If you have children with you there is an activity pack/quiz available to do along the trail (a small charge applies).

The forest covers most of the site and has a number of routes through it, including a five-mile way-marked walk. Cycling and horse riding are popular activities in the forest, so be aware of this 'traffic'. There are lots of walkers too, but you can find quieter areas away from the visitor facilities.

There is a good mixture of birds in the forest. Siskins are very common all year round, with smaller numbers of Redpolls. Crossbills can be seen at any time but numbers fluctuate wildly from year to year.

Dartford Warblers breed in the

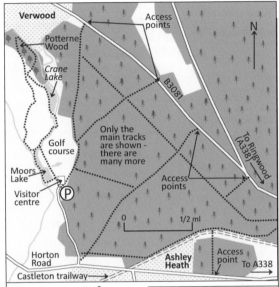

How to get there

(Three miles W of Ringwood).

From Bournemouth head north on A338 to A31 Ashley Heath roundabout. Cross straight over and take the minor road (Horton Road) to Ashley Heath – the entrance to the Park is 1.5 miles along this road on the right hand side (signposted from the roundabout).

From the Ringwood or Wimborne/Poole directions, turn off A31 at the Ashley Heath roundabout.

For alternative parking along the B3081, head towards Ringwood from the Ashley Heath roundabout but keep in the left hand lane, for Verwood, turning left on to the B3081.

Public transport: The Bournemouth-Verwood bus service runs past the Park entrance (Wilts & Dorset).

heathland patches among the forested areas – look for Tree Pipits (summer) and Stonechats in the same areas.

Nightjars breed in the area and Woodcock are occasionally recorded in the winter.

Other nearby sites

Avon Heath Country Park, Cranborne Common, Holt Heath.

129

Key points

- **Multiple ownerships.**
- **Designated SSSI.**
- **Expect 25-30 species in spring/summer.**
- **Access at all times.**
- **Paths can be wet in winter.**
- **Events organised – contact ARC for details.**
- **Facilities close by.**
- **No wheelchair access.**
- **Excellent for reptiles.**

Contacts

ARC 01202 391 319
www.arc-trust.org

East Dorset District Council 01425 470 721
www.dorsetforyou.com

TYPICAL heathland birds such as Dartford Warbler, Woodlark and Nightjar can be found at Parley, though it is more famous for a number of non-avian 'firsts' for Britain. These include the smooth snake (first recorded in 1853 but still present today, along with the other five species of British reptiles), and the mazarine blue butterfly, first discovered in the late-1800s but now extinct.

Target birds *All year* – **Dartford Warbler (90%).** *Summer* – **Nightjar (90% hear, 75% see), Woodlark (90%).**

Other possible bird species

All year		*Summer*
Buzzard	Stonechat	Hobby
Green Woodpecker	Linnet	*Winter*
Meadow Pipit	Reed Bunting	Snipe
	Common passerines	

Background information and birding tips

MOST OF Parley Common's 150ha is a Site of Special Scientific Interest and is under multiple ownership. The northern boundary is bordered by a housing estate but the remainder adjoins farmland, smallholdings and a golf course.

It is an attractive site (if you ignore the line of pylons running through it), and it is fairly long but quite narrow. The heathland habitats range from the dry heath with blocks of gorse on the higher ground, through humid/wet heath to the mire systems.

The site is a remnant of what would have been a continuous block of heathland stretching from the New Forest to Purbeck. A partnership between East Dorset District Council and Amphibian & Reptile Conservation Trust (ARC) which has recently re-introduced low density summer grazing, is responsible for managing most of the site.

The main entrance is located by the Heathlands Community Centre in Trickett's Cross on the northern boundary and immediately on entering the heath one of the major issues on this site is obvious......fire! Evidence of past fires is easily seen, especially the closer you are to the houses.

A second access point, with roadside parking (Lone Pine Drive), lies closer to the southern end of the site. Access is open at all times and the heath is criss-crossed by a number of paths, which can be quite muddy in the wetter areas.

Despite frequent fires, which must have some effect on them, Dartford Warblers should be found quite easily by walking around the obvious paths – the birds are often picked up by their scratchy song or scolding call first. At least one pair of Woodlarks breed here, no doubt benefiting from some of these burnt areas!

A dusk visit should also produce a Nightjar sighting ......but get your bearings first while it is still light, although you shouldn't have to venture too far from the houses before your first sighting.

How to get there

(Five miles N of Bournemouth).

Head south on A31 from Ringwood, taking A347 towards Ferndown. At the next (Sainsbury's) roundabout bear left to a mini-roundabout (named 'Turbary') at Trickett's Cross. Turn left here into Turbary Road, then turn right at the T-junction in to Lockyers Drive. Follow this road round to another T-junction and turn right again onto Barns Road. The entrance to Parley Common is alongside the Heatherlands Community Centre on the bend of Barns Road – park somewhere safely along the road.

Alternatively, from Ferndown take A347 Ringwood Road north towards Ringwood and turn right at the 'Turbary' roundabout in to Turbary Road.

For the Lone Pine Drive entrance, drive down Golf Links Road (just to the south of the 'Turbury' roundabout) until the Lone Pine Drive turning on the left – continue to end of road where a footpath leads out onto the Common.

Public transport: The Poole-Verwood bus service passes through Trickett's Cross on A348. The Bournemouth-Wimborne service passes through Ferndown where you can change to the above service or to the Ferndown-Ringwood service for Trickett's Cross (Wilts & Dorset).

A spring/summer visit will produce Stonechats and Linnets around the drier areas, especially where there is gorse, while Meadow Pipits will be on the more open areas.

Green Woodpeckers may be seen flying to/from the wooded edges of the heath or might even be flushed from the ground where they feed on wood ant nests.

Buzzards, Kestrels and Sparrowhawks are the most likely birds of prey but with luck a Hobby may be found hawking for day-flying moths and dragonflies. Wheatears can be seen on passage.

The areas of woodland and trees along the edge of the site have a good mixture of common woodland species, including Jay, Great Spotted Woodpecker and Treecreeper, while Reed Bunting is resident in the wetter areas.

The site has a strong reptile interest, as most Dorset heathlands do, but with ARC involvement there is more specific management of the heath for the benefit of this group of animals. ARC holds a number of events and work parties both here and elsewhere that are worth joining to find out more about the reptiles and for providing a better chance of actually seeing them!

Check out the stream for several species of dragonflies,

while the site's butterflies include silver-studded blue (wet heath) and grayling (dry heath).

A winter visit will find fewer species about but Dartford Warbler will still be here and there is a good chance of flushing Snipe from the heath and possibly Woodcock around the wooded edges. Short-eared Owl and Hoopoe have been recorded in the past.

Key points

- All boats sail at designated times – allow enough time to get tickets or you may be left behind.

- Sailings may be cancelled due to bad weather.

- Wheelchair users - check with the organisers.

- Refreshments/ toilets available on all sailings.

GETTING ONTO the water is a great way to get a feel for the size of the harbour and a chance to get close views of some of its birds. Winter sailings can find divers and scarcer grebes, Long-tailed Duck, Eider and Common Scoter. Some sailings have the added bonus of landing on Brownsea Island for close encounters with wintering Avocets and other waders. During the summer take the option of a cruise along the Purbeck coast for breeding seabirds. All boats are accompanied by local guides - it may even be me!

Target birds

Summer sailings – Puffin (80%), Peregrine (80%) Gannet (50%). *Winter sailings* – Avocet (90%), Greenshank (90%), Spoonbill (80%), Black-necked Grebe (80%), Spotted Redshank (70%), Great Northern Diver (50%).

Other possible bird species

Coastal sailings – Summer	*Winter harbour sailings*	*Occasional (winter)*
Fulmar	Dark-bellied Brent Goose	Scaup
Shag	Goldeneye	Eider
Guillemot	Red-breasted Merganser	Long-tailed Duck
Razorbill	Great Crested Grebe	Common Scoter
Kittiwake	Little Egret	Goosander
Regular gull species	Black-tailed Godwit	Red-throated Diver
Sandwich tern	Regular gull species	Black-throated Diver
Common Tern	Kingfisher	Red-necked Grebe
		Slavonian Grebe
		Sandwich Tern

Background information and birding tips

POOLE HARBOUR is regarded as the world's second largest natural harbour (behind Sydney Harbour in Australia). A number of companies run boats trips, especially during the summer months when landing is permitted on Brownsea Island.

They are a good way of getting a feel for the area but are not specifically for birders. There is, however, a selection of dedicated birdwatching trips available with guides on hand to point out and explain about the birds and the harbour.

The RSPB Poole Local Group have been organising the very popular Birdboats since 1993. The dates vary but usually run between late October and early March.

Sailings around the harbour last for two hours, while those landing on Brownsea Island last for 3.5 hours. Having approx. two hours on the island gives you enough time to appreciate how important the island's lagoon is to the harbour's birdlife and for a good chance of a close encounter with the island's red squirrels.

Birdboats also run two coastal trips in June, departing from Poole Quay, and the staff at Durlston Country Park organise coastal trips out of Swanage (approx. mid-May

Contacts

RSPB Birdboats (www.rspb.org.uk or www.pooleharbour birdboats.co.uk)

Brownsea Island Ferries 01929 462 383

Durlston Country Park 01929 424 443 (www.durlston.co.uk)

to early July). Both go in search of Puffins and other seabirds.

The Birdboats large vessels carry 100+ passengers and have toilet/refreshment facilities, but the size/facilities of the boats for the Durlston trips depend on the operator used.

Wheelchair access is possible on the larger boats but please check with the organisers before booking.

Each of the winter sailings can be different but the example below is a typical experience.

After leaving Poole Quay the boat heads across to the Arne peninsula, with Great Crested Grebe, Shag, Cormorant, Goldeneye and Red-breasted Merganser the likeliest species to be seen. This section can also be the best area to find some of the harbour's scarcer ducks, such as Long-tailed Duck, Scaup, Common Scoter and Eider.

Off the Arne Peninsula birds can be picked up on the shoreline: Little Egret is often here in good numbers and there is a chance of a Spoonbill.

Goosanders are quite scarce in the harbour but I have seen them on a few occasions here, so it is worth giving the Red-breasted Mergansers a second look.

Leaving Arne the boat heads back towards Brownsea Island then turns south by Furzey and Green Islands, past Fitzworth Point (dark-bellied Brent Goose) and into the South Deep. Again this crossing may pick up grebes

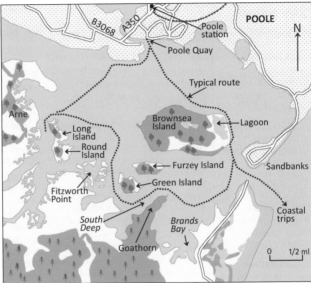

How to get there

(Boats sail from close to Poole/Swanage town centres).

RSPB Birdboats depart from Poole Quay. Swanage trips depart from the town pier. Poole and Swanage town centres have ample parking near to the departure points.

Public transport: **Both locations are served by public transport (for evening**

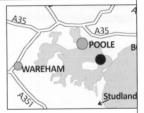

and ducks, with possibly a diver or two (all three species could be around).

It is worth looking at the landing area on Furzy Island as you pass – I have seen Golden Pheasant out in the open here on a couple of occasions.

From the South Deep the boat makes its way up the channel to the harbour

trips check the last train/bus times back to your destination).

mouth. Again more grebes and ducks should be present and there is a very good chance of a Great Northern Diver on this stretch (the more likely diver of the trip) – it is not unusual to have up to a couple of sightings.

Past the harbour mouth the boat will slow down and sit off the Brownsea Island lagoon for a short while

133

Key points

- **Birdboats' winter harbour trips last two hours and Brownsea Island/harbour trips last 3.5 hours.**

- **Summer coastal trips last three hours.**

- **Birdboats leaflets available from RSPB or Brownsea island ferry kiosk on Poole Quay.**

- **A donation per ticket sold is made to the RSPB.**

- **Swanage sailings last about 2.5 hours.**

before returning to Poole Quay. From the top deck it is possible to look over the sea wall to get good views of the birds.

The wintering Avocet flock has reached nearly 2,000 birds in the harbour in recent years and the lagoon usually holds the highest concentrations.

Other waders should include good numbers of Black-tailed Godwits, Oystercatchers and Dunlin with smaller numbers of Grey Plovers, Redshanks and maybe Turnstones, Spotted Redshanks and Greenshanks (although these three are more likely to be picked up on the trips that stop on the island).

There will also be a selection of duck including Shelduck, Wigeon, Teal, Shoveler, Mallard and Gadwall as well as Grey Heron, Little Egret and Spoonbill (often into double figures).

The Brownsea Island landings may also produce sightings of Kingfisher, Water Rail (usually heard), Snipe, Siskins and Redpolls.

When the sailings are due to land on Brownsea Island the boats usually go to the island first before continuing around the harbour, following the route taken above in reverse.

The summer evening cruises along the Purbeck coast go in search of the Puffin. They are only found in very small numbers in Dorset and Dancing Ledge (site 18) is worth a visit for them.

However, being on the boat means birds can be seen at close quarters either flying by, swimming on the water or (if the boat can get in close) on the ledges.

Other breeding seabirds you will definitely see include Guillemot,

Razorbill, Shag, Cormorant, Fulmar and Kittiwake, while Gannet regularly pass by.

Peregrines breed along this stretch of coast and there is a very good chance of a sighting or two.

Note: Contact the individual organisers for further information about dates, sailing times and prices. The exact route taken on any of the sailings may vary depending on the weather and tidal conditions.

Occasionally trips may be substantially altered or cancelled in the event of poor sailing conditions.

In general sea conditions on the winter trips within the harbour are not too bad thanks to the harbour's sheltered, shallow waters (fog is more of a potential problem).

The trips along the coast during the summer are more likely to hit rougher seas and are more prone to being cancelled or altered. Whatever time of the year you go out on the water remember to wrap up well ......it can be very cold!

Other nearby sites

Brownsea Island, Ham Common, Lytchett Bay, Poole Harbour – Poole Quay to Sandbanks, Studland, Upton Country Park & Holes Bay.

SOME OF THE most expensive real estate in the world is found at Sandbanks but don't be put off – alongside the built-up sections you'll find a selection of excellent birding spots that provide the best chance inside the harbour of seeing Great Northern Diver, Bar-tailed Godwit, Knot, Purple Sandpiper, Turnstone and Mediterranean Gull. In a prolonged spell of cold of cold weather check out Poole Park for a chance of an unusual duck or two.

Target birds
Winter – Bar-tailed Godwit (90%), Turnstone (90%), Mediterranean Gull (90%), Great Northern Diver (50%), Knot (50%), Sanderling (50%), Purple Sandpiper (50%).

Other possible bird species

Winter
Greylag Goose
Canada Goose
Dark-bellied Brent Goose
Goldeneye
Red-breasted Merganser
Great Crested Grebe
Cormorant
Shag

Little Egret
Oystercatcher
Ringed Plover
Curlew
Redshank
Regular gull species
Siskin

Summer
Common Tern

Sandwich Tern

Occasional (winter)
Common Sandpiper
Sandwich Tern
Auks
Chiffchaff
Firecrest
Redpoll

Background information and birding tips

THIS SHORELINE is certainly the most disturbed part of Poole Harbour, with as much disturbance nowadays in the winter as in the summer from activities both on and off the water.

Though a few of the species mentioned here may be seen over the summer, the winter is the most productive time. Key sites for birdwatching are covered in detail over the next few pages.

Key points
• **Close to Poole town centre.**
• **Ample local parking.**
• **Toilets/ refreshments along the route.**
• **Wheelchair access to most areas.**
• **A top spot for Med Gull and Purple Sandpiper.**

How to get there
(Sites lie between Poole town centre and Sandbanks).

You can approach Poole Quay, Baiter, Parkstone Bay and Poole Park on foot from Poole town centre where there are ample car parks. Alternatively, follow the signs to Poole Old Town/the Quay and Baiter for additional parking.

FOR POOLE PARK: To park here take the B3093 from the main roundabout by the Dolphin shopping centre/bus station to the next small roundabout and take the 2nd exit along Kingland Road.

The first left turn takes you on to the road around the lake with ample parking along it.

FOR SANDBANKS: Leave Poole town centre on A350 (Parkstone Road) to the main Civic Centre roundabout and follow the road signs to Sandbanks – the B3369 (Sandbanks Road). Pass under the railway bridge and take fourth road on the right, which turns into Whitecliff Road – the car park here can be used to look at Parkstone Bay. Whitecliff Road continues back under the railway line and into Poole Park.

Continues over the page..

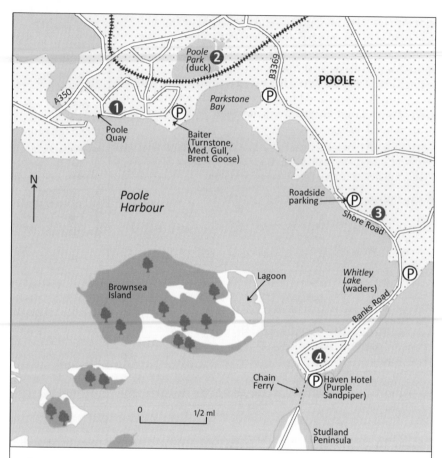

Following the Sandbanks road you will eventually come onto Shore Road (which becomes Banks Road). There is plenty of roadside parking along this stretch of road where Whitley Lake can be viewed.

After Banks Road, continue around the one-way system towards the Sandbanks ferry. There is a small car park by the ferry/Haven Hotel and limited roadside parking just after the turn to the ferry. This area gets very busy in the summer and sometimes on fine winter weekends – you may get caught up in the tailback of vehicles waiting to cross on the ferry to Studland.

Alternatively this site can be approached from the south at Studland over the Sandbanks ferry.

Public transport: Buses from

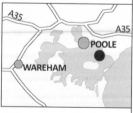

Poole run to Sandbanks (Wilts & Dorset).

136

❶ Poole Quay – Baiter – Parkstone Bay (SZ 021 902)

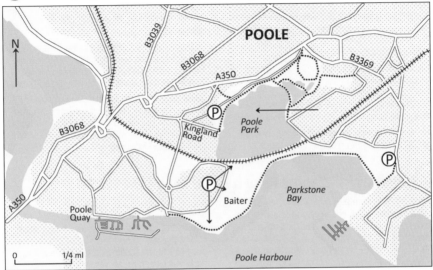

WITHIN EASY reach of Poole town centre, a walk from the Quay around into Parkstone Bay is best made when the tide is out and birds are feeding on the mud. Once the tide is in, disturbance of the available roosting areas usually pushes the birds elsewhere or on to the water.

If you are here at high tide though, check out the various pontoons and the breakwater of the yacht club for Ringed Plovers and Turnstones.

There is usually a Mediterranean Gull somewhere between the yacht club and Baiter, especially in early spring when adults often congregate in the area before moving on to their breeding area further around the harbour. Offshore here, winter gull roosts hold the regular gull species but check amongst them for Mediterranean Gulls.

The usual small numbers of Oystercatchers may be joined by the occasional Curlew, Redshank or Grey Plover. Out on the water Great Crested Grebes, Red-breasted Mergansers and Goldeneyes should be easily seen.

If there is not too much disturbance, dark-bellied Brent Goose often graze on the grass behind the car park at Baiter. If disturbed, they will usually sit out on the water for long periods. A careful check of the flocks can reveal pale-bellied individuals and a Black Brant recently spent part of a winter here.

If it is raining heavily and you don't fancy getting out of the car, Baiter is worth visiting as it can be heaving with birds feeding on the grass, particularly if it coincides with a high tide and little disturbance.

As well as the geese, Oystercatchers (I have seen up to 600), Turnstones and Ringed Plovers may be joined by a small number of Black-tailed Godwits. While in the car park, watch out for the antics of the Carrion Crows dropping shells onto the tarmac to get at the contents.

At the back of Parkstone Bay, Brent Geese, waders and gulls gather on the exposed mud. This is another area where there is a very good chance of a Mediterranean Gull – look through the gulls on the mud or roosting on the small boats anchored in the bay.

② Poole Park (SZ 020 910)

CLOSE TO Baiter, but the other side of the railway line, is Poole Park. The artificial lakes of the park are a favoured spot for Canada Geese and a feral flock of Greylag Geese.

A few ducks use the lakes but apart from regular Mallards and Tufted Ducks there are not usually many species, though Pochards and Goldeneyes are possible and Mandarin Duck has been recorded.

However, during periods of extremely cold weather something more unusual, such as Smew, Goosander, divers and grebes could appear.

The park played host to a Long-billed Dowitcher and a Ring-billed Gull at the same time in early 2011. Check through any Black-headed Gulls you see for colour-ringed birds.

The park itself will attract a few common passerines in the trees and bushes scattered around the park including Siskins and possibly a few Redpolls. A Yellow-browed warbler overwintered here recently.

③ Whitley Lake, Shore Road & Banks Road (SZ 045 891)

THE AREA known as Whitley Lake, off Shore Road/Banks Road, is a very popular area for wind/kite surfing activity, bait digging and even dog walking when the tide is out. Despite this heavy disturbance, it is well worth a look.

An interesting piece of work I was involved with a few years ago looked at the disturbance of birds using this area in daylight and darkness. The tidal states were the same during both periods to make sure the counts were standardised. Dunlin proved to be an interesting species as they were never seen during the day (when there was disturbance), but were found feeding on the shore during darkness (when there was no disturbance).

I still find that this is the best spot in the harbour for Knot and Bar-tailed Godwits, where up to 50 of the former and more than 100 of the latter may be feeding.

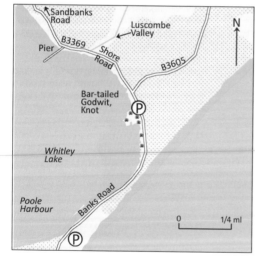

The tide goes well out at low water and birds are scattered across the sandy mudflats but begin to group together as the tide rises.

A small area of higher ground by the road provides a high tide roost site, depending on the levels of disturbance, but birds usually commute between here and the Brownsea Island lagoon. Mediterranean Gulls and Brent Geese are also regular.

Just off Shore Road (access via a stile) there is a small 10ha local nature reserve – Luscombe Valley. Could be worth a look for wintering Chiffchaffs and there is also a chance of a Firecrest.

④ Harbour entrance (SZ 037 871)

CHECK ANY birds on the water inside and outside of the harbour mouth. There may be a diver (usually Great Northern), a grebe or a sea duck close in. Shags are more common here than Cormorants, and look out for the occasional auk (probably a Guillemot or Razorbill but Little Auks have been seen).

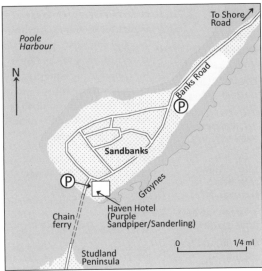

In the right conditions seabirds may come into the bay close to the harbour entrance but a better site for seawatching is a little further along the coast at Branksome Chine (site 8).

If you are here early morning or late afternoon you can see small flocks of Red-breasted Mergansers, Brent Geese and the occasional Great Northern Diver commuting to roost through the harbour mouth from/ to their roost. One or two Sandwich Terns are seen in most winters.

The main target bird here is Purple Sandpiper, quite scarce in the county. You may be lucky and find them feeding on the chain ferry slipway but, if not, you can (taking care) hop over the wall in front of the Haven Hotel and walk around the rocks and out onto the groynes (tide and weather conditions permitting!)

The birds are usually found on the groynes, often with a few Sanderlings and Ringed Plovers. This area is prone to disturbance so an early morning visit may be more successful. If disturbed, the birds sometimes fly over to the Studland side.

Note: if you are visiting Studland (site 53) but want to try for the Purple Sandpipers by the hotel, leave your car in the Shell Bay car park and cross on the ferry as a foot passenger. Alternatively, from the beach by the Studland side of the ferry crossing, scan with a telescope on the rocks across the water for the birds – sometimes they can be picked up from here, albeit at a distance.

Other nearby sites

Branksome Chine, Brownsea Island (from Sandbanks or Poole Quay), Studland, Upton Country Park & Holes Bay.

Key points

- An important geological site.
- Historical locations.
- One of the UK's top birdwatching spots.
- Excellent seawatching.
- Spring and autumn migration hotspot.
- Excellent bird observatory.
- An annual bird report.
- Easy public transport access to all areas.
- Plenty of facilities on the island.
- Limited disabled access.
- Good butterflies, flora and other wildlife.

Contacts

Portland Bird Observatory 01305 820 553. www.portlandbirdobs.org.uk

Butterfly Conservation 01929 400 209. www.butterfly-conservation.org

WITHOUT a doubt one of the best birding sites in the UK (never mind Dorset), Portland is blessed with an excellent bird observatory at The Bill, while the island is a magnet for common, uncommon and rare birds at migration time and can turn up excellent birds at any time of the year – many birds new to the Dorset list have been added here. Little Owls and Purple Sandpipers are regularly seen and it is also Dorset's best site for seawatching with divers, shearwaters, petrels, skuas, terns and auks often passing in good numbers and variety. Portland is definitely a 'must do' site on any birding trip to Dorset.

Target birds

All year – Little Owl (75%), Peregrine (75%), Raven (75%). *Summer* – Guillemot (100%), Razorbill (95%), Puffin (30%). *Winter* – Purple Sandpiper (75%), Black Redstart (30%), Firecrest (30%). *Passage* – Spring/autumn migrants and rarities, seabird movements.

Other possible bird species

All year
Fulmar
Gannet
Cormorant
Shag
Common Scoter
Sparrowhawk
Buzzard
Kestrel
Oystercatcher
Turnstone
Regular gull species
Kittiwake
Barn Owl (scarce)
Little Owl
Skylark
Meadow Pipit
Rock pipit
Stonechat
Linnet
Bullfinch
Yellowhammer

Summer
Puffin
Whitethroat
Lesser Whitethroat

Winter
Red-throated Diver
Brent Goose
Eider

Lapwing
Mediterranean Gull
Little Gull
Common Gull
Winter thrushes

Passage migrants
Sanderling
Bar-tailed Godwit
Whimbrel
Common Sandpiper
Turtle Dove
Cuckoo
Hirundines
Tree Pipit
Yellow Wagtail
Grey and 'Alba' wagtails
Black Redstart
Redstart
Whinchat
Wheatear
Ring Ouzel
Wood Warbler
Yellow-browed Warbler
Firecrest
Spotted Flycatcher
Pied Flycatcher
Siskin
Redpoll

Passage seabirds
Manx Shearwater

Balearic Shearwater
Storm Petrel
Pomarine Skua
Arctic Skua
Great Skua
Sandwich Tern
'Commic' Terns

Scarce migrants
Sooty Shearwater
Leach's Petrel
Honey Buzzard
Marsh Harrier
Hen Harrier
Osprey
Merlin
Hobby
Quail
Grey Phalarope
Black Tern
Short-eared Owl
Great Spotted Woodpecker
Hoopoe
Wryneck
Woodlark
Tawny Pipit
Nightingale
Icterine Warbler
Melodious Warbler
Barred Warbler

Dartford Warbler
Red-breasted Flycatcher
Coal Tit (continental race)
Golden Oriole
Woodchat Shrike
Tree Sparrow
Serin
Hawfinch
Lapland Bunting
Ortolan Bunting

Occasional
Cory's Shearwater
Long-tailed Duck
Velvet Scoter
Black Kite
Red Kite
Goshawk
Long-tailed Skua
Sabine's Gull
Iceland Gull
Glaucous Gull

Roseate Tern
Little Auk
Long-eared Owl
Alpine Swift
Bee-eater
Red-rumped Swallow
Bluethroat
Subalpine Warbler
Rose-coloured Starling
Common Rosefinch

Background information and birding tips

THE PHRASE 'Go everywhere and expect anything' is probably all that needs to be said about Portland! Bobolink, Desert Wheatear, Collared Flycatcher and Rose-coloured Starling are among my own lifers on the island and I have seen many other not-so-common species such as Wryneck, Bluethroat, Red-breasted Flycatcher and Subalpine Warbler.

Portland, joined to the mainland by a causeway from Wyke Regis (Weymouth), is roughly four miles long by 1.5 miles wide and covers about 1200ha. The north end of the island rises sharply to 130m above sea level and then slopes away to Portland Bill in the south, where the cliffs are only a few metres above sea level.

Limestone is the island's main natural resource with past (and present) quarrying activities shaping the island's landscape. Most of the central area of the island that hasn't been settled has been quarried. Open farmland remains to the south of Southwell.

There are a few interesting birds resident on the island including Peregrine, Little Owl and Raven, but it is for migrants (on land and sea) that the island is best known. The island's importance for these birds has been recognised for a hundred years but serious birding really took off in the 1950s. The first bird observatory was established in 1955, moving to its present location in the Old Lower Light in 1961.

The original recording area of the island refers to The Bill – the southern end of the island beyond Southwell. Now recording covers the whole island, including Ferrybridge and Portland Harbour, which I have treated as a separate site (see site 44).

An excellent annual bird report is produced by the Portland Bird Observatory (the 'Obs') and if you are planning a visit it is worth checking out the Obs website, or one of the birdline services, for up-to-date information on what birds are about, to point you in the right direction.

Accommodation is available at the Obs - a great place to stay to be 'in the thick of it'. Birds can turn up anywhere ......including private gardens. If a rarity turns up in a sensitive area, the local birders will often make viewing arrangements, but please be considerate to resident's privacy and requests.

The 'right' weather conditions during migration will make a difference as to whether Portland has a 'good' year or not. In the spring, birds will usually move straight through in clear skies, while rain and mist will ground them and can hold them up for a while.

In the autumn, easterlies and south-easterlies are eagerly awaited in case any interesting species are blown over from their normal migration routes in the east. An early morning start in the spring and autumn is best for migrants but they do turn up unexpectedly anywhere, at any time.

Other nearby sites
Lodmoor, Portland Harbour & Ferrybridge, Radipole Lake, The Fleet, The Nothe & Weymouth Bay.

How to get there

(S of Weymouth).

From Weymouth, follow A354 through Wyke Regis, across the causeway and onto Portland. The A354 and minor roads link up the settlements and The Bill [clockwise: Fortuneswell – Easton – Southwell - Portland Bill – Weston – Chiswell].

PORTLAND HARBOUR (see site 44):

VERNE COMMON:
Once over the causeway go straight on across three roundabouts – after crossing the third (Victoria Square) stay in the left lane into Victory Road, then take the bend to the right into Castle Road and first left into Verne Common Road (signed HM Prison/ RN Cemetery). Continue through the housing estate (the road winds up the hill), cross over the road bridge of the old railway line and pull up on the left. Park carefully off the road, walk down the track to the entrance gate for the common.

NORTH WOODS:
Continue on A354 through Fortuneswell and up the steep hill. At the roundabout at the top turn left and follow the road behind the Portland Heights Hotel, where there are a number of parking areas (free) on the left, overlooking the North Woods.

BROADCROFT QUARRY AREA:
Continue on A354 towards Easton, but turn left into Grove Road. After about 250m (past the fire station and playing field) turn right and drive 150m down the track to a small parking area (free) by the Broadcroft Quarry butterfly reserve. Note: Quarry lorries use the track, do not enter the working quarry area.

PENNSYLVANIA CASTLE/ CHURCH OPE COVE:
Continue through Easton along

Wakeham (road) and into Pennsylvania Road. There is a parking area (free) just on the right opposite the Castle. On the Castle side of the road take the footpath down to the cove, passing through woodland.

PORTLAND BILL:
Continue on this road for about a mile into Southwell and take the next left to The Bill – the only road in and out. The Obs is on the left side of the road

after about 0.75 mile, the car park at The Bill another half mile beyond. There is limited parking at the Obs for guests and members only, the large car park at The Bill is pay & display – also refreshments and toilets here.

BARLEYCRATES LANE - REAP LANE & SUCKTHUMB QUARRY:
Return to the Southwell junction and turn left towards Weston and follow the road around to the right (Avalanche Road). Take the next main road off to the right (Weston Street) and park up. Barleycrates

Lane is on the opposite side of Avalanche Road. The footpath leads out to the cliffs and circles southwards to Reap Lane. The Suckthumb Quarry area can be accessed by footpaths to the south off Weston Street and to the east off Avalanche Road. Note: Do not enter the working quarry areas.

TOUT QUARRY:
Continue on through Weston and take the left turn by the church into Wide Street. After 400m turn left into the industrial area, follow the road around to the right and then take the right fork and carry on until reaching the parking area (free).

CHESIL COVE:
Leave the industrial area and turn left to the next roundabout (by the Portland Heights Hotel). Turn left back on to the A354 and continue down the hill. At Fortuneswell the road forks left (a one way system) and carries on to Chiswell. Just after the end of the one Way system turn left into Brandy Row.

There is parking (free) immediately on the left or further along on the right. Walk to the promenade at the end of Brandy Row – overlooking the cove. There is an alternative car park (free), with toilets, 250m further along the road (turn in by the restaurant on the corner).

If you only intend visiting Chesil Cove, or want to go there first, keep in the right hand lane after the Victoria Square roundabout, and turn left into Chiswell (Road) and right again into Brandy Row (passing the alternative car park first).

To leave Portland turn left onto the A354 and head towards Wyke Regis/Weymouth.

Public transport: Regular bus services between Weymouth and Portland (First: Hampshire & Dorset, South West Coaches).

❶ Verne Common (SY 688 737)

THE COMMON is located on the steep sheltered slopes on the north of the island. A path which runs through it eventually reaches a locked gate. The area is very overgrown with scrub and bramble, providing plenty of cover for resident birds and migrants alike. Unfortunately, there is no access for wheelchair users.

There is a Royal Navy cemetery here with a number of sycamore trees in the grounds. Bird records in the past have included Corncrake, Wryneck, Yellow-browed Warbler and Dorset's only Cliff Swallow (in 2000).

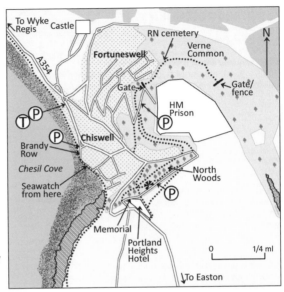

❷ North Woods (SY 689 730)

THE VIEW north from the top of Portland (by the Portland Heights Hotel) is an impressive sight with Portland Harbour below and Chesil Beach/The Fleet stretching away into the distance.

The steep slope below the viewpoint is covered in woodland with a path running through it – access it from the left hand side of the memorial. The path is steep and unsuitable for wheelchairs.

If you do walk down to the bottom of the hill, turn right and take the (steep) road back to the viewpoint. The area behind the viewpoint consists of open grassland and old quarry workings and can be worth a look.

This can be a good spot to look for birds as they leave the island, either making their way through the woods or flying over.

The viewpoint is a good spot to scan for passing birds of prey which have included Osprey, Marsh Harrier and Honey Buzzard.

❸ Chesil Cove (SY 683 732)

THOUGH not usually as productive as The Bill, the cove is a good spot for seawatching. Passing seabirds often follow the coast along Chesil Beach before turning south for The Bill. In the spring it is best to seawatch here in the early morning when there is a gentle wind from the SW to SE.

In the late spring/summer Storm Petrels sometimes come into the bay and autumn gales can blow birds in here too – Grey Phalaropes and Little Gulls are virtually annual.

In the winter divers use the cove and it is always worth searching through any flocks of Common Scoters for a sighting of a Velvet Scoter.

4 Broadcroft Quarry area (SY 695 723)

THERE is a small (7ha) Butterfly Conservation nature reserve here which holds a good number of butterflies including Lulworth skipper and silver-studded blue. Check out the scrub and old quarry workings around the area for birds – including Whitethroats, Stonechats and possible migrants.

5 Tout Quarry (SY 685 724)

THIS IS another disused quarry but with a difference. The area was turned into a stone sculpture park when quarrying ceased working in the early 1980s – there are now more than 70 sculptures spread around the site.

There is a trail through the quarry (and information boards) – keep to the paths.

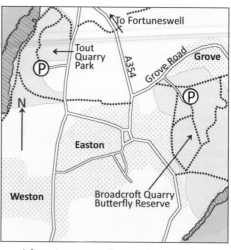

A few migrants usually pass through here, including Ring Ouzel, and it's also good for butterflies.

6 Reap Lane – Barleycrates Lane - Suckthumb Quarry (SY 686 709)

THIS AREA lies just to the north of The Bill and can be reached on foot from there by following the coastal path along the western cliffs. On its day the site can be as good as The Bill. There is a good circular walk here of just over 1.5 miles.

Start at Barleycrates Lane (off Avalanche Road, by the hall). The narrow lane is lined with brambles and rough field margins, fences and walls (all ideal for skulking warblers) and has open fields behind. The path comes out by the cliffs, where you should turn left and head south.

Ignore two lanes leading off to the left (after 100m and 450m) and walk to the end of the 'Lawnsheds' where you'll see another path off to the left – take this one and follow the field round into Reap Lane. The lanes are worth checking as you pass –

look for birds on the fences, in the rough field margins and on the open grassland.

Bird species here have included Red-footed Falcon, Dotterel, Tawny Pipit, Golden Oriole, Woodchat Shrike, Ortolan and Lapland

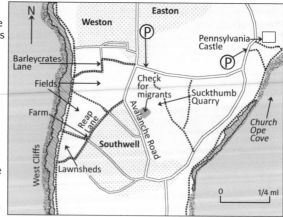

Buntings. Check out the farm for Black Redstart.

Suckthumb Quarry lies on the opposite side of Avalanche Road and is another disused quarry.

If you wander around the area, be sure to check the clump of trees by the road – this can be a good spot for migrants (Dorset's first Eastern Bonelli's Warbler was found here in 2009).

⑦ Pennsylvania Castle/Church Ope Cove (SY 695 711)

THE FOOTPATH by the castle passes through a small wood and on down to the cove. The general area is good for Firecrests and I have seen a Red-breasted Flycatcher in the wood in the past.

Other interesting bird species here have included Hoopoe, Nightingale, Black Redstart, 'Siberian' Chiffchaff and Serin.

⑧ Portland Bill (SY 681 690 – Obs, SY 677 684 Bill)

BY FAR the greater portion of birds recorded on Portland each year come from this area. It is heavily watched throughout the year, especially during passage times, by both locals and visiting birders.

Open farmland and cliffs dominate the habitat and access around the area is by a network of public and permissive footpaths (many of the fields are private and shouldn't be entered). There is no stopping, or parking, permitted on the road from Southwell to The Bill car park.

Explore the whole area if you visit in spring or autumn. Early migrants begin arriving in March, with Sand Martins, Wheatears and Chiffchaffs usually the first, and is in full flow through April and May.

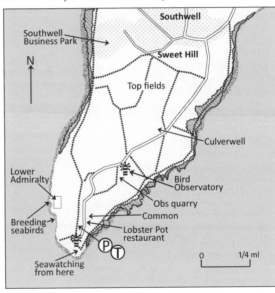

Some species, such as Ring Ouzel, Redstart, Grasshopper Warbler and Willow Warbler are more numerous in April, while Garden Warblers, Wood Warblers and Spotted Flycatchers favour May.

By August autumn migration is underway and tends to be busier than September. Some of the short-distance migrants such as Ring Ouzels, Blackcaps and Chiffchaffs, usually come through later in September and into

October – a small number of Blackcaps and Chiffchaffs, along with Firecrests, can over-winter.

Aside from the regular migrants it is the unexpected that draws birders to Portland and The Bill in particular. Spring overshoots from the continent may include species such as Alpine Swift, Bee-eater, Hoopoe, Red-rumped Swallow, Subalpine Warbler, Golden Oriole and Serin.

Other species more likely in the autumn are: Wryneck, Tawny Pipit, Melodious Warbler, Yellow-browed Warbler, Pallas's Warbler, Rose-coloured Starling and Ortolan Bunting. A number of UK firsts have been found on Portland, including Calandra Lark, Desert Warbler, Lesser Short-toed Lark and the first modern-day record of Egyptian Nightjar.

A typical route from The Bill car park (unless seawatching) is to head north along the landward side of the Lower Admiralty compound and then follow the coast path along the top of the cliffs until reaching the fence of the Southwell Business Park – look out for Peregrines and Ravens along the way.

Head inland at the fence to Sweet Hill where the footpath continues eastwards towards the road.There are two footpaths along this stretch heading south through the Top Fields – take either of these and head towards Culverwell.

Keep checking the vegetation and scrub as you walk around the fields and the field themselves – Skylarks, Stonechats and Whitethroats breed here. Culverwell has a sizeable area of scrub and is worth checking thoroughly.

From Culverwell head back along the road to the Obs – call in and have a look at the facilities. The Observatory leases the field opposite, using it to plant arable strips. Birds can be found here in good numbers – view from the road or the footpath that runs up the side. In the autumn birds include flocks of finches and possibly a Short-eared Owl.

There is no entry into the Obs garden but it can be viewed from the terrace. The scrub from the garden spills out towards the nearby quarry. Check out this scrub and look into the quarry for any lurking migrants – it's also a good spot for Little Owl (check out the crevices).

Continue on past the coastguard cottages to the Pulpit Pub (there is another clump of scrub here worth checking out) and cross over the Common back to the car park. The Common is a good spot when Wheatears and wagtails are moving through and check out any gulls loafing there for Yellow-legged.

Another route to take from the car park is to walk east along the cliffs. These are lower than the western side and may hold a few waders including Whimbrels and Common Sandpipers on passage and Rock Pipits.

The cliffs around the southern tip are a reliable wintering area for Purple Sandpipers and, virtually all year, for Turnstones.

The Bill is the best place for seawatching in Dorset as birds move through the English Channel. Watch from the landmark on the Point which gives a little shelter against the worst of any weather, and be careful looking to the south into the sun's reflection off the water.

Gannets and Common Scoters are seen virtually throughout the year, as are Fulmars, Shags, Kittiwakes, Guillemots and Razorbills which, along with a few Puffins, nest on the cliffs at The Bill.

The peak time for passing seabirds is April-May when Manx Shearwaters, Arctic and Great Skuas, Sandwich and 'Commic' Terns reach their highest numbers – smaller numbers pass through in the autumn.

The spring can be good for Pomarine Skuas, while Balearic Shearwaters pass in reasonable numbers from May to October. Sooty Shearwaters are quite scarce from August to November, peaking in September. Storm Petrels are slightly later (May to July) with Leach's Petrels in October-November, usually in stormy weather. Little Gulls are more likely in the winter.

Scarce seabirds sighted from here have included Cory's Shearwater, Long-tailed Skua, Glaucous, Iceland and Sabine's Gulls, Black Guillemot and Little Auk. Winter and spring passage is the time to look for divers: Red-throated are reasonably common during both periods, Great Northern and Black-throated are more likely during passage.

Grebes are scarce at all times, as are wildfowl – Brent Goose is the most likely during the winter with the occasional Eider or Long-tailed Duck.

Wheelchair access around the area is difficult because of the terrain, but there is good access to the Point for seawatching.

THE SHELTERED waters of Portland Harbour have long been one of the best sites for wintering divers in the county. Black-throated and Great Northern Divers are regularly seen, but Red-throated less so. All five species of grebe can also be picked up here, along with a variety of sea duck and auks sheltering in the harbour. I have even seen Black Guillemots on a few occasions. From Ferrybridge, which connects Portland to the mainland, look for pale-bellied and Black Brant among the large numbers of dark-bellied Brent Geese in winter and Dorset's only breeding colony of Little Terns in summer.

Target birds
Summer – Little Tern (95%). *Winter* – Mediterranean Gull (90%), Great Northern Diver (75%), Black-necked Grebe (75%), Pale-bellied Brent Goose (50%), Black Brant (50%), Black-throated Diver (25%), Slavonian Grebe (25%), Red-necked Grebe (10%), Firecrest (10%).

Other possible bird species

All year
Cormorant
Shag
Little Egret
Rock Pipit

Summer
Sandwich Tern
Common Tern

Winter
Little Grebe
Great Crested Grebe
Red-breasted Merganser

Oystercatcher
Ringed Plover
Grey Plover
Dunlin
Regular gull species
Guillemot
Razorbill
Black Redstart
Chiffchaff

Passage
Little Ringed Plover
Curlew Sandpiper

Dunlin
Little Stint
Knot
Sanderling

Occasional
Eider
Red-throated Diver
Kentish Plover
Black Guillemot
Yellow-browed Warbler

Background information and birding tips

OVER THE YEARS I have had the impression that Portland Harbour has become busier with leisure activities on the water. With the area being the centre for the 2012 Olympic sailing events this is undoubtedly likely to continue.

The long term effects on bird numbers in the harbour remains to be seen. The harbour is huge and, although birds can sometimes be seen close to shore, a telescope is a great asset. Calm, cloudy days will give the best viewing conditions.

The harbour is at its best during the winter and can easily be combined with a trip to Portland and/or the Weymouth sites.

Though I have seen fewer Black-necked and Slavonian Grebes in recent years, they still occur, along with Great Crested, Little and the occasional Red-necked Grebes.

Great Northern and Black-throated Divers are regularly seen, especially the former, but Red-throated are not so regular.

The harbour (and Ferrybridge) holds a good population of Red-

Key points
• Best viewing spots at Sandsfoot Castle, Sailing Club, Ferrybridge visitor centre and Portland Castle: sites good for wheelchair users.

• Best in winter – expect 25-30 species.

• Can walk from Weymouth or take a bus.

• Pay & display at Ferrybridge.

• Visitor centre, toilets & cafe kiosk at Ferrybridge.

Contacts
Chesil Beach Visitor Centre
01305 760 579.
www.chesilbeach.org

147

breasted Mergansers, but other ducks are found in much smaller numbers and are not necessarily annual visitors: look for Common and Velvet Scoters, Long-tailed Duck, Eider and Goldeneye. A handful of auks – usually Razorbills and Guillemots – may shelter in the harbour in winter.

Waders are few and far between but Turnstones, Oystercatchers and Ringed Plovers are usually seen, along with the occasional Common Sandpiper (spring/autumn). Shag and Cormorant and regular gull species are present all year round and terns are in the area in the summer.

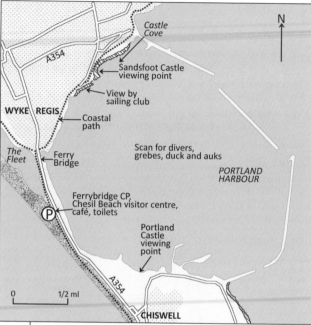

Other interesting birds turn up from time to time, especially in periods of bad weather – usually in the autumn/winter. Species such as Little Auk, Grey Phalarope, Storm and Leach's Petrel and Goosander may be among them, but Black Guillemots were once more regular than they are now.

First stop should be Sandsfoot Castle (roadside parking). Views of the harbour are now more obscured by foliage but scan where you can, especially into Castle Cove where grebes are often close in.

Continue down the road to the entrance of the Castle Cove Sailing Club and park here – again scan out into the harbour for grebes, divers and duck. The scrub on the slopes above Castle

How to get there

From Weymouth follow A354 to Portland. For Sandsfoot Castle take the Old Castle Road (signposted off A354). Continue on A354 into Wyke Regis, following the road to Portland.

Just after leaving Wyke Regis, the Chesil Beach Visitor Centre is a short way along the causeway (on the right).

For Portland Castle continue along A354 to the island, turn left on to Castle Road towards Portland Castle (signposted).

It is possible to walk from Weymouth to Ferrybridge

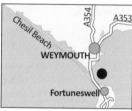

along South West Coast Path which runs along the edge of the harbour.

Public transport: Regular bus services between Weymouth and Portland (First: Hampshire & Dorset) and also between Dorchester and Portland.

Cove (a footpath leads down to the shore from Old Castle Road almost opposite Sudan Road) and along the road to the sailing club entrance

is worth checking out for wintering Chiffchaffs and Firecrests. Yellow-browed Warblers have also been seen here.

148

Portland Harbour is a great place for all the British grebe species, including elegant Black-necked Grebes.

At Ferrybridge, view the harbour from the Weymouth side of the bridge (park by the centre and walk back along the road). Little Grebes usually gather here and Red-breasted Mergansers may be close in. Walk northwards along the shore, scanning as you go.

On Portland itself, the only real place to view the water is from Portland Castle. Park up in the car park (free) and walk through the gap in the wall. Look out for Black Redstart on the nearby buildings, the jetty or the beach during the winter months.

Ferrybridge, described here though it is actually part of The Fleet (site 56), is also at its best during the winter. There will be more waders here than in the harbour (but not in huge numbers), including Oystercatchers, Dunlins, Grey Plovers, Ringed Plovers, Curlews and Turnstones.

There is usually a good selection of gulls, including Mediterranean Gull which has become much more common on The Fleet in recent years – on one occasion I saw more than 200 birds roosting on the shore here.

Other waders tend to pass through in the spring or autumn (some more regularly than others). They have included Kentish and Little Ringed Plovers, Little Stints, Curlew Sandpipers, Knot and Sanderlings. In 2010 a summer-plumaged Red-necked Stint was found here ......but identified from a photograph only after it had departed the scene!

The main challenge on The Fleet is to search through the flock(s) of dark-bellied Brent Geese for the handful of pale-bellied/Black Brants that accompany them annually.

When birds are at Ferrybridge there is a better chance of picking them out as they can be fairly close. Red-breasted Goose has been recorded with the Brents and will be a little more obvious.

If you walk over the shingle bank you can look out over the sea. Usually there is very little to be seen apart from an occasional diver, grebe or seabird – it will be more productive to visit Chesil Cove (just south of Ferrybridge on Portland) or Portland Bill.

There is usually very little around in the summer but Little Terns breed on Chesil Beach by Ferrybridge (subject of a species protection scheme) and may be joined by feeding Common and Sandwich Terns.

Park (pay & display) by the Chesil Beach visitor centre at Ferrybridge (a new centre is planned) and view from here or by walking along the road back towards Weymouth. This area is tidal so birds are somewhat distant at low tide and when full in they tend to move back up The Fleet, so try to catch a rising or falling tide.

Other nearby sites
Portland, Radipole Lake, The Fleet, The Nothe & Weymouth Bay.

Key points

- Owned/ leased by Dorset Wildlife Trust.
- Designated SSSI and SAC.
- Expect 25-30 species in the summer.
- Limited parking for ca. 8 cars (can be busy).
- Two way-marked trails, allow at least two hours for the longer one.
- Main track/ dismantled railway line suitable for wheelchairs.
- Other paths can be wet, some steep.
- Information board.
- Good for butterflies.

Contacts

Dorset Wildlife Trust 01305 264 620. www. dorsetwildlifetrust.org. uk/reserves

T HIS ANCIENT common has superb views over the West Dorset countryside as far as Golden Cap on the coast, nearly ten miles away. Its mixture of woodland and meadow habitat supports a good variety of common birds and it is one of Dorset's best sites for butterflies - including marsh fritillary and wood white. This was where I saw my last Willow Tit in the county – sadly now probably extinct in Dorset.

Target birds *All year* – Green Woodpecker (90%), Bullfinch (90%), Marsh Tit (80%), Yellowhammer (80%), Lesser Spotted Woodpecker (25%). *Summer* – Tree Pipit (90%), Garden Warbler (75%).

Other possible bird species

All year	Common woodland	Fieldfare
Buzzard	birds	Redwing
Tawny Owl	*Summer*	Siskin
Great Spotted	Blackcap	Redpoll
Woodpecker	Whitethroat	
Nuthatch	Chiffchaff	*Occasional*
Treecreeper	Willow Warbler	Cuckoo
Raven		Nightjar
Linnet	*Winter*	Yellow Wagtail
	Woodcock	

Background information and birding tips

A VARIETY of tracks, paths and rides run through the Dorset Wildlife Trust's landholding, which covers 115ha, so you have a number of options of where to walk. It is worth spending half a day here to explore the woodland and meadow habitats.

From the car park, follow the obvious track for just over 300m, passing an information board/map, to a junction – at this point it is possible to take one of two way-marked trails. The longer trail is just under two miles, taking in the dismantled railway line, woodland and open meadow.

The shorter trail is just over half a mile around part of the meadows. The main 'forestry' track and the dismantled railway line are suitable for wheelchair users. The first stretch of track from the car

park will give a good idea of what birds are found here. Chiffchaffs, Willow Warblers, Bullfinches and Yellowhammers are likely, along with some of the expected common passerines including thrushes, tits (including Marsh), Nuthatches and Treecreepers. Once at the junction, look/listen out for Tree Pipits.

My choice from here is to first follow the dismantled railway line which runs through the site for about a mile. The line, built in 1857 to take trains from Maiden Newton to Bridport, ceased to run in 1975 after which the tracks were removed. The shelter afforded by the railway cutting provides a good display of wildflowers and butterflies can be numerous.

The first 500m section covers open grassland before it leads into woodland. After another 500m look for the gate into the southern woodland area – this track joins up with the main forestry track and rides into the woodland. A further 300m down the line is another gate (just beyond is an old railway bridge). Leave the railway line at this gate and walk along the edge of the woodland (not suitable for wheelchairs).

On the right is an open area of grassland (formerly a conifer plantation). Views open out here to the south – the prominent feature in the distance is Eggardon Hill, an Iron Age hill fort. Buzzards soaring overhead are worth a second look as Red Kites are occasionally seen. Continue along the woodland edge until the end of the forestry track comes into view – the way-marked trail returns along here.

Instead of taking this track, walk for another 100m to a small gate. Follow the obvious path, initially with a short steep climb which can be muddy, as it wends its way through the woodland. The mature trees hold a good selection of common woodland birds and possibly, even a Lesser Spotted Woodpecker.. The path leads out into the open (there is an option of turning left along another section of the forestry track).

Continue following the path to the right. Views open up to the north and east, so look for birds of prey soaring overhead, as well as for Raven, and listen out for Garden Warblers in the scrub. The path eventually joins up with the main forestry track which continues through the meadows back to the first junction.

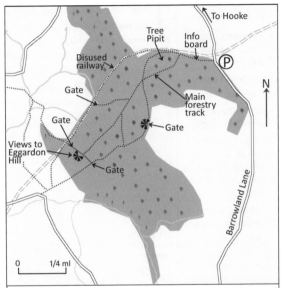

How to get there

(10 miles NW of Dorchester).
Take A37 Yeovil road from Dorchester and turn left on to A356 just past Grimstone. About a mile after leaving Maiden Newton turn left (Toller Lane) to Toller Porcorum and continue on to a T-junction. Turn right here – the car park located on the left hand side after

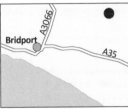

about half a mile (before the railway bridge).

Though a spring/summer visit is the best time for birds, winter visit may produce a Woodcock sighting – usually flushed from the woodland floor – and Redwings, Fieldfares, Siskins and Redpolls will be around.

Nightjar has been recorded in the summer and in the autumn Yellow Wagtails sometimes drop in among the cattle if they are grazing on the meadows. The cattle

were introduced in 1990 to allow grazing of the meadows to increase species diversity and a number of ponds were dug to provide water for them. These ponds are now good habitats in their own right, holding newts and dragonflies.

Marsh fritillary can be found on the damp meadows, while along the woodland rides look out for wood white and silver-washed fritillary butterflies.

151

Key points

- A designated Marine Nature Reserve.
- Toll road to the car park.
- Refreshments in Kimmeridge.
- Visitor centre open all year (check winter hours): disabled access.
- Toilets, with disabled access.
- Cliff path steep in places – no access for wheelchair users.
- Rock pools are slippery.
- Events (check website).
- A fossil hunter's paradise (look on beach only – do not stand under the cliff base as cliffs are not stable).

Contacts

Dorset Wildlife Trust
01305 264 620
Marine Centre
01929 481 044
www.
dorsetwildlifetrust.
org.uk/reserves

THE WATERS around Kimmeridge Bay are designated as a Marine Wildlife Reserve and is certainly worth a visit in summer if you have children. The Bay's visitor centre has interactive displays plus an aquaria and there are plenty of rock pools to dip into and fossils to search for on the beach. The open grassland and scrub above the cliffs can be productive for birds and Peregrines breed along this stretch of coast.

Target birds *All year* – **Raven (75%), Yellowhammer (75%), Peregrine (50%), Grey Partridge (<10%).**

Other possible bird species

All year	Whitethroat	Turnstone
Cormorant		
Shag	*Passage*	*Occasional*
Little Egret	Whimbrel	Divers & grebes
Buzzard	Hirundines	Eider
Sky Lark	Wheatear	Sanderling
Rock Pipit		Hoopoe
Corvids	*Winter*	Wryneck
	Ringed Plover	Corn Bunting
Summer	Dunlin	
Stonechat	Curlew	

Background information and birding tips

THE PURBECK Marine Wildlife Reserve, managed by the Dorset Wildlife Trust, was set up in 1978 because of the nature conservation value of the area and specifically in Kimmeridge Bay because of its suitability for marine education.

It was the first established Voluntary Marine Nature Reserve in the UK but now has legal protection under the Marine Bill.

For those so inclined, there is a chance to follow a snorkelling trail that takes you through the shallow waters of the bay (check the details and get advice from the Marine Centre). The best time to explore the rock pools and ledges along the shoreline is at low water. Look under the exposed seaweeds which are home to shrimps and small fishes and look among the shale pebbles on the beach for

fossils – ammonites are the most common. The Marine Centre is only open at limited times during the winter, so check before planning a visit.

Although the site is obviously known for its underwater life, rather than its birds, it is worth a visit to experience the two, especially if you have children with you. The centre runs a number of events and guided 'rock pool' walks if you want to find out more about the marine environment. The reserve itself actually extends back to the cliff tops and from here there are footpaths across the fields leading back into the village.

In the summer it is worth making a half day visit to enjoy the marine environment but combine it with a circular walk from the car park to the village and back – there is a nice café/farm shop in the village to take a break from your walk.

Kimmeridge is one place where I have seen Grey Partridge over the years – but they are very scarce though. Corn Bunting is another species that has virtually disappeared from Purbeck but again there may be a chance of one here.

More likely during the summer are Skylark, Stonechat, Whitethroat, Linnet and Yellowhammer among the expected common species. Buzzard, Peregrine and Raven are also regularly seen.

At passage times there is a chance of a fall of migrants and hirundines can pass in their hundreds. On the ground, look for Wheatears, Whinchats, Meadow Pipits, flycatchers, wagtails (including Yellow – especially if there are cows around!) There may be something more unusual, as recently Hoopoe and Wryneck have been recorded.

Whimbrels can sometimes be found resting in the nearby fields along with Lapwings. Check the scrub along the top of the cliffs, and anywhere else you walk, between the cliffs and the village for the migrants.

Looking for birds offshore probably won't be too productive but it's worth a scan. Cormorants and Shags should be easily found and there is a chance of passing Gannets, Fulmars, Kittiwakes and auks during rougher weather. In the past Slavonian Grebes and Eiders have been seen on the water and I have observed up to 14 Mediterranean Gulls on the beach and in the bay.

A few birds can be found

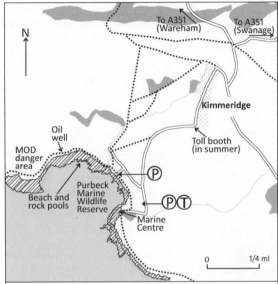

How to get there

(7.5 miles S of Wareham).

From the A351 at Wareham take the bypass towards Corfe Castle. Turn right on the minor road signposted for Grange-Creech (passing the Springfield Hotel). Continue on this road until reaching the top of a steep hill and bear left around the hairpin bend towards Church Knowle. (There is a car park by this hill where it is worth stopping for great views over the Purbeck heathlands). After just over a mile, turn

right to Kimmeridge. Carry on through the village for another mile - passing a toll booth (a parking fee is payable to the Smedmore Estate) – until reaching the car park.

through the autumn and winter as waders come in to the beach to feed on insects washed up in the seaweed. These may include Turnstones, Ringed Plovers,

Dunlin and Curlews and there is a chance of Sanderlings as well. Scan offshore for the chance of wintering divers and grebes.

Other nearby sites

Coombe Heath & Lulworth Lake, Corfe Common, Creech, Stoborough & Grange Heath, Worth Matravers coastal walks.

153

Key points

- Allow an hour for Buddleia Loop Trail.
- Allow two hours to include the North Hide Trail.
- Over 260 species recorded here/Lodmoor.
- Expect 40-60 species depending on time of year .
- Pay-and-display parking in Swannery car park (W&PBC).
- Access available at all times except path to north hide (open 8.30-4.30).

THE RSPB leaflet describes Radipole as 'an oasis in the heart of Weymouth' and it is all true. Despite being surrounded by busy roads, a retail park, housing and a large busy car park, this is undoubtedly one of the best birding sites in the county and, I would say, probably the top urban birding site in the UK. This is Dorset's best place to see Bearded Tit and Water Rail, while Bittern is a regular winter visitor and the site has a record for turning up rarities too.

Target birds

All year – Cetti's Warbler (95% hear, 75% see), Little Egret (75%), Marsh Harrier (50% - more in summer if breeding), Bearded Tit (50%). *Summer* – Reed Warbler (95% hear, 75% see), Sedge Warbler (95% hear, 75% see), Hobby (30%). *Winter* – Bittern (50%), Water Rail (50% see), unusual gulls, including Mediterranean Gull (75%).

Other possible bird species

All year	*Summer*	Green Sandpiper
Mute Swan	Common Tern	Yellow Wagtail
Cormorant	Hirundines	
Grey Heron	Summer warblers	*Occasional*
Little Grebe		Scaup
Great Crested Grebe	*Winter*	Ruddy Duck
Buzzard	Pochard	Osprey
Peregrine	Lapwing	Merlin
Water Rail	Snipe	Jack Snipe
Regular gull species	Black-tailed Godwit	Black Tern
Kingfisher	Common Gull	Sandwich Tern
Stonechat	Winter thrushes	Red-rumped Swallow
Bullfinch	Chiffchaff	Grasshopper Warbler
Reed Bunting		Firecrest
	Passage	
	Common Sandpiper	

Background information and birding tips

ON MY FIRST foray into Dorset back in the mid 1980s I picked up Ring-billed Gull and Wilson's Phalarope on the same day at Radipole and even now the tradition of the reserve turning up rarities continues.

Radipole Lake has been managed by the RSPB since 1976 but its importance for birds was first recognised in 1929 when it was declared a bird sanctuary. The site is designated a SSSI and is part of the former estuary of the River Wey. When sluices were installed on Westham Bridge in the 1920s the lake was formed, and was soon colonised by reeds. Scrub and wet grassland are also important habitats on the site.

Your starting point should be the visitor centre in the north-west corner of the council-owned Swannery car park. It is worth going in to check the sightings board/diary to see what is about ... it also makes a good hide (I have often seen Bearded Tit from here).

Contacts

RSPB Weymouth Visitor Centre 01305 778 313
www.rspb.org.uk/reserves

One trail of about a mile takes you around the 'Buddleia Loop', where there is a viewing shelter, while a second goes out to the North Hide (1,200m from the centre). The stone paths have a good walking surface but can flood in the winter or during periods of high rainfall.

Part of the lake can also be viewed from along Radipole Park Drive – turn left out of the car park and walk along the pavement to scan the lake.

Spring has arrived when the first Reed and Sedge Warblers are heard, though Sand Martins are usually the first migrants to turn up in mid/late-March, quickly followed by Swallows and House Martins. I have seen Red-rumped Swallow here on a couple of occasions, so check the hirundines carefully.

Grasshopper Warbler is virtually an annual visitor and can usually be heard for a short time in the spring when an early morning search is best.

Reed Bunting, Bearded Tit and Cetti's Warbler are resident, the latter common along the scrub-lined paths – their burst of song is unmistakable at any time of the year. Bearded Tits become easier to see in the autumn when family groups roam the reedbeds but, at any time of the year listen for their distinctive pinging call.

I have probably actually seen more Water Rails here than anywhere else in Dorset. They are usually heard squealing from the reeds but in the winter, particularly during cold spells, check out the edges of the water/reeds as they will often come out in to the open – these edges are also good for Snipe.

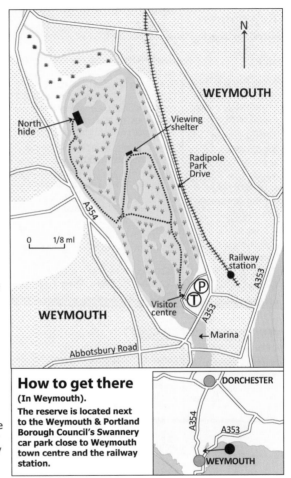

How to get there
(In Weymouth).

The reserve is located next to the Weymouth & Portland Borough Council's Swannery car park close to Weymouth town centre and the railway station.

Bitterns have wintered for many years and may be picked up in flight or seen feeding along the fringes of the reedbeds, particularly from the North Hide.

Little Egrets used to regularly roost near North Hide – often up to 60 birds – but the roost has become more erratic recently. You should certainly see some egrets on a visit but the numbers are now hard to predict.

Radipole isn't as suitable as Lodmoor (site 31) for waders because water levels usually remain quite high and there are few areas of

155

Key points

- Toilets nearby (Swannery car park).

- Visitor centre open 9am-5pm (summer), 9am-4pm (winter).

- Books, bird food, optics & other RSPB goods on sale. Hot/cold drinks & snacks available.

- Easy to reach by public transport.

- Whole site is wheelchair accessible.

- Trail leaflet available.

- Events organised – check website for details.

exposed mud. They do turn up in small numbers, mainly in the area in front of the visitor centre, and more so in the autumn as water levels are lowered to allow access for reed cutting. Lapwing, Dunlin, Black-tailed Godwit and Common Sandpiper are regular but occasionally something more unusual, such as a Curlew Sandpiper or Knot, may drop in.

Great Crested and Little Grebes breed, together with a few pairs of duck which are more in evidence in the winter, especially during periods of cold weather when numbers may increase substantially.

There are usually good counts, which can be into the hundreds, of Mallard, Gadwall, Teal, Tufted Duck and Pochard and smaller numbers of Shoveler, Shelduck and Wigeon. More unusual species may include Scaup and Ruddy Duck.

Marsh Harrier has been a regular visitor over the years but in 2009 a pair bred, the first breeding record of the species in Dorset since 1962. In 2010 they moved to nearby Lodmoor and in 2011 a male split his time between a female on Radipole and another on Lodmoor.

Other birds of prey are seen regularly with Buzzards, Kestrels and Sparrowhawks frequent, Peregrines less so, while Ospreys come through on passage. In the summer look for Hobbies hawking for dragonflies over the lake.

Radipole has long been a Mecca for gull enthusiasts – it is worth spending time to look for that next rarity – and it is a great place to practise your identification skills by checking out the the various adult/immature plumage stages at close quarters. In the winter birds

will come to the lake (or even loaf about in the car park) before flying out into Weymouth Bay to roost for the night.

There are always gulls around but winter into early spring has the best numbers. Common and Black-headed Gulls are the most numerous but search through them for Mediterranean (regular), Yellow-legged and Little.

Dorset's first Ring-billed Gull was identified here in 1976 and they were fairly regular until the late 1990s. They still turn up but are more irregular, as are sightings of Iceland and Glaucous Gulls. There have been sporadic sightings of Franklin's, Laughing, Bonaparte's and, more recently, Caspian.

There is always a reasonable selection of small birds and among the regular migrants something a little more unusual, such as a Wryneck or Hoopoe, can turn up.

In the winter, Pied Wagtails gather at times in large numbers around the car park/visitor centre before heading into town to roost for the night and Starlings roost in the reedbeds, sometimes in their thousands.

Some great progress has been made recently on the management of the site, after a few years in the doldrums, which should benefit many of the key bird species. Butterflies and dragonflies will add to the interest of a summer visit. Recently, otters have made their way back on to the River Wey and are occasionally sighted on the reserve, as are water voles.

Other nearby sites

Lodmoor, Lorton Meadows & Two-Mile Copse, Portland, Portland Harbour & Ferrybridge, The Fleet, The Nothe & Weymouth Bay.

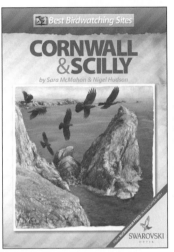
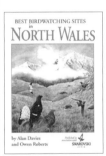 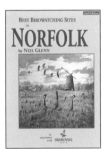  

Key points

- Part owned by National Trust.

- Good coastal walks - three to five miles.

- Spring and autumn passage are key birding periods.

- Coastal Nightingales.

- Information boards.

- Steep slopes.

- Easy parking.

- Wheelchairs users can view from NT car park and can reach shore from lower car park.

- Summer café/ facilities in Ringstead.

Contacts

National Trust 01297 489 481. www. nationaltrust.org.uk

RINGSTEAD BAY, which has superb views looking over towards Weymouth and Portland, attracts a variety of migrants in both spring and autumn – in October 1997 a Siberian Rubythroat turned up (at Osmington Mills) which I managed to miss as I was in Japan ......watching Siberian Rubythroat! It is still a reliable coastal site for Nightingale and good for other scrub birds.

Target birds
Summer – Lesser Whitethroat (90%), Nightingale (75%). *Passage* – spring 'falls' and autumn 'movements'

Other possible bird species

All year	Common woodland birds	Redstart
Cormorant		Whinchat
Shag	*Summer*	Wheatear
Fulmar (most of year)	Redstart	Ring Ouzel
Buzzard	Garden Warbler	Spotted Flycatcher
Kestrel	Willow Warbler	Pied Flycatcher
Skylark	Chiffchaff	
Meadow Pipit		*Occasional*
Stonechat	*Passage*	Great Northern Diver
Cetti's Warbler	Whimbrel	Slavonian Grebe
Bullfinch	Sandwich Tern	Hobby
Yellowhammer	Hirundines	Merlin
	'Alba' wagtails	Firecrest
	Yellow Wagtail	

Background information and birding tips

THOUGH Ringstead Bay is the main birding focus of this site, walks can be extended to the east, out to White Nothe, and westwards to Osmington Mills. I prefer to use the free National Trust car park, where your walk can start after taking in the fantastic scenery. Also look out for Buzzards and Kestrels hanging on the wind. The slopes down towards the sea are quite steep from here.

Alternatively there is a car park close to the beach in Ringstead village (parking charge) where there is a shop, café and toilets (open between Apr-Oct).

A network of footpaths provide a few options as far as routes go. Initially head east from the car park to the track leading down to Holworth House and the South West Coast Path. If you turn left here the path will take you out along the cliff top to White Nothe, and a path leads down to the beach (1.5 miles from car park).

If you turn right here you will soon arrive at Burning Cliff. The path runs along the top but part of the way along you will pass a National Trust sign where you can get down into the cliffs. This stretch is usually the best area for the Nightingales (mid/late April to mid/late June is the best time).

Beyond Burning Cliff is Ringstead village (1.5 miles from car park). About 50m back from the beach is the lower car park with (summer) shop, café and toilets. For a shorter walk, leave the car park and walk to the bend in the road and a footpath to the right that will take

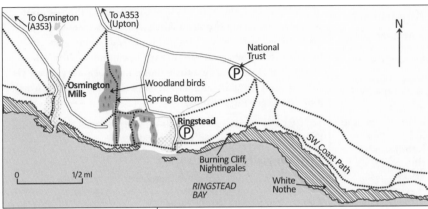

you back up the slope to the top car park (2.5 miles round trip).

For a longer walk continue along the coast path – this will eventually take you in to Osmington Mills (nice pub here). Just after Ringstead there are two strips of woodland running north-south with footpaths through them. If you go up one and back down the other, you'll certainly add a few common woodland species to your day's tally.

It is possible to continue in woodland through Spring Bottom up to the Upton road where you can return to the car park (four miles round trip/ five miles if via Osmington Mills).

Aside from the Nightingales (and great scenery), the main attraction here is the spring and, more particularly, autumn migration. Whitethroats, Lesser Whitethroats and Blackcaps tend to stay but most migrants will pass through.

In the spring, the areas of scrub above and below the cliff tops provide resting places for newly-arrived migrants while the

How to get there

(5.5 miles NE of Weymouth).

From Weymouth take A353 north-eastwards through Preston and Osmington until a right turn is signposted to Upton. Follow this minor road to the main National Trust (viewpoint) car park. There is alternative parking by the coast – after leaving Upton, take the next turning to the right and follow this road to the end.

Public transport: The Poole-Exeter Coastlink bus service passes along the A353 (First: Hampshire & Dorset).

open grassland will attract Wheatears, pipits, 'Alba' wagtails and the occasional Hobby. When there is a good fall of birds, Redstarts, Garden Warblers, Willow Warblers and Chiffchaffs can turn up in good numbers and may be joined by smaller numbers of Yellow Wagtails, Ring Ouzels, Whinchats, Spotted Flycatchers, Pied Flycatchers and Firecrests (though these are more likely to be seen during the autumn). Whimbrels and Sandwich Terns may pass along the shore.

Apart from departing

migrants, the autumn also sees movements of birds: Skylarks, Meadow Pipits, Linnets and hirundines can pass in their hundreds. This is usually the time of year when something a little more unusual may pass through – in recent years these have included Dotterel, Lapland Bunting ......and Tree Sparrow.

Peregrines, Ravens, Stonechats, Bullfinches, Yellowhammers and Cetti's Warblers all breed in the area and Fulmars and Cormorants nest on the cliffs of White Nothe.

159

Key points

- An example of general farmland birdwatching.

- Combine walking with driving.

- Birders should not try tape luring Quail – this is strictly illegal.

FARMLAND may not be as productive as in the past, but areas bordering the River Allen as it flows from springs north of Wimborne St. Giles southwards to where it meets the River Stour are good for a range of common birds with a possibility of something a little more unusual such as Barn Owl ......or even Quail. Along its way is Crichel Lake that is worth a look for wintering wildfowl.

Target birds *Winter* – **Barn Owl (30%).** *All year* – **Yellowhammer (75%), Corn Bunting (50%).**

Other possible bird species

All year		
Mute Swan	Green Woodpecker	Tufted duck
Mallard	Skylark	Lapwing
Red-legged Partridge	Common corvids	Regular gull species
Grey Heron	Common woodland birds	Winter thrushes
Buzzard		
Kestrel	*Summer*	*Occasional*
Moorhen	Migrant warblers	Grey Partridge
Coot		Quail
Stock Dove	*Winter*	Hen Harrier
	Gadwall	Merlin
	Teal	Golden Plover

Background information and birding tips

DURING THE late 1990s the RSPB carried out a breeding bird survey in the north-east and south-west downland farming belt of Dorset to repeat part of a survey carried out a decade before. The aim was, in particular, to reassess Grey Partridge, Lapwing, Tree Sparrow and Corn Bunting numbers.

Unfortunately, the survey highlighted further declines but the experience of working on the project made me appreciate just how many 'non-birded' areas there are in the county. I would encourage readers to break out an OS map and give the River Allen valley/Crichel Lake area a try. You should be rewarded with a nice mixture of common birds and the possibility of something a little more unusual.

Park your the car along the road just outside the village of New Town and walk back to the entrance gate into Crichel Manor – the small side gate takes you along a public footpath. Any ploughed fields in winter/spring will have a mixture of birds picking over the ground – among the Wood Pigeons look for Stock Dove.

A short way along the footpath, where it turns right, you'll see the lake from the corner and through the hedge (the tarred track beyond is private). Wintering birds such as Gadwall, Teal and Tufted Duck, should be present.

The next stretch of the walk passes through woodland, eventually coming to a bridge over the river. You should pick up a good mixture of common woodland birds along here – by spring they will include Blackcaps and Chiffchaffs. The river bank scrub

Circular walk

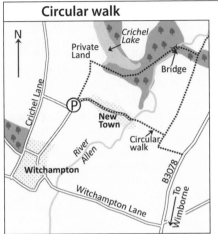

Surrounding villages

How to get there

(Five miles N of Wimborne).

From Wimborne town centre take B3078 northwards towards Cranborne. After just over 3.5 miles turn left into

Witchampton Lane continue on through Witchampton to New Town – park on the roadside between the 'gate' and the end of the road. A circular walk will give views of the river and Crichel Lake.

and patches of reed usually hold Reed Buntings and, in summer, Reed and Sedge Warblers.

Continue to a crossroads and then take the path to the right, heading south. After about half a mile there is another footpath, on the right, crossing the field back to the river/village. Take the road back to where you left the car. The circular route is about 2.5 miles, so allow a good hour to walk it.

Precise locations for farmland birds are hard to suggest. Corn Buntings and Lapwings are quite scattered, Grey Partridges are very scarce and Tree Sparrows are now virtually 'extinct'.

In the winter months these

large tracts of farmland may hold flocks of Lapwings, possible Golden Plovers, thrushes, finches and buntings and there is always a chance of a Hen Harrier, Merlin or even Short-eared Owl.

During summer, Whitethroats and Yellowhammers are common in hedgerows. Around the fields Skylarks are widespread, but Corn Buntings are more localised. With patience, there is a chance of hearing Quail calling from the cereal fields.

The roads west of the B3081, taking in the villages of Witchampton, Long Crichel,

Gussage St Michael, Gussage All Saints and Wimborne St Giles, are worth exploring. Drive along, stop where practical and follow footpaths out into the fields (the local OS map will be useful).

One bird of interest, Barn Owl, is fairly common in the area and winter is often a good time to see them, particularly if they are hunting in the late afternoon. Over the years I have had a number of sightings in the car headlights while driving along the B3078 between Cranborne and Wimborne after dark.

Other nearby sites

Badbury Rings, Garston Wood, Holt Heath, Martin Down.

Key points

- Easily watched from the road. Telescope useful.
- Wheelchair users can view from bridge and minor road.
- Option of a walk along part of the valley (footpath can be very wet).
- A chance of winter swans and grey geese.
- Nearest public toilets in Wareham.

THIS CHARMING chalk river meanders for more than 30 miles through the county from its source north-west of Dorchester eastwards, via Wareham, and out into Poole Harbour. You may find a Grey Wagtail, a Kingfisher or a few common waterfowl at various places but the best birding location is at Holme Bridge. Winter is by far the best time when a selection of duck and a few waders are present. In some years grey geese species, plus Bewick's and Whooper Swans, are a possibility.

Target birds *Winter* – Green Sandpiper (30%), Kingfisher (30%), Bewick's Swan, Whooper Swan, Bean Goose, Pink-footed Goose, White-fronted Goose (all very irregular).

Other possible bird species

Winter	Little Egret	Finches
Wigeon	Lapwing	
Gadwall	Snipe	*Occasional*
Teal	Grey Wagtail	Goosander
Pintail	Stonechat	Water Rail
Shoveler	Winter thrushes	Black-tailed Godwit

Background information and birding tips

THE BEST PART of the site, also known among local birders as East Holme, can be viewed from the bridge and by walking east along the minor road south of the bridge, towards the village. The land in this immediate area is private but you can view from the roads (a telescope is useful).

The valley is prone to flooding from late autumn to early spring and this is usually when this site is at its best. With water lying on the ground, a variety of ducks are attracted, including Pintail and Shoveler. On the river, Goosander, a scarce bird in this part of Dorset, has been seen occasionally.

There is a resident herd of Mute Swans in the valley and it is always worth checking them out as both Bewick's and Whooper Swans have turned up, but they are by no means annual.

Flocks of geese are likely to be the local Canada or Greylag Geese, but other grey geese do appear very irregularly.

Waders from Poole Harbour, usually Black-tailed Godwits, sometimes venture up the valley later in the winter when tides are particularly high in the harbour, though they don't tend to stay around for long. Lapwings and Snipe in the fields are more likely and Green Sandpipers are often seen on the floods.

Little Egrets are regular – but check them carefully. During the 2007/08 influx of Cattle Egrets into Dorset, they were seen here. In recent years, there have been winter sightings of Great Bustards in Dorset (from the introduced population on Salisbury Plain) – at the end of 2008 a bird turned up in the valley!

Water Rails, Kingfishers and Grey Wagtails can be seen by the river

Other nearby sites

Coombe Heath, Higher Hyde Heath, Wareham Forest, Wareham Meadows & Swineham Point.

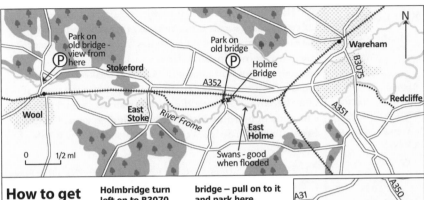

How to get there

(1.5 miles W of Wareham).

Leave Wareham on A352 heading towards Wool. At Holmbridge turn left on to B3070 towards East Holme. Just over the railway line a new bridge crosses the River Frome, next to it is the old bridge – pull on to it and park here.

Public transport: The Poole-Weymouth-Exeeter bus serice runs along A352 between Wareham and Wool.

and the fields and hedgerows in the immediate area usually hold a good mixture of passerines including Redwings and Fieldfares. Look through any mixed flocks of birds that you come across as Lesser Spotted Woodpecker, Firecrest and Chiffchaff have been seen on occasions.

A site visit doesn't usually take very long, but if you want to spend a little more time in the area I would recommend a walk from Holme Bridge, westwards towards Stokeford (a 2.5 mile round trip).

The public footpath does not actually run along the river but it is a pleasant walk with plenty of views over the valley.

Outside of the winter months the bird interest lessens but

it can still be worth calling in. Lesser Spotted Woodpeckers have bred nearby and a Woodchat Shrike turned up in May 2008. From May to late summer look for banded demoiselle and other dragonflies from the bridge.

Further up the valley, just to the north of Wool, it is worth making a quick stop at Wool Bridge to check out the river and surrounding fields. Continue on A352 to Wool. Just before the Texaco garage (and railway crossing), turn right onto the old road bridge (SY 845 871).

Mute Swans, Mallards and Coots are always here, Little Grebes are regular and there is always a chance of a passing Kingfisher or a Grey Wagtail.

Historically, the Frome Valley

has been home to breeding Lapwings and Snipe (all but gone now).

This area, and other parts of the valley, has been the subject to initiatives under the Purbeck Keystone Project (PKP) to improve the water level management of the flood plain.

Working with local farmers, plans have been drawn up and some works started to remove scrub, clean out or reinstate ditches and to install sluices to help manage water levels to benefit breeding and wintering waders and other wildlife.

The lower reaches of the River Frome (from Wareham to Poole Harbour) is covered by Wareham Meadows & Swineham Point (site 63).

163

Key points

- Sherborne Castle & gardens – open to the public April to October (not daily, so check before visiting).

- Entrance fees apply.

- Wheelchair access possible to gardens, though some slopes are steep.

- Season ticket available for all year round access.

- Easy parking.

- Café, toilets and shop facilities on site.

- Events (check website or local tourist office).

Contacts

Sherborne Castle Estates 01935 813 182
www.sherbournecastle.co.uk

SHERBORNE LAKE isn't really a traditional birdwatching site because access is pretty much tied in with the opening times of the two castles on its shores. A large ornamental lake, created by Capability Brown in 1753, is set within the attractive grounds of Sherborne Castle, its lakeside gardens on the southern shore and partially overlooked by the ruins of the Old Sherborne Castle on the northern shore. The lake holds a number of breeding bird species, including Great Crested Grebe, Reed and Sedge Warblers and attracts a few wildfowl in winter.

Target birds *All year* – Great Crested Grebe (95%), Little Egret (30%). *Winter* – Brambling (20%).

Other possible bird species

All year	*Sedge Warbler*	Pochard
Mute Swan	Blackcap	Wigeon
Canada Goose	Chiffchaff	Little Grebe (scarce)
Feral geese (now scarce)	Willow Warbler	Regular gull species
Grey Heron	Goldcrest	Brambling
Cormorant		
Coot (scarce)	*Passage*	*Occasional*
Moorhen	Common Sandpiper	Black Swan
Reed Bunting	Terns	Mandarin
Common passerines		Goosander
	Winter	Peregrine
Summer	Little Grebe	Mediterranean Gull
Hirundines	Teal	Black Tern
Reed Warbler	Tufted Duck	Cetti's Warbler

Background information and birding tips

THIS IS NOT a site you would visit for the birds alone, but with the added interest of the castles and the gardens it is a pleasant day out if you are in the Sherborne area.

The main access to the site, via Sherborne Castle, is open to the public from April 1 to October 31 (but not daily) and a visit between these dates will allow you to walk around the western part of the 50-acre lake.

Old Sherborne Castle (managed by English Heritage) has the same opening dates but visibility of the lake from here is limited. Entrance fees apply to both properties.

The Sherborne Castle estate, which was created by Sir Walter Raleigh in 1594, has all the facilities that tourists expect (cafe, shop and loos), and wheelchair access is possible around the 30 acres of gardens, though some assistance may be needed to negotiate steeper paths to some areas.

The paths are well laid out and a map is available to show where you can walk. You should find a good selection of common passerines

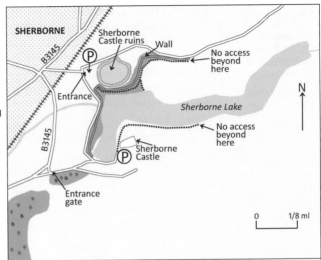

around the grounds and on the times I have visited they have included Nuthatches, Blackcaps, Chiffchaffs, Willow Warblers and Goldcrests, as well as Buzzards overhead.

The lake holds breeding Great Crested Grebes and hirundines regularly hawk over the water – these may include hundreds of Sand Martins.

Reed Warblers, and occasionally Sedge Warblers, can be heard or seen around the fringes of the lake and Cetti's Warbler has been recorded on occasions in the winter, but must still be considered a very scarce species.

In the spring and autumn, Common Sandpipers are fairly regular visitors and occasionally terns pass through – usually they are Common Terns, but occasionally Black, Arctic or Sandwich Terns may put in an appearance.

Access to the lake and gardens outside of the public opening dates/times is possible by purchasing a season ticket, but for the occasional visit this may not be an option (contact the estate office for current information).

The lake holds a few wildfowl species during the winter period, which may include Teal, Tufted Duck and Pochard – but usually

How to get there

(SE outskirts of Sherborne).

On approaching Sherborne, on the A352 from the north or south, turn off on to the B3145 (New Road) to the main entrance to Sherborne Castle.

For Sherborne Old Castle continue on the road to the crossroads turn right and immediately right again.

Public transport: The nearest

train station is Sherborne (a 10 minute walk to Sherborne Castle).

only in very small numbers.

Goosanders were regular visitors in the past but they are now very scarce. On occasions a Mandarin Duck has been seen here. The gulls are worth checking through for the possibility of

a Mediterranean Gull or two, a Kittiwake or Yellow-legged Gull.

Other nearby sites

Blackmoor Vale, Brackett's Coppice, Sutton Bingham Reservoir.

Key points

• **Owned by Dorset Wildlife Trust/Forestry Commission.**

• **Designated SSSI.**

• **Combine Sopley Common with Ramsdown Plantation on a visit.**

• **Terrain makes disabled access difficult.**

• **Typical heathland species.**

• **Some birding across the Avon Valley.**

• **Spectacular views.**

Contacts

Dorset Wildlife Trust
01305 264 620
www.
dorsetwildlifetrust.org.
uk/reserves

BOASTING the usual array of heathland birds, Sopley Common is a small Dorset Wildlife Trust reserve lying close to Bournemouth airport. The adjacent Ramsdown Plantation, growing around a steep hill, will add a few more birds to the list and from the viewpoint at the top you can get a great perspective of the surrounding area. Sopley Common is also an excellent site for dragonflies.

Target birds *All year* – **Dartford Warbler** (80%), **Crossbill** (50%). *Summer* – **Nightjar** (90%), **Hobby** (50%), roding **Woodcock** (50%).

Other possible bird species

All year	Common passerines	Goosander
Little Egret		Black-tailed Godwit
Lapwing	*Summer*	
Snipe	Tree Pipit	*Occasional*
Redshank	Chiffchaff	Bewick's Swan
Meadow Pipit	Willow Warbler	Whooper Swan
Siskin		Grey geese
Redpoll	*Winter*	Barn Owl
	Wigeon	Woodlark

Background information and birding tips

PART OF THE complex of Avon Valley heathlands that run along the Dorset side of the River Avon, Sopley Common is a small (33ha) Dorset Wildlife Trust site but, together with the adjoining 50ha of Ramsdown Plantation (Forestry Commission), it forms part of a larger area of heathland and forest.

Sopley Common and Ramsdown Planatation are separated from Town Common & St Catherines Hill (site 59) by the busy A338. The Common is bisected by the Avon Causeway road that continues eastwards across the Avon Valley and into Hampshire.

Much of the western part of Sopley Common is largely dominated by dry heath and this is where the usual heathland specialities can be found: Nightjars, Dartford Warblers and Stonechats.

This is also one of the few reliable sites where Woodcocks can be found conducting their roding display flights at dusk. Any time between March and June should produce a sighting.

Tree Pipits and, occasionally, Woodlarks are also found here. There is a network of footpaths to follow across the site.

In contrast, the eastern part of the reserve drops down towards the river valley and the ground conditions are much wetter.

These areas of wet heath are far richer botanically and are an interesting contrast to the drier areas. They are excellent for dragonflies and damselflies – so keep an eye out for Hobbies in summer as they can sometimes be seen hawking for them.

Dotted around the site are areas of scrubby woodland which will add to the variety of birds seen.

As Sopley Common is a small site, it is worth continuing a walk into Ramsdown Plantation, a mixed forest spread around a steep hill.

It is a popular place where you can take a circular walk from the car park to the plateau where a viewing platform offers spectacular views in all directions over the surrounding countryside including the Avon Valley.

In the woods there is a good chance of finding Crossbills, Siskins and Redpolls, as well as a selection of common woodland birds.

The River Avon forms the Dorset boundary with Hampshire and this part of the valley can be viewed from the Avon Causeway and from the B3347 between the villages of Avon and Sopley (Note: this village is in Hampshire if you are purist when it comes to keeping county bird lists).

Lapwings, Redshanks and Snipe breed in the valley but numbers have been in decline for a while now and the latter may no longer breed. Barn Owls are found in the area and can at times be seen hunting over the causeway – try towards dusk for the best prospects of success.

In winter, wildfowl, particularly Wigeon, and waders use this part of the valley. Bewick's and Whooper Swans and grey geese (except Greylag) are infrequent but can turn up and it is worth looking for Goosanders on the river.

Black-tailed Godwits can sometimes be found in the valley in their hundreds, with Curlews, Redshanks, Lapwings, Snipe and,

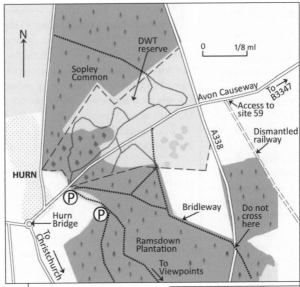

How to get there

(Eight miles S of Ringwood).

Heading north from Bournemouth, or south from Ringwood/A35, take the A338 and then turn off onto B3073 (at Blackwater), taking this road towards Hurn.

At the Hurn Bridge roundabout turn right and head east along the Avon Causeway. After about 200m there is a parking area on the right hand side. Alternatively, take the track just past the parking area into the Forestry Commission car park for Ramsdown Plantation.

Public transport: From Bournemouth take the Hurn Airport bus service (Discover Dorset).

occasionally Ruff, in smaller numbers. Periods of cold weather and flooding usually provide the best conditions to attract the birds in good numbers.

It is possible to access Town Common and St Catherine's Hill (site 59) from the Avon Causeway along the dismantled railway line.

Other nearby sites

Avon Heath Country Park, Coward's Marsh, Christchurch Harbour, Parley Common, Town Common & St Catherine's Hill.

Key points

- **100 species have been recorded on a single winter's day.**

- **Leaflets available at Knoll Beach cafe and shop.**

- **Variety of paths dry & wet.**

- **Wheelchair access limited to car park areas.**

- **Regular National Trust events – see website for details.**

- **Hides at Brand's Bay and Little Sea.**

- **Plenty of parking (some roadside). Pay & display in National Trust car parks (members free).**

THE STUDLAND AREA, which can lay claim to being one of the county's best birding spots as well as being among the most scenically attractive, is one of my top rated sites in Dorset. A variety of habitats includes heathland, forestry, bays and mudflats of Poole Harbour, coastal waters and a freshwater lake. Any time of the year can produce good birds, though the winter months tend to be the best: Studland Bay is one of Dorset's most important sites for Black-necked and Slavonian Grebes, Great Northern Diver is almost guaranteed and Mediterranean Gulls are regular visitors.

Target birds *All year* – Ring-necked Parakeet (75%). *Summer* – Dartford Warbler (90%), Nightjar (90% hear, 75% see), Hobby (30%). *Winter* – Black-necked Grebe (95%), Mediterranean Gull (95%), Great Northern Diver (80%), Slavonian Grebe (50%), Peregrine (50%).

Other possible bird species

All year	Summer warblers	Winter thrushes
Shelduck		
Gadwall	*Winter*	*Passage*
Pochard	Brent Goose	Osprey
Tufted Duck	Wigeon	Whimbrel
Little Grebe	Teal	Hirundines
Cormorant	Pintail	Redstart
Shag	Eider	Whinchat
Little Egret	Common Scoter	Wheatear
Buzzard	Red-breasted Merganser	Ring Ouzel
Kestrel	Great Crested Grebe	Spotted Flycatcher
Oystercatcher	Avocet	Pied Flycatcher
Redshank	Ringed Plover	
Siskin	Grey Plover	*Occasional*
Redpoll	Knot	Red-crested Pochard
Reed Bunting	Sanderling	Velvet Scoter
Common passerines	Black-tailed Godwit	Red-throated Diver
	Bar-tailed Godwit	Black-throated Diver
Summer	Curlew	Red-necked Grebe
Sandwich Tern	Greenshank	Spoonbill
Common Tern	Turnstone	
Cuckoo	Regular gull species	

Background information and birding tips

IT IS POSSIBLE to spend a whole day exploring the Studland area or you can, as I usually do, make specific stops at different points depending on what you want to see or how much time you have.

The area can be easily reached from Poole (via the Sandbanks ferry), the historic village of Corfe Castle or the seaside town of Swanage. A significant part of the Studland peninsula is owned and

Contacts

The National Trust
01929 450 123.www.
nationaltrust.org.uk

managed by the National Trust and has open access. In contrast, Rempstone Forest is a private estate with the forests managed by the Forestry Commission and there are some access restrictions in the area.

Both areas are covered by a good network of public footpaths and bridleways. There is ample car parking off the main Studland road but don't forget your National Trust membership card …… the cost of parking can soon mount up!

A number of eating places along the Studland road will keep you well fuelled, while there is the chance of seeing Ring-necked Parakeets near the café by the Middle Beach car park.

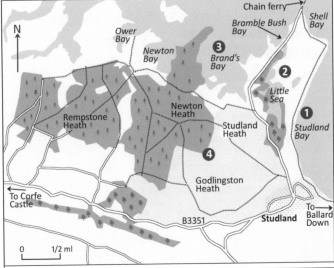

How to get there

(Two miles N of Swanage).

From Wareham take A351 to Corfe Castle. Turn left just before the castle onto B3351 – this is the main road through the peninsula to the Sandbanks-Studland chain ferry.

From Poole-Bournemouth follow the road signs to Sandbanks and cross on the chain ferry (charges apply).

From Swanage head north along the seafront, continue past Ulwell, until the road joins the B3351, turn left or right depending on where you are heading to.

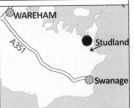

Public transport: The Bournemouth-Sandbanks-Swanage bus service stops along the Studland peninsula (Wilts & Dorset).

Nearest railway station is Wareham.

The southern end of the site adjoins Ballard Down (site 4) which can easily be added to a full day visit. This is a very busy area all year round – especially in the height of the summer when traffic can be very heavy.

Apart from birdwatchers, the area attracts walkers, dog walkers (restrictions on beach use in the summer), horse riders, cyclists and beach goers …… including nudists (there is a designated/marked area for this activity!)

Brand's Bay holds wintering waders and wildfowl and, at passage time, Whinchat, Wheatear, Ring Ouzel and other migrants can come through in good numbers.

Over the next four pages you'll find my guide to the most promising specific Studland sites for birds.....

Other nearby sites

Ballard Down, Brownsea Island (from Sandbanks), Corfe Common, Durlston Country Park.

169

① Studland Bay-Shell Bay and beach car parks (South SZ 038 825, Middle SZ 036 829, Knoll SZ 034 836, Shell Bay SZ 035 863)

IT IS POSSIBLE to walk the length of the beach making frequent stops to scan the bays. This is a good option if you are travelling on foot or by public transport. However, if you are driving your time will be best spent by making the short drives along the peninsula to the four National Trust (NT) car parks.

These provide easy access to view the bays (South, Middle and Knoll beach car parks for Studland Bay and Shell Bay car park for Shell Bay). Each of the car parks has toilet facilities and Knoll Beach has a National Trust shop and café that is open all year. Wintering divers, grebes and sea-duck are the main attractions in the bays.

Middle beach car park gives the best views across Studland Bay due to its height above sea level but the other car parks shouldn't be overlooked. Wintering Black-necked Grebe is virtually guaranteed here and by March many are changing into full summer plumage. This is now one of the most important wintering sites for them in the UK.

It is not unusual to see 10-20 birds on a visit but I have seen up to 50. Other birders have counted up to 80 birds – the best time for peak numbers is late in the afternoon as birds are gathering to roost off Knoll Beach.

Check the Black-necks carefully and you may pick out a Slavonian Grebe, and the occasional Red-necked Grebe may be with the Great Crested Grebes. With Little Grebes on Little Sea, it can be possible to see all five species in a day.

Among the divers, the most likely is Great Northern though both Red-throated and Black-throated are found from time to time. I have seen three species of scoter here: Common Scoter is the most likely, with an occasional Velvet Scoter but Surf Scoter is very unlikely.

Mixed in with the dark-bellied Brent Geese could be an individual pale-bellied or Black

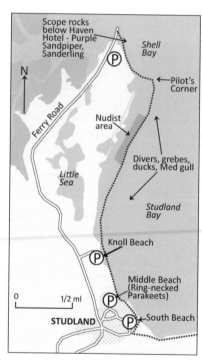

Brant – birds are often feeding close to the shore. Red-breasted Mergansers are common and Eiders turn up occasionally.

An ideal time to visit is a calm, sunny winter's day with good visibility. Birds can be a way out from the shore (but not always), so a telescope is recommended. The beach and bays attract wintering gulls, with Mediterranean Gulls plentiful.

It is possible to walk the length of the beach from the South to Shell Bay car parks. If there isn't too much disturbance, you may pick up Ringed Plovers or Sanderlings on the beach.

Sometimes Purple Sandpipers can be seen

on the rocks by the chain ferry (but they are more likely to be over by the Haven Hotel on the north shore (site 42) – scope across to the hotel or take the chain ferry across to have a closer look).

Seawatching into the bays is not particularly productive. Common and Sandwich Terns, that breed on nearby Brownsea Island (site 9), can be seen feeding along the shore and out in the bays in the spring/summer, while Shags and Cormorants are about all year. If any Sandwich Terns are over-wintering then there is a good chance they will be here.

Other seabirds are sighted infrequently and are usually associated with bad weather, particularly strong easterlies/south-easterlies: Fulmars, Gannets, Kittiwakes, skuas (passage times) and auks are the most likely.

A walk above the cliffs from the Middle Beach car park to the South Beach car park, via Fort Henry (a wartime bunker), may find the Ring-necked Parakeets (a scarce bird in the county) that breed here but are around all year.

The woodland and fields along the way will add a few passerines to a day's tally, particularly thrushes in the winter......this is the only place I have actually had five species of thrush together in one binocular view!

2 Little Sea (SZ 026 843 or SZ 034 836)

ONE IMPORTANT feature on the peninsula is the freshwater lake behind the sand dunes as the birds here will add variety to a day's birdwatching.

Coots, Grey Herons, Mallards, Little Egrets and Little Grebes are about all year, but the winter months bring in a number of duck. Pochard and Tufted Ducks are the most numerous, sometimes reaching three figures, with smaller numbers of Gadwall, Shovelers, Wigeon, Teal and Pintails usually present.

More unusual species have included Ruddy Duck, Red-crested Pochard and Scaup and, in 1992, 2001/02 and 2002/03, Lesser Scaup.

In periods of really cold weather duck numbers can build up substantially but there is always a chance that the water may freeze over and most of the birds will disappear.

You can view the water from a number of places on the adjoining heath, accessible from the road, or alternatively there is a small nature trail, with hides, starting from

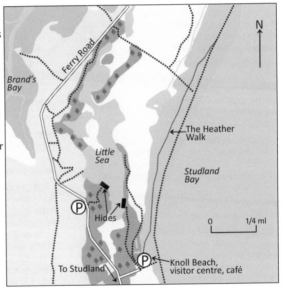

Knoll Beach car park. This is a good area for woodpeckers, tits, Redpolls and other common woodland species. Check out any gulls on the water – apart from the regular gull species, there may be a Mediterranean Gull among them.

❸ Brand's Bay (SZ 025 850) & Bramble Bush Bay (SZ 035 863)

THIS IS AN important wintering area of Poole Harbour that can be watched from a hide at its southern end (the best area to view the waders). There is limited pull-off parking by the road, but alternatively, you can walk along the shore or adjacent heath.

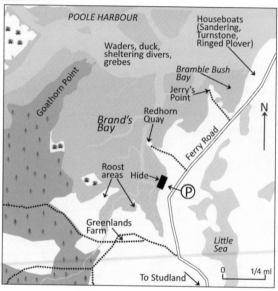

Do not walk along the shore between the hide and Redhorn Quay as you will just flush the birds you were hoping to see!

Between Redhorn Quay and Jerry's Point, the best policy is to view as much as possible from the adjacent heath. Walk along the shore around Bramble Bush Bay, but look out for groups of waders on the shoreline.

The state of the tide has an effect on what you might see. At high water a few birds roost on the southern saltmarsh but most waders will be on Brownsea Island.

Curlews are the exception, as most of them will roost here at high water. There are sometimes good numbers of Redshanks and other waders if the tides are not too high.

Once the tide starts to drop, waders will start arriving or move out of the saltmarsh to feed on the exposed mud.

During low water, especially on the spring tides, the water goes well out into the bay, so feeding birds can be distant but a rising tide will push them back in towards the shore. You can certainly expect to see Curlews, Black-tailed Godwits, Grey Plovers, Oystercatchers, Dunlins and Redshanks in good numbers.

This is a fairly reliable site in the harbour for Knot and there is sometimes a Greenshank or two about (check out the area to the left of the hide).

If there is a lot of disturbance on the beaches then Sanderlings and Ringed Plovers often gather in Bramble Bush Bay (along with Turnstones) – check out the area close to the house boats in the bay.

The bay is always worth checking for divers and grebes. If conditions out to sea are bad, birds often shelter in here. Look for Great Northern and Black-throated Divers, Black-necked, Slavonian and Red-necked Grebes, Eiders (usually females and immature males), Common Scoters, Goldeneyes, Red-breasted Mergansers and perhaps a Long-tailed Duck or Velvet Scoter.

A number of other duck, including Shelducks, Teal, Wigeon and Pintails, plus Brent Geese also use this bay. The strip of heath, between the bay and the road, usually has Dartford Warblers and Stonechats.

④ Studland & Godlingston Heaths & Rempstone Forest

(main access points SY 974 842 & SY993 837 (no vehicles beyond here), SY 018 819, SZ 026 843 or via Studland village/Ferry Road)

STUDLAND'S heathland stretches from the chain ferry southwards to the B3351 and can be accessed at a number of points which lead on to a series of public footpaths, bridleways and tracks.

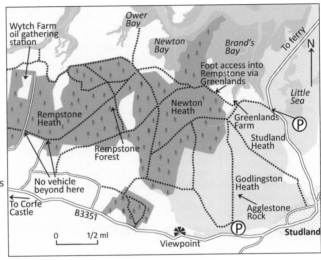

Many of these continue into Rempstone Forest. Birding will be better on the heaths in the spring/summer.

The best point of access is by the Greenlands Farm track (you can also park here for Little Sea) where a path heads south towards the Agglestone Rock, an interesting block of sandstone perched on top of a hill and an obvious landmark to get your bearings.

You should start to pick up the typical heathland species as you wander about – Meadow Pipits, Stonechats, Dartford Warblers and Linnets and, at dusk, Nightjars.

The area by Greenlands Farm is covered by acid grassland rather than heather – a good example how agricultural land has been claimed from the heath in the past. This is a good area in the spring and autumn for passing Wheatears, Whinchats and Ring Ouzels.

Rempstone Forest is part of a large private estate and is a mosaic of forestry plantation and heathland with some access to the harbour shoreline. There are plenty of public footpaths and bridleways over the area but vehicular access is limited (private roads).

Oil operations are active throughout the area,

so the oil company vehicles, including security guards, are regularly seen on the roads. The trails through the area are well marked (including a national cycle network route).

Unless you want to put time aside to explore the wider area, I would recommend the walk from the Greenlands Farm track across to Ower Bay, about 2.5 miles. The walk gives a different perspective of the Poole Harbour and a further chance of finding the breeding heathland specialities – Dartford Warblers, Stonechats, Nightjars and, occasionally, Woodlarks.

The forest can be good for Crossbill, Siskin and Redpoll. In the winter, birds in Ower Bay will be similar to those of Brand's Bay, with a better chance of Avocets and Lapwings here, but try to catch the tide on the fall/rise after high/low waters.

Return to Greenlands Farm the way you went or take one of the other tracks back through the forest.

Key points

- Owned by Wessex Water.

- Access available at all times.

- Expect 25-30 species.

- Wheelchair access and disabled facilities in car park.

- Hide accessible to wheelchairs.

- Main car park/ toilets closed in winter.

O NLY THE southern tip of the reservoir lies within the county – the rest is in Somerset – but it is one of only a handful of sites in this area and unless you are being a purist and only ticking Dorset birds it is worth dropping in. Though more unusual birds are becoming less regular, it is still notable for wintering wildfowl and gulls and passage Osprey. The 'Dorset End' has turned up a number of decent rarities in the past, including Broad-billed Sandpiper, Wilson's Phalarope and Whiskered Tern.

Target birds

All year – **Great Crested Grebe (95%), Grey Wagtail (50%), Kingfisher (40%).** *Passage* – **Osprey (20%), Hobby (20%), Green Sandpiper (20%), Common Tern (20%).**

Other possible bird species

All year	Chiffchaff	Regular gull species
Cormorant		Siskin
Shelduck	*Winter*	Redpoll
Common passerines	Wigeon	
	Teal	*Occasional*
Summer	Pintail	Garganey
Hirundines	Shoveler	Scaup
Reed Warbler	Pochard	Goosander
Whitethroat	Tufted Duck	Peregrine
Blackcap	Goldeneye	Merlin
Willow Warbler	Lapwing	Little Ringed Plover
	Snipe	Black Tern

Background information and birding tips

J UDGING from past records (and before my time), Sutton Bingham Reservoir has probably had its heyday. The 1970s and 1980s turned up some birding gems but since 1990 there has been little of note to set the pulse racing.

During this time waders fared well – with Broad-billed, Buff-breasted, Semi-palmated, (possible) Western and Terek Sandpipers, Long-billed Dowitcher and Wilson's Phalarope putting in appearances. Added to these, White-winged Black Tern, Whiskered Tern and Franklin's Gull all put the reservoir firmly on the local birding map.

Nowadays the birding is lower key but it is still a pleasant site in which to spend a couple of hours. The causeway across the north-western end is best for wintering ducks and gulls: look both sides of the road, especially the smaller area to the west. Among the expected species there may be a chance of a Scaup, Goosander or something else a little more unusual.

The main body of water at this end can be good for a pre-roost gathering of gulls. Take a while to scan through the flock (in the past Glaucous, Iceland, Ring-billed and, more regularly, Mediterranean Gulls have been seen). If you are lucky, you may see the ducks and gulls being buzzed by a Peregrine.

Contacts

Wessex Water (Ranger)
01935 872 389

The best time for waders here is during passage time in the spring and more so in the autumn. More than 35 species have been recorded over the years, including those rarities mentioned above, but no species, probably with the exception of Common and Green Sandpipers and Redshank, could really be called regulars.

For the waders I suggest viewing the reservoir from the southern end in the autumn as the water levels drop and the mud is exposed. A telescope will be useful here.

A car park, toilets and an old Norman church are located just south of the causeway over the reservoir. In the spring and summer this can be a good place to pick up a few common passerines among the trees and bushes. (The car park is closed in the winter).

Mid-way along the reservoir, heading southwards, there is a bird hide (with a facility for wheelchairs). Park in the small lay-by and follow the path to the hide.

Kingfishers sometimes perch just outside of the hide so approach quietly and you should find a selection of ducks (winter) and Great Crested Grebes (all year round) on the open water.

Elsewhere along the road there are areas where you can

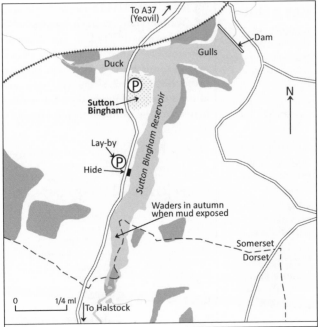

How to get there

(4 miles S of Yeovil)

Sutton Bingham lies S of Yeovil and W of the main Yeovil-to-Dorchester road (A37). From Dorchester take a left turn to Netherton/East Coker (Netherton Lane) just after you cross the Somerset border. Continue on this road (under the railway bridge) to a T-junction, then turn left to pass under a second railway bridge – the reservoir's north end is in front of you.

Just over the causeway there is a car park and toilets. Continue south along the road, stopping where practical.

pull in to view the reservoir but watch out for passing vehicles.

Osprey on passage is still the best bird I have seen here but making a visit at any time of the year should produce a nice selection of species with a chance of something a little more unusual.

Other nearby sites

Brackett's Coppice, Cattistock Churchyard & Maiden Newton, Kingcombe Meadows, Powerstock Common.

175

THOUGH THIS Dorset Wildlife Trust site holds Dartford Warblers and excellent numbers of Nightjars, the flood meadows alongside Tadnoll Brook are becoming increasingly important for birds. A project to re-wet the meadows is already paying dividends with Lapwings and Curlews returning to breed. Both species, along with Snipe and Green Sandpipers, also use the meadows in the winter. The site should only get better over the coming years. A hide now overlooks the wetland area.

Target birds
All year – Dartford Warbler (80%), Yellowhammer (80%). *Summer* – Nightjar (90% hear, 75% see), Tree Pipit (80%).

Other possible bird species

All year	*Summer*	Snipe
Mallard	Cuckoo	
Buzzard	Green Woodpecker	*Occasional*
Meadow Pipit	Chiffchaff	Peregrine
Stonechat	Willow Warbler	Hobby
Linnet		Jack Snipe
Reed Bunting	*Winter*	Green Sandpiper
Common scrub birds	Lapwing	Woodlark

Background information and birding tips

MEASURING 155ha, the largest piece of heathland in the west of the county is often overlooked by birders who choose the Purbeck heaths close to the coast. However if you are travelling between Weymouth and Wareham you will pass right by Tadnoll and Winfrith and it is worth calling in.

The site is generally very open and has some stunning views, albeit against a backdrop of the decommissioned Winfrith nuclear power station. From the eastern (Winfrith) side of the site, the heath drops away to flood meadows beside the Tadnoll Brook before rising again on the western (Tadnoll) side.

There are two main parking areas – one on the Tadnoll side and one on the Winfrith side (with other parking spots further along this road). I would recommend parking on the Winfrith side and following the David Limb Trail.

This will take you across open heath to the top end of the meadows, over the brook and on to the heath and parking area on the Tadnoll side.

From here you can retrace your steps over the brook and then either explore the heath at the northern end of the Winfrith side or continue on your original route back to the car.

Alternatively you can walk back along the minor road from the Tadnoll parking area to the Winfrith parking area.

With the new wetland work already completed, a dog-friendly walk has been created within one of the drier fields so dogs can be run off a lead and owners are encouraged to use this new route. There is a hide overlooking the wetland area.

The suite of heathland birds are here. Both Nightjars and Dartford Warblers are found in good numbers but Woodlarks are irregular. Green Woodpeckers, Tree Pipits, Stonechats, Linnets and Yellowhammers also breed. Hobbies come through occasionally, as do Peregrines, while Buzzard is a resident species in the area.

The wetland area is starting to attract more waders in the winter – look out for Lapwings, Snipe (and possibly Jack Snipe), Curlews and Green Sandpipers.

After construction work in 2008 on the wetland features, including scrapes and sluices to hold up the water levels, Lapwings and Curlews bred again for the first time after an absence of eight and 20 years respectively. Snipe and Redshanks are the other target breeding species.

Ducks here are usually Mallards but a Mandarin turned up on one occasion in the Brook.

Though the site is largely open, there are a few patches of scrub and trees dotted around the heath, with areas of mainly birch woodland/scrub around the edge of the meadows. These are worth checking out for a mixture of other birds to bump up your list.

Reed Buntings and Ravens are regular and you'll see a mixture of common scrub birds such as Chiffchaffs and Willow Warblers in the summer. In the spring, but mainly in the autumn, a few migrants will be moving through

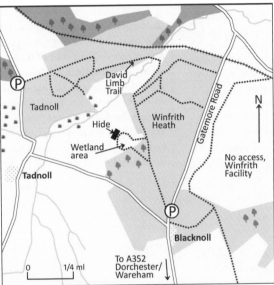

How to get there
(Seven miles W of Wareham).

Approach off A352 from either the Weymouth/ Dorchester or the Wareham/ Wool directions. For Tadnoll, take the first left turn to the east of Owermoigne.

After passing Tadnoll Mill Farm (on left) continue on for another 500m and park on the left hand side of the road. The Tadnoll reserve is on the right hand side (opposite a derelict barn).

For Winfrith, turn onto the road opposite the Red Lion pub (on corner of turning to

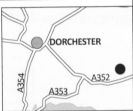

Winfrith Newburgh). There is parking just after a left hand turn (which will also take you to the Tadnoll parking area).

Public transport: The Poole-Weymouth-Exeter bus services run along the A352 and pass the site (First Hampshire & Dorset).

the area with Wheatears, Whinchats, Redstarst and Whitethroats the most likely. Cuckoos are usually heard in April and may stay to breed.

Other nearby sites
Bere Regis, Tincleton & Waddock Cross Cress Beds, Coombe Heath, Ringstead Bay, River Frome - Holme Bridge.

177

Key points

- **Highly designated: SSSI, SAC, SPA, Ramsar.**

- **Expect 40-50 species depending on time of year.**

- **Choose a single ten mile walk or a number of shorter options.**

- **Leaflets available at Chesil Beach centre (Ferrybridge).**

- **Disabled access difficult.**

Contacts

Abbotsbury Swannery
01305 871 858
www.abbotsbury-tourism.co.uk

ENCLOSED by the shingle of Chesil Beach, The Fleet is the largest tidal lagoon in the UK and for the energetic, a walk from one end to the other, especially on a nice sunny winter's day, is an excellent way of finding the birds that the site has to offer. With less time and energy though, there are a number of sections that can be reached independently. Wintering wildfowl are the main attraction to birders. The large flock of dark-bellied Brent Geese usually holds a few pale-bellied birds and a Black Brant or two. Ducks of interest include Scaup, Long-tailed Duck and occasionally Smew, and Dorset's first Bufflehead spent time here in 2010.

Target birds

All year – Mediterranean Gull (80%), Peregrine (50%). *Winter* – Pale-bellied and Black Brant races of Brent Goose (50%), Scaup (50%), Short-eared Owl (<10%), Black Redstart (10%). *Passage* – migrants.

Other possible bird species

All year
Mute Swan
Shelduck
Mallard
Great Crested Grebe
Cormorant
Little Egret
Grey Heron
Sparrowhawk
Buzzard
Kestrel
Coot
Moorhen
Oystercatcher
Ringed Plover
Redshank
Regular gull species (exc. Common)
Skylark
Meadow Pipit
Stonechat
Raven
Other corvids
Yellowhammer
Reed Bunting
Common scrub birds

Summer
Little Tern
Sandwich Tern
Common Tern

Hirundines
Summer warblers

Winter
Brent Goose
Wigeon
Gadwall
Teal
Pintail
Shoveler
Pochard
Tufted Duck
Goldeneye
Red-breasted Merganser
Grey Plover
Lapwing
Knot
Dunlin
Snipe
Black-tailed Godwit
Bar-tailed Godwit
Common Gull
Winter thrushes

Passage
Marsh Harrier
Hen Harrier
Osprey
Merlin
Hobby
Little Ringed Plover
Little Stint

Curlew Sandpiper
Common Sandpiper
Green Sandpiper
Offshore seabirds
Yellow Wagtail
Whinchat
Wheatear
Pied Flycatcher
Spotted Flycatcher

Occasional
Whooper Swan
White-fronted Goose
Barnacle Goose
Long-tailed Duck
Smew
Goosander
Ruddy Duck
Black-necked Grebe
Spoonbill
Avocet
Sanderling
Jack Snipe
Wood Sandpiper
Little Gull
Firecrest
Bearded Tit

How to get there

(Immediately W of Weymouth).

Directions to all of the locations are from minor roads off the B3156 and B3157. These roads run along the length of The Fleet, and beyond, from the A354 roundabout at Wyke Regis (Weymouth/ Portland) to the A35 at Bridport.

Individual sections from south to north:

FERRYBRIDGE: See site 44 for full site details and directions.

BRIDGING CAMP: From the Wyke Regis roundabout take B3156 to the next T-junction and turn left. After 75m, where the main road veers to the right, continue straight on into Camp Road.

Follow the road for just over half a mile to the end and park up on the side of the road. Walk from here to Littlesea/ Tidmoor.

EAST FLEET: From B3157, just before leaving Chickerell, turn left at the small roundabout to East Fleet. Just after East Fleet, the road bends to the right – either park carefully on the roadside or drive to a small car park by the church (please make a contribution).

Walk back down the road to the bend and follow and the footpath past the houses out to the shore.

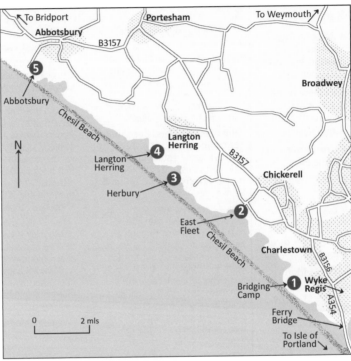

HERBURY: Continue from East Fleet towards Moonfleet Manor (hotel). On the last bend before reaching the hotel pull off the road and park – follow the footpath down to shore.

LANGTON HERRING: From B3157, turn off to Langton Herring. Drive through the village and past Lower Farm, where the road bends to the right. Just after the bend park carefully on the side of the road and walk back towards the village, before taking the footpath to the right just before the farm.

ABBOTSBURY SWANNERY AND ABBOTSBURY BEACH: Take the minor road in the centre of Abbotsbury to the Swannery car park (signposted). For the beach leave the village

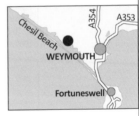

heading west and turn left into Cloverlawns, past the Tropical Gardens (signposted) and down to the beach car park on the left.

Public transport: The Poole-Exeter Coastlink bus service runs along the B3157 via Weymouth. Nearest railway station is Weymouth.

179

Key points

- Abbotsbury Swannery only open in summer. Entrance fee.

- Refreshments & toilets (inc disabled) at Abbotsbury.

- Children's activities.

- Information & leaflet.

- Disabled access.

- Swan feeding sessions.

- Two hides (access by request) – not accessible to wheelchairs.

Background information and birding tips

THE FLEET stretches for eight miles from Ferrybridge to Abbotsbury and it is possible to walk its length along the South West Coast Path. It covers about 480ha, ranges from between 75m to 900m in width and is no more than a few metres in depth.

The Fleet and Chesil Beach has been in the continued ownership of the Ilchester Estate for more than 400 years and is protected by, among others, SSSI, SPA and Ramsar designations.

Conditions at the southern end are tidal, with the main inflow of seawater coming through a narrow channel linking Ferrybridge to Portland Harbour, but further north the conditions are less tidal and saline. Though seawater percolates through the shingle along its length, the water gradually becomes brackish and then, at Abbotsbury, virtually fresh.

The southern part of the site is covered under Portland Harbour & Ferrybridge (site 44) but many of the birds seen at Ferrybridge use other parts of The Fleet. It is possible to walk its length, from Ferrybridge to Abbotsbury, along a section of the way-marked South West Coast Path. The path follows the landward shore but makes detours away from the water in places and if you were to cover the entire length it would come to around ten miles.

A walk from south to north is the best direction to take in the winter so you can keep the low sun behind you for as much as possible. Walking the length of The Fleet is a great way to get an appreciation of the site in a single visit but if you are short of time you can just visit smaller sections.

Access along the shingle on the Chesil Beach side of The Fleet is very limited between Ferrybridge and Abbotsbury. So as not to disturb breeding birds there is no access at all from May to August. Access is limited to the seaward side (below the bank) for the remainder of the year so that birds on The Fleet are not disturbed. The sea can be viewed from the beach at Ferrybridge and Abbotsbury though.

Most of the surrounding countryside is open farmland, pasture and arable, with areas of scrub dotted around. The most varied habitat lies within Abbotsbury Swannery where there is a sizable reedbed, a wet meadow and woodland.

Wintering waders and, particularly, wildfowl on The Fleet itself are the main interest of the area. Due to the distances at which the birds are viewed, a telescope is recommended.

Wigeon is the most numerous duck species (nearly 5,000 birds) but there are also good numbers of Mallard, Teal, Pochard and Tufted Duck (hundreds), and smaller numbers of Gadwall, Pintail and Shoveler. Numbers of all species can increase in periods of cold weather and there is a better chance of something more unusual, such as Smew.

Wader numbers are not particularly high but most of the common species turn up on passage, or in the winter, including Oystercatcher, Grey Plover, Bar- and Black-tailed Godwits and Knot. Little Ringed Plovers, Little Stints,

Curlew Sandpipers and Wood Sandpipers are less common but are usually seen annually on passage. Coot can reach numbers into the thousands.

Away from the water you will pick up a good selection of common birds throughout the year. Raven is frequently seen and birds of prey may include Osprey, Marsh Harrier, Hen Harrier, Hobby and Merlin, usually passing through.

Sparrowhawks, Buzzards, Peregrines and Kestrels are regular throughout the year.

Look out for migrants during the spring and autumn. As well as the expected hirundines, Yellow Wagtails, Whinchats, Wheatears, summer warblers and flycatchers, there is always the chance of something rarer. In 2009, Marsh, Radde's and Yellow-browed Warblers were all found at the Swannery.

❶ Bridging Camp (SY 653 773) - Camp Road to Littlesea & Tidmoor

THE NARROWEST point on The Fleet runs below the Bridging Camp and can be viewed from the end of Camp Road. The camp, used for training military personnel, is a regular wintering spot for Black Redstart - but as there is no access into the camp, you'll need to check the buildings from along the footpath.

This section starts from the road just before the camp entrance. Follow the path along the boundary fence to the end, turn left and walk down to the shore.

Scan along the opposite shore, including the small headland – I have often seen a gathering of Little Egrets and Mediterranean Gulls here – and across the water for ducks, particularly Goldeneyes and Red-breasted Mergansers, plus Brent Geese.

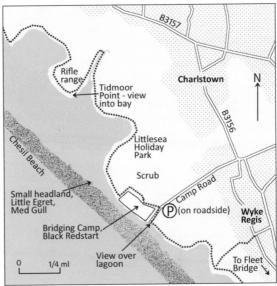

Follow the edge of the field, walking away from the camp, checking the scrub on the left as you go, until you reach a gate. Go through the gate into the scrub – after 50m you are back out in the open overlooking the Littlesea Holiday Camp.

Continue walking past the holiday camp along the shore to Tidmoor, where there is an active rifle range. If the red warning flag is not flying, I usually continue around the Point until I can see into the next bay ......but do not enter the area if it is flying!

This part of The Fleet is best watched a couple of hours before high tide when mud is exposed and waders, including Oystercatchers, Dunlin, Ringed Plovers and Curlews, are moving in with the tide. From Tidmoor retrace your steps to the car, having another look at the scrub and water on the way – the round trip is about 2.5 miles.

The scrub holds a selection of common birds and is a good place for an early Chiffchaff in the spring. Check out the open areas and fences for Stonechats and passing Wheatears. A wintering Short-eared Owl is as likely in this area as anywhere in Dorset.

❷ East Fleet (SY 635 801) - Butterstreet Cove to Chickerell Hive Point

ON REACHING the shore from East Fleet (250m from the road) you are looking out into Butterstreet Cove, the widest part of The Fleet.

Aside from Ferrybridge, this is the best area to find large numbers of Brent Geese and, as it is still tidal, there are usually plenty of waders about – again try to catch a rising tide for the latter.

The geese can be distant but careful searching through them may reveal pale-bellied birds or a Black Brant among the dark-bellied Brents or even, as in 2006, a Red-breasted Goose.

A good number of ducks are also found here, especially Wigeon.

Walk south along the footpath around Butterstreet Cove to Chickerell Hive Point and view into the next bay. From here you can either return along the shore (a round trip of 2.5 miles) or follow the track from the landing stage inland.

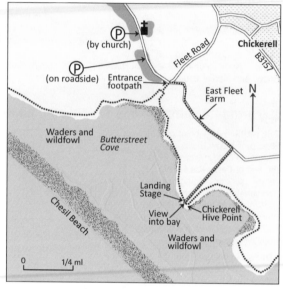

At the junction turn left and walk along the lane, past East Fleet Farm, to the road at East Fleet. This is a 2.75 mile circuit.

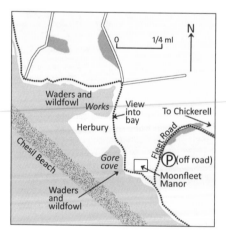

❸ Herbury (SY 619 807)

FROM the parking area just before the Moonfleet Manor (hotel), follow the footpath down to the shore and turn right. Walk around the first bay, Gore Cove, and continue along the path which cuts across the headland to the next bay – the Works. This is another good spot to scan for waders. Little Stints, Sanderlings, Curlew Sandpipers, Knot and Jack Snipe have all been found among the commoner species.

Listen out for Cetti's Warbler in areas of scrub, but don't expect to see one of these skulkers very easily. Mediterranean Gulls are possible over the water. Retrace your steps to the car (a round trip of just over a mile).

4 Langton Herring (SY 610 828)

FROM THE road by Lower Farm, walk for 250m until you reach a gate on your left. Go through the gate and walk diagonally across to the right towards an area of scrub. Check out this habitat for small birds – Bullfinches are often here.

Walk through the scrub and continue along the field (with a row of scrub on your right) until you reach the shore (just over half a mile from the gate).

Water levels in this area are becoming much less influenced by the tidal state. A few waders tuck themselves into Rodden Hive Bay, so look to the right when you reach the shore – I saw a Long-billed Dowitcher here in 2008.

Carry on walking south along the shore to Langton Hive Point and then just beyond so you can look into the Works. Scan over the water for wildfowl – Dorset's first Bufflehead spent time here in March 2010.

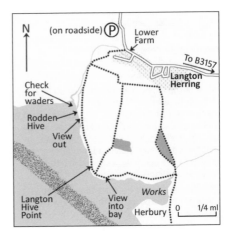

To get back to the road, either retrace your steps or take the option of an inland path – both routes are about 2.5 miles.

5 Abbotsbury Swannery (SY 577 847) & Abbotsbury Beach (SY 550 846)

A MONASTRY was founded at Abbotsbury in the 11th Century and the first reference to the Swannery dates back to 1354. Mute Swans are the obvious attraction here – around 150 pairs breed and there is a wintering flock on The Fleet of 800-1,000 birds.

The Swannery is open from mid-March to late October but a large part of the area can be viewed from the beach and the adjacent road (the only option in the winter).

It is a popular tourist attraction, especially when the swans are hatching in the spring, and so gets very busy.

For the more serious birdwatcher though, there are two outlying hides that are accessible (on

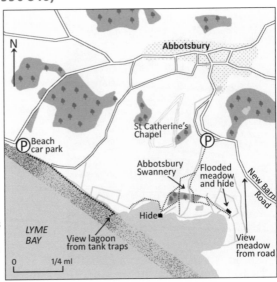

183

request – ask a member of staff) during normal opening times. The paths to them are very muddy, so take boots.

They both pass through areas of reedbed – listen out for Reed and Sedge Warblers which are common and there is the possibility of a Bearded Tit, though they are very scarce.

One of the hides looks out over The Fleet towards an artificial island where Common Terns breed (numbers fluctuate year by year). The other overlooks a flooded meadow which can also be seen from the road (but views are partially obscured). This can be a good area for geese (I have seen Barnacle and White-fronts here) and winter swans.

As The Fleet isn't tidal here there are no large areas of mud exposed, so the meadow can be the best area for waders. Scarce waders may turn up on passage and Lapwings, Snipe and Redshanks are quite common in the winter – look out for Jack Snipe among them. Waders can also be picked up along the shingle shore.

The fresh water at this end of The Fleet, and the relative shelter given by the reedbeds, encourages larger concentrations of wildfowl in the winter. This is the best section for Pochards and Tufted Ducks, and there is a chance of something more unusual, such as Long-tailed Duck or Smew. This is often a good spot for Garganey on passage.

There is no access into the Swannery during winter, so you will need to view the open water from the tank traps on Abbotsbury Beach. From the beach car park walk just over half a mile eastwards to the tank traps (a row of concrete blocks across the landward side of the shingle beach).

It is hard walking on the shingle, so stay close to the base of the beach and approach the traps carefully – if birds are grouped in this corner they can easily be disturbed.

As well as looking into The Fleet from the beach it is worth scanning offshore (into Lyme Bay). In the winter look for divers (especially Red-throated), grebes and Common Scoter and during passage times there is a chance of shearwaters, petrels and skuas.

AS WELL AS the nature reserves which make Weymouth one of the best urban birding areas in the UK, the town's seafront shouldn't be overlooked. In winter divers and grebes can usually be spotted in Weymouth Bay, while at different times Storm Petrels, shearwaters, skuas, unusual gulls and terns may be seen. The Nothe peninsula provides an area overlooking the bay and a chance to pick up passerines in the gardens – a good site to look for wintering Black Redstart.

Target birds
Winter – **Great Northern Diver (75%), Black Redstart (30%), Black-throated Diver (25%), Red-necked Grebe (10%).** *Spring/autumn passage (when conditions right)* – **Seabirds.**

Other possible bird species

All year
Cormorant
Shag
Gannet
Mediterranean Gull
Regular gull species (exc. Common)
Rock Pipit

Summer
Little Tern
Common Tern

Winter
Eider

Common Scoter
Velvet Scoter
Red-throated Diver
Slavonian Grebe
Common Gull
Guillemot
Razorbill
Chiffchaff
Firecrest

Occasional birds offshore
Manx Shearwater
Balearic Shearwater

Storm Petrel
Leach's Petrel
Whimbrel
Grey Phalarope
Pomarine Skua
Arctic Skua
Great Skua
Little Gull
Black Tern
Roseate Tern
Arctic Tern

Background information and birding tips

THE NOTHE is tucked away just to the south of the town centre, on the southern side of the river. Though it sticks out a little into the bay, it is well sheltered from the prevailing winds by Portland and its harbour.

The area is relatively small but it has an excellent bird list of more than 200 species. Unfortunately it probably isn't as well watched now as it used to be.

A website, Birding the Nothe, is still online and even though it hasn't been updated since 2005 it is worth a look (www.naturalist.co.uk/nothe/nothe1.htm).

The Nothe Fort sits on the end of the peninsula. Constructed in the mid 1800s, it was active as a coastal defence structure until 1956. In 1961 it was sold to the local council and is now open as a visitor attraction.

There is no benefit of going into the fort for birds, but it makes an interesting detour (open April to September, plus most Sundays in winter. Admission charges apply). There is disabled access to the Fort.

The public gardens of The Nothe overlook Newton's Cove and are worth checking for any migrants coming through in the spring and autumn.

Key points
- Good for seabirds if the conditions are right.
- Gull roost worth checking.
- Wintering Black Redstart.
- Wheelchair access good on paths.
- Plenty of facilities in Weymouth town centre and along parts of the seafront.

Contacts
Nothe Fort 01305 766 626
www.nothefort.org.uk

In the winter there is a good chance of finding a Black Redstart along the shore, or on the Fort, and Blackcaps, Chiffchaffs or Firecrests in the bushes ...... and don't be surprised if a Yellow-browed Warbler or Pallas's Warbler turns up!

Weymouth Bay stretches more than 2.5 miles from the town centre seafront to Bowleaze with the South West Coast Path following the shore. If you are visiting Lodmoor and Radipole Lake (sites 31 & 47), walking the path is a good alternative to driving.

Wintering ducks, grebes and divers provide the main bird interest in the bay, but if conditions are right, there can be some interesting seabirds around. A telescope is virtually essential as the birds can be some distance from the shore.

Great Northern Diver is the most likely species to be seen, at times reaching double figures, but Black-throated and Red-throated Divers can be expected as well. Great Crested is the most likely grebe to be found, with an occasional Red-necked or Slavonian.

Eider, Common Scoter and the occasional Velvet Scoter are the more interesting duck species to look for. Calm sea conditions are best for spotting these birds but a sunny winter's day can make viewing difficult with the low sun shining off the sea.

Cormorants and Shags are to be seen close to shore all year round, but for other seabirds, a good easterly/south easterly

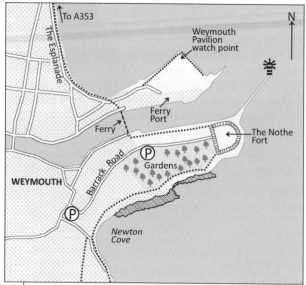

How to get there
(In Weymouth).

There is a car park by The Nothe but the tourist attraction can easily be reached on foot from any of the town's main car parks (or from the railway station).

Parking is also available at the Bowleaze end of the bay – at Preston turn right into Bowleaze Coveway and park on the roadside or in one of the car parks along this road.

Public transport: The distance from the town centre to Bowleaze Cove is about 2.5 miles, with a path all the way along the sea front.

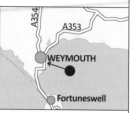

If you don't want to walk both ways, there is a frequent local bus service between Weymouth seafront (by the King's statue) and Bowleaze (First: Hampshire & Dorset).

Nearest railway station is Weymouth.

in the spring and autumn is usually needed to push birds into the bay away from their normal flight paths further to the south past Portland.

In such conditions, you can confidently expect Gannets

and Fulmars but look out for Arctic, Pomarine and Great Skuas, Manx and Balearic Shearwaters and a variety of gulls, terns and auks.

Common Terns breed on Lodmoor and so remain in

the area from April through to the autumn. Sandwich Terns are frequently recorded, with occasional winter records as well, and Little Terns breed nearby on Chesil Beach at Ferrybridge. Many distant terns are likely to be recorded as 'Commics' but a few Arctic Terns are identified annually, along with irregular sightings of Roseate Tern.

On occasions a 'seabird wreck' may occur in westerly/southerly gales in the autumn – Storm and Leach's Petrels, Grey Phalarope and Sabine's Gull are species that have been picked up by keen-eyed observers.

Weymouth Bay has a regular winter gull roost and is best watched from the Pavilion Pier. The roost can be a way out – but a strong offshore wind usually brings the birds closer to shore.

In the late afternoon birds come in from their daytime activities and numbers can build up into the thousands. The flock is mainly composed of Black-headed, Common and Herring Gulls, but patience, and dedication, may be rewarded with something more unusual – Glaucous, Iceland, Ring-billed and Franklin's have been found among them.

Very few waders use the beaches or shoreline in the bay, because much of it is disturbed, even in winter, but Turnstones can usually be found on the rocks below the Nothe.

Other encounters with waders are likely to be with birds flying by – including Oystercatchers, Curlews and, during passage, Whimbrels.

Fulmar is one of the seabird species blown close to land during spring and autumn.

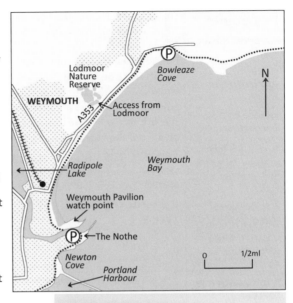

Other nearby sites

Lodmoor, Portland Harbour & Ferrybridge, Radipole Lake, Portland, The Fleet.

Key points

- **A Local Nature Reserve.**
- **Expect 20-25 species in the spring.**
- **Close to Dorchester.**
- **Easy parking.**
- **Allow 60 to 90 minutes for a visit.**
- **Trail (some steep slopes).**
- **Very limited wheelchair access.**
- **Information boards.**
- **Nearest toilets in Dorchester.**

Contacts

Dorset County Council
Rangers Office
01305 251228
www.dorsetforyou.com

TWO OF Thomas Hardy's most famous novels, *Under the Greenwood Tree* and *Far From the Madding Crowd*, were written in the cottage of his birth, located on the northern boundary of Thorncombe Wood, and this must have had an influence on his writing. One of the few broad-leaved woodlands in the Dorchester area that is open to the public, it adjoins the south-west boundary of Puddletown Forest. And its star bird is the elusive Lesser Spotted Woodpecker, which is still seen from time to time.

Target birds
All year – **Marsh Tit (80%), Bullfinch (50%), Yellowhammer (50%), Lesser Spotted Woodpecker (10%).** *Summer* – **Spotted Flycatcher (50%), Nightjar (50%), Wood Warbler (<10%).**

Other possible bird species

All year	Other common woodland birds	*Occasional*
Buzzard		Hobby
Great Spotted Woodpecker	*Summer*	Woodcock
Nuthatch	Blackcap	Redstart
Treecreeper	Chiffchaff	Firecrest
Linnet	Willow Warbler	Siskin
		Redpoll
		Crossbill

Background information and birding tips

THIS Local Nature Reserve holds a good selection of common woodland birds and on occasions something a little more unusual may be found.

The site is only 26ha in size but it adjoins the more extensive Puddletown Forest if you want to take a longer walk (although I have always found Wareham Forest to be far more productive for birds).

Thorncombe is listed as an ancient woodland site and a SNCI with deciduous and mixed woodland, a block of heathland and a pond providing a variety of habitat. Part of the Durnovaria (Dorchester) to Londinium (London) Roman road runs through the middle of the wood – watch out for the ghost of a Roman centurion if here after dark!

The trail from the car park leads off in three directions, with a short wheelchair-accessible section heading out from the eastern corner by the fire gate.

I normally prefer to take the path closest to the information boards. Go past the first path off to the right and the second path off to the left until you reach a crossroads where there are a number of swallet holes (natural sinkholes). The second path takes you to Thomas Hardy's Cottage (signposted), now owned by the National Trust and open to the public during the summer.

By now you should have come across a selection of birds – Great Spotted Woodpeckers are regularly seen (and always watch out for Lesser Spotted) and in spring there will be a good mixture of bird song, possibly including Wood Warbler. Reaching the crossroads turn left, go through the old Victorian iron fence and up the track into the heathland area.

The heathland, known as Black Heath, is only a small remnant of what would have been a much more extensive area in past times. There is usually a pair of Nightjars in this part of the wood – more are found in Puddletown Forest – and Yellowhammers probably breed here as well.

Adder, grass snake and common lizard are found in the heather and on the bracken/birch slopes. The 'Rushy Pond' at the top of the heathland can attract birds down to drink and in the summer holds a good selection of dragonflies.

Behind the pond a footpath leads into Puddletown Forest. After a short distance you'll see Rainbarrow and Duddle Heaths to the right. Extensive views to the south are good for raptor watching and the heath holds Nightjars, Dartford Warblers, Stonechats and Tree Pipits.

Back in the Thorncombe Wood area, carry on the path along the top of the heathland, turning right at the junction where a footpath continues down to Lower Bockhampton.

After passing through the iron fence again turn left and then left again. The loop here passes through an area of managed hazel coppice before leading back to the car park. There are a number of short-cuts round the trail if your time is limited.

Apart from the expected common woodland birds (which could include Spotted Flycatcher

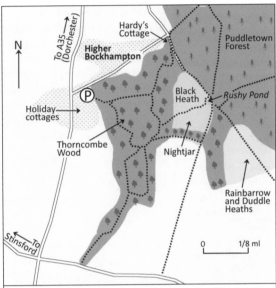

How to get there

(2.5 miles NE of Dorchester).
From the A35(T), to the east of Dorchester, take the minor road off the Stinsford Hill roundabout towards Stinsford/Kingston Maurward.

Stay on this road for just under a mile to the crossroads signposted to Higher Brockhampton, turn left. After half a mile, turn right (just past the hotel) and right again (100 metres) into the car park.

If approaching from the

east, leave the A35(T) just before the bridge where the dual carriageway merges into a single carriageway and follow the signs to High Brockhampton. The turn to the car park by the hotel is half a mile off the A35(T).

and Bullfinch) keep an eye (and ear) open for Siskin, Redpoll and Crossbill anywhere along the route and for Buzzard or Hobby (summer) overhead.

A visit during the winter should produce a similar list of resident birds plus Woodcock, Firecrest and Tawny Owl (often vocal during the day).

Other nearby sites

Bere Regis, Tincleton & Waddock Cross Cress Beds, Lorton Meadows & Two-mile Copse, Maiden Castle.

Key points

- Allow a good two to three hours to do a full circuit.
- Paths not suitable for wheelchairs.
- Shops and facilities nearby.
- Accessible by public transport.
- Great views over the Avon Valley.
- Good for dragonflies and reptiles.

LYING CLOSE to Christchurch, these two adjacent sites are a mix of woodland and heathland with a substantial bird interest including breeding Nightjars, Tree Pipits and Dartford Warblers. The eastern side of St Catherine's Hill provides a good viewpoint to look over Town Common and the Avon Valley and you can pick up passing raptors, which have included Honey Buzzard and Red Kite.

Target birds *All year* – Dartford Warbler (80%). *Summer* – Nightjar (95% hear, 75% see), Tree Pipit (80%), Hobby (20%).

Other possible bird species

All year	Redpoll	Chiffchaff
Sparrowhawk	Crossbill	Willow Warbler
Buzzard	Common passerines	Spotted Flycatcher
Kestrel		Linnet
Meadow Pipit	*Summer*	
Stonechat	Hobby	*Occasional*
Raven	Cuckoo	Snipe
Siskin	Hirundines	Woodcock
	Blackcap	Green Sandpiper

Background information and birding tips

THERE ARE two options here – take the high road or take the low road! To really appreciate the site, I usually take the high road first – walking northwards from the parking area on Marsh Lane along St Catherine's Hill, a 35ha site managed by Christchurch Countryside Service.

After continuing to the northern boundary, I then return southwards through Town Common (140ha, managed by the Amphibian & Reptile Conservation Trust) along the dismantled railway, making detours off into the heath along the way.

The main public footpath runs the length of the hill, much of it passing through the pine woodland which covers a good proportion of the hill. Some pockets of heathland lie to the left of the main path, with side paths down the slopes to a housing estate. The heath

here is worth checking out for Dartford Warblers and Nightjars and you should pick up a mixture of common birds, including Siskins, and maybe Crossbills.

The site has been a conservation battleground in recent years, with tree-felling activities causing a lot of friction with the local community. While the trees on the hill are likely to remain in the foreseeable future, recent clearance work on the eastern slope has opened up some amazing views over Town Common and the Avon Valley below.

The first time I visited after the clearances I was very impressed by the views from the first viewpoint (about 600m from the parking area - along St Catherine's Hill Lane, past the houses and through the gate on to the hill itself).

Continue walking northwards along the edge of the hill for the

Contacts

ARC 01202 391 319
www.arc-trust.org

Christchurch
Countryside Service
01425 272 479

views or through the woodland and heathland pockets (or more likely take in a combination of the two if you have time). St Catherine's Hill is a great vantage point to watch for raptors coming through the Avon Valley.

In May 2005, Red Kite, Honey Buzzard and Marsh Harrier were seen on the same day. Buzzards, though, are more likely, along with Sparrowhawks and Kestrels.

Eventually the footpath reaches the A338. It is possible to cross this very busy road to get to Ramsdown Plantation (site 52) – the footpath is still a right of way across the road – but I would NOT recommend trying it. Instead, continue on the track to the dismantled railway which runs northwards to the Avon Causeway road and southwards back to Marsh Lane.

The habitat here is open heathland, with plenty of boggy areas and ponds. The choice is to either stay on the old railway route or follow obvious tracks through the heath either side of it, gradually wending your way back to Marsh Lane.

To get the best out of your visit, the latter option can be the more interesting. Tree Pipits, Dartford Warblers and Stonechats should be fairly easy to see on the heath and watch out for a Hobby hawking for dragonflies.

The scrub along the old railway route may hold a mixture of common passerines, particularly at the southern end where there is more scrub. In the summer listen out Blackcaps, Chiffchaffs, Willow Warblers and Spotted Flycatchers and in winter look out for flocks of Siskins and Redpolls.

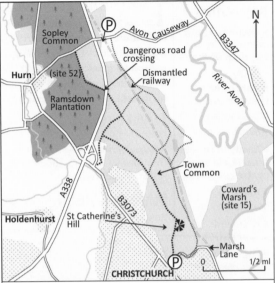

How to get there

(1.5 miles NW of Christchurch).

From A35 in Christchurch take B3073 off the Fountain Roundabout (heading towards Hurn) into Bargates Road which runs into Fairmile Road. After a mile and a quarter, turn right, signposted to Dudmoor Leisure Centre, into Marsh Lane and park here.

An alternative parking area lies to the north. Follow the directions to Sopley Common (site 52), but continue on the Avon Causeway road and 130m after crossing the bridge over the A338 turn right into a parking area at the north end of the dismantled railway line.

Public transport: **The Bournemouth-Christchurch service runs through Fairmile, with a stop just 150m from Marsh Lane (Yellow Buses).**

Nearest railway station is Christchurch, just over one mile from Marsh Lane, along Fairmile Road.

Other birds include Cuckoo (summer), Green Sandpiper (autumn) and Snipe (winter). Woodcock have bred here in the past but I have seen no recent records.

Check out the ponds and wet areas of heath for dragonflies and grass snake and the drier areas for other reptiles.

191

Key points

- Owned/ managed by Borough of Poole (UCP).

- Part of Poole Harbour SSSI.

- Free parking (UCP).

- Easily accessed from Poole town centre.

- Allow 2-3 hours.

- Hide and screens (UCP).

- Leaflet available (UCP).

- Events organised (UCP). See website for details.

- Refreshments/ toilets (UCP).

 Paths suitable for wheelchairs.

- Good numbers of wildfowl and waders.

- Best site for Yellow-legged Gull.

Contacts

Borough of Poole
Leisure Services
01202 261 306
www.
boroughofpoole.com

JUST A STONE'S THROW from Poole railway station, this site is worth a visit at any time of the year but is at its best during the winter when it frequently produces the harbour's highest counts of Teal and Wigeon and consistently turns up wintering Spotted Redshanks, Greenshanks and Common Sandpipers. For the gull watchers, Yellow-legged Gull and Mediterranean Gull are among the regulars.

Target birds
All year – Black-tailed Godwit (90%), Water Rail (75% - heard). *Summer* – Reed Warbler (95%). *Winter* – Spotted Redshank (90%), Kingfisher (90%), Yellow-legged Gull (75%), Greenshank (50%), Common Sandpiper (20%). *Passage* – Osprey (75%), Whimbrel (75%).

Other possible bird species

All year	Great Spotted	Fieldfare
Mute Swan	Woodpecker	
Canada Goose	Green Woodpecker	*Occasional*
Shelduck	Reed Bunting	Great Crested Grebe
Cormorant		Peregrine
Little Egret	*Summer*	Jack Snipe
Buzzard	Common Tern	Whinchat
Sparrowhawk	Sandwich Tern	Wheatear
Moorhen	Blackcap	Garden Warbler
Redshank	Chiffchaff	Lesser Whitethroat
Herring Gull	Willow Warbler	Pied Flycatcher
Black-headed Gull		Bearded Tit
Grey Wagtail	*Winter*	Firecrest
	Little Grebe	
	Redwing	

Background information and birding tips

HOLES BAY is separated from the main area of Poole Harbour by a narrow channel dividing Hamworthy and Poole Town. The site is easily accessed if you don't have transport – Poole's main railway and bus stations are just a few minutes walk from the south-east corner of the bay.

In recent years I have been involved with various surveys in the bay and it is particularly good in the winter for its wildfowl and waders which are often viewed at close quarters.

It is a reliable site to find over-wintering Spotted Redshanks and Greenshanks (they are regularly seen in front of the hide in Upton Country Park or by the small inflow into the bay north of the railway line), and Common Sandpipers (usually found by scanning along the railway embankment).

The edge of the shore sometimes attracts Jack Snipe but you need to examine the area very carefully as they will sit tight and can easily be overlooked.

Land around the bay has been reclaimed in the past and a busy main road runs along its eastern shore, together with a cycle route/footpath which eventually reaches

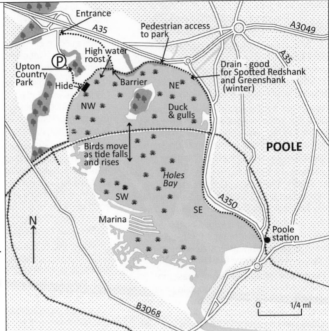

How to get there

(Next to/W of Poole town centre).

Upton Country Park is situated on the south side of the A35/A3049, signposted with brown tourist signs.

The Park is open daily from 9am to dusk, though the car park is usually opened earlier.

Public transport: A town bus service stops at the park.

By foot: **From Poole, cross the road from the railway station (behind platform 2) – you are immediately in the SE corner of Hole's Bay – the path alongside the bay takes you into Upton Country Park.**

Upton Country Park. The bay is conveniently divided into four sections: two north and two south of the main London-Weymouth railway line.

The most productive areas are the NW and NE sections, with the former best viewed from Upton Country Park.

The SE section will be covered if you approach the bay from Poole town centre but, unless you have time to spare, give the SW section a miss (you can easily walk there from the park but Common Sandpiper in winter is the only species you may have a better chance of picking up from this side).

The Harbour's intricate tidal system means that high waters tend to be later (and shorter) than other parts of the Harbour while low water is earlier (and longer).

At high water many birds will be hidden away around the saltmarsh but as the tide falls they will move out into the open.

At low water birds will spread out over the exposed mud or cluster around the water-filled creeks. A rising or falling tide a couple of hours either side of high water is often the best time to be here.

A good option in winter is to walk from the south-

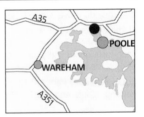

east corner by Poole railway station, starting at low water as the tide is turning, along the cycle route/footpath into Upton Country Park. Alternatively park at Upton Country Park and walk back to at least the railway embankment.

The bay holds good numbers of wildfowl, regularly 500-1,000 each of Teal and

193

Wigeon plus smaller numbers of Pintail, Red-breasted Mergansers and Goldeneyes, and the occasional Pochard and Tufted Duck.

A variety of waders use the bay with Curlews, Black-tailed Godwits, Redshanks, Dunlins and Oystercatchers more in evidence than Avocets (but now a regular visitor), Grey Plovers, Ringed Plovers and Bar-tailed Godwits.

Watch out for Kingfisher anywhere along the route and Yellow-legged Gulls can be picked out among the regular gull species – also look across the road on the top of the roofs (especially the Kerry Foods building) for them.

In the summer the bay is a lot quieter – a few summering Black-tailed Godwits are usually present and both Common and Sandwich Terns may be feeding in the bay in small numbers.

The small pockets of reedbed hold breeding Reed Warblers and listen out for 'pinging' Bearded Tits – although scarce in the harbour they are recorded here from time to time.

During the spring and autumn passage periods Whimbrels come through in small numbers. Ospreys are also likely – there are fewer sightings in the spring but the fish-eating raptors can be regular visitors from mid-July to as late as early November, but bear in mind that they do move around the harbour.

Little Egrets, Grey Herons, Cormorants, Mediterranean Gulls and Water Rails can be seen throughout the year (though the latter is likely to be heard rather than seen).

Upton Country Park has its own facilities – parking, toilets and a café. The site covers about 40ha where, together with the bay, more than 150 species of birds have been recorded. Behind the mudflats and saltmarsh of the park's shoreline is a mixture of gardens and parkland, woodland and a small number of freshwater ponds.

Common woodland species may be seen here all year including Green and Great Spotted Woodpeckers and Nuthatches and in the summer Willow Warblers, Chiffchaffs and Blackcaps breed.

On passage, Wheatears and Whinchats are usually recorded annually and occasional Pied Flycatchers and Nightingales have been seen, while Firecrests are a little more regular. Wintering Fieldfares and Redwings reach good numbers in the fields to the north of the shoreline trail (sometimes Little Egrets and Curlews use these fields as well).

Keep an eye to the sky for Buzzards and Sparrowhawks throughout the year. Peregrines are reasonably regular and can sometimes be seen perching on the high rise buildings to the south of the quay.

The cycle route/footpath along the eastern side of the bay is a hard surface and ideal for wheelchairs to reach the entrance of the park. The paths in the park are firm enough for wheelchairs too.

However, wheelchair users cannot access the park from the Poole side due to a metal kissing gate barrier, but a detour can be made along the cycle path which comes out at the park entrance.

Other nearby sites

Ham Common, Lytchett Bay, Poole Harbour (Poole Quay to Sandbanks), Upton Heath.

THIS URBAN heathland holds good numbers of Nightjars and Dartford Warblers and, more erratically, the odd pair of Woodlarks but sadly it has suffered from a number of major fires. Common migrants, such as Redstarts, Whinchats and Wheatears come through at passage times but the star bird recorded here was a Black-eared Wheatear in 2000.

Target birds *All year* – Dartford Warbler (80%), Raven (50%), Redpoll (50%). *Summer* – Nightjar (90% hear, 75% see), Hobby (75%).

Other possible bird species

All year	Corvids	Passage
Sparrowhawk	Siskin	Hirundines
Buzzard	Linnet	Redstart
Kestrel	Common woodland birds	Whinchat
Green Woodpecker		Wheatear
Great Spotted	*Summer*	
Woodpecker	Hobby	*Occasional*
Meadow Pipit	Chiffchaff	Hen Harrier
Stonechat	Willow Warbler	Woodcock

Background information and birding tips

THIS URBAN heathland site, which covers 200ha, is under a number of ownerships but primarily managed by the Dorset Wildlife Trust. Though one of the larger blocks of heathland remaining in Dorset today, it suffers periodically from arson. This site is a good example of the fragility of these internationally important habitats.

The site is a great example of a heathland mosaic with large areas of dry, humid and wet heath and some scattered boggy pools and ponds.

Management work here is ongoing to make sure that the site remains open and grazing has been introduced in the southern corner.

Upton Heath is bordered on its eastern and northern boundaries mainly by housing and there is a large working landfill site on the north-western boundary. Though there are a number of access points on to the site, there are three that I would recommend using.

This is a good site to visit without a vehicle, as you can reach it easily from Poole town centre by taking a short bus journey or by walking along Holes Bay and through Upton Country Park (site 60).

There are plenty of obvious tracks and paths to explore or, for something more formal, there are three circular routes, varying from 1.4 to 3.3 miles (plus an easy access trail of 570m suitable for pushchairs and wheelchairs) – each route is way-marked with metal symbols.

The southern entrance, off Longmeadow Lane, will take you to a meeting point of the three routes. From the parking area, walk through to the Castleman Trailway. Just off to the right is a

Key points

- **SSSI managed/part owned by Dorset Wildlife Trust.**

- **Allow a good half day to cover all of the way-marked routes.**

- **Information boards and marked routes.**

- **Information leaflet available from Wildlife Trust.**

- **Short route designed for wheelchairs.**

- **Nearest toilets at Upton Country Park.**

- **Excellent for dragonflies.**

Contacts

Dorset Wildlife Trust 01305 264 620. www. dorsetwildlifetrust.org. uk/reserves

DWT (Urban Wildlife Centre) 01202 692 033.

sign board – walk past the board until you reach the raised bank of the dismantled railway. Walk along this to the left for about 170m and you come to the meeting point of the routes.

From here you get a good overview of the site – looking northwards up the slopes or southwards into the grazing area. The shorter Lizard route (1.4 miles) continues along the dismantled railway to a gate leading into the grazing area. The circular route joins up with the Castleman Trailway, taking you back to the Longmeadow Lane parking area.

The Warbler route (1.8 miles) picks its way northwards, across an area of wet heath and up the dry slope towards the Beacon Road entrance before turning off to the eastern boundary then southwards along the Castleman Trailway.

The Dragonfly route (3.3 miles) continues along the dismantled railway to the A35 then turns northwards, circling around the boundary, and joins up with the Warbler route.

Alternatively the Warbler and Dragonfly routes can be easily reached from the Beacon Road entrance (where the Easy Access trail starts/ends).

The main path on to the site from the Springdale

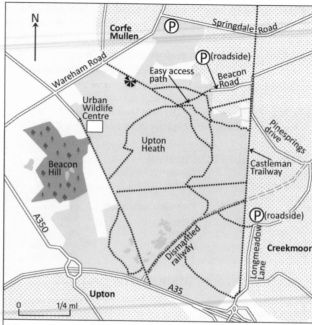

How to get there

(Two miles NW of Poole).

From A35 turn off to Creekmoor and drive along Longmeadow Lane until the junction with Beech Bank Avenue. There is parking at the end of Longmeadow Lane and access to the heath from here.

For the Beacon Road entrance, continue past Longmeadow Lane into Beechbank Avenue – over the first small roundabout to the next roundabout and turn left into Pinesprings Drive. Follow this road for half a mile and turn left into Beacon Road (Take care: the entrance is slightly obscured on the rise of a hill, just beyond where a piece of woodland comes down to the road). Park at the far end - there is a large map at the entrance to the heath (SY 988 951).

Alternatively, from the southern end of the main road running

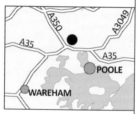

through Corfe Mullen, turn off Wareham Road into Springdale Road, there is a car park 250m on the right (SY 985 958).

Public transport: The Upton-Creekmoor-Poole bus service runs by the Longmeadow Lane end of the site (Wilts & Dorset). The nearest railway station is Poole. Upton Country Park (site 60) can be reached on foot from here, and Upton Heath (Longmeadow Lane) is a further 500m on from the main entrance of the Park.

Road car park heads south for about 500m through a narrow block of heathland to a viewpoint. There are great views from here – overlooking the site and beyond to Poole Harbour and the Purbeck Hills in the distance. Paths continue down from the viewpoint into the main block of heathland.

Whether you chose to wander around yourself or decide to follow a marked route there will be plenty of opportunities to pick up the heathland specialities.

If your time is limited though, I would suggest sticking to the Lizard route. Dartford Warbler, Stonechat and Nightjar are all species found in good numbers and are widespread across the site.

Woodlarks have bred on occasions in the past but can't be considered as regular visitors – but keep an eye out for them, especially in areas of cleared ground. Hobbies and Ravens have bred in recent years and, along with the local Buzzards, are regularly seen.

Other birds that should be picked up include Green Woodpeckers, Meadow Pipits, Chiffchaffs, Willow Warblers and Linnets. During the spring and autumn a few migrants come through, including Wheatears, Whinchats, Redstarts and passing hirundines.

Around the edges of the site, particularly along the woodland of the Castleman Trailway, look out for a variety of common woodland birds including thrushes, Great Spotted Woodpeckers, Treecreepers, Jays and Bullfinches.

The summer months are good for dragonflies and the site is worth a visit in the winter months when Dartford Warblers will still be around and there is also a possibility of picking up a Hen Harrier or Woodcock, the latter often flushed up from the scrubby edges.

Short-eared Owl has occasionally been seen in the winter and Siskin and Redpoll flocks are regularly encountered.

FIRE A CONSTANT THREAT

SINCE completing the draft of this site in June 2011, a huge fire (the largest here since 1976) spread over Upton Heath, destroying a third of it: arson was the likely cause.

The damage caused to breeding birds, reptiles, invertebrates and other wildlife was considerable.

The area affected lies to the north-east of the dismantled railway as far up as the Beacon Road entrance. The Warbler route and the eastern side of the Dragonfly route were wiped out.

The vegetation should recover over a short period of time but it may take up to 20 years or even longer for the full range of species to re-colonise the burnt areas.

I have not changed the original draft as the birds mentioned should still be found, particularly in the area to the south of the dismantled railway. A visit now though will highlight the fragility of these internationally important heathland sites and it will be interesting to see how the site recovers over the coming years.

Other nearby sites

Canford Heath, Ham Common, Hatch Pond, Lytchett Bay, Upton Country Park & Holes Bay.

Key points

- **Multi-purpose working forest (Forestry Commission).**
- **Includes a National Nature Reserve.**
- **Multiple free parking areas.**
- **An extensive network of footpaths, bridleways and forestry rides.**
- **Wheelchair access difficult due to rough ground. Best area is Great Ovens.**
- **Nearest toilets in Wareham.**
- **Good for walking and cycling.**
- **Leaflet & information boards (Morden Bog).**
- **Grazing stock – close all gates.**

Contacts

The Amphibian and Reptile Conservation Trust (Great Ovens)
01202 391 319
www.arc-trust.org

Forestry Commission
023 8028 3141
www.forestry.gov.uk

THE WAREHAM FOREST complex covers around 14-square miles of predominantly coniferous forest and open heathland, all of which is worth exploring for birds. The forest is a reliable site for Woodlarks and Hobbies and, in good years, Crossbills can be very common. Ravens, Peregrines and Redstarts breed and it is one of the few sites in the county where there is still a chance of Lesser Spotted Woodpecker. For many years, it has been the most reliable site for wintering Great Grey Shrike.

Target birds
All year – Dartford Warbler (80%), Raven (75%), Peregrine (50%), Crossbill (20%), Lesser Spotted Woodpecker (<10%). *Summer* – Nightjar (95% hear, 75% see), Tree Pipit (90%), Hobby (80%), Woodlark (80%), Redstart (50%). *Winter* – Great Grey Shrike (50%), Hen Harrier (30%).

Other possible bird species

All year		Passage
Teal	Linnet	Woodcock
Red-legged Partridge	Yellowhammer	Winter thrushes
Sparrowhawk	Common woodland birds	Redpoll
Buzzard	*Summer*	*Passage*
Kestrel	Cuckoo	Osprey
Snipe	Hirundines	Redstart
Kingfisher	Blackcap	Whinchat
Meadow Pipit	Chiffchaff	Wheatear
Grey Wagtail	Willow Warbler	Spotted Flycatcher
Stonechat	*Winter*	Pied Flycatcher
Marsh Tit	Tufted Duck	*Occasional*
Siskin	Little Grebe	Red Kite
	Merlin	Firecrest

Background information and birding tips

BIRDERS who love a good walk will find Wareham Forest a great site – it is just a 15 minutes stroll north-west from the town's railway station and once in the forest the terrain is fairly flat and reasonably dry, though in the winter, or during wet spells, some areas can be a little soggy.

If you have time in the spring/early summer, I would recommend putting a packed lunch in your bag and spending the whole day exploring the area. If your time is more limited though, there are some areas that are particularly good for birds.

Most of the forest is managed by the Forestry Commission with two areas under the management of Natural England and The Amphibian and Reptile Conservation Trust (ARC). Though a high priority is placed on amenity and conservation use, this is a working forest, so restrictions may be placed on access from time to time for operations such as tree felling: please abide by any signs you find.

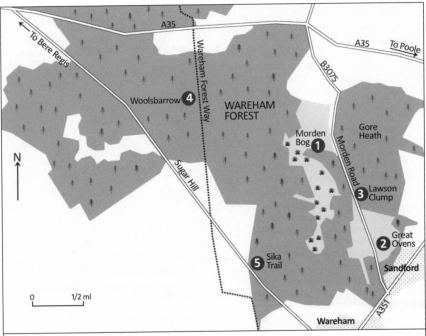

How to get there

(Immediately N of Wareham).

Two minor roads bisect the forest. Leave Wareham on the A351 towards Sandford and once over the railway line turn left towards Bere Regis. This road runs through the forest and there are a number of parking spots along the road.

For the second road, take the A351 to Sandford then turn left onto B3075 towards Morden. Again this road runs through the forest and there are a number of parking spots along the road.

Public transport: The nearest railway station is at Wareham and buses running between Poole and Swanage stop here as well (Wilts & Dorset). The southern end of the forest can be reached easily from here – follow the blue walking signs

from the bus stop/platform two side of the station. The walk is just over half a mile.

Grazing is an important part of heathland management and large areas of the forest are now stocked – please ensure that gates are closed at all times.

The heathland areas hold all six species of the UK's reptiles and the wetter areas and ponds are very good for dragonflies. Sika and roe deer are regularly encountered and the forest is good for bats.

Other nearby sites
Bere Regis, Tincleton & Waddock Cross Cress Beds, Higher Hyde Heath, River Frome - Holme Bridge, Wareham Meadows & Swineham Point.

① Morden Bog National Nature Reserve (SY 929 926)

THIS IS THE MAIN, and most popular, birdwatching area within the forest. It has been a NNR since 1956 and covers 150ha. There is informal off-road parking by Sherford Bridge, on the B3075 Morden road – park on the right hand side of the road and cross carefully (blind bend ...... fast cars!).

The northern edge of the NNR follows the route of the bridleway. The Sherford River, lined with alders, flows just to the north of the bridleway with grassland and mature oak trees in between.

This is the place to look for Lesser Spotted Woodpecker, especially in late winter or early spring when they may be calling. They are by no means guaranteed but just when they seem to have disappeared, they are seen again.

In winter, the alders are popular with Siskin flocks and, not so regularly, with Redpolls. Tawny Owl, Green Woodpecker and Mistle Thrush are resident species while Spotted Flycatcher, and sometimes Pied Flycatcher and Redstart, favour this area in the autumn (late–August and into September). Red-legged Partridge turn up from time to time and Kingfisher and Grey Wagtail may be found on the river.

Continue walking along the bridleway, through the metal gate where the NNR starts (there is a reserve sign here), and along the wooded edge. Walk past the first metal gate (after 200m), then the second one (locked/ under the power lines) and the third gate (after half a mile) and turn left onto the heath here.

You should find a good selection of common woodland birds along this stretch including Jays, Treecreepers, Nuthatches, Marsh Tits and Goldcrests, plus Blackcaps and Chiffchaffs in summer. Firecrests also turn up from time to time.

Once on the heath, the path heads south. After 150m a clump of trees on the right are being thinned out – in the autumn look for birds flitting around in here (I have had some great views of Crossbill). After another 150m

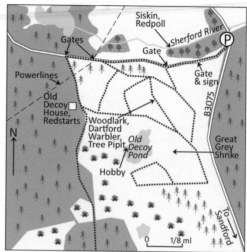

there is a small clearing – the site of the Old Decoy House. This has been a reliable spot for breeding Redstarts for many years and is worth checking in the spring.

On the left side of the path is another sign – walk out on to the heath here. Follow the path eastwards, keeping the large Old Decoy Pond and the adjacent bog on your right (Teal and Snipe breed in here). In the summer, the area is a favoured feeding site for Hobbies, and during the winter, check out the pond for duck (usually Tufted Duck and Teal) and Little Grebes.

The immediate area around the pond is a favourite spot for wintering Great Grey Shrike. Scan the tops the trees carefully and watch for its undulating flight as it moves around. When a bird overwinters, there is a good chance of finding it, but bear in mind that it can wander over quite a wide area.

From this path you should pick up Woodlarks (especially February to June), Dartford Warblers and Stonechats (all year) and Tree Pipits (summer). The ground rises to the left and there are a number of paths running to the top of the ridge – take one of these to get back the bridleway by the gate (200m from the sign) and return to the parking area.

Other raptors (and Raven) are frequently seen over the area. Buzzards, Sparrowhawks and Kestrels are regular, but Peregrines less so. Osprey sightings are more likely in the autumn than the spring and Hen Harriers and Merlins are occasionally seen in the winter.

Check out any large raptors you see as Red

Kite sightings are becoming more regular.

Hirundines and Wheatears pass through in the spring and autumn, while Whinchats are more likely in the autumn.

Occasionally rarities will turn up – the best I have seen has been a Crane by the Old Decoy Pond.

❷ Great Ovens (SY 922 903)

GREAT OVENS is mainly open heathland and lies in the south-east corner of the site, straddling the B3075 Morden road. There is a small car park on the west side of the road, from which a track will take you deeper into the southern part of the forest.

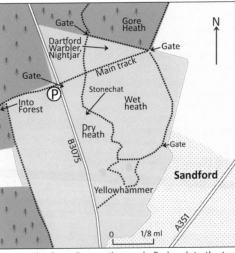

The area to the east of the road is managed by ARC. Start your walk here but take care when crossing on foot, or pulling out in the car – vehicles travel fast along the road which has a blind summit, and the view is obscured by vegetation.

The track is the main route through the site but after 170m there is an obvious crossroads. The path to the left climbs up the hill to a gate into Forestry Commission land (Gore Heath). Walk up to the gate and scan over the slopes before returning to the main track.

Take the right turn and follow the path into the heath – the area to the left is largely wet heath, to the right dry heath – it is good for Stonechats along here. After about 600m this path forks: there is a pond straight ahead (another 150m along the right fork). The area beyond the pond is good for Yellowhammers, so take the circular route around the ponds even though the paths are indistinct in places.

Take the left fork and continue to the gate leading into Sandford. Just before the gate turn left and follow the path along the boundary which eventually joins the far end of the main footpath.

A stand of dead pines in the corner by the main footpath shows the evidence of a previous fire. From here you can either return to the car along the main footpath or follow

the fence line up the sandy firebreak to the top of the hill and walk along to the Gore Heath gate and then return to the main footpath down the hill.

North of the track is the best place to look for Dartford Warblers, Tree Pipits and, possibly, Woodlarks. The top of the hill is a good vantage point to look for a Hobby hawking over the heath.

Nightjars are widespread across all of the heathland areas within the forest and they regularly travel quite large distances over the forest to feed. Great Ovens is a particularly good area to look for them at dusk on both sides of the road.

They should be heard easily enough just before dusk, especially on reasonably calm nights, but look out for them in flight or sitting on the wires or tree tops.

❸ Lawson's Clump (SY 921 909)

THERE IS a small signposted car park here, 550m further along the B3075 (on the right hand side of the road) from the Great Ovens parking area. This block of forest continues northwards to the Sherford River.

There are plenty of paths throughout the area – the southern half of this block, known as Gore Heath, is likely to be the more productive.

This area usually offers the best chance of finding Crossbill flocks in the forest - I have seen them on many occasions in, and just beyond, the car park.

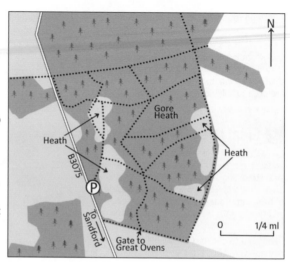

❹ Woolsbarrow (SY 888 917)

THE EARTHWORKS of this hill fort date back to the Iron Age. It has one of the highest elevations in the forest, so is worth a visit to look at the surrounding views and, at any time of the year it is one of the best spots for raptor watching.

There are two small parking areas at Stroud Bridge, on the Wareham-Bere Regis road. From here it is possible to do a circular walk out to Woolsbarrow, taking in a mixture of standing forest, clear felled areas and heathland.

Dartford Warblers and Stonechats should be found along the way and Woodlarks are possible in the clear-felled areas and watch out for Crossbills.

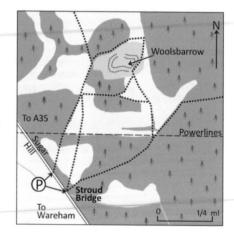

❺ Sika Trail (SY 906 893)

THE LARGEST car park in the forest is located at Cold Harbour, on the Wareham-Bere Regis road, and is locked overnight. This is the start of a seven mile long cycle (and walking) route (which can also be easily be reached on foot or bike from Wareham).

The trail, which is well laid out and signposted, passes through heathland and forest. A good selection of birds should be found along the way, but it can be busy here so take care not to get knocked over by a bike!

YOU CAN EXPECT an array of interesting birds that may include Scaup, Marsh and Hen Harriers, Little Gull, Cetti's Warbler and Bearded Tit in this area between Wareham, the Rivers Frome and the Piddle and Poole Harbour. There are also good views across the western end of the harbour towards the Purbeck Hills. Within a short distance of the town centre, there is a river walk, a freshwater gravel pit, wet grassland and a large reed bed – a variety of habitats that always ensures a good bird list.

Target birds *All year* – Cetti's Warbler (80%), Marsh Harrier (30%), Bearded Tit (30% - higher in spring), Kingfisher (30%). *Summer* – Sedge Warbler (95%), Reed Warbler (95%), Hobby (30%). *Winter* – Hen Harrier (30%).

Other possible bird species

All year	Common passerines	Snipe
Mute Swan	Bullfinch	Winter thrushes
Greylag Goose		
Canada Goose	*Summer*	*Passage*
Little Grebe	Sandwich Tern	Whinchat
Great Crested Grebe	Common Tern	Wheatear
Little Egret	Hirundines	
Buzzard	Summer warblers	*Occasional*
Kestrel		Black Swan
Water Rail	*Winter*	Garganey
Coot	Gadwall	Scaup
Stonechat	Pochard	Ruddy Duck
Reed Bunting	Tufted Duck	Greenshank
	Lapwing	Little Gull

Background information and birding tips

THIS SITE offers a choice of three circular walks starting from the town centre, but if your time is limited a fourth, shorter, option is available.

The longest route (four miles) follows the path along the sea wall (with the River Frome on one side and wet grassland on the other), reaching the gravel pits, after two miles.

The route then continues on to Swineham Point. From the Point, the walk continues around the north side of the pits to North Bestwall and then back into town.

The two shorter routes (three miles each) offer a walk along the river to Swineham Point, returning along the south side of the pits into Bestwall Road.

Alternatively, head along Bestwall Road to Swineham Point and continue to the north side of the pits, returning to town by North Bestwall.

The river up to Wareham is tidal and a walk along it in the spring and summer should virtually guarantee Reed and Cetti's Warblers – I have had up to six territories of the latter along here.

Key points

• Part of the site is an RSPB reserve.

• Easily accessed from Wareham town centre.

• Parking in Wareham.

• A choice of walks.

• Allow two to three hours for the longest walk.

• The river path is passable, but not in good repair.

• Other paths can be wet/muddy.

• Toilets available in Wareham.

• Overlooks an important reed bed.

• Freshwater gravel pits.

Contacts

RSPB Arne office
01929 553 360
www.rspb.org.uk/reserves

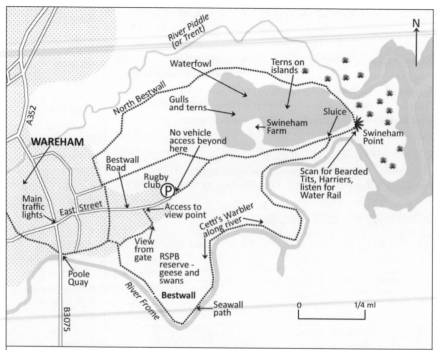

How to get there

(Next to/E of Wareham).

At the crossroads (traffic lights) in Wareham drive down East Street, and on into Bestwall Road to the end (by the rugby club entrance). Park on the roadside – do not drive down the lane. Continue on foot along the lane towards the pits and Swineham Point. Alternatively park in one of the town car parks and walk down East Street/Bestwall Road or take the river walk to Swineham Point.

Public transport: There are bus and rail links to Wareham.

Both are very vocal but take a little patience to actually see.

The river, apart from Mute Swan, Mallard and Moorhen doesn't have too much to offer but keep an eye out for a flash of blue of a Kingfisher flying by or listen out for squealing Water Rail in the reed fringes (they are sometimes flushed).

The sea wall path is fairly narrow, quite uneven and can be wet and muddy. In places it is in a poor condition, so walk with care.

The height of the path gives views over the wet grassland, which is partly owned by the RSPB. Waders haven't bred here for a while but during the winter they sometimes use the site, especially when there are very high tides in the harbour.

The sea wall eventually reaches the end of the grassland by the Swineham Farm sluice.

Curlew is the wader most likely to be seen in winter or passage periods. Snipe are always about but are usually well hidden and best seen when they move around.

Black-tailed Godwits sometimes use the fields at very high tides but they are just as likely to fly further inland up the Frome Valley.

Among the water birds, Mute Swans, Mallards and Moorhens are about all that nest here.

As an alternative to viewing the wet grassland from the sea wall there is a gap in the houses on Bestwall Road that takes you to a gate overlooking the RSPB section. A White Stork paid a brief visit to these fields in June 2001 and another was in the general area in late 2010.

The workings on the gravel pits finished in 2007, followed by re-instatement work. To view the pits you have to pick your way along the footpath (on the southern side) and scan through the vegetation where possible.

At the eastern end of the pits the footpath rises onto the sea wall which gives much better views over the eastern end but a telescope is essential as most of the birds are at distance from this point. It would be nice to think that in the future some viewing provisions would be put in place.

Despite the extensive size of Poole Harbour there is little by the way of freshwater in the area, so the pits are important for a number of species. A good selection of duck species is present during the autumn and winter: Pochard, Tufted Duck, Teal, Shoveler, Gadwall and Mallard are all usually about, along with Coot, Little and Great Crested Grebes.

The inevitable flock of Canada Geese are worth checking for any feral geese or an occasional straggler – Pink-footed and Bean Geese have been seen in the area.

A Ring-necked Duck turned up in the spring of 2009. In periods of very cold weather the pits can freeze over.

A few waders drop in to the pits from time to time, so they are always worth checking. Who knows, you may strike lucky with a bird such as a Pectoral Sandpiper, which turned up in 2008. In the summer, Sandwich and Common Terns fly over the pits and large numbers of hirundines can gather, especially in the late summer.

Other interesting birds that turn up almost annually include Slavonian and Black-necked Grebes, Garganey, Scaup, Ruddy Duck and Little Gull, while Black Swan is not infrequent.

At the eastern end of the pits is Swineham Point which has one of the more extensive areas of reedbed in the harbour. The reeds hold Reed Buntings and a few pairs of Bearded Tit.

The best time to see the Beardies can be spring and autumn on a reasonably still, sunny day. Listen out for their distinctive 'pinging' call and watch for birds flying over the reeds. With a bit of luck they may land close by. Keep an eye over the reeds for passing harriers – Hen (winter), Marsh (all year).

To complete the long circular walk continue on the footpath between the pits and the harbour which takes you into the Piddle Valley. The path continues around the northern side of the pits through fields, along woodland edge, and finally back to the old Saxon walls of Wareham. This part of the walk tends to be fairly quiet.

Whichever route is taken there will be a good selection of common passerines along the way, the species, depending on the time of year, including summer warblers, Stonechats and Bullfinches.

If your time is limited, park at the end of Bestwall Road and continue on foot along the path to Swineham Point, passing the pits en route. Do not drive beyond the end of the houses on Bestwall Road (private road). The return trip is just over 1.5 miles.

Other nearby sites

Arne, Creech, Stoborough & Grange Heaths, Hartland Moor & Stoborough Heath NNR, Middlebere, River Frome, Wareham Forest.

Key points

- **Some National Trust ownership & a small DWT reserve.**

- **A good coastal walk. Any good places for wheelchair users?**

- **Allow half a day to cover area well.**

- **Parking (pay & display), toilets and a café at West Bexington.**

- **Good for visible migration.**

THE SHINGLE beach of the Fleet continues westwards towards Lyme Regis and the stretch of coast either side of West Bexington is well worth a visit. The areas of reedbed and mere, backed by farmland with plenty of hedgerows and scrub, always have rarity potential and there are plenty of days of visible autumn migration when birds often pass over in high numbers. This is also one of the best places to do some seawatching out into Lyme Bay – I have seen Surf Scoter here.

Target birds
All year – **Raven (80%), Yellowhammer (80%), Peregrine (50%), Cetti's Warbler (50%), Barn Owl (25%), Little Owl (25%).** *Spring and autumn* – **Passage migrants.** *Autumn* – **Visible Migration.** *Winter* – **Red-throated Diver (75%), Common Scoter (50%).**

Other possible bird species

All year
Shag
Cormorant
Regular gull species
Stonechat
Reed Bunting
Common passerines

Summer
Reed Warbler
Sedge Warbler
Whitethroat

Winter
Great Crested Grebe
Black Redstart

Passage
Garganey
Common Sandpiper

Green Sandpiper
Hirundines
Yellow Wagtail
Grey Wagtail
'Alba' wagtails
Redstart
Whinchat
Wheatear
Grasshopper Warbler

Seabird Passage
Sooty Shearwater
Manx Shearwater
Balearic Shearwater
Storm Petrel
Leach's Petrel
Gannet
Arctic Skua
Great Skua

Grey Phalarope
Little Gull
Terns

Occasional
Velvet Scoter
Honey Buzzard
Marsh Harrier
Hen Harrier
Osprey
Merlin
Hobby
Wood Sandpiper
Glaucous Gull
Wryneck
Firecrest
Serin
Lapland Bunting

Background information and birding tips

OVERLOOKING Lyme Bay, the village of West Bexington lies between The Fleet (site 56) to the east and Lyme Regis (site 34) to the west. The Dorset Wildlife Trust has a small 20ha nature reserve here – West Bexington Mere – and The National Trust owns other parts of the coastline.

There is car parking at West Bexington, where there are toilets and a café or, alternatively, you can park above Cogden Beach (National Trust) - both are pay & display facilities.

From the West Bexington car park walk to the east at least as far as the coastguard cottages (about a mile). The cottages are a regular place for Black Redstarts in the autumn/winter ......if you continue on for another 1.5 miles you will reach the Abbotsbury beach car park (site 56).

For the meres and Cogden Beach (two miles away) head west from

Contacts

Dorset Wildlife Trust 01305 264 620. www.dorsetwildlifetrust.org.uk/reserves

National Trust 01297 489 481. www.nationaltrust.org.uk

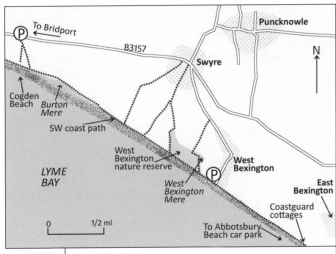

the car park. The first mere is the DWT reserve, close to the car park. Burton Mere is at the Cogden end of the walk. Walk along the beach (this can be hard work on the shingle) or take the footpath/tracks behind the beach.

The summer is the quiet birding season and the beach can be busy with people but there are still a few birds around. The reedbed areas around the meres have breeding Sedge, Reed and Cetti's Warblers (and possibly Bearded Tit) as well as Reed Bunting and Little Grebe.

The scrub and open farmland behind the beach has a good mixture of common birds including Stonechats, Whitethroats and Yellowhammers. Ravens breed in the area.

This stretch of coast has been well watched over the years and has turned up a lot of good birds, in particular during migration periods.

The spring tends to be quieter but a good selection of common migrants pass through. Garganey is more likely in spring on the Meres, and Grasshopper Warbler will often sing for a brief time.

Other migrants include Redstarts, Wheatears and Firecrests, with Whinchats, flycatchers and Yellow Wagtails more likely in the autumn.

Waders along this stretch of

How to get there
(10 miles NW of Weymouth).
From Bridport on A35 take the B1357 to Swyre. From Swyre turn right to West Bexington and follow the road to the beach car park. From Weymouth take B3157 through Chickerell, via Portesham/Abbotsbury to Swyre. From Dorchester take the A35 towards Bridport. Just before Winterbourne Abbas, turn left on B3159 to Portesham, then turn right onto B3157 to Swyre.

Public transport: The Poole to Exeter Coastlink bus service runs along the B3157 (First: Hampshire & Dorset). Nearest railway station is Weymouth.

coast are not particularly common but a few may pass through, including Whimbrels and Ringed Plovers.

The meres also attract waders, with Common and Green Sandpipers and Snipe the most likely, but look out for the occasional Jack Snipe and Wood Sandpiper.

It also pays to keep your eyes peeled for birds of

prey: Ospreys, Marsh and Hen Harriers, Merlins, Hobbies and occasionally a Honey Buzzard pass through, while Buzzards, Kestrels and Peregrines may be seen all year round.

Among the owls, Barn and Little are in the general area and Short-eareds are sometimes seen during the spring/autumn.

207

Visible migration (Vis Mig) in October/November can be staggering at times, with birds passing over or along the beach, in their hundreds if not thousands (numbers will depend on time in the field as well).

In general choose a day with light-ish northerly or westerly winds and good visibility. A regular watch point is located at East Bexington (see the excellent Trektellen website www.vismig.org), just to the west of the Abbotsbury beach car park.

Finches are well represented – Chaffinches and Linnets are usually the most numerous (occasionally over 1,000 birds), with smaller numbers of Bramblings, Redpolls and Siskins. Hirundines, Skylarks, Starlings and Meadow Pipits often reach the hundreds.

In November 2010 a staggering 47,000 Wood Pigeons and nearly 1,000 Stock Doves passed in a 4hr 30min period – but a movement like this is exceptional. Apart from the numbers of birds involved, it is the occasional goodies that add an extra interest to Vis Mig: Woodlark, Tree Sparrow, Crossbill and Lapland Bunting have been recorded,

The West Bexington car park is as good a place as any to do a seawatch out into Lyme Bay but anywhere along the coastal path is worth a scan. Lyme Bay is important for wintering Red-throated Divers and Great Crested Grebes are regularly seen.

Common Scoters are a little more hit and miss but, if found, worth checking out for Velvet Scoter and even Surf Scoter (the last one was seen in 2008). The sun is quite low in the winter, so visibility can be affected on bright days.

In the spring and autumn (generally better), seabird passage usually occurs when moderate winds are blowing onshore from the south-east/south/south-west. Birds may include Gannets, shearwaters, skuas and terns but they tend to be quite distant, so a telescope is essential.

During autumn gales look out for any seabirds that might get pushed close into the shore or onto the meres – these have included Storm and Leach's Petrels as well as skuas, Little Gulls and Grey Phalaropes. If conditions are too rough, seawatching can be difficult due to lack of shelter and sea spray.

Though mainly found at heathland sites, there's a good chance of seeing Stonechat on the scrub and open farmland behind the beach here at West Bexington.

Other nearby sites
Lyme Regis, Powerstock Common, The Fleet.

A SERIES of footpaths radiates from the village of Worth Matravers to stunning coastal scenes at Seacombe, Winspit, St. Aldhelm's Head and Chapman's Pool, so birds can almost be treated as a bonus! Sheltered scrub-lined valleys, open fields and coastal cliffs make the area attractive to passage migrants and one of my first memories of Winspit was standing in line on its narrow track waiting to see Dorset's first Red-flanked Bluetail. There is a good local pub in the village for refreshments after a long hard walk.

Key points

- **Choice of two car parks, one with toilets.**
- **Small parking charge.**
- **Refreshments at local pub.**
- **Variety of walks available, but no wheelchair access.**
- **Good migration spot.**
- **Stunning scenery.**

Target birds

All year – **Raven (80%), Yellowhammer (80%), Peregrine (50%).** *Passage* – **Wheatear (80%), Gannet (50%), Kittiwake (50%), Guillemot (50%), Redstart (50%), Common Scoter (20%), Hobby (20%), Yellow Wagtail (20%).**

Other possible bird species

All year
Red-legged Partridge
Cormorant
Shag
Buzzard
Kestrel
Sky Lark
Meadow Pipit
Rock Pipit
Grey Wagtail
Stonechat
Bullfinch
Common passerines

Passage
Cuckoo
Hirundines
Whinchat
Ring Ouzel

Grasshopper Warbler
Sedge Warbler
Reed Warbler
Spotted Flycatcher
Pied Flycatcher
Brambling
Siskin
Redpoll

Seabirds
Common Scoter
Fulmar
Regular gull species
Sandwich Tern
Common Tern
Razorbill

Summer
Lesser Whitethroat
Whitethroat

Summer warblers

Winter
Merlin
Black Redstart
Chiffchaff
Firecrest

Occasional
Grey Partridge
Sooty Shearwater
Manx Shearwater
Balearic Shearwater
Pomarine Skua
Arctic Skua
Great Skua
Little Owl
Wryneck
Corn Bunting

Background information and birding tips

THE VILLAGE of Worth Matravers is the ideal starting point for walks around this attractive part of the Purbeck coast. Each of the areas can be covered individually or in a number of combinations.

Drivers can choose between the car park at the entrance to the village (with toilets), or if you want to centre your visit on Chapman's Pool or St Aldhelm's Head, the car park to the east of the village by Renscombe Farm will be the better choice.

The section of walk along the coast itself is part of the South West Coast Path. Some of the walks are steep, particularly the coastal valley to the north of St Aldhelm's Head.

As well as the option of taking short walks there are a number

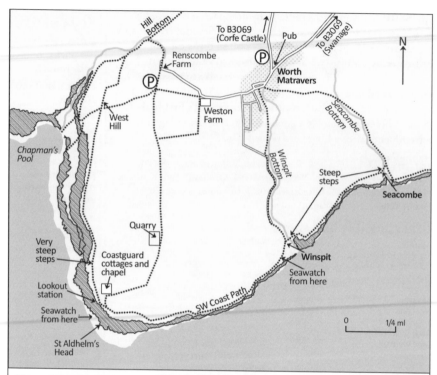

How to get there

(3.5 miles W of Swanage).

From Wareham head south on A351 towards Swanage. Immediately after passing through Corfe Castle, turn right onto B3069 to Kingston. The road veers to the left at the Scott Arms pub and after a mile turn right to Worth Matravers. The car park is on the right hand side just as the road enters the village.

From the Swanage direction, take B3069, through Langton Matravers, to Acton and turn left to Worth Matravers. At the Square & Compass pub, turn right for the car park just up the hill.

Public transport: The regular Poole-Wareham-Swanage bus service (Wilts & Dorset) passes along B3069 (a mile walk into Worth Matravers) and a limited service runs from Swanage to Worth Matravers (Mon to Sat).

Walkers can take the South West Coast Path from

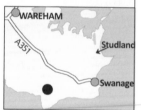

Swanage (eight miles to Chapman's Pool) which also takes in Durlston Country Park (site 20) and Dancing Ledge (site 18).

of longer circular walks available, their lengths varying from about three miles to seven miles. For the full circular walk which covers each of the areas, and to leave plenty of time to check out the scrub for birds, you should put aside a full day. My usual choice when I visit the area is to walk one of the shorter circular walks or, if time is particularly limited, to just do one of the short walks.

Main access details

For Seacombe:
From Worth Matravers car park, turn right and walk down the hill to the T-junction (by the Square & Compass pub) and turn right. After about 80m, turn left into Pikes Lane (just before the village pond). Turn left after 30m and follow this road for another 50m to pick up the Seacombe footpath.

For Winspit:
As above but walk past the Seacombe turn for another 30m then turn left and walk down past a row of houses to a stile.

For St. Aldhelm's Head:
From Renscombe car park, head south along the track, passing a quarry, the coastguard cottages and St. Aldhelm's chapel before reaching the coastguard lookout station.

For Chapman's Pool:
The valley is best reached via Hill Bottom. From Renscombe car park head east, across the fields, to the top of the slope that overlooks Chapman's Pool (West Hill). A path does wend its way down the steep (slippery) slope but go with great care if you decide to attempt this route!

The easiest option is to head northwards along the top of the slope and follow the main coast footpath down into the valley.

At the bottom turn left and follow the track to the shore (to leave, retrace your steps past this turn and after 200m the track veers to the right, coming out just to the north of Renscombe Farm, a short walk back to the car park.

- Walk options (approx. distances)

- **Full circular**
Seacombe, Winspit, St Aldhelm's and Chapman's Pool (seven miles).

- **Shorter circular walks:**
Seacombe & Winspit (3 miles); Seacombe & St Aldhelm's Head (5 miles); Winspit & St. Aldhelm's Head (4 miles); Winspit & Chapman's Pool (5 miles); St. Aldhelm's Head & Chapman's Pool (3.5 miles) R*

- **Short walks:**
Seacombe (2 miles return); Winspit (2 miles return); St. Aldhelm's Head (3 miles return) R*; Chapman's Pool (2 miles) R*

* All walks start in Worth Matravers except *R (Renscombe)

- **The local OS map is very useful for this site.**

Suggested walk route for a wide range of bird sightings

BY WAY of an example, the following describes the full circular walk, in a clockwise direction. One thing to bear in mind is that the area gets very busy with walkers, so an early start is advisable to miss some of the rush.

Leaving Worth in the direction of Seacombe, take the path across the field to the stone wall, over the stile and continue across the next field to the bushes. The path drops down the slope here – it can be wet and slippery in places – through scattered bushes, to a gate at the bottom.

From here, it continues along Seacombe Bottom eventually reaching a gate leading into the old cliff quarry – this is a dead end but worth a look around the area – stay out of the caves.

The valley can be a migrant trap in spring and autumn. From the gate, head back up the valley for 170m to a gate and path on the left that takes you over to Winspit. There are two sets of steep steps – out of Seacombe and down into Winspit.

This is another scrub-lined valley with an old quarry by the cliffs. If on the long circuit, it is worth walking up the valley at least as far as the small sewage works (look for Grey Wagtail here) before returning to the coast.

Again more migrants may be found in the valley when conditions are right. It can be worth a seawatch from here when the winds are blowing onshore – in spring the best period is mid-April to mid-May, or in the autumn during unsettled weather.

The next stretch of the walk follows the coast path to St Aldhelm's Head, the most southerly point of Purbeck. This is another good spot for seawatching and is usually a better option than Winspit, though passing seabird numbers are not generally very high.

Common Scoters, Fulmars, Gannets and the commoner auks, gulls and terns are most likely seabirds to be seen but other interesting birds have including Manx, Balearic and Sooty Shearwaters, Arctic and Pomarine Skuas, Little Gull, Sabine's Gull and Black Tern.

Two of Dorset's scarcer birds that may just be hanging on at St Aldhelm's Head are Grey Partridge and Corn Bunting – though I have seen both of them here, they are by no means certain.

Make a detour off the coast path along the track, past the coastguard cottages, at least as far as the quarry (half a mile), to have a look for them and anything else that may be in the fields.

From St. Aldhelm's Head continue along the coast, first negotiating the very steep valley (steps) just to the north of the coastguard cottages, before coming to West Hill. Follow the directions (see opposite page) into Chapman's Pool where the scrub in the valley is another potential migrant trap.

Once back at Renscombe Farm follow the road back into Worth Matravers, turning left at the Square & Compass, or call in for well-earned refreshments, and back to the car park.

Migration starts in the first half of April with the early passage of hirundines, Wheatears, Blackcaps and Chiffchaffs.

Through the rest of April and into May other migrants follow and may include species such as Hobby, Cuckoo, Turtle Dove, Tree Pipit, Yellow Wagtail, Ring Ouzel, Redstart and Whinchat, a variety of warblers plus Pied and Spotted Flycatchers.

September and October are the best months for returning migrants. Similar species may be encountered as in the spring but this is a good time for finch movements including Siskins, Redpolls and occasionally Bramblings.

Apart from passing migrants there is a good selection of birds breeding along the walks. Buzzards, Peregrines, Kestrels and Ravens are usually encountered at some point and check the scrub for Stonechats, Lesser Whitethroats, Whitethroats, Linnets, Bullfinches and Yellowhammers.

Little Owls still hang on in the area and Red-legged Partridges are much more likely to be found than Grey.

A winter visit is usually less rewarding bird-wise but the walk is still worth the effort for the scenery alone.

There is always a chance of a Black Redstart – check out the quarry areas and the coastguard cottages and search through any flocks of larks, pipits, finches and buntings you come across in case there is something a little more unusual among them. Winspit, in particular, may hold a wintering Firecrest or Chiffchaff and can be good for Merlin.

Other nearby sites

Corfe Common, Dancing Ledge, Durlston Country Park, Purbeck Marine Wildlife Reserve.

Checklist of bird species recorded in Dorset

This list assesses the status of Dorset's birds and is based on the current county avifauna (Green, G 2004: The Birds of Dorset), Dorset Bird Club Annual Reports ......and my own opinion! All 417 species on the Dorset list (as of the end of 2010) are listed here – many of them are rarities but the full list will give an idea of how frequently and where birds have turned up. Under each species, the sites listed in ( ) are those where there is a good chance of seeing them but these are only the main sites and they do turn up elsewhere.

There are two pending records not yet accepted to the Dorset list: Elegant Tern (2005/Christchurch Harbour) and Paddyfield Warbler (2011/The Fleet).

Categories

Very Common	Occurs in large numbers and is usually very widespread
Common	Occurs in fairly large numbers or is widely distributed in suitable areas
Fairly common	Occurs in moderate numbers in suitable areas and season
Locally common	Occurs in reasonable numbers but is restricted to certain areas
Uncommon	Occurs in small numbers
Scarce	Usually one to five records annually
Rare	Recorded less than annually
Very rare	Recorded between 6-25 times since 1950
Accidental	Recorded five times or less since 1950

A Quick Guide to Dorset's Birds

What are your chances of seeing .....?

Two blank columns have been added to allow you to record your own sightings. The third column contains a scoring system that will give you an idea of what you might see and the likelihood of seeing them [sightings will depend on time of year, the sites visited and how long you spend in the field].

1 = should see	blank = unlikely, sub-rarities /rarities
2 = a good chance of seeing	# = feral birds
3 = possible, but scarce/irregular	

			British Name	Scientific Name	Status and Key Locations
		1	Mute Swan	*Cygnus olor*	Common breeding resident and winter visitor - important population on The Fleet
		3	Bewick's Swan	*Cygnus columbianus*	Scarce winter visitor - has become less regular (River Frome)
			Whooper Swan	*Cygnus cygnus*	Scarce winter visitor - annual in recent years on The Fleet
			Bean Goose	*Anser fabalis*	Very rare winter visitor – four 19th Century records then ca20 records 1976-2009
			Pink-footed Goose	*Anser brachyrhynchus*	Rare winter visitor and passage migrant
		3	White-fronted Goose	*Anser albifrons*	
			(European)		Uncommon winter visitor
			(Greenland)		Accidental – 1992, 1998, 2008 Abbotsbury, 2002 Lodmoor, 2007/8 Lodmoor/Frome Valley
	#		Greylag Goose	*Anser anser*	Locally common feral breeding resident (Poole Hbr, Avon Valley)
	#		Snow Goose	*Anser caerulescens*	Formally rare feral resident (from 1972) but not recorded for many years

			British Name	Scientific Name	Status and Key Locations
		1	Canada Goose	*Branta canadensis*	Very common breeding resident
		#	Barnacle Goose	*Branta leucopsis*	Rare winter visitor and passage migrant or scarce feral resident
		1	Brent Goose	*Branta bernicla*	
			(dark-bellied)		Locally common winter visitor and passage migrant (Christchurch Hbr, Poole Hbr, Studland, Ferrybridge/The Fleet)
			(pale-bellied)		Uncommon winter visitor and passage migrant (Ferrybridge/The Fleet)
			(Black Brant)		Very rare winter visitor - annual in recent years at Ferrybridge/The Fleet
			Red-breasted Goose	*Branta ruficollis*	Accidental (1983/4 Avon Valley, 2003 Studland, 2006/7 Poole Hbr and Ferrybridge/The Fleet)
		#	Egyptian Goose	*Alopochen aegyptiacus*	Scarce feral visitor (Lower Avon Valley)
			Ruddy Shelduck	*Tadorna ferruginea*	Rare feral visitor
		1	Shelduck	*Tadorna tadorna*	Locally common breeding resident and fairly common winter visitor (Poole Hbr)
		3	Mandarin Duck	*Aix galericulata*	Scarce breeding resident (Stour Valley)
		1	Wigeon	*Anas penelope*	Common winter visitor and passage migrant (Christchurch Hbr, Poole Hbr, The Fleet)
			American Wigeon	*Anas americana*	Very rare winter visitor and passage migrant (13 records 1984-2000)
		1	Gadwall	*Anas strepera*	Uncommon breeding resident (Lodmoor, Radipole), locally common winter visitor and passage migrant
		1	Teal	*Anas crecca*	Scarce breeding resident, common winter visitor and passage migrant
			Green-winged Teal	*Anas carolinensis*	Very rare winter visitor and passage migrant (ca20 records 1948-2007)
		1	Mallard	*Anas platyrhynchos*	Very common breeding resident and winter visitor
		1	Pintail	*Anas acuta*	Locally common winter visitor and passage migrant (Poole Hbr, The Fleet)
		2	Garganey	*Anas querquedula*	Uncommon passage migrant – has occasionally bred (Christchurch Hbr, Coward's Marsh, Lodmoor, Radipole)
			Blue-winged Teal	*Anas discors*	Accidental (1982 Sutton Bingham, 1989, 2001 Stanpit, 1991,1999 Abbotsbury)
		1	Shoveler	*Anas clyptea*	Scarce breeding resident (Lodmoor, Radipole), locally common winter visitor and passage migrant (Poole Hbr, The Fleet)
		3	Red-crested Pochard	*Netta rufina*	Scarce visitor - esp winter, probably from feral populations in Europe
		1	Pochard	*Aythya farina*	Scarce breeding resident (Lodmoor, Radipole), common winter visitor and passage migrant (Lodmoor, Radipole, Studland, The Fleet)

THE DORSET BIRD LIST

			British Name	Scientific Name	Status and Key Locations
			Ring-necked Duck	*Aythya collaris*	Very rare winter visitor and passage migrant (ca21 records 1977-2009)
			Ferruginous Duck	*Aythya nyroca*	Rare winter visitor
		1	Tufted Duck	*Aythya fuligula*	Uncommon breeding resident (Lodmoor, Radipole), common winter visitor and passage migrant (Lodmoor, Radipole, Studland, The Fleet)
		2	Scaup	*Aythya marila*	Uncommon winter visitor and passage migrant (Lodmoor, Poole Hbr, The Fleet)
			Lesser Scaup	*Aythya affinis*	Accidental (1992 Hatch Pond, 2001/02 and same bird 2002/03, 2003/04 Studland)
		2	Eider	*Somateria mollissima*	Uncommon winter visitor and passage migrant (Hengistbury, Portland, Studland)
			King Eider	*Somateria spectabilis*	Accidental (2005 Chesil Beach/Ferrybridge and Portland)
		2	Long-tailed Duck	*Clangula hyemalis*	Uncommon winter visitor and passage migrant – esp good sightings from Poole Birdboats
		1	Common Scoter	*Melanitta nigra*	Locally common non-breeding resident, winter visitor and passage migrant (Hengistbury, Portland)
			Surf Scoter	*Melanitta perspicillata*	Very rare winter visitor and passage migrant (12 records, nine since 1961, five since 2000)
		3	Velvet Scoter	*Melanitta fusca*	Uncommon winter visitor and passage migrant
			Bufflehead	*Bucephala albeola*	Accidental (2010 West Bexington/The Fleet)
		1	Goldeneye	*Bucephala clangula*	Fairly common winter visitor and passage migrant (Poole Hbr, The Fleet)
		3	Smew	*Mergellus albellus*	Scarce winter visitor, subject to cold weather influxes
		1	Red-breasted Merganser	*Mergus serrator*	Locally common winter visitor and passage migrant (Poole Hbr, The Fleet)
		3	Goosander	*Mergus merganser*	Uncommon winter visitor and passage migrant (Avon Valley, The Fleet)
		3	Ruddy Duck	*Oxyura jamaicensis*	Uncommon breeding resident, uncommon winter visitor and passage migrant (Lodmoor, Radipole)
			Black Grouse	*Tetrao tetrix*	Former uncommon resident, now long extinct
		2	Red-legged Partridge	*Alectoris rufa*	Common, but declining, resident - augmented by releases
		3	Grey Partridge	*Perdix perdix*	Uncommon, declining resident (Maiden Castle)
		3	Quail	*Coturnix coturnix*	Uncommon breeding visitor (numbers vary year to year) and passage migrant (Cranborne Chase area)
		1	Pheasant	*Phasianus colchicus*	Very common breeding resident
		3	Golden Pheasant	*Chrysolophus pictus*	Scarce introduced breeding resident on Poole Hbr islands (Brownsea, Furzey - scan Furzey from RSPB Birdboats) – usually very secretive

			British Name	Scientific Name	Status and Key Locations
		2	Red-throated Diver	*Gavia stellata*	Uncommon winter visitor (Studland, West Bexington) and passage migrant (Durlston, Hengistbury, Portland)
		2	Black-throated Diver	*Gavia arctica*	Uncommon winter visitor (Portland Hbr) and passage migrant
		1	Great Northern Diver	*Gavia immer*	Uncommon winter visitor (Portland Hbr, Studland, Weymouth Bay) and passage migrant (Durlston, Hengistbury, Portland)
			White-billed Diver	*Gavia adamsii*	Accidental (1997 Portland)
			Pied-billed Grebe	*Podilymbus podiceps*	Accidental (1980 Radipole/Studland)
		1	Little Grebe	*Tachybaptus ruficollis*	Locally common breeding resident, winter visitor and passage migrant
		1	Great Crested Grebe	*Podiceps cristatus*	Uncommon breeding resident (Hatch Pond, Longham Lakes, Radipole) and locally common winter visitor
		3	Red-necked Grebe	*Podiceps grisegena*	Uncommon winter visitor and passage migrant (Poole Hbr, Portland Hbr)
		1	Slavonian Grebe	*Podiceps auritus*	Uncommon winter visitor and passage migrant (Poole Hbr, Portland Hbr, Studland)
		1	Black-necked Grebe	*Podiceps nigricollis*	Uncommon winter visitor and passage migrant (Poole Hbr, Portland Hbr, Studland)
			Black-browed Albatross	*Thalassarche melanophris*	Accidental (1980 Durlston)
		1	Fulmar	*Fulmarus glacialis*	Locally common breeding resident and passage migrant (Durlston, Purbeck cliffs, Portland, West Dorset cliffs)
			Cory's Shearwater	*Calonectris diomedea*	Very rare passage migrant (2002, 2008, 2009 Portland the only records since 1994)
			Great Shearwater	*Puffinus gravis*	Very rare passage migrant (five modern records: 1963, 1991, 1999 Portland, 1999 Seatown, 2009 Lyme Bay pelagic)
		3	Sooty Shearwater	*Puffinus griseus*	Uncommon autumn passage migrant
		2	Manx Shearwater	*Puffinus puffinus*	Fairly common passage migrant and non-breeding summer visitor
		2	Balearic Shearwater	*Puffinus mauretanicus*	Uncommon non-breeding summer visitor, autumn passage migrant and occasional winter visitor (Portland)
			Macaronesian Shearwater	*Puffinus baroli*	Accidental (1984 Hengistbury)
		3	Storm Petrel	*Hydrobates pelagicus*	Uncommon non-breeding summer visitor and autumn passage migrant
		3	Leach's Petrel	*Oceanodroma leucorhoa*	Rare autumn and winter visitor, subject to 'wrecks' in adverse weather
		1	Gannet	*Morus bassanus*	Fairly common offshore all year
		1	Cormorant	*Phalacrocorax carbo*	Fairly common breeding resident, winter visitor and passage migrant
		1	Shag	*Phalacrocorax aristotelis*	Locally common breeding resident, winter visitor and passage migrant

		British Name	Scientific Name	Status and Key Locations
	2	Bittern	Botaurus stellaris	Uncommon winter visitor - now regular at Hatch Pond, Lodmoor, Radipole and possible other suitable sites, esp during very cold weather
		American Bittern	Botaurus lentiginosus	Accidental (1804 Puddletown, 1980 Tincleton)
		Little Bittern	Ixobrychus minutes	Very rare passage migrant (ca10 records before 1900, then 10 since 1970, one in 2008 at Lodmoor)
		Night Heron	Nycticorax nycticorax	Very rare passage migrant (21 records, 16 between 1960-2006)
		Squacco Heron	Ardeola ralloides	Very rare passage migrant (ca11 records, only four since 1905: 1977 Longham Bridge, 1982 Radipole, 1996 Hengistbury, 2007 Weymouth area)
		Cattle Egret	Bubulcus ibis	Very rare passage migrant but annual since 2005, with an influx of birds in 2007
	1	Little Egret	Egretta garzetta	Locally common breeding resident (first bred 1996 on Brownsea) - spread through county but mainly coastal sites
		Great White Egret	Ardea alba	Very rare passage migrant and winter visitor
	1	Grey Heron	Ardea cinerea	Common breeding resident, winter visitor and passage migrant
		Purple Heron	Ardea purpurea	Rare passage migrant
		Black Stork	Ciconia nigra	Very rare passage migrant (ca10 records: two in 19th century and eight since 1977)
		White Stork	Ciconia ciconia	Rare passage migrant
		Glossy Ibis	Plegadis falcinellus	Very rare passage migrant (ca20 records: seven since 1956)
	1	Spoonbill	Platalea leucorodia	Uncommon passage migrant and winter visitor (Arne, Brownsea)
	3	Honey Buzzard	Pernis apivorus	Uncommon passage migrant – has bred
		Black Kite	Milvus migrans	Very rare passage migrant, mainly spring - ca27 records since 1980
	3	Red Kite	Milvus milvus	Uncommon passage migrant and winter visitor - increasing
		White-tailed Eagle	Haliaeetus albicilla	Formally a very rare winter visitor, no records since 1941
	2	Marsh Harrier	Circus aeruginosus	Scarce breeding resident (Lodmoor, Radipole), uncommon passage migrant and winter visitor
	1	Hen Harrier	Circus cyaneus	Uncommon winter visitor and passage migrant (Hartland, Middlebere)
		Pallid Harrier	Circus macrourus	Accidental (1938 Blandford)
		Montagu's Harrier	Circus pygargus	Uncommon passage migrant – no breeding records since 2004
		Goshawk	Accipiter gentilis	Scarce passage migrant and winter visitor – has bred
	1	Sparrowhawk	Accipiter nisus	Common breeding resident, winter visitor and passage migrant

217

			British Name	Scientific Name	Status and Key Locations
		1	Buzzard	*Buteo buteo*	Common breeding resident
			Rough-legged Buzzard	*Buteo lagopus*	Very rare winter visitor and passage migrant (ca24 records, only four since 1997)
		2	Osprey	*Pandion haliaetus*	Uncommon passage migrant (Poole Hbr)
		1	Kestrel	*Falco tinnunculus*	Fairly common breeding resident and passage migrant
			Red-footed Falcon	*Falco vespertinus*	Rare passage migrant, esp spring – 32 records
		2	Merlin	*Falco columbarius*	Uncommon winter visitor and passage migrant (Durlston, Hartland)
		1	Hobby	*Falco subbuteo*	Locally common breeding visitor and passage migrant (Hartland, Wareham Forest)
			Gyr Falcon	*Falco rusticolus*	Accidental – no modern records
		1	Peregrine Falcon	*Falco peregrinus*	Locally common breeding resident (ca30 pairs), winter visitor and passage migrant
		1	Water Rail	*Rallus aquaticus*	Locally common breeding resident, winter visitor and passage migrant (Hatch Pond, Lodmoor, Poole Hbr, Radipole, The Fleet) Spotted Crake Porzana porzana Rare passage migrant, mainly in autumn
			Spotted Crake	*Porzana porzana*	Rare passage migrant, mainly in autumn
			Little Crake	*Porzana parva*	Accidental (1888 Alderholt, 1975 Lodmoor, 1994 Stanpit)
			Baillon's Crake	*Porzana pusilla*	Accidental (1893 record Swanage)
			Corncrake	*Crex Crex*	Rare passage migrant
		1	Moorhen	*Gallinula chloropus*	Very common breeding resident
			Allen's Gallinule	*Porphyrula alleni*	Accidental (2002 Portland)
		1	Coot	*Fulica atra*	Common breeding resident and winter visitor
			Crane	*Grus grus*	Rare passage migrant and winter visitor (ca25 records since 1972)
			Little Bustard	*Tetrax tetrax*	Accidental (three very old records and 1987 Coward's Marsh)
			Great Bustard	*Otis tarda*	Former resident, long extinct but birds from Salisbury Plain re-introduction programme cross the border
		1	Oystercatcher	*Haematopus ostralegus*	Uncommon breeding resident, common winter visitor and passage migrant
			Black-winged Stilt	*Himantopus himantopus*	Very rare passage migrant (nine records: 1837 then eight between 1956-1990)
		1	Avocet	*Recurvirostra avosetta*	Locally common winter visitor and uncommon passage migrant (mainly Poole Hbr, scarce elsewhere)
			Stone Curlew	*Burhinus oedicnemus*	Scarce passage migrant
			Cream-coloured Courser	*Cursorius cursor*	Accidental (1853 Batcombe Down)
			Collared Pratincole	*Glareola pratincola*	Accidental (three old records, then 1974 Lodmoor, 1977 Holes Bay, 1990 Abbotsbury, 1992 Portland)

		British Name	Scientific Name	Status and Key Locations
	2	Little Ringed Plover	*Charadrius dubius*	Scarce breeding visitor and uncommon passage migrant
	1	Ringed Plover	*Charadrius hiaticula*	Scarce breeding resident, locally common winter visitor and passage migrant
		Kentish Plover	*Charadrius alexandrinus*	Scarce passage migrant, esp Ferrybridge (no records 2008/2009)
		Dotterel	*Charadrius morinellus*	Rare passage migrant
		American Golden Plover	*Pluvialis dominica*	Accidental (1992 Ferrybridge and Stanpit, 1998 Stanpit)
		Pacific Golden Plover	*Pluvialis fulva*	Accidental (1990 Stanpit, 1996 two birds at Lodmoor)
	2	Golden Plover	*Pluvialis apricaria*	Locally common winter visitor and passage migrant (Maiden Castle)
	1	Grey Plover	*Pluvialis squatarola*	Locally common winter visitor and passage migrant
		Sociable Plover	*Chettusia gregaria*	Accidental (1961 Wimborne, 1975 The Fleet, 1995 Radipole/Lodmoor/Wareham Water Meadows/Brand's Bay)
		White-tailed Plover	*Vanellus leucurus*	Accidental (1979 Abbotsbury)
	1	Lapwing	*Vanellus vanellus*	Locally common, but declining, breeding resident, common winter visitor and passage migrant
	1	Knot	*Calidris canutus*	Uncommon winter visitor and passage migrant (Poole Hbr)
	1	Sanderling	*Calidris alba*	Uncommon passage migrant and winter visitor
		Semipalmated Sandpiper	*Calidris pusilla*	Accidental (1982 Sutton Bingham, 1989 Ferrybridge/East Fleet, 2002 Ferrybridge, 2010 Lodmoor)
		Western Sandpiper	*Calidris mauri*	Accidental (2004 Brownsea)
		Red-necked Stint	*Calidris ruficollis*	Accidental (2010 Ferrybridge)
	2	Little Stint	*Calidris minuta*	Uncommon passage migrant, mainly in autumn, and rare winter visitor
		Temminck's Stint	*Calidris temminckii*	Rare passage migrant, mainly in spring
		White-rumped Sandpiper	*Calidris fusciollis*	Accidental (1974, 1999 Ferrybridge, 1982, 2000 Lodmoor, 2007 Brownsea)
		Baird's Sandpiper	*Calidris bairdii*	Accidental (1967 Portland, 1988, 1999 Christchurch Hbr)
		Pectoral Sandpiper	*Calidris melanotos*	Rare autumn passage migrant
		Sharp-tailed Sandpiper	*Calidris acuminata*	Accidental (1978 Langton Herring)
	2	Curlew Sandpiper	*Calidris ferruginea*	Uncommon passage migrant, mainly in the autumn
		Stilt Sandpiper	*Calidris himantopus*	Accidental (2006 Brownsea)
	1	Purple Sandpiper	*Calidris maritima*	Uncommon winter visitor and passage migrant (Hengistbury, Lyme Regis, Poole Hbr, Portland)
	1	Dunlin	*Calidris alpina*	Common winter visitor and passage migrant

		British Name	Scientific Name	Status and Key Locations
		Broad-billed Sandpiper	Limicola falcinellus	Accidental (1973 Sutton Bingham, 1975 Herbury Gore, 1986 Ferrybridge, 1986 Stanpit)
		Buff-breasted Sandpiper	Tryngites subruficollis	Very rare autumn passage migrant (10 records 1955-2005)
	3	Ruff	Philomachus pugnax	Uncommon passage migrant and winter visitor
	3	Jack Snipe	Lymnocryptes minimus	Uncommon winter visitor and passage migrant – usually flushed
	1	Snipe	Gallinago gallinago	Scarce breeding resident, fairly common, but declining, winter visitor and passage migrant
		Great Snipe	Gallinago media	Rare winter visitor and passage migrant prior to 1900, no recent records
		Long-billed Dowitcher	Limnodromus scolopaceus	Accidental (1976 Arne, 1977 Lodmoor/Radipole, 1977/78 Herbury Gore/Langton Herring, 2000 Middlebere, 2008 Rodden Hive, 2010/11 – Lodmoor/Poole Park/Radipole/The Fleet)
	2	Woodcock	Scolopax rusticola	Scarce breeding resident (Holt Heath, Sopley), winter visitor and passage migrant
	1	Black-tailed Godwit	Limosa limosa	Locally common winter visitor and passage migrant (Christchurch Hbr, Poole Hbr) Some birds over-summer Icelandic race
	1	Bar-tailed Godwit	Limosa lapponica	Uncommon winter visitor (Poole Hbr) and passage migrant
	2	Whimbrel	Numenius phaeopus	Locally common passage migrant and rare winter visitor
	1	Curlew	Numenius arquata	Scarce breeding resident (Holt Heath), common winter visitor and passage migrant
		Upland Sandpiper	Bartramia longicauda	Accidental (1976 Portland)
		Terek Sandpiper	Xenus cinereus	Accidental (1974 Radipole, 1988, 1998 Stanpit)
	1	Common Sandpiper	Actitis hypoleucos	Fairly common passage migrant and scarce winter visitor (Holes Bay)
		Spotted Sandpiper	Actitis macularia	Accidental (1973 The Nothe, 1976 Christchurch Hbr, 1984, 2005 Stanpit)
	2	Green Sandpiper	Tringa ochropus	Locally common passage migrant and winter visitor (cress beds)
	1	Spotted Redshank	Tringa erythropus	Uncommon passage migrant and winter visitor
	1	Greenshank	Tringa nebularia	Locally common passage migrant and uncommon winter visitor (Brownsea, Poole Hbr)
		Lesser Yellowlegs	Tringa flavipes	Very rare passage migrant and winter visitor – eight records 1963-2000
		Marsh Sandpiper	Tringa stagnatalis	Accidental (2000 Stanpit)
	3	Wood Sandpiper	Tringa glareola	Uncommon passage migrant, mainly in the autumn
	1	Redshank	Tringa totanus	Uncommon, but declining, breeding resident, fairly common winter visitor and passage migrant

			British Name	Scientific Name	Status and Key Locations
		1	Turnstone	*Arenaria interpres*	Locally common winter visitor and passage migrant – a few non-breeders over summer
			Wilson's Phalarope	*Phalaropus tricolour*	Accidental (1984 Radipole/Lodmoor, 1987 Radipole, 1988 Holes Bay and Sutton Bingham, 2007 Stanpit)
			Red-necked Phalarope	*Phalaropus lobatus*	Very rare passage migrant, mainly in the autumn (three old records then 24 between 1960-2006)
		3	Grey Phalarope	*Phalaropus fulicarius*	Uncommon autumn passage migrant and rare winter visitor, subject to large scale 'wrecks' in adverse weather
		2	Pomarine Skua	*Stercorarius pomarinus*	Uncommon passage migrant, mainly spring (Portland)
		2	Arctic Skua	*Stercorarius parasiticus*	Locally common passage migrant (Portland, Hengistbury)
			Long-tailed Skua	*Stercorarius longicaudus*	Rare passage migrant
		2	Great Skua	*Catharacta skua*	Uncommon passage migrant, and scarce winter migrant (Portland)
			Ivory Gull	*Pagophila eburnean*	Accidental (five 19th Century records, then 1932 Weymouth Bay, 1980 Chesil Cove)
			Sabine's Gull	*Larus sabini*	Rare offshore migrant, usually storm driven
		1	Kittiwake	*Rissa tridactyla*	Uncommon breeding resident, fairly common passage migrant and winter visitor
			Bonaparte's Gull	*Larus philadelphia*	Accidental (1970 Durlston, 1975 Christchurch Hbr, 1981 Weymouth/Hengistbury, 1990 Portland, 2006 Weymouth Bay)
		1	Black-headed Gull	*Larus ridibundus*	Very common breeding resident, winter visitor and passage migrant
		3	Little Gull	*Larus minutus*	Uncommon passage migrant and winter visitor
			Ross's Gull	*Rhodostethia rosea*	Accidental (1967 Portland Hbr, 1974 Christchurch Hbr)
			Laughing Gull	*Larus atricilla*	Very rare (six records, 1969–2005, all in Weymouth area)
			Franklin's Gull	*Larus pipixcan*	Accidental (1982, 2000 Radipole/Weymouth Bay, 2004 Radipole, 1990 Sutton Bingham, 2008 Poole Hbr)
		1	Mediterranean Gull	*Larus melanocephalus*	Locally common breeding resident (Poole Hbr), passage migrant and winter visitor (Brownsea, Ferrybridge/The Fleet, Poole Hbr, Studland)
		1	Common Gull	*Larus canus*	Common winter visitor and passage migrant
			Ring-billed Gull	*Larus delawarensis*	Rare winter visitor and passage migrant - first recorded 1976
		1	Lesser Black-backed Gull	*Larus fuscus*	Scarce breeding resident, fairly common winter visitor and passage migrant
		1	Herring Gull	*Larus argentatus*	Common breeding resident, very common winter visitor and passage migrant

			British Name	Scientific Name	Status and Key Locations
		1	Yellow-legged Gull	*Larus michahellis*	Scarce breeding resident (one pair Brownsea), locally common passage migrant and winter visitor (Holes Bay, Middlebere)
			Caspian Gull	*Larus cachinnans*	Accidental (2001, 2008 (3 birds) Radipole, 2003 Corfe Mullen)
			American Herring Gull	*Larus smithsonianus*	Accidental (2002 Corfe Mullen)
			Iceland Gull	*Larus glaucoides*	Scarce winter visitor and passage migrant
			Glaucous Gull	*Larus hyperboreus*	Scarce winter visitor and passage migrant
		1	Great Black-backed Gull	*Larus marinus*	Scarce breeding resident, fairly common winter visitor and passage migrant
			Sooty Tern	*Sterna fuscata*	Accidental (1935 Abbotsbury)
			Bridled Tern	*Sterna anaethetus*	Accidental (1984 Lodmoor)
		1	Little Tern	*Sterna albifrons*	Uncommon, declining, breeding visitor (Ferrybridge), and uncommon passage migrant
			Gull-billed Tern	*Sterna nilotica*	Very rare passage migrant (10 records 1961-1996, 2010 West Bexington/The Fleet)
			Caspian Tern	*Sterna caspia*	Very rare passage migrant (14 records, 11 between 1974-2001)
			Whiskered Tern	*Chlidonias hybridus*	Accidental (six records, 1836 then 1983, 1987, 1988 (2 birds), 2008)
		2	Black Tern	*Chlidonias niger*	Uncommon passage migrant
			White-winged Black Tern	*Chlidonias leucopterus*	Very rare passage migrant (27 records, four since 2000)
		1	Sandwich Tern	*Sterna sandvicensis*	Fairly common breeding visitor (Brownsea) and passage migrant
			Lesser Crested Tern	*Sterna bengalensis*	Accidental (1995 Hengistbury)
			Forster's Tern	*Sterna forsteri*	Accidental (1995/96 The Fleet)
		1	Common Tern	*Sterna hirundo*	Locally common breeding visitor (Abbotsbury, Brownsea, Lodmoor) and common passage migrant
		3	Roseate Tern	*Sterna dougallii*	Uncommon passage migrant – occasionally breeds
		2	Arctic Tern	*Sterna paradisaea*	Fairly common passage migrant
		1	Guillemot	*Uria aalge*	Locally common breeding resident (Durlston, Portland), common winter visitor and passage migrant
		1	Razorbill	*Alca torda*	Uncommon breeding resident (Durlston, Portland), fairly common winter visitor and passage migrant
			Black Guillemot	*Cepphus grylle*	Rare winter visitor and passage migrant
			Little Auk	*Alle alle*	Scarce passage migrant, mainly in autumn, and winter visitor
		2	Puffin	*Fratercula arctica*	Uncommon breeding visitor (Dancing Ledge, Portland) and scarce passage migrant
			Pallas's Sandgrouse	*Syrrhaptes paradoxus*	Accidental (four records from influx of 1888-1889)

			British Name	Scientific Name	Status and Key Locations
		#	Rock Dove	*Columba livia*	Fairly common breeding resident (Feral Pigeon)
		1	Stock Dove (Stock Pigeon)	*Columba oenas*	Common, but declining, breeding resident, passage migrant and winter visitor
		1	Wood Pigeon	*Columba palumbus*	Very common breeding resident, passage migrant and winter visitor
		1	Collared Dove	*Streptopelia decaocta*	Common breeding resident
		2	Turtle Dove	*Streptopelia turtur*	Uncommon, but declining, breeding visitor (Martin Down) and passage migrant
		2	Ring-necked Parakeet	*Psittacula krameri*	Uncommon breeding resident (Studland)
			Great Spotted Cuckoo	*Clamator glandarius*	Accidental (1989 St Aldhelm's Head, 1994 Hengistbury)
		1	Cuckoo	*Cuculus canorus*	Fairly common, but declining, breeding visitor and passage migrant
			Yellow-billed Cuckoo	*Coccyzus americanus*	Accidental (1895 Bridport, 1979 Portland, 1991 Weymouth)
		1	Barn Owl	*Tyto alba*	Locally common breeding resident
			Scops Owl	*Otus scops*	Accidental (1990 caught on fishing boat 25km offshore, released on Portland)
		1	Little Owl	*Athene noctua*	Fairly common breeding resident (Portland)
		1	Tawny Owl	*Strix aluco*	Common breeding resident
			Long-eared Owl	*Asio otus*	Scarce passage migrant and winter visitor
		2	Short-eared Owl	*Asio flammeus*	Uncommon passage migrant and winter visitor
		1	Nightjar	*Caprimulgus europaeus*	Fairly common breeding visitor and scarce passage migrant (on most heathlands)
			Egyptian Nightjar	*Caprimulgus aegyptius*	Accidental (1984 Portland)
			Common Nighthawk	*Chordeiles minor*	Accidental (1983 Studland)
		1	Swift	*Apus apus*	Common (but declining) breeding visitor and passage migrant
			Pallid Swift	*Apus pallidus*	Accidental (1984, 2004 Portland, 2002 Stanpit)
			Alpine Swift	*Apus melba*	Rare passage migrant, predominantly coastal records
			Little Swift	*Apus affinis*	Accidental (1983 Studland, 1997 Hengistbury)
		1	Kingfisher	*Alcedo atthis*	Fairly common breeding resident
			Bee-eater	*Merops apiaster*	Scarce passage migrant, mainly in spring and summer
			Roller	*Coracias garrulus*	Accidental (1868 Dorchester, 1955 Yetminster, 1966 Wareham Forest, 1967 Hartland Moor, 1975 West Milton)
		3	Hoopoe	*Upupa epops*	Uncommon passage migrant, mainly in spring
		3	Wryneck	*Jynx torquilla*	Uncommon passage migrant, mainly in autumn
		1	Green Woodpecker	*Picus viridis*	Common breeding resident – esp on heathlands

			British Name	Scientific Name	Status and Key Locations
		1	Great Spotted Woodpecker	*Dendrocopos major*	Common breeding resident and rare passage migrant
		3	Lesser Spotted Woodpecker	*Dendrocopos minor*	Uncommon, declining breeding resident (Arne, Wareham Forest)
			Calandra Lark	*Melanocorypha calandra*	Accidental (1961 Portland)
			Short-toed Lark	*Calandrella brachydactyla*	Very rare passage migrant (14 records since 1985, mainly Portland)
			Lesser Short-toed Lark	*Calandrella rufescens*	Accidental (1992 Portland)
		1	Woodlark	*Lullula arborea*	Locally common breeding resident (Avon Heath, Cranborne Heath, Grange Heath, Wareham Forest) and uncommon passage migrant
		1	Skylark	*Alauda arvensis*	Common breeding resident, winter visitor and passage migrant
			Shore Lark	*Eremophila alpestris*	Very rare winter visitor and passage migrant (a few pre-1968 records then 20 records until 1997, one in 2005 and one in 2010)
		1	Sand Martin	*Riparia riparia*	Fairly common breeding visitor and passage migrant
		1	Swallow	*Hirundo rustica*	Common breeding visitor and passage migrant
		1	House Martin	*Delichon urbica*	Common breeding visitor and passage migrant
			Red-rumped Swallow	*Hirundo daurica*	Rare migrant, mainly in spring and summer (45 records since1972)
			Cliff Swallow	*Hirundo pyrrhonota*	Accidental (2000 Portland)
			Richard's Pipit	*Anthus novaeseelandiae*	Scarce passage migrant, mainly in the autumn
			Blyth's Pipit	*Anthus godlewskii*	Accidental (1998 Portland)
			Tawny Pipit	*Anthus campestris*	Rare passage migrant, mainly in the autumn
			Olive-backed Pipit	*Anthus hodgsoni*	Accidental (five records, 1970-1992 all from Portland)
		1	Tree Pipit	*Anthus trivialis*	Locally common breeding visitor (esp heathlands) and fairly common passage migrant
			Pechora Pipit	*Anthus gustavi*	Accidental (1983, 1990 Portland)
		1	Meadow Pipit	*Anthus pratensis*	Common breeding resident, passage migrant and winter visitor
			Red-throated Pipit	*Anthus cervinus*	Very rare passage migrant, mainly in autumn (15 records since 1961)
		1	Rock Pipit	*Anthus petrosus*	Locally common breeding resident (coastal), winter visitor and passage migrant
		2	Water Pipit	*Anthus spinoletta*	Uncommon winter visitor and passage migrant (cress beds, Lodmoor)
		1	Yellow Wagtail	*Motacilla flava (flavissima)*	Fairly common passage migrant – other races rare
			Citrine Wagtail	*Motacilla citreola*	Accidental (2009 Lodmoor)
		1	Grey Wagtail	*Motacilla cinerea*	Locally common breeding resident, passage migrant and winter visitor

			British Name	Scientific Name	Status and Key Locations
		1	Pied/White Wagtail	*Motacilla alba*	(Pied) Common breeding resident, passage migrant and winter visitor; (White) Fairly common passage migrant
		3	Waxwing	*Bombycilla garrulus*	Rare winter visitor and passage migrant, subject to irruptions into UK
		3	Dipper	*Cinclus cinclus*	Uncommon breeding resident in the west of the county (Lyme Regis)
		1	Wren	*Troglodytes troglodytes*	Very common breeding resident and passage migrant
			Brown Thrasher	*Toxostoma rufum*	Accidental –(1966/67 Durlston)
		1	Dunnock	*Prunella modularis*	Very common breeding resident and passage migrant
			Alpine Accentor	*Prunella collaris*	Accidental (1978 Portland)
		1	Robin	*Erithacus rubecula*	Very common breeding resident, passage migrant and winter visitor
			Thrush Nightingale	*Lusinia luscinia*	Accidental (1994, 2008 Portland, 1996 Abbotsbury)
		2	Nightingale	*Luscinia megarhynchos*	Uncommon, declining, breeding visitor (Deadmoor and Lydlinch Commons, Ringstead Bay) and passage migrant
			Siberian Rubythroat	*Luscinia calliope*	Accidental (1997 Osmington Mills)
			Bluethroat	*Luscinia svecica*	Rare passage migrant
			Red-Flanked Bluetail	*Tarsiger cyanurus*	Accidental (1993 Winspit)
		1	Black Redstart	*Phoenicurus ochrurus*	Uncommon passage migrant and winter visitor – occasionally breeds
		1	Redstart	*Phoenicurus phoenicurus*	Scarce breeding visitor (Lambert's Castle, Wareham Forest) and fairly common passage migrant
		2	Whinchat	*Saxicola rubetra*	Fairly common passage migrant
		1	Stonechat	*Saxicola torquata*	Fairly common breeding resident, passage migrant and winter visitor
		1	Wheatear	*Oenanthe oenanthe*	Rare breeding visitor and common passage migrant
			Pied Wheatear	*Oenanthe pleschanka*	Accidental (1954, 1996 Portland)
			Black-eared Wheatear	*Oenanthe hispanica*	Accidental (1975, 1985 Portland, 1998 Winspit Valley, 2000 Upton Heath)
			Desert Wheatear	*Oenanthe deserti*	Accidental (1991, 1994 Portland, 1997 Studland)
			Rufous-tailed Rock	*Thrush Monticola saxatilis*	Accidental (1988, 1989 Portland)
			Grey-cheeked Thrush	*Catharus minimus*	Accidental (2008 Portland)
		2	Ring Ouzel	*Turdus torquatus*	Uncommon passage migrant, esp autumn
		1	Blackbird	*Turdus merula*	Very common breeding resident, winter visitor and passage migrant
			Dark-throated Thrush	*Turdus ruficollis*	Accidental – 1994 Bournemouth
		1	Fieldfare	*Turdus pilaris*	Common winter visitor and passage migrant

			British Name	Scientific Name	Status and Key Locations
		1	Song Thrush	*Turdus philomelos*	Common breeding resident, winter visitor and passage migrant
		1	Redwing	*Turdus iliacus*	Common winter visitor and passage migrant
		1	Mistle Thrush	*Turdus viscivorus*	Common breeding resident, winter visitor and passage migrant
			American Robin	*Turdus migratorius*	Accidental (1966 Brand's Bay/Canford Cliffs)
		1	Cetti's Warbler	*Cettia cetti*	Locally common breeding resident (Lodmoor, Radipole, Swineham)
			Zitting Cisticola	*Cisticola juncidis*	Accidental (1977 Lodmoor, 2000 Portland, 2000 Hengistbury)
			Pallas's Grasshopper	*Warbler Locustella certhiola*	Accidental (1996 Portland)
		3	Grasshopper Warbler	*Locustella naevia*	Uncommon passage migrant – occasionally breeds
			Savi's Warbler	*Locustella luscinioides*	Rare passage migrant and summer visitor
			Aquatic Warbler	*Acrocephalus paludicola*	Rare autumn passage migrant (first recorded 1953 and annual 1969 to 2007, usually trapped/ringed)
		1	Sedge Warbler	*Acrocephalus schoenobaenus*	Common breeding visitor and passage migrant
			Blyth's Reed	*Warbler Acrocephalus dumetorum*	Accidental (1989, 2001 (2 birds), 2004 Portland)
			Marsh Warbler	*Acrocephalus palustris*	Rare passage migrant
		1	Reed Warbler	*Acrocephalus scirpaceus*	Common breeding visitor and passage migrant
			Great Reed	*Warbler Acrocephalus arundinaceus*	Very rare passage migrant and summer visitor (eight records 1959-2002)
			Eastern Olivaceous	*Warbler Hippolais pallida*	Accidental (1999, 2003, 2008 Portland)
			Booted Warbler	*Hippolais caligata*	Accidental (1980, 1987, 1999, 2002 Portland, 1984 St Aldhelm's)
			Sykes' Warbler	*Hippolais rama*	Accidental (2000 Portland)
			Icterine Warbler	*Hippolais icterina*	Rare passage migrant, mainly in autumn, since 1958
			Melodious Warbler	*Hippolais polyglotta*	Scarce passage migrant, mainly in autumn, since 1954
		1	Blackcap	*Sylvia atricapilla*	Common breeding visitor and passage migrant, and uncommon winter visitor
		1	Garden Warbler	*Sylvia borin*	Fairly common breeding visitor and passage migrant
			Barred Warbler	*Sylvia nisoria*	Rare autumn migrant since 1955
		1	Lesser Whitethroat	*Sylvia curruca*	Fairly common breeding visitor and passage migrant
			Orphean Warbler	*Sylvia hortensis*	Accidental (1955 Portland)
			Desert Warbler	*Sylvia nana*	Accidental (1970/71 Portland)
		1	Whitethroat	*Sylvia communis*	Common breeding visitor and passage migrant
		1	Dartford Warbler	*Sylvia undata*	Locally common breeding resident (on most heathlands)

THE DORSET BIRD LIST

		British Name	Scientific Name	Status and Key Locations
		Subalpine Warbler	*Sylvia cantillans*	Rare passage migrant (26 records since 1964)
		Sardinian Warbler	*Sylvia melanocephala*	Accidental (1988 Cogden Beach, 1993, 1995 (2 birds) Portland)
		Greenish Warbler	*Phylloscopus trochiloides*	Very rare passage migrant (10 records 1975-2003, mainly Portland)
		Arctic Warbler	*Phylloscopus borealis*	Accidental (1984, 2005 Portland)
	3	Pallas's Warbler	*Phylloscopus proregulus*	Scarce autumn migrant
	3	Yellow-browed Warbler	*Phylloscopus inornatus*	Uncommon autumn passage migrant, occasionally overwinters
		Hume's Warbler	*Phylloscopus humei*	Accidental (1994 Winspit, 1999, 2000, 2001, 2003 Portland)
		Radde's Warbler	*Phylloscopus schwarzi*	Very rare autumn migrant (13 records since 1976)
		Dusky Warbler	*Phylloscopus fuscatus*	Very rare autumn migrant (15 records since 1984, has overwintered)
		Western Bonelli's	*Warbler Phylloscopus bonelli*	Very rare passage migrant (eight records 1955-1989)
		Eastern Bonelli's	*Warbler Phylloscopus orientalis*	Accidental (2009 Portland)
	3	Wood Warbler	*Phylloscopus sibilatrix*	Uncommon passage migrant and sporadic breeder
	1	Chiffchaff	*Phylloscopus collybita*	Very common breeding visitor, passage migrant and uncommon winter visitor; (Siberian) Scarce autumn migrant and winter visitor
		Iberian Chiffchaff	*Phylloscopus ibericus*	Accidental (1999 Portland)
	1	Willow Warbler	*Phylloscopus trochilus*	Common breeding visitor and passage migrant
	1	Goldcrest	*Regulus regulus*	Common breeding resident, winter visitor and passage migrant
	2	Firecrest	*Regulus ignicapillus*	Uncommon passage migrant and winter visitor (Durlston) – occasionally breeds
	1	Spotted Flycatcher	*Muscicapa striata*	Fairly common, but declining, breeding visitor and passage migrant
		Red-breasted Flycatcher	*Ficedula parva*	Scarce passage migrant, mainly in the autumn
		Collared Flycatcher	*Ficedila albicollis*	Accidental (2009 Portland)
	2	Pied Flycatcher	*Ficedula hypoleuca*	Uncommon passage migrant
	2	Bearded Tit	*Panurus biarmicus*	Scarce breeding resident, uncommon passage migrant and winter visitor (Radipole, Lodmoor, Swineham)
	1	Long-tailed Tit	*Aegithalos caudatus*	Common breeding resident
	1	Blue Tit	*Parus caeruleus*	Very common breeding resident
	1	Great Tit	*Parus major*	Very common breeding resident
	1	Coal Tit	*Parus ater*	Common breeding resident and scarce passage migrant (continental race)
	1	Marsh Tit	*Parus palustris*	Fairly common breeding resident

			British Name	Scientific Name	Status and Key Locations
			Willow Tit	*Parus montanus*	Former breeding resident, probably now 'extinct' – rarely recorded
		1	Nuthatch	*Sitta europaea*	Fairly common breeding resident
			Wallcreeper	*Tichodroma muraria*	Accidental (1920 Chilfrome, 1968 Winspit-Seacombe-Dancing Ledge)
		1	Treecreeper	*Certhia familiaris*	Fairly common breeding resident
			Short-toed Treecreeper	*Certhia brachydactyla*	Accidental (1970, 1979 Portland)
			Penduline Tit	*Remiz pendulinus*	Very rare autumn migrant and winter visitor (nine records since 1988)
		3	Golden Oriole	*Oriolus oriolus*	Scarce passage migrant, mainly in the spring and summer
			Isabelline Shrike	*Lanius isabellinus*	Accidental (1959 Portland, 1978 Winspit, 1985 Portland, 1988 Durlston)
		3	Red-backed Shrike	*Lanius collurio*	Scarce passage migrant
			Lesser Grey Shrike	*Lanius minor*	Accidental (1965 Bere Regis, 1988 The Nothe, 1989 Stoford (Somerset border), 2008 Corfe River Meadows)
		3	Great Grey Shrike	*Lanius excubitor*	Scarce passage migrant and winter visitor – can be long staying (Arne/Hartland Moor, Wareham Forest)
			Southern Grey Shrike	*Lanius meridionalis*	Accidental (1989 Portland)
			Woodchat Shrike	*Lanius senator*	Scarce passage migrant
		1	Jay	*Garrulus glandarius*	Common resident and scarce passage migrant, subject to autumn influxes
		1	Magpie	*Pica pica*	Very common resident – large winter roost at Hatch Pond
			Nutcracker	*Nucifraga caryocatactes*	Accidental (seven records, all during the 1968 influx)
			Chough	*Pyrrhocorax pyrrhocorax*	Former breeding resident, now accidental (two records since 1925: 2001 Portland and 2003 St Aldhelm's Head)
		1	Jackdaw	*Corvus monedula*	Common breeding resident, winter visitor and passage migrant
		1	Rook	*Corvus frugilegus*	Very common breeding resident, winter visitor and passage migrant
		1	Carrion Crow	*Corvus corone*	Very common breeding resident, winter visitor and passage migrant
			Hooded Crow	*Corvus cornix*	Rare winter visitor and passage migrant
		1	Raven	*Corvus corax*	Fairly common breeding resident - now increasing
		1	Starling	*Sturnus vulgaris*	Very common breeding resident, winter visitor and passage migrant
			Rose-coloured Starling	*Sturnus roseus*	Rare passage migrant – esp Portland
		1	House Sparrow	*Passer domesticus*	Common, but declining, breeding resident
		3	Tree Sparrow	*Passer montanus*	Scarce local breeding resident and uncommon passage migrant

		British Name	Scientific Name	Status and Key Locations
		Red-eyed Vireo	*Vireo olivaceus*	Accidental (1987 Hengistbury, 1988 Portland, 1995 Weymouth)
	1	Chaffinch	*Fringilla coelebs*	Very common breeding resident, winter visitor and passage migrant
	2	Brambling	*Fringilla montifringilla*	Locally common winter visitor (Badbury Rings) and passage migrant (Durlston, Hengistbury, Portland)
	3	Serin	*Serinus serinus*	Scarce to uncommon passage migrant (first recorded 1960, has bred)
	1	Greenfinch	*Carduelis chloris*	Very common breeding resident, winter visitor and passage migrant
	1	Goldfinch	*Carduelis carduelis*	Common breeding resident, winter visitor and passage migrant
	1	Siskin	*Carduelis spinus*	Locally common resident, fairly common passage migrant and winter visitor, esp conifer forests (Avon Heath, Moors Valley, Wareham Forest)
	1	Linnet	*Carduelis cannabina*	Fairly common, but declining, breeding resident, common passage migrant and winter visitor
		Twite	*Carduelis flavirostris*	Rare passage migrant and winter visitor
	2	Lesser Redpoll	*Carduelis cabaret*	Scarce breeding resident, fairly common winter visitor and passage migrant
		Mealy Redpoll	*Carduelis flammea*	Rare winter visitor and passage migrant
		Arctic Redpoll	*Carduelis hornemanni*	Accidental (1996 (2 birds) Studland)
		Two-barred Crossbill	*Loxia leucoptera*	Accidental (1966 Arne)
	2	Crossbill	*Loxia curvirostra*	Uncommon breeding resident, irruptive passage migrant and winter visitor – esp conifer forests (Avon Heath, Moors Valley, Wareham Forest)
		Common Rosefinch	*Carpodacus erythrinus*	Rare passage migrant, esp Portland, since 1967
	1	Bullfinch	*Pyrrhula pyrrhula*	Fairly common breeding resident
	3	Hawfinch	*Coccothraustes coccothraustes*	Scarce passage migrant (Durlston and Portland) and winter visitor (formerly Cattistock Churchyard)
		Northern Parula	*Parula americana*	Accidental (1968, 1988 Portland, 1985 Hengistbury)
		Northern Waterthrush	*Seiurus noveboracensis*	Accidental (1996 Portland)
		Savannah Sparrow	*Passerculus sandwichensis*	Accidental (1982 Portland)
		Dark-eyed Junco	*Junco hyemalis*	Accidental (1983 Christchurch, 1989 Portland, 1993 Dorchester)
	3	Lapland Bunting	*Calcarius lapponicus*	Uncommon passage migrant, mainly autumn and rare winter visitor
		Snow Bunting	*Plectrophenax nivalis*	Uncommon passage migrant, mainly autumn and rare winter visitor
		Pine Bunting	*Emberiza leucocephalos*	Accidental (1975 Portland)

			British Name	Scientific Name	Status and Key Locations
	1		Yellowhammer	*Emberiza citronella*	Common, but declining, breeding resident and passage migrant
			Cirl Bunting	*Emberiza cirlus*	Former breeding resident, now a rare passage migrant and winter visitor (four records since 1994: 2003, 2008 Portland, 2003 Hengistbury, 2007 Abbotsbury
			Ortolan Bunting	*Emberiza hortulana*	Uncommon passage migrant, mainly in the autumn
			Rustic Bunting	*Emberiza rustica*	Accidental (1976, 1987, 1990, 1998 Portland, 1993 Stanpit)
			Little Bunting	*Emberiza pusilla*	Rare passage migrant and winter visitor, esp Portland, since 1976
			Yellow-breasted Bunting	*Emberiza aureola*	Accidental (1977, 1993, 2003 Portland)
	1		Reed Bunting	*Emberiza schoeniclus*	Common, but declining, breeding resident, winter visitor and passage migrant
			Black-headed Bunting	*Emberiza melanocephala*	Very rare passage migrant (nine records 1970-2000, mainly Portland)
	1		Corn Bunting	*Miliaria calandra*	Locally common breeding resident – esp the central chalk belt (Badbury Rings, Maiden Castle)
			Bobolink	*Dolichonyx oryzivorus*	Accidental (1992 Portland, 2002 Christchurch Hbr)

DEFINITIONS OF BIRD GROUPS USED IN THIS BOOK

IN THE GUIDES to particular sites, space may be limited, so we have adopted some group names. Here is an explanation of the species included for each of the general terms used in the 'Target Birds', 'Other likely species' sections and the main body of the text. For some sites, individual species may be listed as well as the group names.

AUKS
Guillemot, Razorbill, Puffin (rarely)

COMMON PASSERINES
A mixture of common species including hirundines, Wren, Dunnock, Robin, thrushes, warblers, Goldcrest, tits, Nuthatch, Treecreeper, corvids, Starling, finches, etc

COMMON FINCHES
Chaffinch, Greenfinch, Goldfinch, Siskin, Linnet, Bullfinch

REGULAR GULL SPECIES
Black-headed Gull, Common Gull (winter only), Lesser Black-backed Gull, Herring Gull, Great Black-backed Gull

COMMON WOODLAND BIRDS
Wood Pigeon, Tawny Owl, Great Spotted Woodpecker, Wren, Robin, Dunnock, Blackbird, Song Thrush, Goldcrest, Long-tailed Tit, Blue Tit, Great Tit, Coal Tit, Nuthatch, Treecreeper, Chaffinch

COMMON CORVIDS
Magpie, Jackdaw, Rook, Carrion Crow

HIRUNDINES
Sand Martin, Swallow, House Martin + Swift

COMMON SCRUB BIRDS
Wren, Dunnock, Robin, Stonechat, Blackbird, Song Thrush, Mistle Thrush, summer warblers, Long-tailed Tit, Blue Tit, Great Tit, common finches, Yellowhammer

SUMMER WARBLERS
Blackcap, Chiffchaff, Willow Warbler (other warblers usually mentioned separately)

TITS
Long-tailed Tit, Blue Tit, Great Tit, Coal Tit, (Marsh Tit usually mentioned separately)

DEFINITIONS OF BIRD GROUPS USED IN THIS BOOK

WADERS & WILDFOWL
A general term used for a mixture of locally common birds of these groups such as Oystercatcher, Curlew and Redshank, Shelduck, Wigeon and Teal and scarcer species

WINTER THRUSHES
Blackbird, Fieldfare, Song Thrush, Redwing, Mistle Thrush

GLOSSARY / BIRDSPEAK

LIKE MANY OTHER activities, birding has generated a language of its own and this is an attempt to explain terms used in the birding world; some of these may not be familiar to beginners and less experienced birders.

AUK: The general name for Guillemots, Razorbills, Little Auks and Puffins; often used on seawatches when viewing conditions are poor and the passing birds cannot be identified to species level.

BB RARITY: Rare bird of which a full description is required for the British Bird Rarities Committee (BBRC), in order for a record to be officially accepted.

BBRC: British Bird Rarities Committee. Sometimes referred to as 'the ten rare men' they sit in judgement over the rarity records.

BINS: Binoculars.

BIRDER: Someone who is keen but not obsessive, usually knowledgeable about identification, songs, calls and behaviour and well acquainted with the local birding sites. Birders often find rarities for twitchers and are usually happy to help dudes with the LBJs.

BIRDLINE: Telephone information service with the latest update on the whereabouts of significant birds. For Birdline Southwest, call 09068 700 241.

BIRDRACE: A competition between groups of birders to see how many species of birds can be seen (and heard) in 24 hours or other designated time period.

BIRDS: With around 10,000 species inhabiting nearly every type of ecosystem around the globe and ranging in size from 5cm to 2.7m, they are truly amazing creatures and worth a second look.

BONXIE: Great Skua, Shetland name in common use.

BOP'S: Birds of prey.

BTO: British Trust for Ornithology.

CATEGORY A: Species that have been recorded in an apparently natural state at least once since January 1, 1950.

CATEGORY B: Species that were recorded in an apparently natural state at least once between January 1, 1800 and December 31, 1949, but have not been recorded subsequently.

CATEGORY C: A category on the official British bird list containing species that have escaped from captivity or been introduced in the past and now have self-sustaining populations (e.g. Canada Goose).

CATEGORY D: A category not on the official British bird list, it contains species that would otherwise appear in Category A except that there is reasonable doubt that they have ever appeared in a natural state. (Always worth making a note of in case sightings are requested by BBRC at a later date).

CATEGORY E: A category not on the official British bird list, it contains species that have been recorded as introductions, human-assisted transportees or escapees from captivity, and whose breeding population (if any) are thought not to be self-sustaining.

CATEGORY F: A category not on the official British bird list containing species recorded before 1800.

COMMIC TERN: A non-identifiable tern which could have been an Arctic or a Common Tern.

CREPUSCULAR: Active in dim light, dawn or dusk.

CRIPPLER: A bird of extreme beauty, size or rarity.

CRIPPLING VIEWS: Extremely good views of any bird.

231

DIP: To go on a 'twitch' and not see the bird you went for.

DIPPER: One who 'dips' – a person who 'twitches' but misses the target bird. Not good!!

DIURNAL: Active in daylight.

DUDE: A person who has all the top birdwatching equipment and is keen, but not particularly good at identification; occasionally irritating dudes who think they know far more than they really do can cause a run of stringy records for a site.

DUFF GEN: Incorrect information about a bird or location.

DWT: Dorset Wildlife Trust.

ECLIPSE: Male duck species moult out of breeding plumage in summer, donning a dowdy, female-type plumage known as eclipse.

FALL: A mass grounding of migrating passerines, usually as a result of fog or heavy rain.

FIRST: First record of a species in the UK, a county, etc.

FENCE-HOPPER: A bird that has escaped from captivity.

FLUSH: To disturb a bird.

GRIP OFF: To see something that someone else has missed. Being 'gripped off' is particularly annoying if it happens to you on your 'local patch'.

HECTARE (HA): A unit of area 100m x 100m. One unit = 2.47 acres.

HIRUNDINE: The general name for swallows and martins.

ID: Identification.

IRRUPTION: An arrival of birds due to a population increase and a lack of food in their native area. Irruptions vary greatly from year to year in both numbers of birds and species. Irruptive species include Crossbill, Waxwing, Jay and Nutcracker.

JIZZ: A term used to describe the immediate recognition of a bird from (usually) the briefest of views. This perception of the essential characteristics of a bird, whether colour, size, shape, sound or likeness, is something that comes with experience.

LIFER: A bird species you have never seen before and can now add to your life list.

LISTER: Someone who keeps a list of everything they see, everywhere they see it! Garden list, life list, world list, county list, year list, birds seen while gazing out of the office window, etc.

LOCAL PATCH: An area regularly covered by a birder, usually close to home. The feeling when something new turns up on your patch, rare or not, is exciting, particularly to a 'lister'!

LOW LISTER: Someone who hasn't seen many species of bird.

LBJ: A shortened version of the affectionate term Little Brown Job, given to any bird with dowdy plumage. Even in summer plumage they all appear to look exactly like at least a dozen other species (Dunnock, pipits, Garden Warbler, etc). Female and immature birds are likely to be LBJs and identification can be tricky even for the experts.

LNR: Local Nature Reserve.

LRP: Shortened term for Little Ringed Plover.

MEGA: A very rare bird which is a good tick for any birder, even the most miserable of veterans!

MIPIT: Slang for a Meadow Pipit.

"MUCH ABOUT?": Traditional greeting from one birder to another.

MUCKY DUCK: A hybrid or farmyard duck.

NNR: National Nature Reserve.

NOCTURNAL: Active at night.

PAGER: Subscription-only bird sightings information service. Will usually bleep with a new message at the most inopportune moments!

PELAGIC: Trip by boat out of sight of land in search of seabirds.

PLASTIC: Can refer to an escaped cage bird, or a Category C, D or E species.

PUFFIN PATTER: Holiday makers desperate to see Puffins; that they often think they're the size of penguins!

RAMSAR: A wetland site of international importance as defined at the convention in Ramsar, Iran.

REDHEAD: A female or immature of certain duck

species (Goldeneye, Red-breasted Merganser, Goosander, Smew).

ROBIN STROKER: A name for people who usually belong to the RSPB and only feed their back garden birds.

RODING: The display flight of the Woodcock. Usually seen at dawn and dusk.

RSPB: Royal Society for the Protection of Birds

RSPCA: Royal Society for the Prevention of Cruelty to Animals. The organisation to contact in the unfortunate event of finding an injured or sick bird.

SAC: Special Area of Conservation under EC Habitats Directive.

SEAWATCH: A prolonged period of looking at the sea from a headland with bins and a scope in the hope of seeing passing seabirds. This can be very rewarding if the timing is right, as many thousands of birds can pass by a given spot.

SCOPE: Telescope.

SIBE: A bird that is normally found in Siberia, but has got lost along the way; they often turn up in housing estates!

SNCI: Sites of Nature Conservation Interest.

SPA: Special Protection Areas under EC Birds Directive.

SSSI: Site of Special Scientific Interest.

STRINGER: A person who misidentifies a bird and sticks to that identification, turning a common bird into a more exciting rarity.

STRINGY: Suspect identification. A claimed bird that turns out to be a different, usually, commoner species. Birders doing this on a regular basis have a bad name and are tagged stringers.

SUM PLUM: Summer plumage, many of the birds seen on migration or wintering in this country have lost most of their beautiful summer plumage, so to get a bird in sum plum is a bonus for many species.

TART'S TICK: A bird thought by others to be easy to add to one or other of your lists, but which you have found difficult to pin down.

TICK: To see a bird or birder. Probably derived from 'listers' seeing a bird then ticking it off on one or more of their lists.

TRASH BIRDS: Gaudy, easy-to-identify species. Unfortunately more usually seen in exotic locations overseas.

TWITCH: Travel to see a specific bird (usually a rare species) as soon as news of it breaks. Can involve a journey of many miles, or can just be to your 'local patch' to see something you have never seen there before. Has gained a bad name with beginners and birders who don't 'twitch', but is usually well organised, friendly, and great fun (if you don't 'dip').

TWITCHER: Someone who goes on a twitch. Fanatic 'twitchers' set off as soon as news breaks of a rare bird, anywhere in the country. Others go when they can, usually at the weekend, after the target bird has flown on the Friday night! Twitchers are not always good at identifying birds for themselves unfortunately and sometimes know little about the species they have twitched.

VIS MIG: Visible migration, when the birds can actually be seen on the move; coming in off the sea for example. An exciting phenomenon to watch.

WESTERN P: Western Palearctic, the zoogeographical area to which Britain belongs in the broader context of birding.

WRECK: The unfortunate arrival of exhausted, hungry seabirds after prolonged gales at sea; usually close to the shore but occasionally birds can be blown many miles inland.

WWT: Wildfowl and Wetlands Trust.

YANK: An American species that has turned up over here, often larger and more colourful that our resident counterpart!

YEAR LIST: A record of birds seen (in Britain) from January 1 to December 31.

YEAR LISTER: Someone who tries to see as many species of bird in a year as possible. This has sometimes involved people seeing a rare bird on December 31, and then travelling again to see it

COUNTY BIRD RECORDER

Kevin Lane, 42 Twin Oaks Close, Broadstone BH18 8JF. Tel: 07901 614 629
dorsetbirdclub@hotmail.com
www.dorsetbirds.org.uk

BIRDS & WILDLIFE GROUPS (DORSET)

Abbotsbury Swannery
New Barn Road, Abbotsbury, Nr Weymouth DT3 4JG. Tel: 01305 871 858
www.abbotsbury-tourism.co.uk

Amphibian & Reptile Conservation Trust (ARC)
655A Christchurch Road, Boscombe, Bournemouth BH1 4AP. Tel: 01202 391 319
www.arc-trust.org

Dorset Bird Club (DBC)
Diana Dyer, Membership Secretary, The Cedars, 3 Osmay Road, Swanage BH19 2JQ.
Tel: 01929 421 402
www.dorsetbirds.org.uk

Dorset Natural History & Archaeological Society (DNH&AS)
Dorset County Museum, High West Street, Dorchester DT1 1XA. Tel: 01305 262 735
www.dorsetmuseum.org

Dorset Wildlife Trust (DWT)
HQ: Brooklands Farm, Forston, Dorchester DT2 7AA. Tel: 01305 264 620
www.dorsetwildlifetrust.org.uk

Fine Foundation Marine Centre: Purbeck Marine Wildlife Reserve, Kimmeridge, Wareham BH20 5PF. Tel: 01929 481 044

Lorton Meadows Wildlife Centre: Lorton Lane, Upwey DT3 5QH. Tel: 01305 816 546

The Kingcombe Centre: Toller Porcorum, Dorchester DT2 0EQ. Tel: 01300 320 684
www.kingcombe.org

The Villa: Brownsea Island Nature Reserve, Poole BH13 7EE. Tel: 01202 709 445

Portland Bird Observatory (PBO)
The Old Lower Light, Portland Bill DT5 2JT.
Tel: 01305 820 553.
www.portlandbirdobs.org.uk

RSPB SW Regional Office
Keble House, Southernhay Gardens, Exeter, Devon EX1 1NT. Tel: 01392 453 759.

Arne Nature Reserve: RSPB Work Centre, Arne BH20 5BJ. Tel: 01929 553 360.

Radipole Lake Visitor Centre: Swannery Car Park, Radipole Park Drive, Weymouth DT4 7TZ.
Tel: 01305 778 313.

RSPB Birdboats/ Brownsea Island Ferries: Hethfelton Offices, East Stoke, Wareham BH20 6HJ. Tel: 01929 462 383.
www.pooleharbourbirdboats.co.uk
www.brownseaislandferries.com

The National Trust
Brownsea Island: Poole BH13 7EE
Tel: 01202 707 744.

Kingston Lacy Estate: Wimborne BH21 4EA
Tel: 01202 840 630.

Purbeck Office: Currenden Farm, Currenden Hill, Swanage BH19 3AA. Tel: 01929 450 123

West Dorset Office: Filcombe Farm, Muddyford Lane, Morcombelake DT6 6EP. Tel: 01297 489 481.

Wiltshire Countryside Office: West Kennett Farm, West Kennett, Wiltshire SN8 1QF
Tel: 01672 539 167.

BIRDS & WILDLIFE GROUPS (REST OF UK)

Birding For All (formerly Disabled Birders Association)
Bo Boelens, 18 St Mildreds Road, Margate, Kent CT9 2LT.
www.disabledbirdersassociation.org.uk

British Dragonfly Society
Lynn Curry, BDS Membership Office, 23 Bowker Way, Whittles.ey, Peterborough PE7 1PY.
Tel: 01733 204 286.
www.british-dragonflies.org.uk

British Trust for Ornithology (BTO)
The Nunnery, Thetford, Norfolk IP24 2PU
Tel: 01842 750 050. www.bto.org

Butterfly Conservation
Manor Yard, East Lulworth, Wareham BH20 5QP.
Tel: 01929 400 209.
www.butterfly-conservation.org

Joint Nature Conservation Committee (JNCC)
Monkstone House, City Road, Peterborough PE1 1JY. www.jncc.gov.uk

Natural England
Head Office, 1 East Parade, Sheffield S1 2ET

Tel: 0300 060 6000.
www.naturalengland.org.uk

Royal Society for the Protection of Birds (RSPB)
Headquarters, The Lodge, Potton Road, Sandy, Bedfordshire SG19 2DL. Tel: 01967 680 551.
www.rspb.org.uk

The Woodland Trust
Headquarters, Kempton Way, Grantham NG31 6LL. Tel: 01476 581 111.
www.woodlandtrust.org.uk

OTHER USEFUL CONTACTS

Birdline Southwest
Tel: 09068 700 241 (premium rate number).
Tel: 0845 4567 938 (to report news).

Chesil Beach Visitor Centre
Portland Beach Road, Portland DT4 9XE.
Tel: 01305 760 579.
www.chesilbeach.org

Disabled toilets leaflet
RADAR, 12 City Forum, 250 City Road, London EC1V 8AF. Tel: 0207 125 0322.

Dorset Environmental Records Centre (DERC)
Library Headquarters, Colliton Park, Dorchester DT1 1XJ. Tel: 01305 225 081.
www.derc.org.uk

English Heritage
SW Regional office, 29 Queen Square, Bristol BS1 4ND. Tel: 0117 975 0700.
www.english-heritage.org.uk

Forest Enterprise
New Forest, The Queen's House, Lyndhurst, Hants SO43 7NH. Tel: 02380 283 141.
www.forestry.gov.uk

RSPCA
National contact number for all sick and injured birds and animals. Tel: 08705 555 999.

Sherborne Castle Estates
New Road, Sherborne, Dorset DT9 5NR.
Tel: 01935 813 182.
www.sherbornecastle.co.uk

The National Trust
Headquarters, PO Box 39, Warrington WA5 7WD.
Tel: 0844 800 1895.
www.nationaltrust.org.uk

TOURIST INFORMATION CENTRES

For information about getting around, accommodation, places to go and events in Dorset the network of Tourist Information Centres is a good starting point:

Blandford: 1 Greyhound Yard, DT11 7EB.
Tel: 01258 454 770.

Bournemouth: Westover Road, BH1 2BU.
Tel: 01202 451 700.

Bridport: 47 South Street, DT6 3NY.
Tel: 01308 424 901.

Christchurch: 49 High Street, BH23 1AS.
Tel: 01202 471 780.

Dorchester: 11 Antelope Walk, DT1 1BE.
Tel: 01305 267 992.

Lyme Regis: Guildhall Cottage, DT7 3BS.
Tel: 01297 442 138.

Poole: Enfeco House, Poole Quay, BH15 1HJ.
Tel: 01202 253 253.

Shaftesbury: 8 Bell Street, SP7 8AE.
Tel: 01747 853 514.

Sherborne: 3 Tilton Court, Digby Rd, DT9 3NL.
Tel: 01935 815 341.

Swanage: The White House, Shore Rd, BH19 1LB. Tel: 08704 420 680.

Wareham: Holy Trinity Church, South St, BH20 4LU. Tel: 01929 552 740.

Weymouth: The King's Statue, The Esplanade, DT4 7AN. Tel: 01305 785 747.

Wimborne: 29 High St, BH21 1HR.
Tel: 01202 886 116.

LOCAL AUTHORITIES

Bournemouth Borough Council
Tel: 01202 451 451.
www.bournemouth.gov.uk
Hengistbury Head Nature Reserve: Bournemouth BH6 4EW. Tel: 01202 420 909

Poole Borough Council
Tel: 01202 265 265.
Upton Country House. Tel: 01202 261 306.
www.boroughofpoole.com

Dorset County Council
Tel: 01305 221 000
www.dorsetforyou.com

USEFUL CONTACTS

Avon Heath Country Park: Birch Road, St Ives, Ringwood BH24 2DA. Tel: 01425 478 082. (Rangers) Tel: 01425 478 470 (Visitor Centre).

Durlston Country Park: Lighthouse Road, Swanage BH19 2JL. Tel: 01929 424 443.
www.durlston.co.uk

DORSETFORYOU.COM

The following councils can be found under the 'dorsetforyou' website

Christchurch Borough Council
Tel: 01202 495 000.

Christchurch Countryside Service (Stanpit Marsh): Steamer Point Woodland Nature Reserve, End of

Seaway Avenue, Friar's Cliff, Christchurch BH23 4JQ. Tel: 01425 272 479.

East Dorset District Council
Tel: 01202 886 201.

North Dorset District Council
Tel: 01258 454 111.

Purbeck District Council
Tel: 01929 556 561.

West Dorset District Council
Tel: 01305 251 010.

Weymouth and Portland Borough Council
Tel: 01305 838 000.

BIBLIOGRAPHY

I HAVE selected a small number of books and reports that may be of interest. Up-to-date annual reports can be obtained from the relevant groups who may also hold a few back issues. Some of the books are now out of print but are available in the second hand market.

BIRDS

The Birds of Dorsetshire by Mansel-Pleydell, J.C. (Pub: R.H. Porter 1888).

The Birds of Dorset by Prendergast, Col E.D.V & Boys, J.V. (Pub: David & Charles 1983).

The Birds of Dorset by Green, G. (Pub: Christopher Helm 2004).

Dorset Bird Report (Pub: Dorset Bird Club since 1977).

Portland Bird Observatory and Field Centre Annual Report (published since 1963).

The Birds of Christchurch Harbour Annual Report (Pub: Christchurch Harbour Ornithological Group since 1956).

OTHER TITLES OF INTEREST

Butterflies of Dorset by Thomas, J. & Webb, N. (Pub: DNH&AS 1984).

New Atlas of Dorset Butterflies by Thomas, J. et al. (Pub: DNH&AS 1998).

The Dragonflies of Dorset by Prendergast, E.D.V. (Pub: DNH&AS 1991).

The Flora of Dorset by Bowen, H.M.J. (Pub: Pisces Publications 2000).

The Natural History of Dorset by The Dorset Wildlife Trust (Pub: The Dovecote Press Ltd. 1997).

The Reptiles and Amphibians of Dorset by Wareham, D.C. (Pub: British Herpetological Society 2002).

The Wild Flowers of the Isle of Purbeck, Brownsea and Sandbanks by Pratt, E.A. (pub: Brambleby Books 2008)

MAPS

In addition, the following Ordinance Survey Maps are relevant for Dorset.

Explorer Map 25,000:1 scale

OL15 Purbeck & South Dorset: Poole, Dorchester, Weymouth & Swanage

OL22 New Forest (includes Christchurch & Bournemouth)

116 Lyme Regis & Bridport: Chard (showing part of the South West Coast Path

117 Cerne Abbas & Bere Regis: Blandford Forum & Beaminster

118 Shaftesbury & Cranborne Chase: Poole, Wimborne Minster & Blandford Forum

129 Yeovil & Sherborne: Somerton & Wincanton

SITES ACCESSIBLE BY PUBLIC TRANSPORT

AS IN MANY areas of the UK, using public transport to go birdwatching in Dorset has its limits (and challenges!)

I have listed the sites that I consider are reasonably practical to get to by public transport from a main town (which themselves can be relatively easily reached by bus or train). The towns are Blandford Forum, Bournemouth, Christchurch, Dorchester, Poole, Ringwood, Salisbury, Sherborne, Swanage, Wareham, Weymouth and Wimborne.

The information in this section has been taken from the most recent timetables issued prior to the publication of this book but please bear in mind that routes and/or timings can change without warning. A short walk (usually less than one mile) may be required to reach the site from the nearest drop-off point.

A number of companies run bus routes through the county but the frequency of services vary, especially away from the main centres. Many services are often reduced/or may not run on Saturdays, Sundays and public holidays. The times of the first and last buses vary from route to route as well, so don't forget to check the time of the last bus home!

Each of the bus (and train) companies publishes their own timetables - on their websites and in leaflet form. Dorset County Council produces a series of bus-train guides covering rural Dorset, including the services to/from the Poole-Bournemouth-Christchurch conurbation. Most timetables can be obtained from Tourist Information Centres (see Contacts).

GENERAL TRAVEL INFORMATION

Traveline
Public Transport Information 0871 200 2233
www.travelinesw.com

BUS COMPANIES

Coach House Travel
16 Poundbury West Ind. Est, Dorchester DT1 2PG
Tel: 01305 267 644

Damory Coaches
Unit 1, Clump Farm, Higher Shaftesbury Road,
Blandford DT11 7TD
Tel: 01258 452 545
www.damorycoaches.co.uk

Discover Dorset (Bournemouth Airport shuttle)
Lowther House, 110 Lowther Road, Bournemouth
BH8 8NS
Tel: 01202 557 007
www.discoverdorset.co.uk

First Hampshire & Dorset
Edward Street, Weymouth DT4 7DP
Tel: 0870 010 6022
www.firstgroup.com

NORDCAT
Unit 4A, Butts Industrial Estate, Sturminster
Newton DT10 1 AZ
Tel: 01258 472 164

South West Coaches
Southgate Road, Wincanton BA9 9EB
Tel: 01963 33 124
www.southwestcoaches.co.uk

Transdev Yellow Buses
Bus Depot, Yeomans Way, Bournemouth BH8 0BQ
Tel: 01202 636 060
www.bybus.co.uk

Wilts & Dorset Bus Company
Nelson Road, Newport, Isle of Wight PO30 1RD
Tel: 01983 827 005
www.wdbus.co.uk

RAIL COMPANIES

First Great Western Trains
Customer Services Team, First Great Western,
Freepost SWB40576, Plymouth PL4 6ZZ
Tel: 08457 000 125
www.firstgreatwestern.co.uk

South West Trains
Customer Relations, South West Trains, Overline
House, Southampton SO15 1GW
Tel: 0845 600 0650
www.southwesttrains.co.uk

Swanage Railway
Station House, Swanage BH19 1HB
Tel: 01929 425 800
www.swanagerailway.co.uk

SITES ACCESSIBLE BY PUBLIC TRANSPORT

THE SITES

2 Avon Heath Country Park
Wilts & Dorset, route 38 (not Sun): The Ringwood-Ferndown-Heatherlands Estate service runs along the A31. Get off by the St Leonards Hotel and walk about half a mile down Brock's Pine Road to the North Park visitor facilities.

4 Ballard Down
Wilts & Dorset, route 50 (daily): The Bournemouth-Sandbanks-Swanage service runs through Studland village (get off by the Studland Stores/PO) – the start of the Ballard Down walk is about 500m from the main road. The site can also be reached on foot from Swanage.

5 Bere Regis, Waddock Cross & Tincleton Cress Beds
Wilts & Dorset/operated by Damory Coaches, route 387 (not Sun/public holidays): The Poole-Dorchester service passes through Bere Regis. Alight by the Church Cottages – the cress beds are less than 100m down the road. There are no services to Waddock Cross or Tincleton.

8 Branksome Chine
Wilts & Dorset, route 50 (daily): The Bournemouth-Sandbanks-Swanage service runs past the turn into the car park – get off at the Canford Cliffs/Branksome Dean Chine stop, walk down into the car park.

Wilts & Dorset, route 52 (daily): The site can also be reached from the Poole-Sandbanks service but there is a mile walk from the Canford Cliffs/Parade stop. Walk along Western Road/Pinecliff Road to the car park on the sea front, and along the sea front to the Branksome Chine car park.

9 Brownsea Island
Access to the island is via boats running from Poole Quay-Poole is easily reached by rail and bus. A shorter crossing runs from Sandbanks, by the chain ferry. Wilts and Dorset: route 50 (daily) Bournemouth-Swanage and route 52 (daily) Poole-Sandbanks services stop by the Brownsea Island kiosk.

10 Canford Heath
Wilts & Dorset: Route 3, Poole-Wimborne (daily) and route 32, Poole-Bournemouth (not Sun/public holidays) services pass along Gravel Hill. Wilts & Dorset: Routes 5 & 6 Poole-Canford Heath services (daily) stop in Canford Heath Estate.

Alight in Knowlton Road and walk through on to the southern end of the heath.

11 Cattistock Churchyard & Maiden Newton
South West Coaches, route 212 (not Sat/Sun/public holidays): The Dorchester-Yeovil service stops at both Cattistock and Maiden Newton.

First Great Western rail service between Weymouth/Dorchester and Bristol stops at Maiden Newton (daily).

12 Christchurch Harbour
For Hengistbury/Wick - Yellow Buses, route 1C (daily): The Poole-Bournemouth-Christchurch-Somerford service runs past The Broadway. Get off at the Tuckton Bridge or Belle Vue stops and walk to The Broadway junction. Continue down The Broadway for a mile to the main Hengistbury Head car park.

For Stanpit/Mudeford – Yellow Buses, route 111 (not Sun/public holidays): The Hurn-St Catherines-Highcliffe service runs through Christchurch and Stanpit/Mudeford.

14 Corfe Common
Wilts & Dorset, route 40 (daily): The Poole-Wareham-Swanage service runs through Corfe Castle. Get off on East Street or by the Castle View visitor centre. The entrance to the Common is a short walk through the village.

If you are staying in Swanage, as an interesting alternative, take a steam train to Corfe Castle – check operating times with the Swanage Railway as they vary through the year.

15 Coward's Marsh
Yellow Buses, route 21 (daily): The Bournemouth-Christchurch service runs along Fairmile Road, passing the site entrance in Marsh Lane. Get off at The Grove Top and walk back towards Christchurch for about 150m to the Marsh Lane (off Fairmile Road) parking area. Walk for another 650m down Marsh Lane to the viewing gate.

If walking from Christchurch railway station along Fairmile Road, turn into Suffolk Avenue and enter Marsh Lane from this direction (about 0.5 mile to the gate from Fairmile Road).

17 Creech, Grange & Stoborough Heaths
Wilts & Dorset, route 40 (daily): The Poole-Wareham-Swanage service runs to Stoborough

Green. The nearest access point onto the heath is a short walk through the Stoborough Green housing estate. The same access point can be reached on foot from Wareham (about one mile) – walk from the South Bridge over the causeway to Stoborough/Stoborough Green. There is a railway station in Wareham where the bus can be picked up.

18 Dancing Ledge
Wilts & Dorset, route 40 (daily): The Poole-Wareham-Swanage service runs through Langton Matravers. Get off at the Durnford Drove stop. The starting point (the car park) is a 500m walk down Durnford Drove.

Wilts & Dorset, route 44 (not Sun/public holidays): A limited service runs from Swanage to Worth Matravers, stopping at Langton Matravers (as above).

20 Durlston Country Park
The park lies immediately to the south of Swanage town centre - there are no public transport services from the town. 'The Victorian Trail' (1.75 miles) is way-marked to the park - the trail starts at the Tourist Information Centre on the seafront and follows the coast, via Peveril Point, to the park. Alternatively, walk along the roads to the park (just over one mile). Either walks involve climbs up quite steep hills.

21 Fontmell Down
NORDCAT, route 83 (not Sun/public holidays): A limited service runs from Shaftesbury to Wimborne, via Blandford. Get off in Compton Abbas, by the church, and walk from the village to the western side of the site (picking up route 1).

22 Garston Wood
Wilts & Dorset, route 184 (daily): The Blandford Forum-Salisbury service passes through Sixpenny Handley. There is a one mile walk from the village along the Broad Chalke road to reach the southern end of the wood.

23 Ham Common
Wilts & Dorset, route 152 (not Sun/public holidays): The Poole-Hamworthy-Rockley Park service runs along Napier road – get off at Rockley Caravan Park and walk a 150m further along the road to the entrance to the top car park.

24 Hambledon Hill & Hod Hill
Damory, route 309/310 (not Sun/public holidays): The Blandford Forum-Sturminster Newton-Gillingham (railway station)-Shaftesbury service

runs through Child Okeford. There are two access points from the village up to Hambledon Hill (500m or 700 m from The Cross bus stop). It is possible to walk to Hod Hill via Hambledon Hill.

25 Hartland Moor & Stoborough Heath NNR
Wilts & Dorset, route 40 (daily): The Poole-Wareham-Swanage service runs to Stoborough Green. The nearest access point onto the heath is a short walk along New Road. The same access point can be reached on foot from Wareham (about one mile) – walk from the South Bridge over the causeway to Stoborough/Stoborough Green.

Alternatively walk from Wareham (South Bridge) along the south side of the River Frome to Redcliffe and walk through to Ridge and the nearest access point on to the site (one mile).

There is a railway station in Wareham where you can connect with the bus.

26 Hatch Pond
Wilts & Dorset, routes 4 & 8 (daily) & Damory, route 347 (not Sun/public holidays): These services run from Poole Bus Station and stop at The Fleetsbridge roundabout (south side). The roundabout is crossed through a number of underpasses out into Waterloo Road (east side). There is about a half mile walk to Hatch Pond.

Wilts & Dorset, route 32 (limited - not Sun/public holidays): This service continues along the A349 (to Merley), with a bus stop just before the traffic light turn into Hatch Pond Road.

28 Holt Heath
Wilts & Dorset, route 37 (not Sun/public holidays) Poole-Verwood & route 36A (Sun/public holidays only) Bournemouth-Verwood: both services pass through West Moors. Get off at the Memorial Hall (Station Road) stop or the Gullivers Farm stop and walk through to the heath.

31 Lodmoor
First Hampshire & Dorset, route 31 (daily): The Weymouth-Dorchester-Axminster service runs along the seafront to Overcombe, get off by Lodmoor Country Park/Sealife Centre or by the Overcombe Corner.

32 Longham Lakes
Wilts & Dorset, route 37 (not Sun/public holidays): The Poole-Verwood service passes through Longham. Get off at the Longham Bridge (by the hotel).

33 Lorton Meadows & Two-mile Copse
The Weymouth-London Waterloo rail service stops at Upwey station which is a 1.25 mile walk from the Wildlife Centre. From the station walk up to the entrance on Littlemoor Road and turn left. Turn left again at the traffic lights and walk along the A354 Dorchester Road, towards the town centre, until reaching a left turn into Lorton Lane (follow the lane 0.5 mile to the centre).

First Hampshire & Dorset, route 10 (daily): The Weymouth-Dorchester service runs along the A354 - get off at the Broadway (church) and walk back 300m towards the town centre to the Lorton Lane turn.

34 Lyme Regis
First Hampshire & Dorset, route X53 (daily) Poole-Exeter and route 31 (daily) Weymouth-Dorchester-Axminster services both call in at Charmouth and Lyme Regis.

35 Lytchett Bay
Wilts & Dorset, route 8 (daily): The Poole-Creekmoor-Upton service runs along Sandy Lane in Upton (north side of the bay).

Wilts & Dorset, route 9 (daily): The Poole-Hamworthy-Turlin Moor service runs into Turlin Moor (east side of the bay).

36 Maiden Castle
Coach House Travel: The no.1 and 2 Dorchester Town services (not Sun/public holidays) stop on Maiden Castle Road/Celtic Crescent. Continue on foot along Maiden Castle Road (over the bridge) to the Maiden Castle car park – 0.75 miles (most of the route is through open countryside so you can birdwatch along the way).

Alternatively the car park is a 1.5 mile walk from the railway stations (Dorchester South & Dorchester West)/or a 1.75 mile walk from the town centre.

37 Martin Down
Wilts & Dorset, route 184 (daily): The Blandford-Salisbury service runs along the A354 - get off at the Woodyates, Martin Down Nature Reserve stop.

39 Moors Valley Country Park
Wilts & Dorset, route 36 (not Sun/public holidays) and route 36A (Sun/public holidays only): The Bournemouth-Ringwood-Verwood service passes the Moors Valley entrance,

40 Parley Common
Wilts & Dorset, route 37 (not Sun/public holidays): The Poole-Ferndown-Verwood service passes Trickett's Cross. Route 13 (daily), Bournemouth-Wimborne service stops in Ferndown where Route 37 service or Route 38 (not Sun) Ferndown-Ringwood service can be picked up for Trickett's Cross.

41 Poole Harbour & Coastal Boat Trips
Boats leave from the Quay at Poole and from Swanage Pier, both easily reached from the town centres.

42 Poole Harbour – Poole Quay to Sandbanks
The Quay, Poole Park, Baiter and Parkstone Bay are all within walking distance of Poole town centre and the main railway and bus stations. For Shore Road/Sandbanks take the Wilts & Dorset, route 52 (daily) Poole-Sandbanks service and get off at the junction of Shore Road/Banks Road.

43 Portland
First Hampshire & Dorset, route 1, 10 & 501 (all daily): Regular services run from Weymouth to Portland (1 & 10 do not go to The Bill - get off in the Sweet Hill area and walk south to The Bill).

South West Coaches, route 205: A limited service runs between Weymouth and Portland Bill (not Sun/public holidays. Sat service does not go to the Bill).

44 Portland Harbour & Ferrybridge
First Hampshire & Dorset, routes 1, 10 & 501 (all daily): all run between Weymouth and Portland. Route 10 runs from Dorchester. Get off at the Ferrybridge stop and walk to either site from here.

47 Radipole Lake
The reserve lies in the heart of Weymouth – a short walk from the main bus stands and the railway station.

48 Ringstead Bay
First Hampshire & Dorset, route X53 (daily): The Poole-Weymouth-Exeter service runs along the A353 through Osmington. Get off at the Mill Road stop – there is a one mile walk down to the shore at Osmington Mills.

50 River Frome - Holme Bridge
First Hampshire & Dorset, route X53 (daily): The Poole-Weymouth-Exeter service runs along the

A352 between Wareham and Wool. There is a bus stop at Stokeford Village Hall 100m from the start of the walk from Stokeford to Holme Bridge. Walk down the lane, cross over the railway line – the walks starts here.

51 Sherborne Lake

Sherborne Castle and the old castle ruins are both within easy walking distance of the town centre and the railway station.

52 Sopley Common, Ramsdown Plantation & Avon Causeway

Discover Dorset, Airport Shuttle Bus (daily): This service runs from Bournemouth – get off at Hurn Bridge and walk the short distance to Sopley Common (the Airport is 0.75 mile from the site).

53 Studland

Wilts & Dorset, route 50 (daily): The Bournemouth-Sandbanks-Swanage service runs through Studland village and to the Sandbanks ferry – get off along this road depending on where you want to go first.

57 The Nothe & Weymouth Bay

Both areas are within an easy walk of Weymouth town centre/railway station.

First Hampshire & Dorset, route 503 (daily): The Weymouth-Bowleaze service runs along the seafront as an alternative to walking the whole way.

55 Tadnoll & Winfrith Heath

First Hampshire & Dorset, route X53 (daily): The Poole-Weymouth-Exeter service runs along the A352 between Wareham and Wool. Buses stop on this road by the Red Lion at Portway (the Winfrith Newburgh turning) – walk 0.5 mile from the main road to Blacknoll and the Winfrith parking area.

56 The Fleet

First Hampshire & Dorset, route X53 (daily): The Poole-Weymouth-Exeter service runs along the B3157 between Weymouth and Abbotsbury but a walk is required from the various bus stops along this road down to the shore of The Fleet.

59 Town Common & St Catherine's Hill

Yellow Buses, route 21 (daily): The Bournemouth-Christchurch service runs along Fairmile Road, passing the site entrance in Marsh Lane. Get off at The Grove Top and walk back towards

Christchurch for about 150m to the Marsh Lane parking area.

60 Upton Country Park & Holes Bay

Exit Poole railway station from platform 2 – you are looking at Holes Bay! Cross the busy road and follow the shore to the right, this path continues on into Upton Country Park.

Wilts & Dorset, route 128 (not Sun/public holidays): The Poole–Upton Country Park/Dacombe Drive service runs to the park. Wilts & Dorset, route 8 (daily): The Poole-Creekmoor-Upton service drops off at the park entrance.

61 Upton Heath

Wilts & Dorset, route 8 (daily): The Poole-Creekmoor-Upton service runs along Longmeadow Lane.

62 Wareham Forest

Wilts & Dorset, route 40 (daily): The Poole-Wareham-Swanage service stops at Wareham railway station – it is a 0.5 mile walk from here to get to the southern end of the forest.

63 Wareham Meadows & Swineham Point

This site is easily reached on foot from Wareham town centre.

64 West Bexington

First Hampshire & Dorset, route X53 (daily): The Poole-Weymouth-Exeter service runs along the B3157. Get off at Swyre and walk down to the coast or alternatively get off at Cogden Beach.

65 Worth Matravers coastal walks

Wilts & Dorset, route 40 (daily): The Poole-Wareham-Swanage service along the B3069 but there is a mile walk into Worth Matravers from the nearest bus stop.

Wilts & Dorset, route 44 (not Sun/public holidays): A limited service runs from Swanage to Worth Matravers (not Sun).

BEST SITES WITH DISABLED ACCESS

THE SITES that I consider to have reasonable access for wheelchair users are listed below, but please bear in mind that some sites will be more difficult than others. In many cases access will be along tracks which may be firm but uneven and may be capped with stone.

I would recommend that any readers with mobility problems should contact the phone number (where listed) on the Site Guide page to get up-to-date advice, especially in respect to the ground conditions at the time of your visit.

THE SITES

1 Arne
There is a disabled parking area at Shipstal Point that will take you closer to the shore - permission is required to drive here - contact the RSPB office. Part of the Shipstal trail is accessible by wheelchair. The Coombe Trail is not suitable for wheelchairs.

2 Avon Heath Country Park
The main way-marked trails on North Park are suitable for wheelchairs, as are the facilities here. The trails on South Park are unsuitable.

5 Bere Regis, Tincleton & Waddock Cross Cress Beds
All of the cress beds can be viewed from the roadsides.

8 Branksome Chine
Seawatching can be undertaken from the car park area.

9 Brownsea Island
Boats to the island: Wheelchair access should be checked with the boat companies – it may not be possible to get up to the top deck of the boat. Users should be able to walk a few steps (assisted if required) to access the boarding gates. Each wheelchair must be accompanied by an attendant.

On the island: Paths leading to the Visitor Centre are fairly level and smooth. Beyond this the island tracks are rough in places and can be difficult to negotiate, including to the DWT hides. It is possible to hire a wheelchair (free) for your visit. The shop, café and toilets are accessible.

10 Canford Heath
There are a few wheelchair friendly gates from where some tracks are negotiable. The gates are all locked and are opened with a RADAR key – contact the site for details of obtaining a key and the routes available.

11 Cattistock Churchyard & Maiden Newton
There are suitable paths through Cattistock Churchyard for wheelchairs. The river at Maiden Newton can be viewed from the road only – the footpath to Chilfrome is not suitable for wheelchairs.

12 Christchurch Harbour
The main track from the parking area at Hengistbury Head out to Mudeford Spit is tarred and easily accessible for wheelchairs. The Mudeford Quay area can be viewed from the car park.

15 Coward's Marsh
Access for wheelchairs along Marsh Lane is a little tricky as the surface is quite badly potholed (which are often filled with water). It is possible to drive along Marsh Lane to the viewing gate but disabled passengers should be dropped/picked up here and the car removed to the parking areas.

19 Duncliffe Wood
There is limited to access through the wood along the main bridleway but there are quite steep gradients in places.

20 Durlston Country Park
Wheelchair access is restricted around the park - where path surfaces are suitable for them fairly steep slopes are involved. A 'Tramper' mobility vehicle is available for hire from the visitor centre.

22 Garston Wood
Access is limited along some of the rides, contact the RSPB for further information.

23 Ham Common
Tracks across the site are not suitable for wheelchairs but the heath/harbour can be viewed from the main viewpoint car park on Napier Drive and the harbour can be viewed from Hamworthy Pier car park.

25 Hartland Moor & Stoborough Heath NNR
There are two disused tramways that have reasonable surfaces for wheelchair access. Some of the area can also be viewed from the roadside along Soldier's Road.

26 Hatch Pond
This is a relatively small site and most of it can be

viewed from the tarmac path along the southern boundary of the pond. The best viewing area for the Bittern though is from amongst the trees along the eastern boundary which can be reached over a grassy path (which can be muddy). The ground amongst the trees is covered in leaf litter and slopes down to the water – care would need to be taken if attempted in a wheelchair.

27 Higher Hyde Heath
There is access into the hide overlooking the pond and for a short way along the track beyond the hide.

29 Kingcombe Meadows
The 'Tramper route' on the reserve is designed for use by mobility vehicles and consists of a mile log circuit over some of the meadows. It is still quite rough and should be used with caution.

30 Lambert's Castle
There is no wheelchair access as such but the open ground from the car park gate to the fort is relatively flat.

31 Lodmoor
There is good access around the site by wheelchair – the surfaces over the site are constructed of compacted stone. Southdown Avenue and along the sea front are part of the public highway (tarred paths).

33 Lorton Meadows & Two-mile Copse
The Wildlife Centre has disabled facilities and the short Green Hill Trail is over relatively flat ground.

34 Lyme Regis
There is suitable access for wheelchairs around the Lyme Regis part of this site but away from the town paths are steep and uneven and not suitable.

35 Lytchett Bay
The 'Pools' off Slough Lane are visible from the roadside.

36 Maiden Castle
Access on to the fortifications is not possible with a wheelchair but the surrounding area can be scanned from the car park area and the Monkey's Jump lay-by.

37 Martin Down
The main tracks from the two car parks are reasonably good for wheelchairs. There is no suitable access to the Vernditch Chase side of the road.

38 Middlebere
The access to the 'Avocet' hide is along a 0.75 mile track - it is rough (with some potholes) but passable with a wheelchair – alternatively contact the National Trust for permission to drive down to the cottages, a short distance from the hide.

39 Moors Valley Country Park
The park is well geared up to wheelchair access around the lakes and visitor facilities with excellent tarmac paths. The tracks around the forest areas are rough.

41 Poole Harbour & Coastal Boat Trips
Wheelchair access should be checked with the boat companies – it may not be possible to get up to the top deck of the boat. Users should be able to walk a few steps (assisted if required) to access the boarding gates. Each wheelchair must be accompanied by an attendant.

42 Poole Harbour – Poole Quay to Sandbanks
Most of the recommended areas for birdwatching are accessible by wheelchair on good paths. The exception is the area around the Haven Hotel where it is not possible to view the rocky shore.

43 Portland
All areas on the island are generally unsuitable for wheelchairs but it is possible to seawatch from The Bill and Chesil Cove. The viewpoint above North Woods can be watched from the car park.

44 Portland Harbour & Ferrybridge
Both of these areas can be viewed from the parking areas, or footpaths that are suitable for wheelchairs. Specifically: Sandsfoot Castle, the Sailing Club entrance, Ferrybridge and Portland Castle.

45 Powerstock Common
Wheelchair access is possible from the parking area along the main track through the site and along the old dismantled railway.

46 Purbeck Marine Wildlife Reserve
The beach and rock pools are not accessible to wheelchair users but there is good access to the Marine Centre,

47 Radipole Lake
Wheelchair access is possible across the reserve's stone paths. Most of the year they are dry and passable but, in prolonged periods of rain, sections may become flooded from time to time. Access is also possible into the visitor centre/shop.

48 Ringstead Bay

Wheelchair users can view the immediate area around the National Trust car park and can reach the shore from the lower car park but it is not possible to get to Burning Cliff/White Nothe.

49 River Allen – Crichel Lake

It is not possible to walk around the Crichel Lake loop but there are plenty of opportunities to view the farmland areas to the west from the roadside.

50 River Frome – Holme Bridge

The main part of the site (Holme Bridge) is viewable from a bridge and a minor road where it is possible to park a car. The river at Wool is also viewable from a bridge (with parking).

51 Sherborne Lake

It is possible to use wheelchairs on the public paths around the castle and by the lake, some steeper gradients.

53 Studland

Access is quite difficult for wheelchairs over most of the area but it is possible to view Studland Bay from the Knoll and Middle Beach car parks. There are a number of pull-ins along the Ferry Road where is it possible to view the heath.

54 Sutton Bingham Reservoir

The reservoir can be viewed from the roadside over the causeway and along the western side. In the summer, the car park area is open and there are disabled facilities here. The bird hide, towards the southern end of the reservoir has wheelchair access.

55 Tadnoll & Winfrith Heath

There is no suitable wheelchair access over the heath but it can be viewed from along the roadside (Gatemore Road).

56 The Fleet

Access to most areas is not possible by wheelchair. The exceptions are the end of the road by the Bridging Camp (reached by car) and the grounds of Abbotsbury Swannery.

57 The Nothe & Weymouth Bay

There are good tarmac paths around The Nothe gardens and along the length of the seafront that are suitable for wheelchairs. If you want to visit the Nothe Fort there is a lift allowing access to its three floors.

58 Thorncombe Wood

There is very limited wheelchair access for a few hundred metres along the path out of the southern end of the car park.

60 Upton Country Park & Holes Bay

The majority of the paths around the bay or in the park are passable by wheelchair. There is a metal kissing gate barrier along the shore that is not passable in a wheelchair - a detour along the cycle route (towards Broadstone) to the park's main entrance would have to be made. It is best to treat the east side of Holes Bay and the country park as separate sites.

61 Upton Heath

There is a short (570m) easy access trail out from Beacon Road which will give great views over the site. It should also be possible to get to the viewpoint from the Springdale Road car park (500m). Other tracks and paths are unsuitable for wheelchairs.

62 Wareham Forest

The paths are generally rough, with slopes and are difficult for wheelchair access. The easiest area for wheelchairs is across the main track at Great Ovens.

63 Wareham Meadows & Swineham Point

There is very limited access for wheelchairs – restricted to the private road from the end of Bestwall Road to Swineham Farm.

64 West Bexington

The coastal path is unsuitable for wheelchairs but seawatching can be undertaken from the car park area at West Bexington.

Birds mentioned in the index are generally those that are featured as Target Birds in the site reports. Commonly occuring species are omitted to keep the index to a manageable size.